From Damaged Life

CRITICAL THEORY AND THE CRITIQUE OF SOCIETY SERIES

In a time marked by crises and the rise of right-wing authoritarian populism, **Critical Theory and the Critique of Society** intends to renew the critical theory of capitalist society exemplified by the Frankfurt School and critical Marxism's critiques of social domination, authoritarianism, and social regression by expounding the development of such a notion of critical theory, from its founding thinkers, through its subterranean and parallel strands of development, to its contemporary formulations.

Series editors: **Werner Bonefield**, University of York, UK and **Chris O'Kane**, John Jay College of Criminal Justice, City University of New York, USA

Available titles:

Right-wing Culture in Contemporary Capitalism, Mathias Nilges
Adorno and Neoliberalism, Charles Andrew Prusik
Toward a Critical Theory of Nature, Carl Cassegård
Spectacular Logic in Hegel and Debord, Eric-John Russell
Adorno and Marx, Werner Bonefeld and Chris O'Kane
Walter Benjamin and the Critique of Political Economy, Duy Lap Nguyen
The Adventures of the Commodity, Anselm Jappe
Critical Theory and the Critique of Antisemitism, Marcel Stoetzler
Open Marxism, Christos Memos

From Damaged Life

The Critical Theory of Theodor W. Adorno

Jordi Maiso

BLOOMSBURY ACADEMIC
LONDON • NEW YORK • OXFORD • NEW DELHI • SYDNEY

BLOOMSBURY ACADEMIC
Bloomsbury Publishing Plc, 50 Bedford Square, London, WC1B 3DP, UK
Bloomsbury Publishing Inc, 1359 Broadway, New York, NY 10018, USA
Bloomsbury Publishing Ireland, 29 Earlsfort Terrace, Dublin 2, D02 AY28, Ireland

BLOOMSBURY, BLOOMSBURY ACADEMIC and the Diana logo are trademarks of Bloomsbury Publishing Plc

First published in 2022 in Spain as Desde la vida dañada by Siglo XXI

First published in Great Britain 2026

Series design by Ben Anslow

A catalogue record for this book is available from the British Library.

A catalog record for this book is available from the Library of Congress.

ISBN: HB: 978-1-3505-6277-6
PB: 978-1-3505-6278-3
ePDF: 978-1-3505-6279-0
eBook: 978-1-3505-6280-6

Series: Critical Theory and the Critique of Society

Typeset by Newgen KnowledgeWorks Pvt. Ltd., Chennai, India
Printed and bound in Great Britain

For product safety related questions contact productsafety@bloomsbury.com.

To find out more about our authors and books visit www.bloomsbury.com and sign up for our newsletters.

For José Antonio Zamora,
without whom this book would not exist.

Contents

Abbreviations

Works by Theodor W. Adorno

ÄT:	Th. W. Adorno: *Ästhetische Theorie* (GS 7)
DA:	M. Horkheimer y Th. W. Adorno: *Dialektik der Aufklärung* (GS 3)
ES:	Th. W. Adorno: *Einleitung in die Soziologie*
GS:	Th. W. Adorno: *Gesammelte Schriften* (20 vols.)
IG:	Th. W. Adorno: «Individuum und Gesellschaft. Entwürfe und Skizzen»
LGF:	Th. W. Adorno: *Zum Lehre von der Geschichte und von der Freiheit*
MM:	Th. W. Adorno: *Minima Moralia* (GS 4)
ND:	Th. W. Adorno: *Negative Dialektik* (GS 6)
PETG:	Th. W. Adorno: *Philosophische Elemente einer Theorie der Gesellschaft*
PhS:	Th. W. Adorno, *Philosophie und Soziologie*
PMP:	Th. W. Adorno, *Probleme der Moraphilosophie*

Correspondence Volumes

ABB:	Th. W. Adorno y W Benjamin: *Briefwechsel 1928–1940*
AHB:	Th. W. Adorno y M. Horkheimer: *Briefwechsel* (4 vols.)

Works by Other Authors

BGS:	W. Benjamin: *Gesammelte Schriften* (7 vols.)
HGS:	M. Horkheimer: *Gesammelte Schriften* (19 vols.)
MEW:	*Marx Engels Werke* (44 vols.)

Introduction

While Adorno has long held a recognizable place among the classics of twentieth-century thought, this does not imply that his critical theory is well understood. As so often happens, the clichés that have enabled a certain image of his work to circulate widely have also obscured it. For decades, platitudes and stereotypes have smothered his legacy, standing in the way of a more productive engagement with his texts. This vulgarization of the figure of Adorno has tended to portray him as an author who, though perhaps subtle and brilliant, no longer has much to say to us. In short, he has become a *classic*—enshrined and forgotten as such. This has undoubtedly resulted in a neutralization of his critical potential. Various accusations of pessimism, elitism, aestheticism, and political resignation—repeated to the point of exhaustion—have played a major role in this regard. There is also a certain unease with his prose, which has a reputation for being unintelligible and obscure. At the same time, he is often portrayed as a mandarin of high culture who arrogantly disdains emerging mass culture—one who retreats into art, turning his back on political struggles. None of this has made it easy to approach his work without the burden of preconceptions. Neither has the fact that for decades there was a certain belief that anything that might still be of contemporary relevance in his critical theory had already been assimilated and indeed updated by those who presented themselves as the "successors" of so-called Frankfurt School critical theory—above all Jürgen Habermas and Axel Honneth—despite their having very little in common with it. Nevertheless, interest in Adorno's work has not died out; rather, it has continued to gain traction. Over the past two decades, engagement with his work has steadily increased, opening up fruitful avenues of enquiry in the reception of his thought. This may seem perplexing for an author whom many have sought to dismiss for over half a century, at least as far as critical theory is concerned. However, reality is stubborn, and whereas the theory of communicative action has aged at a surprisingly fast rate and the theory of recognition has never been more than a neatly integrated niche in the academic market, Adorno's work—which is much more distant from us chronologically—seems better placed to confront a historical moment characterized by the return of manifestly authoritarian dynamics, the coercions of an increasingly stiffling capitalism, a blind domination of nature that undermines its own foundations, and a social logic that imposes itself on life, leaving it permanently damaged. Thus, while Adorno has hitherto been read primarily as a philosopher or an aesthete, this book addresses his work as a critical theory of contemporary society.

In a way, this book reaffirms Adorno's relevance without denying the historical distance that stands between him and us. There is no room for evasion on that point: his thought responds to a time that is not our own. It was formulated as an attempt to update the tasks of critique after the end of liberal capitalism, which led to the emergence of fascism and societies that crossed new thresholds of barbarism and violence, captured in Adorno's work by the toponym "Auschwitz." In this historical landscape, his critical theory registered the—at least provisional—collapse of the emancipatory hopes that had arisen in modern societies as well as the social integration of antagonism itself and the increasing disempowerment of living subjects. Yet he did not give up on critique. Since reality had reached a new degree of negativity, a form of critique that could measure up to it became necessary. In this regard, his thought makes no concessions but aspires to become a stand-in for a praxis that may one day become possible again. This is what sharpens his theoretical gaze on an era that, despite all its advances, exhibits clear signs of regression. In this regard, his thought has often been reproached for its refusal to treat fascism and advanced capitalism as clearly distinct entities. While they were undoubtedly different regimes, Adorno did not consider them to be divided by such a vast gulf. Rather, he understood them as two variants within a far-reaching process transforming the conditions of modern sociality. These transformations, which lie at the foundation of contemporaneity, are the focus of his critical theory. In them, he detects a tendency toward the concentration of social and economic power, one which relegates individuals to mere interchangeable cogs in the social machinery and increasingly condemns them to a state of powerlessness. As Roberto Schwarz has pointed out, the radical character of Adorno's critique is rooted in this understanding of the trajectory of developed societies.[1] For decades, this made Adorno anathema. His position was taken to be a kind of extravagant radicalism that, traumatized as it was by the catastrophes of the first half of the century, was unable to deal with the consolidation of democracy and the "domestication" of capitalism in the second postwar period. Today, however, it seems rather that this perspective prevented him from succumbing to the delusions of the so-called golden age of capitalism, which assumed that economic growth could go hand in hand with social prosperity and entertained the idea that the rule of capital could acquire a human face. Thus, the very same reasons once invoked to demonstrate the obsolescence of his critique—supposedly obsessed with the most corrosive features of the totalitarian period—now serve to explain why his theory has withstood the test of time. In the meantime, Adorno's warning that advanced capitalism was on its way to becoming a total, ruthless social system has materialized to an extent few could have foreseen.[2]

This book, then, approaches Adorno's critical theory with a special emphasis on his social theory, and in particular on his analyses of advanced capitalism. In so doing, it aims to address a gap in the reception of his work. Although his theoretical output is well regarded for its important contribution to the analysis of authoritarianism and anti-Semitism as well as for the social implications of its critique of the culture industry—and although even the importance of his engagement with Marx has only recently been recognized[3]—the fact remains that few so far have attempted to integrate these perspectives into a unified account of Adorno's critical theory of society. This is what the present book aims to offer, while also addressing other aspects of his thought

[1]Cf. Roberto Schwarz, "On Adorno (An Interview)," trans. Simone Fernandes and Mariana Fidelis, *Dissonância: Revista de Teoria Crítica: Dossiê Teoria Decolonial e Teoria Crítica*, 4 (2020): 437.

[2]Cf. Frederic Jameson, *Late Marxism: Adorno, or, the Persistence of the Dialectic* (London: Verso, 1990), 5–6.

[3]Cf., for example, Werner Bonefeld and Chris O'Kane, eds., *Adorno and Marx: Negative Dialectics and the Critique of Political Economy* (London: Bloomsbury, 2022).

through the lens of his understanding of advanced capitalism. In this way, it aims to make explicit the sociohistorical coordinates of his critical theory and what these imply in order to place Adorno in the tradition of emancipatory thought. From this, in turn, arises the need to clarify his relationship with Marx's critique. Although his dialogue with Hegel and Kant is much more explicit, when confronting them he sought to differentiate the true and false elements of classical bourgeois philosophy, and ultimately it is Marx who sets the tone. Adorno also acknowledged his debt to Marx in his analysis of society in his own time. To a significant extent, his writings on social theory in the 1950s and 1960s draw upon a particular appropriation of the central theses of the critique of political economy. However, Adorno was also aware that Marx's theory could no longer be flawlessly applied to the reality of the twentieth century. It proposed an immanent critique of a bourgeois society whose foundations had long since crumbled. Therefore, in order to keep its transformative impulses alive, they had to be reformulated on the basis of new coordinates. This entailed attending to the specific problems of his historical moment, which presented a qualitatively different social scenario. Hence his analyses of the trend toward total socialization, the deepening of relations of domination and subjugation, the emergence of the culture industry, the rise of authoritarian and anti-Semitic tendencies, the anthropological mutation under advanced capitalism, and the historical decline of the individual. The result is a critical theory of society that cannot be understood without Marx but that also cannot be explained within the parameters of Marxist thought alone. In fact, nothing could be more fruitless than to treat Adorno as an epigone of Marx. This would mean sacrificing the distinctive traits of his work, which responds to the impulses of a theoretical and aesthetic radicalism rooted in very different coordinates and which makes it possible to address elements that lie beyond the reach of the critique of political economy: for example, the impact of social logic on the constitution of living subjects, the transformations in the forms of experience and the growing authoritarian potential, which today prove more relevant than ever.

However, highlighting the ways in which Adorno's critical theory can be distinguished from Marx's stance not only allows us to clarify the specific features of his understanding of advanced capitalism, but also illuminates the way in which his thought frames the position of critique in the societies of the twentieth century. While the emancipatory thought of the nineteenth century had still been able to contest the implications of progress and modernization, by the mid-twentieth century, prospects for transformative change had been constricted. Modernity no longer embodied the promise of a better future, but revealed itself as a potential breeding ground for barbarism; likewise, the possibility of a transformative or revolutionary praxis seemed to have vanished. For anyone who has not abandoned all emancipatory purpose, Adorno's analysis of these historical developments cannot fail to matter. For all of these reasons, the present book aims to offer a way of approaching Adorno's thought that is also capable of locating the political pulse that beats throughout his theoretical output. The possibility of a more fruitful relationship with his thought is also undermined when his theory is subjected to the processes of exhaustive exegesis that adhere to the model of forensic academic dissection. A rigorous approach to Adorno's critical theory requires not only the reconstruction of his texts and arguments, which are certainly subtle and often complex, but also the preservation of the very impulse that breathes life into his thought. This can still be sensed in many of his writings, which still retain a notable capacity for provocation and critical engagement. Adorno's analytical finesse is also frequently revealed in his ability to register the imprint of social processes in spheres that appear to be far removed from them: "how must a world be made in which even questions of counterpoint bear witness to irreconcilable conflicts?" he asks in the foreword to *Philosophy of New Music* (GS 12, 11).[4] This book aims to present an approach to Adorno that is not only capable of making his analyses and arguments intelligible, but also of showing how they are rooted in specific theoretical, social, and political constellations in which they gain significance.

In this light, one of the core concerns of Adorno's critical theory can be found in the concept of "damaged life." Yet when Adorno introduces the term in the subtitle of *Minima Moralia* he is not talking about reflections *on* damaged life, but *from* it. The critic does not place himself in a position of

[4]Theodor W. Adorno, *Philosophy of New Music*, trans. Robert Hullot-Kentor (Minneapolis: University of Minnesota Press, 2006), 5.

sovereignty, purity, or exteriority; he cannot speak *ex cathedra*, because neither he himself nor his theoretical work can be considered safe from socially produced damage. The only thing he can wield in the face of an implacable and harmful social reality is his capacity for reflexivity, which creates the space for a minimal margin of freedom. Adorno noted that "the mechanism of domination inherently suppresses any recognition of the suffering it inflicts" (MM, 70).[5] His reflections strove to recast the experience of this damage into a source of knowledge, tracing the imprint of the social process in the scars and wounds it leaves behind. However, Adorno's conception of damaged life should not be misunderstood. It does not refer to particular lives, or to the painful situation of intellectuals forced into exile, but to new living conditions in the face of the omnipotent emerging social order. This order reduced individuals to social functions, turning them into fungible and substitutable entities. Essentially, the concept of "damaged life" refers to how the logic of the social system intersects individual biographies. This encounter between a relentless social logic and living subjects, forced to live out their lives under the sign of heteronomy, thwarts their yearnings and expectations and inflicts lingering wounds that often take a long time to heal. Adorno realized that in his era there was no longer any sphere of life that could be considered safe from the demands of the social system. "Life does not live," he pointed out, quoting Ferdinand Kürnberger. "At bottom what happens is that the very concept of life, understood as a unity of meaning that develops out of itself, no longer has any reality."[6] The social conditions of existence no longer allow lives to be developed autonomously and understood through the prism of a continuous and coherent life. On the contrary: the life trajectories are increasingly defenseless in the face of the demands of the concentrated social apparatus, which are imposed on them with a force beyond appeal. This imbalance in social relations of force leads to lives marked by anguish and fear and tends to induce individuals to yield to the shifting demands of the social apparatus, to seek to come out on top in the dynamics of competition. However, if this

[5]Theodor W. Adorno, *Minima Moralia*, trans. E. F. N. Jephcott (London: Verso, 2005), 63.

[6]Theodor W. Adorno, letter to Leo Löwenthal on November 25, 1942, in L. Löwenthal, *Schriften 4* (Frankfurt: Suhrkamp, 1984), 158.

tendency were to impose itself completely, it would entail the capitulation of the living and, ultimately, the death of critique. While Adorno recognizes this situation, his thinking does not reject it outright through moral condemnation in the name of an impossible rigor. Rather, his perspective stems from a reflective understanding of the fragile foundation upon which a life of non-resignation—and thus critique itself—rests. For the latter is always in danger of being co-opted and subsumed by the social logic that bears down on it. Without this reflexivity, without vigilant and lucid awareness, critical theory of society is not possible. However, this awareness is not an end in itself. It responds to the desires of a life that may be wounded and damaged, yet has not given up. If Adorno insisted on the significance of individual experience for the development of theory, this was perhaps because he believed that when thought is nourished by aspirations toward an untruncated life and manages to articulate them self-reflexively, it can prove to be an extraordinarily sensitive and valuable seismograph for registering the antagonisms and contradictions at work at a given historical moment. Hence the importance of the untamed tenacity of living subjectivity, which clings to the hopes for happiness and resists any resignation.

***

This book consists of seven chapters, which are divided into two main parts. The first, "The core of experience and the coordinates of critique," aims to clarify some of the misunderstandings that have hindered the reception of Adorno's thought to date. To this end, it attempts to show how his theoretical output is rooted in a very specific set of sociohistorical experiences. Above all, these chapters recover the more political dimension of his thought, which has often been neglected. First, the historical tensions between emancipation and barbarism during the period in which his critical theory emerges are addressed: the significance of Auschwitz as a historical caesura that marks an irreversible rupture in the expectations of emancipatory thought, the relationship of theory with the so-called revolutionary subject, and the resulting epistemological stakes, which point toward the relationship between critical theory and suffering. This is followed by an account of Adorno's distinctive profile as an intellectual, revealing his particular position within the framework of Frankfurt School critical theory, as well as the way in which his theory grapples with the growing difficulties in developing a critique, the crucial importance that the dispute over the political meaning of art acquires in his thought, and his understanding of the relationship between critical theory and praxis, which already sparked extensive polemics in his own time. Finally, a third chapter deals with the controversial critical stance that Adorno outlines in *Dialectic of Enlightenment*, which has often been read as a break with Marx and with his own approach to critical theory. Rather, this work is understood as a response to a new era in the history of domination and subjugation, ushered in by the rise of fascism and advanced capitalism. Its analysis aims to elucidate the distinctive nature of an increasingly stratified social order, which, despite unlocking novel possibilities through its staggering development of the forces of production, confines life to a brutal, vicious struggle for self-preservation.

The second part aims to elucidate what might be called Adorno's critical theory of capitalism and consists of four chapters. Here capitalism appears as something more than a mode of production: it is a configuration of social relations that shapes the forms of life and leaves its imprint on the prevailing modes of social objectivity and subjectivity. The main focus is on the relations between the social whole and living individuals, who, in order to propagate the iniquitous logic of the social system, must reproduce each other. The starting point is the peculiar way in which Adorno's social theory incorporates Marx's critique of political economy. This allows him to account for the logic of socialization in advanced capitalism as a new regime of heteronomy, which is reflected in the logic of the social whole as a "system" and in the evolution of capitalism as a process of "natural history." It is through this framework that the whole centrality of Adorno's diagnosis of advanced capitalism as a logic of "total socialization" can be understood. The following chapters explore the consequences of this regime of socialization, beginning with his analyses of the culture industry, which emerge as a central focus in his critique of capitalism. In this section, the way in which the social system captures living subjects and their needs becomes apparent. The sixth chapter addresses the anthropological transformation of advanced capitalism. The historical decline of liberal capitalism led to the collapse of the figure of the bourgeois individual, giving rise to the emergence of a new type of human being. This led Adorno to assess the shifting constitution of living subjects and to explore its implications for social dynamics. Hence, the increasingly prominent role played by psychoanalysis in his social theory. The last chapter focuses on the way in which Adorno conceives the new figure of ideology within the transformations of capitalism. This requires revisiting his interpretation of certain Marxist theses, especially regarding the problem of fetishism, as well as his analysis of emerging modes of subjectivation, which led him to diagnose an authoritarian potential rooted in the logic of socialization in advanced capitalism, which persisted after the military defeat of fascism. Finally, a brief coda attempts to lay out some reflections on what Adorno's social theory has to offer when it comes to confronting contemporary reality and its crises.

In short, this work aims to provide an understanding of the central features of Adorno's critical theory. In contrast to the widespread tendency to situate his contributions solely in the 1930s and 1940s, a period after which his theory is supposed to have exhausted its potential, this work aims to reaffirm its enduring relevance for a critique of contemporary capitalism, especially with regard to the analysis of subjectivity. However, this book is not the place to bring his positions up to date. The argument here follows one of Adorno's own long-standing insights. Indeed, at the beginning of an essay written in 1956, on the occasion of the 125th anniversary of Hegel's death, Adorno pointed out that in such cases one should be wary of those who place themselves in a position to judge what a great thinker of the past means for the present moment. Such a perspective "makes the impudent claim that because one has the dubious good fortune to live later, and because one has a professional interest in the dead person one is to talk about, one can sovereignly assign the dead person his place, thereby in some sense elevating oneself above him" (GS 5, 251).[7] Such an attitude is commonplace, yet it yields limited insight. It might be more interesting, however, to develop an understanding of a thinker from the past that allows us to interrogate the present through the lens of their ideas. This

[7]Theodor W. Adorno, *Hegel: Three Studies*, trans. Shierry Weber Nicholsen (Cambridge, MA: MIT Press, 1993), 1.

could shed new light on our current situation, distancing it from conventional interpretations and surfacing previously overlooked nuances and perspectives. Perhaps this foreign, temporally dislocated gaze will yield a more productive reflection on the times we live in, their historical origins, and where they have led us. However, it is up to the reader to decide this. In any case, this book is driven by an interest in Adorno as a thinker who, with incisive and subtle precision, identified the entry of advanced societies into barbarism and yet did not abandon the aim of emancipation.

Part One

The Core of Experience and the Coordinates of Critique

Critical Theory as "Science of Mourning"

"there is no category whatsoever, no concept, however true, that is immune to becoming false and even ideological as soon as it is separated from the concrete contexts within which it is actually situated" (LGF, 89).[1] Adorno's statement here does not apply only to the conceptual framework within which philosophical thought unfolds and its categories acquire meaning, but also to its own place within history. Indeed, as Max Horkheimer had earlier asserted, "part of the meaning of theory is the time at which it is developed"

[1]Theodor W. Adorno, *History and Freedom*, trans. Rodney Livingstone (Cambridge: Polity, 2006), 58. Translation modified.

(HGS 5, 305).[2] Theories have a claim to general validity, but they do not fall from the sky. They are the fruit of the urgent demands and expectations of a given historical moment. Hence Walter Benjamin's call to resolutely refuse any notion of "timeless truth" (BGS V, 578):[3] thought cannot be abstracted from the situations to which it responds without doing a certain amount of violence to it. This is especially true for critical theory, which confronts reality with a view toward its emancipatory transformation. This is undoubtedly the case with Adorno's oeuvre in which, as Hans-Jürgen Krahl once pointed out, "biographical experience and the formation of theory, individual experience and the process of theoretical crystallization, were one and the same thing."[4] This introduces a historical index into his thought, meaning it can only be understood in relation to certain social, historical, and political constellations. In fact, Adorno's entire work seeks to remain faithful to the Hegelian maxim of a philosophy that aspires to be its own time comprehended through thought.[5] This implies that thought can no longer aspire to lasting truth, but that its results, however consistent and correct they may be, will always have a dimension that is fragile and ephemeral. This is why Adorno's critical theory distinguishes itself by attributing "a temporal core to truth instead of contrasting truth as something invariable to the movement of history" (DA, 9).[6] Acknowledging this historical dimension of thought, opposed to any notion of *philosophia perennis*, is indispensable when dealing with Adorno's work. Anyone who neglects the task of allowing Adorno's texts to resonate with the implications of their historical moment is bound to misinterpret them.

The strength of Adorno's critical theory lies in its exceptional capacity to reflexively elaborate upon the far-reaching implications of the social and

---

[2]Max Horkheimer, "The Authoritarian State," *Telos*, no. 15 (Spring 1973), 11.

[3]Walter Benjamin, *The Arcades Project*, trans. Howard Eiland and Kevin McLaughlin (Cambridge, MA: Harvard University Press, 2002), 463.

[4]Hans-Jürgen Krahl, *Konstitution und Klassenkampf* (Frankfurt: Neue Kritik, 2008), 303.

[5]G. W. F. Hegel, *Grundlinien der Philosophie des Rechts, Werke 7* (Frankfurt: Suhrkamp, 1989), 26, and *Elements of the Philosophy of Right*, trans. H. B. Nisbet (Cambridge: Cambridge University Press, 2003), 21.

[6]Max Horkheimer and Theodor W. Adorno, *Dialectic of Enlightenment: Philosophical Fragments*, trans. Edmund Jephcott (Stanford, CA: Stanford University Press, 2002), xi.

historical transformations of its time. In this sense, his theoretical work can be read "as a sustained effort to interpret the experience of the subject as a source of knowledge."[7] In his writings, the work of the concept is aimed at grasping the implications of the fractures of his time with a view to developing a critical self-awareness of the social relations of that historical moment. However, this assumes from the outset that Adorno's work is rooted in historical circumstances that are no longer our own: the era of the collapse of revolutionary hopes, the integration of the proletariat, the rise and expansion of fascism, Auschwitz and the failed liberation after the Allied victory, and, later, the triumph of postwar capitalism, in a scenario characterized by post-fascism and the Cold War. It is a moment of historical rupture, where the violent emergence of a new social order undermines the foundations of the old bourgeois world, yet simultaneously shatters the emancipatory aspirations that had arisen with it. In this sense, Adorno's thought bears witness to the consolidation of a model of capitalist socialization that is increasingly all-encompassing and integrative. The conquest of new heights of productivity and scientific-technical development comes at the cost of an enormous concentration of social, political, and economic power that disempowers living individuals and produces conditions increasingly marked by heteronomy. As a result, Adorno was keenly aware that the social and historical disruptions that his thought sought to work through not only affected his object of study, but also threatened the very existence of the nonintegrated critic and of emancipatory theory itself. Social reality, having become ever more hermetically sealed, seemed increasingly impervious to any form of theoretical or practical critique. It is therefore significant that Adorno managed to express a keen awareness of a problem that, in the meantime, has become even more pressing: the realization that the emergence of an increasingly integrated society not only implied the blockage of transformative praxis, but also endangered the very possibility of a critical theory. The constitution of an all-encompassing web of social mediations, which subsumed more and more spheres of life into its operational logic,

[7] Detlev Claussen, *Theodor Adorno: One Last Genius*, trans. Rodney Livingstone (Cambridge, MA: The Belknap Press of Harvard University, 2008), 241.

undermined the autonomy of subjects and permeated the very conditions for producing and transmitting critical knowledge. Consequently, even the intellectual realm saw a creeping conformity take hold. The possibilities of opposing the expansion of a social logic that devours everything in its path with the meager resources of thought became increasingly negligible.

All this cannot merely be understood as the "historical context" of his thought: it points instead to the very substance from which his theory derives. What matters is that it registers unresolved problems that continue to underpin modern life. This is why a model of thought that Adorno, under the impact of these historical experiences, would refer to as a *traurige Wissenschaft* (MM, 13) still concerns us. This concept has often been translated as "melancholy science." Gillian Rose's otherwise highly insightful book already pointed in this direction: Adorno as a melancholic.[8] Such a characterization is problematic, however, as it misses the crux of the matter. Adorno undoubtedly coined this expression in contrast to Nietzsche's "gay science" (*fröhliche Wissenschaft*), which embraced the principle of *amor fati*. But what was at stake in his theoretical model was not primarily sadness or melancholy, but above all the work of mourning (*Trauer*). Indeed, critical theory itself became a "science of mourning" that had to reckon with the implications of a historical transformation that entailed incalculable losses for the emancipatory cause. The expectations of freedom, justice, and the end of subjugation that the bourgeois world had given birth to perished along with it. In this sense, Adorno's critical theory registered the gradual closure of the historical horizon, illustrating how the emancipatory promises implicit in the classical concepts of bourgeois philosophy—history, freedom, spirit, autonomy, or subject—while retaining their validity, were being drained of all historical substance until they lost any purchase on reality itself. However, while Adorno's critique could still draw from the historical tensions between a declining bourgeois world and the then-emerging advanced capitalism, those tensions have long since been resolved—most likely not in the most desirable manner. Nevertheless, his "science of mourning" remains relevant because the

[8]Gillian Rose, *The Melancholy Science* (London: Verso, 2014).

present has inherited the defeats it addressed. This is what enables his critical theory, originally crafted to respond to a specific historical moment, to endure beyond it.

In this sense, it would be a mistake to see this work of mourning as a symptom of abdication. Adorno's theory does not accept a "defeatism of reason" (ND, 15)[9] that makes peace with the status quo. It refuses to present a softened image of social antagonisms and rejects any complicity with an iniquitous society, while maintaining an awareness that it is not alien to it. As a result, Adorno's theory has preserved its critical bite and its capacity to call the present to account. What is at stake in it is the capacity to respond to a singularly bleak historical situation, which presented unprecedented challenges to emancipatory thought. In retrospect, it is evident that when the dichotomy between emancipation and barbarism was originally presented, it was not just a political slogan, but a warning of the real danger that loomed over that historical moment—a danger that would become manifest in the catastrophes that marked the first half of the last century. Adorno's thought emerged at precisely the moment when it became clear on which side the scales were tipping. In fact, his entire body of work can be read in terms of this painfully sharp awareness of the consequences that the failure to achieve social transformation had for the shaping of twentieth-century societies. Everything that emerges in them, even the most seemingly innocuous phenomena, is viewed through the lens of failed emancipation, exposing a social landscape that squanders the potential for creating living conditions free of avoidable suffering, misery, and extreme need, revealing new forms of violence, brutality, and the mutilation of life. This perspective has often been misunderstood, giving rise to clichés—now firmly established—that depict Adorno as a pessimistic and resigned author, secluded in an ivory tower far removed from worldly affairs. In the following pages, I would like to contribute to correcting this image and to resituate Adorno in the historical element that is his own: the realization that emancipation has, for the time being, failed and that what prevails instead is the overwhelming triumph of barbarism. Consequently,

[9] Theodor W. Adorno, *Negative Dialectics*, trans. E. B. Ashton (London: Routledge, 2004), 3.

critical theory must arm itself for a time of resistance. At the same time, when the opportune moment for social transformation seems to have passed and the historical outlook appears foreclosed, thought that refuses to relinquish all hope is called to self-reflection: it must confront its contradictions and delve into the reasons for the failure of emancipation and its subsequent impact on theory. That, for Adorno, "*is* philosophy."[10]

[10]Theodor W. Adorno, *Vorlesung über Negative Dialektik* (Frankfurt: Suhrkamp, 2007), 85 and *Lectures on Negative Dialectics*, trans. Rodney Livingstone (Cambridge: Polity, 2008), 55.

1

Resignation? History, Emancipation, and Barbarism

The most prevalent criticism of Adorno centers on a charge of resignation. According to this view, his critical theory surrenders in the face of a reality it perceives as hermetically sealed: awful but impossible to change. As a result, Adorno's thought is accused of relinquishing any active political intervention and retreating into itself, finding solace in the arts, and indulging in a kind of theoretical refinement that is as radical as it is sterile. This critique finds expression in a well-known passage by Georg Lukács in which he places Adorno within a tradition of a German intelligentsia practicing "a conformism disguised as non-conformism." Lukács reproaches him for having settled in the "Grand Hotel Abyss … a beautiful hotel equipped with every comfort, on the edge of an abyss, a nothingness, of absurdity. And the daily contemplation of the abyss between excellent meals or artistic entertainments can only heighten the enjoyment of the subtle comforts offered."[1] Here, Adorno is depicted as a theorist entirely detached from any transformative vocation. Comfortably installed in this hotel with its haunting views, he indulges in the refined pleasures of high culture. This portrayal is that of a philosopher who seems to have turned away from the struggles of

[1]Georg Lukács, *The Theory of the Novel*, trans. Anna Bostock (Cambridge, MA: MIT Press, 1971), 22.

his era, content merely to recoil in shock at its horrors without getting his hands dirty. Though this caricature of Adorno oversimplifies both his theory and his persona, it has gained significant traction, becoming something of a cliché. Echoes of Adorno as a pessimistic thinker, one lamenting the rise of totalitarianism and the dominance of administered societies while his own defeatist position leads him to seek a compensatory refuge in art, reverberate throughout the works of authors as varied as Jürgen Habermas, Leszek Kołakowski, Manuel Sacristán, Terry Eagleton, and Stuart Jeffries.[2] In some instances, however, this caricature has taken on a grotesque tone, such as in historian Enzo Traverso's book *Left-Wing Melancholia*. Traverso goes so far as to claim, for example, that Adorno "wrote like a vanquished [man] without a *katechon*"[3] and "contemplated the spectacle of decadence with resignation and stoicism, adopting the posture of the meditating damned in Michelangelo's Last Judgement."[4] In this type of sentence, what purports to be a critique of Adorno's political stance devolves into an ad hominem accusation, attributing the theorist's cultural diagnosis to his personal idiosyncrasies. This repeated accusation of pessimism—to which Adorno continues to be subjected—is therefore revealing, since it is not theoretical in nature; it is psychological. As Roberto Schwarz has pointed out, "the obstruction of the revolutionary solution and the sterility of electoral politics are diagnoses, not preferences."[5] Accordingly, Adorno's intellectual position should not be evaluated based on speculative psychological traits, but rather on the strength of his arguments. It is undeniable that the integration of the proletariat, the rise and diffusion of fascism, the concentration of social power, and the universalization of a form of society based on the production and consumption of commodities had dimmed the prospects for revolutionary social transformation. In any

---

[2]Jürgen Habermas, *The Philosophical Discourse of Modernity*, trans. Frederick G. Lawrence (Cambridge: Polity Press, 1987), 106–30; Leszek Kołakowski, *Main Currents of Marxism, vol. III* (Oxford: Oxford University Press, 1978), 357–80; Manuel Sacristán, *Seis conferencias* (Madrid: El viejo topo, 2005), 174; Terry Eagleton, *The Ideology of the Aesthetic* (Cambridge, MA: Basil Blackwell, 1990), 359–65; Stuart Jeffries, *Grand Hotel Abyss* (London: Verso, 2016).

[3]Enzo Traverso, *Left-Wing Melancholia: Marxism, History, and Memory* (New York: Columbia University Press, 2016), 27.

[4]Ibid., 171.

[5]Roberto Schwarz, "On Adorno (An Interview)," 446.

case, Adorno's writings and interventions demonstrate that his thought never ceased to engage with the existing historical conditions, nor did he reconcile himself with capital. Moreover, Adorno's writings and interventions show that his intellectual approach does not shy away from polemics or taking a stand. In fact, nothing could be further from his critical theory than a claim to neutral knowledge, since he himself is aware that "only those who strive for something possible and better can understand what already exists" (GS 20.2, 601). While the tone of Adorno's writings is undeniably marked by an acute awareness that he is confronting a catastrophic epochal horizon with limited prospects for emancipatory thought, the essence of his theoretical position cannot be divorced from the sociohistorical circumstances to which it responds. It is inadequate to dismiss these circumstances solely by pointing to the alleged trauma that the concurrent rise of fascism and Stalinism inflicted on his thinking.[6]

Significantly, Adorno himself addressed these charges of resignation in one of the last texts published during his lifetime:

> We older representatives of what the name "Frankfurt School" has come to designate have recently and eagerly been accused of resignation. We had indeed developed elements of a critical theory of society, the accusation runs, but we were not ready to draw the practical consequences from it. … The objection, effortlessly rattled off, runs along these lines: the person who at this hour doubts the possibility of radical change in society and who therefore neither participates in spectacular, violent actions nor recommends them has resigned. What he has in mind he thinks cannot be realized; actually, he doesn't even want to realize it. By leaving the conditions untouched, he condones them without admitting it. (GS 10.2, 794)[7]

This reproach, formulated in the context of the protest movement of the late 1960s, struck at a vital nerve of any would-be critical theory. Such a theory

---

[6]As Axel Honneth attempts to argue in *Der zerrissene Welt des Sozialen* (Frankfurt: Suhrkamp, 1990), 82 and The Fragmented World of the Social, trans. Charles W. Wright (New York: SUNY Press, 1995), 126.
[7]Theodor W. Adorno, "Resignation," in *Critical Models: Theodor W. Adorno*, trans. Henry W. Pickford (New York: Columbia University Press, 1999), 289.

cannot disregard the categorical imperative formulated by the young Marx: "to overthrow all conditions in which man is a debased, enslaved, neglected, contemptable being" (MEW 1, 385).[8] The motivation behind Marx's statement, which is pre-theoretical and external to academia, is what fuels critical theory; Adorno never relinquishes it. However, the exaggeration of this impulse can sometimes dull one's analytical acumen, compromising the accurate judgment of historical possibilities and the balance of forces, leading critique to lose its connection with reality and become nothing but a "passion of the brain" (MEW 1, 380).[9] At the same time, according to Adorno, these imputations of resignation overlook something crucial: the effective impotence of intellectual and theoretical work. "The fact that true theory refers back to praxis does not make it praxis and does not allow it to claim to be praxis and not mere philosophy."[10] No theory, however critical, can dismantle social structures on its own. The impetus for true transformation requires something more than sheer will or intellectual dedication; it needs to be grounded in historical reality. Adorno's thought serves as a testament to a pivotal realization in this regard: emancipatory thought could now no longer assume its connection with a force capable of altering historical reality. The unique tone of his thought is bound up with his exploration of this loss and his attempt to grapple with its implications without succumbing to silence. This demands that critical theory confront a paradoxical situation: while scrutinizing social relations from the perspective of radical transformation, it must also acknowledge "the actual blockage of that possibility."[11] It finds itself without a subject of transformation to address. This "leads to a rupture in theory itself that should not be eliminated for the sake of overcoming alleged theoretical inconsistencies or inadequacies; nor should it be minimized by declaring it irrelevant."[12] This rupture is the

[8]Karl Marx, "A Contribution to the Critique of Hegel's Philosophy of Right. Introduction," in *Critique of Hegel's "Philosophy of Right,"* trans. Annette Jolin and Joseph O'Malley (Cambridge: Cambridge University Press, 1977), 137.

[9]Ibid., 133.

[10]Theodor W. Adorno, letter to Marcuse 18 July 1948, cited in D. Braunstein, *Adorno's Critique of Political Economy*, trans. Adam Baltner (Leiden: Brill, 2022), 260.

[11]José A. Zamora, "Teoría Crítica: reflexiones en torno a su (in)actualidad," *Diálogo filosófico* 108 (2020), 367.

[12]Ibid.

result of the imposition of the historical situation on a strain of thinking that does not seek to conceal its own powerlessness and, nevertheless, does not fall into resignation and abandon the objective of putting an end to the degradation of life and avoidable suffering.

Adorno remained faithful to Marx in his insistence that emancipatory thought cannot be severed from the unfolding course of history. At the inception of Marx's theoretical endeavors—especially leading up to the setbacks of the Revolutions of 1848—the prospect of an emancipatory transformation of the world almost seemed within reach. However, it soon became evident that in the meantime, social and political conditions had experienced far-reaching transformations. In light of the ascent of fascism and the totalizing logic of advanced capitalism, Adorno asserted that "only stubbornness could still maintain this thesis as Marx formulated it" (GS 10.2, 469).[13] Faced with the integrative prowess of advanced capitalism, the proletariat could no longer embody the "subject-object of history" envisioned by Lukács (VND, 68).[14] In a sense, this might be construed as a regression in theoretical outlook relative to Marx, yet it was a regression instigated by the actual trajectory of history. The historical horizon appeared closed off. Nevertheless, this did not imply that critical thought had become redundant or had lost its purpose, but rather that it was confronting novel historical tasks.

Confronted with the ever-intensifying and unyielding character of the mechanisms of social domination, which heightened their pressure and revealed a newfound potential for inflicting harm upon life, it became imperative to reassess Marx: the history of all preceding societies now seemed to be the story of relations of domination and violence, marked by escalating brutality alongside deepening social disempowerment. Hence Adorno's statement: "The undiminished persistence of suffering, fear, and menace necessitates that the thought that cannot be realized should not be discarded. After having missed its opportunity, philosophy must come to know, without any mitigation, why the world—which could be paradise here and now—can become hell itself tomorrow" (GS 10.2, 470).[15] This imperative underpins his

[13]Adorno, "Why Still Philosophy," *Critical Models*, 14.
[14]Adorno, *Lectures on Negative Dialectics*, 43.
[15]Adorno, "Why Still Philosophy," 14.

entire critical theory. The mention of the "missed opportunity," which returns at the beginning of *Negative Dialectics*, refers to the long-standing hope for the practical fulfillment of philosophy—a hope still upheld by Marx in the wake of Hegel, but ultimately frustrated. Indeed, the anticipation of a scenario wherein reason, finally master of itself, could materialize in history and shape the conditions of existence, thereby making a fully human life possible, collided starkly with a social reality that laid bare the utter impotence of what was once termed spirit. Adorno's "science of mourning" acknowledges this historical disillusionment but does not fall into resignation. Inverting the eleventh thesis on Feuerbach, he points out that the failure of the transformation of the world demanded a renewed interpretation of it (ND, 15).[16] However, the reality that the era offered up for interpretation was far from reassuring.

Adorno's reference to a world with so much promise but such potential to be hellish is far from arbitrary; it alludes to a sociohistorical catastrophe that took shape within the core of the most advanced modern societies. In his writings, this catastrophe appears under the name of Auschwitz, the German name for a place in Poland where, between 1940 and 1945, earthly reality took on truly infernal dimensions. However, this manifestation of hell did not stem from atavistic or uncivilized forces, but from the most methodical and intentional utilization of scientific, logistical, and technological advances. It resulted from the progressively tested and optimized use of poison gas for the "mass production and cost-cutting of death" (MM, 266),[17] the meticulously planned and executed transport of deportees from across Europe, and the most efficient division of labor for the systematic extermination of millions of unarmed and defenseless human beings. Their corpses were then stripped of any economically useful remnants, subjected to final elimination, and reduced to ashes. All this unfolded amid the acquiescence, indifference, or inaction of a world that deemed itself "civilized." Adorno's choice to designate this atrocity with a toponym, "Auschwitz," rather than by employing conceptual terms like "the Holocaust" or "genocide" signifies a recognition that its dimensions surpass mere conceptualization (cf. GS 4, 289). In his thought, the name

[16] Adorno, *Negative Dialectics*, 3.
[17] Adorno, *Minima Moralia*, 223.

Auschwitz signifies a historical break that no longer allows for the idea that history could be redeemed; the only remaining hope lies in the "possibility … of averting the most extreme, total disaster" (GS 10.2, 618).[18] In the aftermath of the systematic and "rational" extermination of millions of human beings, history no longer appears capable of assuming any positive meaning (ND 354),[19] but rather as a succession of catastrophes in which "each of its new forms outdoes the old" (MM, 267).[20] From emancipatory thought, this demands empathetic attention to everything that has been damaged, cut short, and crushed in its course. Here, the interplay between history and violence reaches a new threshold, revealing how civilization's expanding productive capacities are accompanied by increased coercive and destructive potentials that remain unchecked. Redoubled pressure from the forces of domination develops alongside these capacities. Hence, "the critique of violence in all its manifestations, including those within thought and psyche, is essential for Critical Theory."[21] Adorno adamantly refuses to downplay this escalation in violence, resisting the notion of Auschwitz as a historical anomaly (LGF, 14),[22] or "a kind of accident on the road to progress."[23] Instead, he compels us to confront "why humanity, instead of entering a truly human state, is sinking into a new kind of barbarism" (DA, 11).[24] For emancipatory thought, Auschwitz marks a before and an after (MBP, 162).[25] It marks a transition from a time "before the revolution" when the expectation of a forthcoming social transformation provided unassimilated subjects with a trajectory that lent their actions direction and meaning, to a time of barbarism. This era is typified by an growing disproportion between the impotence of living individuals and the power of a relentless social apparatus that displayed a suffocating capacity for integration. For Adorno, this historical horizon

---

[18] Adorno, "Progress," *Critical Models*, 144.

[19] Adorno, *Negative Dialectics*, 361.

[20] Adorno, *Minima Moralia*, 234.

[21] Thorsten Fuchshuber, *Rackets: Kritische Theorie der Bandenherrschaft* (Freiburg: ça ira, 2019), 13.

[22] Adorno, *History and Freedom*, 7–8.

[23] Theodor W. Adorno, "Die menschliche Gesellschaft heute," *Vorträge 1949–1968* (Berlin: Suhrkamp, 2019), 208.

[24] Horkheimer and Adorno, *Dialectic of Enlightenment*, xiv.

[25] Theodor W. Adorno, *Metaphysics: Concepts and Problems*, trans. Edmund Jephcott (Stanford, CA: Stanford University Press, 2001), 116.

compels emancipatory thought to mobilize what remains possible so that this new barbarism might encounter, at the very least, some form of resistance.

"After Auschwitz"

In one of the final texts written before his sudden passing, "Marginalia to Theory and Praxis," Adorno highlighted the historical experiences that had formed the contours of his critical theory, and he did so in relation to Marx:

> In his celebrated letter to Kugelmann, Marx warned of the threat of a relapse into barbarism, which must already have been foreseeable at that time. Nothing could have better expressed the elective affinity between conservatism and revolution. Marx already saw this as the ultima ratio to deflect the collapse he had prognosticated. But the fear, which certainly was not the least of the things motivating Marx, has been eclipsed. The relapse has already occurred. To still expect it in the future, even after Auschwitz and Hiroshima, is to take pitiable consolation in the thought that the worst is possibly yet to come. (GS 10.2, 769)[26]

The toponym Auschwitz refers to the deliberate and systematic extermination of European Jews, as well as Romas, homosexuals, and other lives that the Nazis deemed "unworthy of being lived." Here, a violence and a negativity emerge that defy integration into history, serving no purpose other than pure annihilation. Yet beneath this name something else lies buried: "the hope for a way out, or, echoing the still undamaged language of the nineteenth century, the hope for a social revolution that would fulfill messianic expectations."[27] In light of the magnitude of the horror represented by Auschwitz, the expectations of a "realization of philosophy" are shattered and the old notions of autonomy, freedom, and beauty lose all historical substance. This does not imply that the memory of the millions who died should negate the legitimate right of the living to be happy. Recognizing the significance of this catastrophe

---

[26] Adorno, "Marginalia to Theory and Praxis," *Critical Models*, 267–8. Translation modified.
[27] Detlev Claussen, *Aspekte der Alltagsreligion* (Frankfurt: Neue Kritik, 2000), 19.

does not imply abandoning the search for a world without domination, injustice, or avoidable suffering. Rather, the level of atrocity revealed by Auschwitz puts emancipatory thought in a new situation, one demanding a revision of its former certainties. What happened "has definitively torn away the veil of optimism that once covered the contradictions of the modern emancipatory process,"[28] demonstrating the entanglement between reason and domination, between progress and regression. Barbarism can no longer be conceived as the radical Other of modern society, but as something deeply rooted in its contradictions. The problem is that, faced with an increasingly rigid and impervious social reality, emancipatory praxis seems to have been "indefinitely delayed" (ND, 15).[29] However, if Adorno's theory remains critical, it is because it refuses to resign itself to the triumph of the barbarism laid bare by Auschwitz. "The sole adequate praxis would be to put all energies toward working our way out of barbarism" (GS 10.2, 769),[30] Adorno wrote in 1969. His entire philosophy is articulated as an uncompromising refusal to accept the world that allowed Auschwitz to happen and that provided no grounds to cease fearing a recurrence of similar horrors. Thus, in contrast to Marx's anticipation that the end of capitalism—deemed imminent—would herald the beginning of a truly human history, it could be argued that for Adorno, Auschwitz signifies the onset of a new phase of prehistory.[31] This led him to dissect the objective and subjective causes that had made it possible, which were embedded in the constitutive elements of modern societies and were not eradicated along with the military defeat of fascism. From this arises an acute awareness of both the singular nature of the horror that Auschwitz signifies and of its potential repetition, for "the willingness to commit the unspeakable survives in people as well as in the conditions which enclose them" (GS 10.1, 555).[32] It could be said that the awareness of facing a new phase of prehistory is what sets the distinctive tone of his critical theory, which is so often considered pessimistic or bleak. "One speaks of the threat of a relapse into barbarism,"

[28]José A. Zamora, "Th. W. Adorno: filosofía frente a la catástrofe," *Sociología histórica* 10 (2020): 473.
[29]Adorno, *Negative Dialectics*, 3.
[30]Adorno, "Marginalia to Theory and Praxis," 268.
[31]Cf. Detlev Claussen, *Abschied von Gestern: Kritische Theorie heute* (Bremen: Wassmann, 1988), 18–20.
[32]Adorno, "The Meaning of Working Through the Past," *Critical Models*, 90.

Adorno wrote in 1966. "But it is not a threat—Auschwitz *was* this relapse, and barbarism continues as long as the fundamental conditions that favored that relapse remain essentially unchanged" (GS 10.2, 674).[33]

"After Auschwitz," then, refers not only to a historical rupture, but also to the enduring relevance of the factors that defined the era as a time of barbarism. This also posed a challenge for theoretical endeavors. As Hans-Jürgen Krahl once pointed out, while the conditions leading to the rise of fascism could still be explained within the framework of the critique of political economy and the dynamics of capital accumulation, the same cannot be said for Auschwitz.[34] Attempting to explain it through the lens of the psychology of sadism is equally inadequate. Auschwitz resists any functional explanation that would reduce it to a means to an end, for that would also imply a rationalization of what happened. Therefore, the atrocity denoted by this name confronts any theoretical framework with the limits of meaning; this is precisely what compels us to investigate the conditions that made such a thing possible. This imperative paved the way for the model of critical theory that starts to take shape with *Dialectic of Enlightenment*. This model seeks to examine how the unprecedented levels of atrocity, humiliation, and suffering revealed by Auschwitz could have come about, marking a catastrophic milestone in the history of violence.[35] Once this threshold was crossed, any theory aspiring to confront it could no longer afford any trace of naivety: the horror of Auschwitz demanded looking differently at the society and history in which it germinated.[36] "There is nothing innocuous left,"[37] Adorno wrote in *Minima Moralia* (MM, 26). "Certainly, the unprecedented torture and humiliation of those abducted in cattle-trucks does shed a deathly-livid light on the most distant past" (MM,

---

[33]Adorno, "Education After Auschwitz," *Critical Models*, 191. Translation modified.

[34]Hans-Jürgen Krahl, *Konstitution und Klassenkampf* (Frankfurt: Neue Kritik, 2008), 321.

[35]"In the concentration camps, the boundary between life and death was eradicated. A middle-ground was created, inhabited by living skeletons and putrefying bodies, victims unable to take their own lives, Satan's laughter at the hope of abolishing death. As in Kafka's twisted epics, what perished there was that which had provided the criterion of experience—life lived out to its end" (GS 10.1, 273; "Notes on Kafka" *Prisms*, trans. Samuel and Shierry Weber [Cambridge, MA: MIT Press, 1981], 259).

[36]Few authors have insisted on this point with as much clarity as Detlev Claussen. Cf. "Nach Auschwitz," in *Zivilisationsbruch*, ed. Dan Diner (Frankfurt: Fischer, 1986), 54–68, and José A. Zamora, *Th. W. Adorno. Pensar contra la barbarie* (Madrid: Trotta, 2004), 42–50.

[37]Adorno, *Minima Moralia*, 25.

268).[38] Any thought that failed to grapple with these experiences and the new potential for destruction they unveiled, Adorno believed, was doomed to triviality (LGF, 280).[39] Indeed, as the pinnacle of degradation and suffering, Auschwitz casts a piercing light that exposes the inherent falseness of society, culture, and life itself. Consequently, Adorno's interest here is not to write *about* Auschwitz or turn it into a "topic," showcasing the suffering of the victims anew, who are "tossed out to be gobbled up by the world that did them in" (GS 11, 423).[40] Rather than focusing solely on analyzing the horror of the camps, his theory is grounded in an awareness of the relationship between this "extreme phenomenon" and the "normality" in which it was incubated. For the atrocity epitomized by Auschwitz unveils a perverse constitution of social life in its entirety, revealing it as both an accomplice and a midwife of barbarism. This also implicated cultural production and theoretical activity itself.

Hence Adorno's irritation with attempts to move on, to forget the horror and return to *business as usual* as if nothing had occurred: "Millions of Jews have been murdered, and this is to be seen as an interlude and not the catastrophe itself. What more is this culture waiting for?" (MM, 62).[41] The desire to get back to a "normal course of events" was especially suspicious in spheres that were presumed to be less involved in the horror, such as culture and art. For Adorno, the events in the camps "burned away without consolation any reassuring feature of the spirit and its objectification, culture" (ND, 358).[42] That is why he opposed efforts to resurrect a realm of art, goodness, and beauty that purported to transcend the "somatic stratum of the living being that is distant from meaning" (ND, 358)[43]; as if the revived culture could be used to "cover up the crime" (MBP, 168).[44] The only appropriate response for products of the spirit was shame in the face of what had happened. Auschwitz had unequivocally exposed the failure of culture to grasp hold of human

[38]Ibid., 234.

[39]Adorno, *History and Freedom*, 203.

[40]Theodor W. Adorno, "Commitment," in *Notes to Literature 2*, trans. Shierry Weber Nicholsen (New York: Columbia University Press, 1992), 88.

[41]Adorno, *Minima Moralia*, 55.

[42]Adorno, *Negative Dialectics*, 365. Translation modified.

[43]Ibid., 365.

[44]Adorno, *Metaphysics*, 130.

beings and transform them. This made it impossible to look at its aura of refinement and its claim to transcendence in the same light: culture "abhors stench because it stinks—because, as Brecht put it in a magnificent line, its mansion is built of dogshit" (ND, 359). Adorno's famous dictum on poetry after Auschwitz, frequently not even quoted in full, should be understood under this light: "Cultural criticism finds itself faced with the final stage of the dialectic of culture and barbarism. To write poetry after Auschwitz is barbaric. And this corrodes even the knowledge of why it has become impossible to write poetry today" (GS 10.1, 30).[45] What is at stake in this passage is not a ban on poetry, but the self-reflection of the spirit. If the latter does not want to degenerate into cynicism or ideology, it must refuse any attitude that fosters reconciliation with barbarism or which can feign a false purity that conceals its horror (ÄT, 347–48).[46] Adorno recognized that not even the critic is safe from this peril. Hence the unequivocal formulation in *Negative Dialectics*: "All culture after Auschwitz, including its urgent critique, is garbage" (ND, 359).[47] However, this phrase also has its dialectical counterpoint, for the fact that "culture so far has failed is no justification for furthering its failure" (MM, 49).[48] Renouncing all objectivation of the spirit would effectively grant the triumphant barbarism free rein. Adorno's position navigates between the extremes of this dilemma, aware that the only thing that could measure up to the situation would be a type of cultural and theoretical output capable of confronting the entanglement between culture and barbarism without becoming complicit in brutality and of rejecting any claim to the purity of the spirit in the face of life's degradation and torment.[49]

However, culture and critique merely offer a glimpse of how the new barbarism has infiltrated domains that, at first sight, might seem removed from it. More relevant than the enquiry into culture after Auschwitz is "whether after

[45] Adorno, "Cultural Criticism and Society," *Prisms*, 33.

[46] Theodor W. Adorno, *Aesthetic Theory*, trans. Robert Hullot-Kentor (New York: Continuum, 1997), 152–3.

[47] Adorno, *Negative Dialectics*, 366. Translation modified.

[48] Adorno, *Minima Moralia*, 22.

[49] For Adorno, it was Samuel Beckett who best managed to respond to this new situation in the realm of art, and it was no coincidence that he planned to dedicate his *Aesthetic Theory* to him (cf. Jordi Maiso, "Sismografías de la edad de oro: Adorno y Beckett," *Laocoonte* 7 [2020]: 189–202).

Auschwitz you can go on living" (ND, 355)[50] at all. For in the world that brought forth such barbarity, life itself has been irreversibly scarred. In this sense, the reference to Auschwitz should not be misconstrued. Adorno himself clarified in 1965 that when he invokes this toponym he means "not only Auschwitz, but the world of torture which has continued to exist after Auschwitz and of which we are receiving the most horrifying reports from Vietnam" (MBP, 160).[51] In Adorno's usage, the mention of Auschwitz does not therefore denote a one-off event, but rather a potent trend within society as a whole (GS 10.2, 675). It signifies a new threshold being reached in the history of violence and the potential for living beings to be subjected to suffering—evident both in advances in the destructive technologies exemplified by the atomic bomb and in the growing ability of human beings to tolerate and coexist with such horror. New tasks for any theory with an emancipatory intent emerge from this predicament. Nowhere is this clearer than in Adorno's formulation of the new categorical imperative at the outset of the second meditation on metaphysics in *Negative Dialectics*: "A new categorical imperative has been imposed by Hitler upon unfree mankind: to arrange their thoughts and actions so that Auschwitz will not repeat itself, so that nothing similar will happen" (ND, 358).[52] Each element of this statement warrants careful examination. This imperative does not emanate from the autonomy of the moral agent; its formulation has been *imposed* by historical realities and gains significance in a state of unfreedom, in which individuals are not masters of their own destinies. This resituates the imperative in relation to Kant's version of it, since it no longer refers to an absolutized reason that grounds itself, nor does it constitute an imperative void of content, relying solely on a formal criterion. Adorno's imperative is not based on the freedom of the subject, but on the experience of horrors produced by history. That is why it does not seek to be grounded discursively, like a rational moral law or an abstract principle; instead, it arises from an impulse.[53] It is based purely on a spontaneous reaction prompted by an "impatience with argumentation" and an "unwillingness to allow the horror to continue"

[50] Adorno, *Negative Dialectics*, 363.
[51] Adorno, *Metaphysics*, 101.
[52] Adorno, *Negative Dialectics*, 365.
[53] Sangwon Han, *Konstitutive Negativität* (Bielefeld: Transcript, 2016), 218–22.

(ND, 281)[54]; ultimately its only foundation is solidarity with the living. This introduces an element that is alien to logic, discourse, and reason; without it, these dimensions risk imposing sacrifices on the individual. For "it is only in the unvarnished materialistic motive that morality survives" (ND, 358).[55]

This response to the degradation of living beings, to those who are denigrated, enslaved, helpless, and despised, links Adorno's imperative to the one formulated by the young Marx. Indeed, the latter was also born out of urgency and indignation in the face of unacceptable injustice. Yet there is a fundamental difference between them. Adorno's imperative can no longer simply prescribe "overthrowing social relations." The praxis required to put an end to barbarism appears to be blocked: a connection between moral principle and historical reality can no longer be assumed. All that remains is the need for a new orientation of thought and action to prevent the incessant reproduction of the newly reached threshold of violence, with full awareness of the repeatability of the horror. But this should not lead to misunderstandings. The thrust of Adorno's new categorical imperative is not to "turn us into salt statues, captives of the past,"[56] but to sharpen our focus on the ongoing social catastrophes of the present, preventing them from being trivialized or condoned, and putting an end to everything in social life that continues to break individuals or push them into atrocity. At the same time, its formulation evokes "unfulfilled hopes and unresolved injustices."[57] In short: Adorno's claim amounts to an imperative directed against the lingering presence of barbarism. Nonetheless, the transition from Marx's categorical imperative to Adorno's underscores how the catastrophic course of modern societies has transformed emancipatory thought.

According to a phrase of Adorno's, formulated as early as March 1936, "the goal of the revolution is the elimination of fear" (ABB, 173).[58] The emancipatory goal is already defined here, before Auschwitz, *ex negativo*: liberation from fear,

---

[54]Adorno, *Negative Dialectics*, 286. Translation modified.

[55]Ibid., 365. Translation modified.

[56]Zamora, "Th. W. Adorno: filosofía frente a la catástrofe," 473.

[57]Ibid.

[58]Theodor W. Adorno and Walter Benjamin, *The Complete Correspondence, 1928–1940*, trans. Nicholas Walker (Oxford: Polity Press, 1999), 131. Translation modified.

which reduces individuals and disempowers them. Where there is fear, there can be no freedom. Thus, Adorno advocates a concept of revolution that seeks to eradicate all the forms of oppression and degradation that are inflicted upon humanity: "Revolution must eliminate fear and barbarism; there is no reason to fear it, what should be feared is what exists" (AHB I, 131). This assertion already underscores the idea that it is not the potential transformation of the existing social order that should instill fear, but rather the current order built upon coercive and violent mechanisms of power, which scarcely considers individuals when imposing its rule. If this was Adorno's perspective even before his recognition of the descent into barbarism, Auschwitz was to mark a point of no return in this regard: for what that name signifies is a manifestation of the universalization of fear. The degree to which individual lives have been rendered insignificant becomes evident in the vast disparity between the annihilating violence of systematic genocide and the near-absent capacity for any response from those subjected to it, having been stripped of any semblance of agency and resigned to their demise as passive victims. In this sense, one might speak of the "vacuum between men and their fate" (MM, 61)[59]: merely being marked with the yellow star is sufficient to be consigned—regardless of biographical circumstances or individual trajectories—to the ranks of those fated to have their lungs torn apart in a gas chamber. Faced with such a degree of destruction, indifferent to the value of individual lives, there is little left to fear: "absolute negativity is in plain sight and has ceased to surprise anyone" (ND, 355).[60] However, the terror of this era of pervasive fear extends beyond the industrialized production of death: it forms part of a new frontier in the social capacity for destruction and the "infinite abasement of living" (MM, 41).[61] This is evident in atomic warfare, the development of new forms of torture, the coexistence of increasing prosperity with the persistence of hunger and deprivation of the most basic necessities, as well as in the categorization of countless human beings as "superfluous" or dispensable and the reality of living in a world where the brutality has reached a level where "fearing death

[59]Adorno, *Minima Moralia*, 55.

[60]Adorno, *Negative Dialectics*, 363.

[61]Adorno, *Minima Moralia*, 38.

means fearing worse than death" (ND, 364).[62] In this sense, although Adorno stressed that fear had been "the ultimate lesson of the fascist era" (GS 3, 335),[63] his theory was forced to note that the military defeat of fascism did not put an end to the universalization of fear. It remained embedded in the interaction between individuals and their broader social context, persisting through the arms race of the Cold War, even in those countries that experienced the prosperity of the so-called economic miracles.

Fear always belongs to individuals. It is linked to the principle of self-preservation, to the possibility of staying alive under given circumstances, which always depends on the prevailing social framework in each specific case. In this sense, the model of society emerging in the twentieth century reveals a growing disproportion between an overwhelming social apparatus and increasingly powerless individuals. This undermines the conditions necessary for subjects to determine their existence autonomously and continually exposes the course of their lives to shocks that hinder the notion of a life "lived out to its end" (GS 10.1, 273).[64] Adorno thus points to a situation where the very logic of self-preservation "cannot help suspecting the life to which it attaches is becoming what it shudders at" (ND, 357);[65] for it is the very conditions of subsistence that instill such mounting dread. Given the growing insignificance of individual lives, survival itself becomes a sacrificial act. This phenomenon extends beyond fascism to encompass the forms of capitalist socialization that survived it, a condition Adorno refers to as a "state of unfreedom." While the prosperous postwar societies did not offer such favorable conditions for sadists and torturers to run wild, their forms of socialization were still based on coercion and violence (LGF, 281).[66] Admittedly, one cannot equate the direct coercion of fascist rule with the "mute compulsion of economic relations" (MEW 23, 765),[67] which is imposed on formally free and equal individuals

---

[62]Adorno, *Negative Dialectics*, 371.

[63]Theodor W. Adorno, "The Schema of Mass Culture," trans. Nicholas Walker in *The Culture Industry* (New York: Routledge, 1991), 96.

[64]Adorno, "Notes on Kafka," 259.

[65]Adorno, *Negative Dialectics*, 364. Translation modified.

[66]Adorno, *History and Freedom*, 203.

[67]Karl Marx, *Capital: A Critique of Political Economy, Volume One*, trans. Ben Fowkes (London: Penguin, 1990), 899.

through capital's mechanisms of socialization. However, while Marx relegated direct violence to exceptional occurrences, maintaining that the coercion of "natural laws of production" (MEW 23, 765)[68] sufficed for the normal operation of capitalism, Adorno perceives an "increase in the pressure of domination" (MM, 267)[69] in twentieth-century societies. The growing dominance of the social apparatus submits individuals to increasingly relentless processes of adaptation, which impose the imperatives of the system with as much coercive force as necessary (MBP, 168).[70] Despite the undeniable distinctions between fascism and advanced capitalism, the two ultimately converge in reducing human beings to mere objects of the reproduction of the social whole. This engenders a sense of anguish at being at the mercy of an increasingly closed-off and all-encompassing social system, which determines every single condition of human existence.[71] In this sense, the totalizing character of the social order and its power over individual life is not the exclusive lot of authoritarian regimes but appears as a distinctive feature of a new epoch in Adorno's work. In it the "mechanism for reproducing life, for dominating and for destroying it, is exactly the same, and accordingly industry, state and advertising are amalgamated" (MM, 59).[72] The prohibition against naivety stemming from Auschwitz also shaped the way in which Adorno confronts the persistence of violence and fear within the confines of socialization under advanced capitalism; for the circumstances in which barbarism can emerge persist in that context too.

In the formally democratic societies of the second postwar period, the conditions governing the reproduction of life tend to reduce individuals to mere cogs within the productive apparatus. Their very insertion into the vast machinery of the Fordist employment system often turns them into indistinct specimens, perfectly fungible and replaceable as such. Even when the social apparatus allows individuals to reproduce their lives, and may even provide for them better than ever before, individuals find themselves "entirely

[68]Marx, *Capital Volume One*, 899.

[69]Adorno, *Minima Moralia*, 234. Translation modified.

[70]Adorno, *Metaphysics*, 107.

[71]Adorno, "Contra Paulum," AHB II, 499.

[72]Adorno, *Minima Moralia*, 33.

nullified in the face of the economic powers" (DA, 15).[73] The absolutist logic of capital valorization establishes itself *de facto* as the sovereign power upon which their livelihoods depend; this condition imposes a heavy burden on their consciousness and their unconscious. Fear assumes the form of claustrophobia, the sensation of being ensnared within an increasingly constricting social system that admits no outside (ND, 340).[74] Within this framework, access to employment and social prosperity occurs under a regime of competition that atomizes individuals and sets them against one another, laying the groundwork for a coldness that Adorno famously termed the "basic principle of bourgeois subjectivity, without which Auschwitz would not have been possible" (ND, 356).[75] Consequently, the struggle for subsistence enmeshes individual subjects in a web of guilt, and this is sanctioned by a growing indifference to the fate of others so long as a way of avoiding the most harmful side of a social logic that is known to be implacable. In the end, the problem for Adorno is that the "societal pressure still bears down, although the danger remains invisible nowadays. It drives people toward the unspeakable, which culminated on a world-historical scale in Auschwitz" (GS 10.2, 674).[76] It is the enduring grip of fear and its social determinants that predisposes individuals to perpetuate the very violence they most dread—a violence deeply embedded within the fabric of the social system, qualifying the present as a period of prehistory, a time of barbarism. Any prospect of improvement is therefore contingent upon the arrival of a scenario wherein human beings "will at last be able to breathe a sigh of relief" (GS 10.2, 617),[77] marking the dawn of a "debarbarization of humanity" (GS 10.2, 672).[78] As long as that does not occur, Freud's account of civilization's discontents must be understood in fundamentally social terms. It is no coincidence that the society Adorno had before him had developed the technical means to reach

[73]Horkheimer and Adorno, *Dialectic of Enlightenment*, xvii.

[74]Adorno, *Negative Dialectics*, 346–7.

[75]Adorno, *Negative Dialectics*, 363. Translation modified. Cf. Jordi Maiso, "Zur gesellschaftlichen Produktion von Kälte," in *Grenzsteine. Beiträge zur Kritik der Gewalt*, ed. Theodora Becker, Andreas Franze, Jakob Hayner and Arne Kellermann (Munich: Text+Kritik, 2016), 71–85.

[76]Adorno, "Education after Auschwitz," 191.

[77]Adorno, "Progress," 144.

[78]Adorno, "Education after Auschwitz," 190.

the moon and stars, and to embark on a nuclear arms race that endangered the very possibility of life on Earth, while remaining entirely incapable of creating the conditions for a daily existence free from fear, anguish, and avoidable suffering.[79] In its relentless pursuit of "progress" and increases in productivity, the most basic imperative by which all social progress must be measured remained unfulfilled: "that no-one shall go hungry any more" (MM, 178).[80] This was evidence of the most disastrous features of the current social order: while it "reproduces life," it does so in a way that harbors a constant potential for catastrophe.[81]

This uncompromising diagnosis of the situation, which leaves no room for naivety, imparts Adorno's thought with an urgent tone that refuses to entertain illusions about the nature of theory itself: "Nonetheless it is completely uncertain whether philosophy, as a conceptual activity of the interpretive mind, is still the order of the day, whether it has fallen behind what it should conceptualize—the state of the world rushing toward catastrophe" (GS 10.2, 469).[82] In this vein, one could draw a parallel between Adorno's work and his assessment of Kafka: if history appears as hell in his writings, it is because what could have saved it was allowed to slip away (GS 10.1, 273).[83] Despite the prevailing circumstances indicating, for the time being, that the possibility of a radical transformation of social life has faded from view, Adorno does not overlook the fact that such a transformation would be the only means to halt barbarism and eradicate horror[84]; in fact, all of his thought is articulated from a perspective that refuses to abandon the quest for emancipation. However, Adorno is equally aware that theory alone cannot offer a speculative escape from the impasse of transformative praxis, particularly in the face of profound threats looming on the historical horizon. In this context, his response to

---

[79] Adorno, "Die menschliche Gesellschaft heute," 209.
[80] Adorno, *Minima Moralia*, 156.
[81] Adorno, "Contra Paulum," 477.
[82] Adorno, "Why Still Philosophy," 13.
[83] Adorno, "Notes on Kafka," 259. In a note for his *Arcades Project* where he attempted to elucidate some fundamental historical concepts, Walter Benjamin also defined catastrophe as being a "missed opportunity" (BGS V, 593; Walter Benjamin, *The Arcades Project*, 474). This formulation aptly captures Adorno's perspective on the question.
[84] Adorno, "Contra Paulum," 478.

Lukács' criticisms—penned just months before his untimely demise—is revealing:

> Lukács reproached me with a stupid joke (this stupidity is part of the widespread regressive tendency that considers itself revolutionary today) about how I am supposed to have installed myself in a luxury hotel on the edge of the abyss. That is *worth considering*; Chaplin's cabin in *The Gold Rush* would not be the worst allegory for my thought. Lukács has thrown himself into the abyss and mistaken it for salvation. He is not even here, but crawling around down below, broken like one of Beckett's figures that so enraged him. Where am I to live, then, in the stale air of security? I prefer my rickety luxury hotel. Its luxury, however, consists of nothing other than expressing the most extreme negativity, and even that is begrudged me.[85]

"Where Is the Proletariat?"

Despite this shaky and precarious position, Adorno believed he had good reason to insist on the negativity of the sociohistorical reality. "Only thoughts that go to the utmost extremes are capable of facing up to the all-powerful powerlessness of assured consent" (ND 45),[86] he wrote in *Negative Dialectics*. Developed during a time characterized by the growing destitution of subjects in the face of the social apparatus, his critical theory articulated a distrust of any tendencies dragging thought toward forms of conformity that reduced friction with the prevailing social logic, or even led to overt complicity with it. That is why Adorno was wary of everything that lingered in the comfort zone sanctioned by sound common sense and preferred to grant himself the luxury of confrontation with extreme negativity; this alone prevents thought from reconciling itself with the present reality and becoming an accomplice of barbarism. Hence the famous affirmation that "there is no longer beauty or consolation except in the gaze falling on horror, withstanding it, and in

[85]Theodor W. Adorno, "Graeculus (II). Notizen zu Philosophie und Gesellschaft," *Frankfurter Adorno Blätter*, vol. VIII (Munich: Text+Kritik, 2003), 36.
[86]Adorno, *Negative Dialectics*, 34.

unalleviated consciousness of negativity holding fast to the possibility of what is better" (MM, 26–27).[87] Anyone who has not abandoned the cause of emancipation cannot turn their back on the most atrocious features of a reality that still needs to be changed; to do otherwise would imply a capitulation to these features on the false pretext of avoiding defeatism. In fact, nothing could be more harmful to the cause of emancipation than deluding oneself about the social and historical conditions in which the struggle for transformative intervention takes place.

Considering the triumph and expansion of fascism, the aftermath of Auschwitz, and increasing social integration achieved by advanced capitalism, it was difficult to maintain the belief that the hope for emancipatory transformation remained historically viable. All the assurances that Marxism and the social and political struggles that had emerged in the nineteenth century had formerly been able to count on had been shattered. It was no longer possible to trust that the modernization process would improve the standing of any potentially transformative forces, nor that the working class would be the subject called upon to bring about social transformation. Meanwhile, the course of the Soviet Revolution (especially following the purges of the 1930s) made it increasingly clear that it was drifting ever further from any emancipatory dimension.[88] This affected both communist parties and Marxist theory itself, which, in the hands of those parties, lost all critical potential and merely became a means of legitimizing their own policies. Hence the critical theory project that Max Horkheimer laid out in the 1930s took shape both in opposition to this official Marxism and academic science (HGS 4, 162–216).[89] Faced with a historical situation exhibiting a tendency toward the concentration of power and a growing consolidation of capitalism, it was necessary to redefine how opposition was to be constructed: this was also the case for oppositional theory. In this sense, Adorno agreed with Horkheimer's deep distrust of the triumphalist rhetoric of vulgar Marxism and its political organizations: "The

[87]Adorno, *Minima Moralia*, 25–6.

[88]In this sense, Adorno spoke of the "the revolution's failure even where it succeeded" (ND 316). *Negative Dialectics*, 322.

[89]Max Horkheimer, "Traditional and Critical Theory," in *Critical Theory: Selected Essays*, trans. Matthew J. O'Connell (New York: Continuum, 2002), 188.

further the rational expectation diminishes that society's doom can really be averted, the more reverently they repeat the old prayers: masses, solidarity, Party, class struggle" (MM, 129).[90] Revolutionary impatience, which in its day rejected all caution in the name of the urgency of putting an end to the reigning injustice, now became the demand for blind loyalty to the Party. Faced with a bleak outlook, it insisted that final victory would only arrive through the organization. However, as prospects for emancipation diminished, discipline was detached from the revolutionary struggle and became an end in itself. In the meantime, ruling cliques insisted that theoreticians should not to be doomsayers, should avoid criticism, and should focus on the positive; otherwise, this would amount to a betrayal of the working class. This, in fact, has been the implicit tone of many of the criticisms of Adorno from a certain strain of the left. However, this notion that theory's attempt to build up a clear view of the existing state of affairs could cause discouragement to spread in one's own ranks was nothing but a refusal to confront the real weakness of the revolutionary cause, which cannot rely on any real support from existing forms of subjectivity and consciousness:

> Today, when the enemy's power and control over the consciousness of the masses has been immeasurably strengthened, the attempt radically to alter this consciousness by withholding assent to it is considered reactionary. Suspicion falls on anyone who combines criticism of capitalism with that of the proletariat, which is more and more becoming a mere reflection of the tendencies of capitalist development. (MM, 128)[91]

Strictly speaking, Adorno is not a critic of the proletariat. His thought is extremely sensitive to class injustices, which are not presented as minor or secondary elements in the history of capitalism. For Adorno, disadvantaged and exploited social groups are the focal point of all the injustices of the social system, as well as of its mutilating power. According to him, all history so far has been that of domination and subjugation, and all hierarchy is a "coercive

---

[90]Adorno, *Minima Moralia*, 114.
[91]Ibid., 113.

organization for the appropriation of the labor of others" (GS 8, 373).[92] What Adorno criticizes is the persistence of the confusion that continues to identify the proletariat, as it exists within developed capitalism, with the subject destined to produce emancipatory social transformation. Thus, in deliberate opposition to the mythology of vulgar Marxism, which insisted on presenting an image of the proletariat as a heroic figure, a kind of *deus ex machina* capable of ushering in a new historical era, Adorno had no illusions about what it meant to be proletarian under the social logic of advanced capitalism. As he would insist to Walter Benjamin in their epistolary exchanges from the 1930s, the proletariat is first and foremost "a product of bourgeois society" (ABB, 171).[93] Its class constitution is not characterized by a plebeian character that could have preserved a certain degree of autonomy from the system, but by the subaltern position assigned to it by its function in developed capitalist society. Hence Adorno suspected that, far from being a subject capable of becoming the incarnation and foundation of the emancipated society to come, the proletariat bears "all the marks of mutilation of the typical bourgeois character" (ABB, 173).[94] Their lives play out under the crushing weight of a form of socialization that imposes itself on its members in an increasingly coercive manner and that tends to eliminate anything that might remain in them that is extraterritorial or nonconforming to its order. However, this perspective is not formulated out of elitist disdain, but from the bitter realization of someone who perceives—by virtue of his own privileged position—the harm that actual living conditions inflict both on individuals and on the cause of emancipation.

[92]For Adorno, the echo of the violence that traverses history resounds in the most ancient vestiges of culture, which, as Benjamin pointed out, were always also documents of barbarism: "The archaic silence of pyramids and ruins becomes conscious of itself in materialist thought: it is the echo of factory noise in the landscape of the immutable. Jakob Burckhardt hazards the suggestion that the parable of the cave in Plato's *Republic*, with its sublime symbolism of the doctrine of eternal ideas, derived from the horrendous image of the Athenian silver mines. This implies that the philosophical idea of eternal truth had sprung from the contemplation of present torment. All history is the history of class struggles because it was always the same thing, namely, prehistory" (GS 8, 374 and Theodor W. Adorno, "Reflections on Class Theory," trans. Rodney Livingstone in *Can One Live After Auschwitz? A Philosophical Reader* [Stanford, CA: Stanford University Press, 2003], 94).
[93]Adorno and Benjamin, *The Complete Correspondence*, 130.
[94]Ibid., 131.

Indeed, Walter Benjamin had already written that the experience of his generation revealed that "capitalism will not die a natural death" (BGS V, 819).[95] After the Great War, the stabilization of capitalism, and the rise of fascism, it was no longer possible to trust that the course of history would, by itself, lead to a situation free from injustice and heteronomy; that would require the intervention of a conscious subject. Now, given the enormous integrative power demonstrated by the emerging forms of socialization, the theorist was faced with a "grimly comic riddle: where is the proletariat?" (MM, 221).[96] Wage-earning individuals were finding it progressively more difficult to join the struggles for social transformation, as was becoming apparent; to choose integration was less risky. Undoubtedly, this left critical theory in a state of helplessness, for not only had it lost its connection to a force capable of influencing history, but it had also suddenly found itself without a clear addressee. "To whom shall we say these things?," Horkheimer asked Adorno in 1956, when the two were planning the drafting of a joint political manifesto (HGS 19, 53).[97] Adorno himself wrote to Herbert Marcuse that, even "if we have no other recourse anymore, then we should at least not speak as if the workers' battalions were booming behind our book."[98] While his theory refuses to relinquish the Marxian demand for the "ruthless criticism of all that exists" (MEW 1, 344),[99] the lack of a clear addressee seemed to condemn it to being little more than a powerless testimony. Even if it succeeds in uncovering the truth, any critical theory that fails to resonate with the masses can no longer become a "material force" in history (MEW 1, 385).[100] A painful awareness of this dilemma was therefore already laid out in *Dialectic of Enlightenment*, from which there seemed to be no way to escape: "If today any address is still possible, it is neither to the so-called masses nor to the individual, who is

[95]Benjamin, *The Arcades Project*, 667.

[96]Adorno, *Minima Moralia*, 194.

[97]Theodor Adorno and Max Horkheimer, "Towards a New Manifesto," trans. Rodney Livingstone, *New Left Review* 65 (September/October 2010) 46.

[98]Theodor W. Adorno, Letter to Marcuse July 18, 1948, quoted in Braunstein, *Adorno's Critique of Political Economy*, 261.

[99]Karl Marx, Letter to Ruge, September 1843, "Letters from the *Franco-German Yearbooks*," in *Early Writings* trans. Rodney Livingstone and Gregor Benton (London: Penguin Books, 1992), 207.

[100]Marx, "A Contribution to the Critique of Hegel's Philosophy of Right: Introduction," 137.

powerless, but rather to an imaginary witness, to whom we bequeath it so that it is not entirely lost with us" (DA, 294).[101] In a certain way, the well-known notion of Adorno's critical theory as a message in a bottle must be understood as having resulted from a shipwreck in the struggle for emancipation.

The first consequence of this shipwreck is the social impotence of the proletariat, culminating in its integration into society. Its growing fragility and tendency to conformity were not the product of direct manipulation but of the social conditions that regulate self-preservation in post-liberal capitalism; these left workers in the hands of an increasingly concentrated system of production. Their reduction "to mere objects" of a social apparatus "which preforms every department of modern life right down to language and perception, conjures up an illusion of objective necessity before which they believe themselves powerless" (DA, 56).[102] The Marxist theory of immiseration, which foresaw that the development of capitalist society would place the working class in an increasingly unjust and insufferable situation and predicted that this would lead it to react by organizing itself as a class and opposing the system was not borne out; what emerged in its place was a growing "antithesis between power and impotence" (DA, 56).[103] This placed critical theory in a new situation. Faced with a tendency toward the "total organization of society by big business and ubiquitous technology" (GS 8, 376),[104] the very antagonism between social classes seemed to have been eclipsed. For "the ruling class disappears behind the concentration of capital. This latter has reached a magnitude and acquired a weight of its own that enables capital to present itself as an institution, as the expression of society as a whole" (GS 8, 380).[105] As a result, even though the antagonism between social power and the dispossessed is becoming ever starker and more palpable, wage earners, who are increasingly dependent, no longer recognize themselves as a class (MM, 220). They are wary of solidarity with others like themselves and of getting involved in political struggles, for in their state of increasing

[101]Adorno and Horkheimer, *Dialectic of Enlightenment*, 213. Translation modified.
[102]Ibid., 30.
[103]Ibid.
[104]Adorno, "Reflections on Class Theory," 96.
[105]Ibid., 99.

powerlessness, conformity to the social order is the safest bet. All the while, adaptation offers them new advantages. At the point when the heightened productivity of Fordism began to promote their access to consumption, the proletariat did, in fact, come to have "more to lose than its chains" (GS 8, 384).[106] On this point, the role played by the culture industry, which intensely socializes the time of "leisure" and entertainment as a time for consumption, is key. Likewise, improvements in working and living conditions, together with the emergence of the welfare state, seem to relieve the most pressing threats to their existence. Even though this situation created living conditions that are increasingly subject to the demands of capital reproduction, it nevertheless enabled them to feel part of a society which, while exploitative, offered them access to a share of its fruits. This led them to perceive that the social framework on which their lives depended also granted them a certain amount of leeway to pursue their own interests. For Adorno, this situation—which, against the background of present-day capitalism, tends to be retrospectively idealized—heralded the threat of a total absorption of workers into the social system that would result in their "political and social impotence" (GS 8, 386).[107] The reduction of human beings to objects, to mere functions of the reproduction of social logic, becomes a deceptive image of their equality: "The classless society of car drivers, cinema goers, and fellow citizens (*Volksgenossen*) makes a mockery not only of those who do not belong but even of those who do, the dominated, who no longer dare to admit it to others or to themselves" (GS 8, 377–8).[108] Their condition as a social class persists as a sociological reality. The antagonisms that permeate society have not disappeared; rather, they are intensifying. What is disappearing, however, is class consciousness. In the face of growing social pressure, identification with social dynamics offers workers and wage earners a more "rational" and bearable psychological solution than conflict; but it should not be taken for granted that a renewed awareness of their social situation would suffice to conjure up the political power that this class has lost.

---

[106]Ibid., 103.

[107]Ibid., 105.

[108]Ibid., 97. Translation modified.

The powerlessness of the proletariat had already revealed itself in the absence of any spontaneous resistance to the Nazi seizure of power and the spread of fascism throughout Europe.[109] This situation seemed to suggest that, instead of acting out of class solidarity with a view to transforming the social order, wage earners tended to gravitate toward the privileges and prerogatives that social power could afford them.[110] However, this was not an inherent tendency toward social climbing, but rather the consequence of being subjected to the "immeasurable pressure of domination" (GS 8, 377);[111] this pressure prevents them from extricating themselves from the competition imposed by the system on which their lives depend. In this way, their growing weakness in the face of the social apparatus impacts their own subjective constitution. In order to survive, the dominated have to assimilate themselves body and soul, especially at a time when the system increasingly monopolizes the means of access to the satisfaction of their needs (GS 8, 390).[112] Their own powerlessness makes it difficult for them to distance themselves from the dominant order, to articulate their interests outside of it, and to act autonomously and in solidarity. To do so would require the determination to resist the tide of pressure of the social logic. Therefore, those who occupy the positions most exposed to social pressure have the greatest difficulty in developing the faculties required for the struggle for emancipation; all the forces of socialization promote their tendency to conformity. The possibility of gaining relative autonomy from social imperatives and the minimal freedom that allows for self-reflexivity are then the prerogatives of those who occupy a position of privilege; such is the case of intellectuals. For Adorno (who agrees with Horkheimer on this point), it is crucial for critical theorists to develop a clear awareness of their role in the conflict between emancipation and barbarism. Because although their position in the social division of labor implies a debt to those who remain bound up

---

[109]That situation had already been brought to light in the first empirical study from the Institute for Social Research led by Max Horkheimer, see Erich Fromm, *The Working Class in Weimar Germany: A Psychological and Sociological Study*, trans. Barbara Weinberger (Cambridge, MA: Harvard University Press, 1984).

[110]Max Horkheimer had already pointed this out (cf. HGS 14, 238).

[111]Adorno, "Reflections on Class Theory," 97.

[112]Theodor W. Adorno, "Theses on Need," trans. Devi Dumbadze in *Constelaciones: Revista de Teoría Crítica* 6 (December 2014), 465.

with physical labor, this does not allow them to neglect the specific tasks that fall upon them: those of developing an adequate understanding of social relations and the prevailing constellations of power. In this sense, adopting the standpoint of the proletariat offers "no guarantee of correct knowledge" (HGS 4, 187);[113] on the contrary, as Horkheimer had already pointed out, it may imply a bias in the development of a clear and unequivocal awareness of the predominant social relations and thereby result in a further disempowerment of the masses. According to this point of view, few intellectual stances are as misguided as the identification with the proletariat, which aspires to atone for its guilt over its privileged position in the division of labor by presenting the proletarian condition as if it were a blessing. Against this, Adorno argues that the "glorification of splendid underdogs is nothing other than glorification of the splendid system that makes them so" (MM, 29).[114] If he distrusts those intellectuals who pretend to base their work on the standpoint of the proletariat, it is because "socially, the situation of the intellectual vis-à-vis the proletariat" can only be that of a "failed identification."[115] Ultimately, the problem is that the constitution of the proletarian class comes not from its autonomous articulation as a conscious subject, but from the heteronomous imprint of capitalist social logic; this makes it difficult for its perspective to offer anything more than a reflection of domination—a mere reminder of the damage inflicted. Hence Adorno's suspicion of those intellectuals who, like Brecht, often tried to sound like proletarians, emulating the mannerisms of humble and simple people: "ears that have preserved their sensitivity cannot help hearing that someone is trying to talk them into something. It is arrogant and almost contemptuous toward the victim to talk like them, as though one were one of them. One may play at anything, but not at being a member of the proletariat" (GS 11, 422).[116]

[113]Horkheimer, "Traditional and Critical Theory," 213.
[114]Adorno, *Minima Moralia*, 7.
[115]This is the formula Adorno used in reference to the composer Hanns Eisler, a wayward disciple of Schoenberg who was a close collaborator with Brecht and with whom Adorno wrote *Composition for the Cinema* (cf. Theodor W. Adorno, "Notizen über Eisler," in *Frankfurter Adorno Blätter*, vol. VII [Munich: Text+Kritik, 2001], 125).
[116]Adorno, "Commitment," 87.

This manner of pseudo-proletarian posturing on the part of intellectuals led Adorno, as early as the 1930s, to demand "the total elimination of those Brechtian motifs" (ABB, 173)[117] from Benjamin. For such an attitude can compromise whatever strictly theoretical work might be able to contribute to social transformation, even if it is only capable of doing so through the powerless freedom of the spirit. Hence in March 1936 he wrote to Benjamin that "there is nothing of bourgeois idealism in maintaining solidarity with the proletariat—fully aware and without intellectual inhibitions—instead of turning the own necessity into a virtue of the proletariat, as we are constantly tempted to do; a proletariat that suffers the same necessity, and needs us for knowledge just as much as we need the proletariat for the revolution" (ABB, 174).[118] But these sentences—as well as some of Max Horkheimer's formulations in his programmatic "Traditional and Critical Theory" (cf. HGS 4, 189–90)[119]—were written before the failure of the hope that the alliance of the intelligentsia and the proletariat could lead to a revolution worthy of the name. In Adorno's thought, the collapse of that expectation is signified by the name of Auschwitz; but its far-reaching consequences seem to have been foretold shortly before the beginning of what the Nazis called "the final solution to the Jewish question." Hence, as early as August 1940, Adorno wrote to his friend Horkheimer, with whom he was outlining the collaborative project that would culminate in *Dialectic of Enlightenment*:

> It is gradually becoming the case, especially having heard the latest news from Germany, that I cannot tear my thoughts from the fate of the Jews. I often have the impression that everything we have become accustomed to seeing in terms of the proletariat has now been transferred over to the Jews in a very concentrated way. I wonder if we should not ... say the things we really mean in connection with the Jews, who today embody the polar opposite of the concentration of power. (AHB II, 84)

---

[117]Adorno and Benjamin, *The Complete Correspondence*, trans. Nicholas Walker (Cambridge, MA: Harvard University Press, 1999), 131.

[118]Ibid., 131–2.

[119]Horkheimer, "Traditional and Critical Theory," 215.

Of course, what is at stake in these reflections is not that the Jews should take over from the proletariat as the addressee of theory or as the privileged subject of history; nor is it a question of rearticulating the perspective of a heroic political subject, capable of bringing about a glorious future. What Adorno proposes here is instead a correction of the Marxist notion of history. It is a matter of stripping it of the triumphal bias that leads it to cling to the radiant promises of a supposed "final victory," which always shines from a distant future, instead of attending to the devastation generated by the disasters of the present. It is precisely this correction that makes it possible to trace the link between Marx's categorical imperative "to overthrow all conditions in which man is a debased, enslaved, neglected, contemptable being" (MEW 1, 385)[120] and Adorno's call to arrange our "thoughts and actions so that Auschwitz will not repeat itself, so that nothing similar will happen" (ND, 358).[121]

Indeed, in Marx's early writings, the figure of the proletariat was already quite far from being portrayed in an epic and triumphal manner. Its character as the subject of possible social emancipation was based on the fact that it was a class that embodied "a universal suffering," that was the object "of no particular wrong, but unqualified wrong," and whose degradation implied "the complete loss of humanity" (MEW 1, 390).[122] In short: what qualified the proletariat as the axis of social critique in this regard was not so much its key position in the framework of production as the fact that it embodied all the negativity of the social order; its sufferings under the injustices and outrages of the system of domination in place revealed the true character of "normality." That is why Adorno, confronted in his own time with the implacable concentration of power—a feature shared by fascism, post-liberal capitalism, and the Soviet Union—sought to ground his critical theory in the perspective of those whose experience reveals the most harmful characteristics of the emerging social order. Whereas Walter Benjamin had already pointed out that "the tradition of the oppressed reveals to us that the 'state of emergency' (*Ausnahmezustand*) in which we live is not the exception but the rule"

[120]Marx, "A Contribution to the Critique of Hegel's Philosophy of Right. Introduction," 137.
[121]Adorno, *Negative Dialectics*, 365.
[122]Marx, "A Contribution to the Critique of Hegel's Philosophy of Right. Introduction," 141.

(BGS I, 697),[123] Adorno now observed that the true "exception" of the historical moment, capable of illuminating the "rule" and bringing its true nature to light, was no longer so much the proletariat—which had become increasingly integrated and could aspire to the prerogatives offered by consumption or by integration into various collectives embodying social power—but those who, since the so-called Night of Broken Glass in November 1938, were increasingly persecuted, targeted by racial laws, attacked and expropriated, forced to emigrate without any possessions whatsoever, rejected as undesirable by most of the receiving countries, and finally confined to ghettos, deported, forced to work to the limit of their strength, and systematically exterminated in gas chambers—all this without any social or political agency doing anything substantial to prevent it. This is what turned the Jews into the antithesis of the concentration of power toward which society was tending and what made the study of anti-Semitism a fundamental key to understanding the historical ruptures of the time.

"From the most recent form of injustice, a steady light reflects back on history as a whole" (GS 8, 374),[124] Adorno wrote in 1942. The fate of the Jews revealed the stark and brutal nature of the violence lurking within the social logic, which tends to veil itself beneath the façade of "normality." It highlighted the degree to which individual lives were insignificant in the emerging social order and made it possible to unveil the present as a time of barbarism. Adorno's proposal to frame the fundamental insights of critical theory "in relation to the Jews" did not seek to construct a new subject, nor did it seek to cast the Jews as the essential victim of the social system. Instead, it proposed that their unspeakable torments offered the interpretive key best suited for exposing the true character of the world that inflicted this upon them and what it was capable of. At the same time, his thought was able to perceive in the despair of those who had been persecuted and annihilated the echo of that "weak messianic power" (BGS I, 694)[125] of which Benjamin spoke, which, as is well understood, cannot be dismissed lightly.

---

[123]Walter Benjamin, "On the Concept of History," in *Selected Writings: Volume 4, 1938–1940*, trans. Howard Eiland and Michael W. Jennings (Cambridge, MA: Harvard University Press, 2006), 392.

[124]Adorno, "Reflections on Class Theory," 94.

[125]Benjamin, "On the Concept of History," 390.

"From the Standpoint of Redemption"

The beginning of an interview with the weekly magazine *Der Spiegel*, published three months before his death and shortly after a faction of the German student movement boycotted one of his seminars, captures with precision the disposition of Adorno's critical theory. The journalist begins by noting: "Professor Adorno, two weeks ago the world still seemed to be in order …," to which Adorno replies: "Not to me" (GS 20.1, 402). That lapidary answer says more about the impulse behind his thought than many a monograph. Where the journalist introduces a framework that empathizes with "normality," taking for granted the university professor's complicity with a "legitimate" order allegedly disturbed by the actions of some rebellious students, Adorno withdraws all complicity with that order. His response aims to set the record straight: the problem is the outrageousness of the existing social order, which continues to be based on domination and violence and continues to generate avoidable suffering—not the protests of a few students, who, if anything, tend to unthinkingly reproduce some of its most disastrous features in their attempt to assert themselves against that order. The refusal to legitimize this state of affairs, or even to accept it, is the impulse that drives Adorno's critical theory throughout. To do so would imply minimizing the enormous potential for violence and horror harbored by the very logic of social domination, thereby heaping the scorn of indifference and forgetfulness upon myriad injustices and avoidable suffering. Adorno himself had already pointed out that "forgetting is the adaptation of suffering to domination."[126] Given the fact that his thought recognizes that the dichotomy between emancipation and barbarism was historically resolved in the most ill-fated way, and that the praxis capable of altering this situation appears blocked, critical theory should obey the mandate not to transfigure reality, not to deceive itself about it, and not to make it pass for what it is not. To this extent, theoretical activity is not only a focal point of resistance for Adorno but is also in the service of a possible emancipatory praxis, whose horizon beyond the current blockage remains uncertain, but which cannot be considered definitively closed. Thought that has not fallen into resignation not only opposes conformism that reframes

[126]Adorno, "Contra Paulum," 488.

the existing order as legitimate, but also conformism that denies the possibility of a better reality (LGF, 83).[127]

Up until the caesura represented by Auschwitz, the main enemy of critical theory had been a form of social democracy that believed that the historical unfolding of modernity would by itself lead to emancipation, in a manner that was practically predetermined. According to this view, socially produced suffering was considered something surmountable, its social causes as problems that could be gradually reformed, and thus the hope of an emancipated society—which Marx had conceived in the image of a classless society—became a kind of regulative ideal. Walter Benjamin had already spoken out against the teleology presiding over this notion of history: "Once the classless society had been defined as an infinite task, the empty and homogenous time was transformed into an anteroom, so to speak, in which one could wait for the emergence of the revolutionary situation with more or less equanimity" (BGS I, 1231).[128] Indeed, according to this understanding of politics, the possibility of radical transformation is detached from the coercive dimension of society and its institutions, and the expectation of a better future "assumes the form of religious consolation, even if in a secular garb, the opium that makes possible equanimity in the face of oppression."[129] In order to resist this dissolution of the Marxian idea of the classless society, Benjamin had highlighted its messianic, salvific element as a force whose arrival cannot be anticipated, but which suddenly bursts into history. That is why he went so far as to affirm that "there is no moment in history that would not carry with it *its* revolutionary chance—provided only that it is defined in a specific way, namely as the chance for a completely new resolution of a completely new problem" (BGS I, 1231).[130] Adorno was no stranger to this notion but faced a different situation. He was aware that, in a total and increasingly integrated society, he could no longer immediately connect to this messianic notion of revolution (GS 8, 393),[131] but

[127]Adorno, *History and Freedom*, 60.

[128]Benjamin, "On the Concept of History," 402.

[129]Idit Dobbs-Weinstein, *Spinoza's Critique of Religion and Its Heirs: Marx, Benjamin, Adorno* (Cambridge: Cambridge University Press, 2015), 131.

[130]Benjamin, "Paralipomena to 'On the Concept of History,'" *Selected Writings: Volume 4*, 402.

[131]Adorno, "Theses on Need," 465.

he wanted to conserve its impulse as an epistemological driving force. It is no longer a matter of pinning one's hopes on a radiant future, but of knowing how to present the unredeemed negativity that society and history pose at every moment as a task that cannot be postponed, of facing the avoidable suffering that plagues a large part of humanity as something that generates "shame" (ND, 156)[132] and must not be allowed to continue. In his view, Horkheimer's assertion that emancipatory thought stands "with the desperate, those who have been sentenced to their execution, not with those who have time" (HGS 5, 305)[133] still applied. The task that this situation sets for critical theory is that of an intolerable state of affairs that urgently demands a solution; only a perspective capable of presenting the urgent character of negativity can prevent it from having the last word.

In very few passages is this conception of Adorno's so clearly formulated as in the final fragment of *Minima Moralia*: "The only philosophy which can be responsibly practiced in face of despair is the attempt to contemplate all things as they would present themselves from the standpoint of redemption" (MM, 283).[134] This approach takes on its meaning in the light of a historical situation that Adorno refers to as "consummate negativity" (MM, 283)[135] and which imposes precise tasks on any philosophy that—despite its own powerlessness in the face of a blocked praxis—does not want to abdicate its duties. This passage already formulates an awareness of what "after Auschwitz" means for emancipatory thought. It would therefore be a mistake to interpret this final fragment of *Minima Moralia*—as some distinguished readers have done[136]—as a "flight into theology" or an escape from finite, historical reality. What Adorno is articulating here is a new means of approaching an unredeemed reality, one that implies a new way of understanding the task of theory. What is proposed in this fragment is an epistemological model that aspires to live

[132]Adorno, *Negative Dialectics*, 153.

[133]Horkheimer, "Authoritarian State," 11. Translation modified.

[134]Adorno, *Minima Moralia*, 153.

[135]Ibid.

[136]This is the case for Albrecht Wellmer: see "La unidad no coactiva de lo múltiple," in Albrecht Wellmer and Vicente Gómez, *Estética y teoría crítica* (Madrid: Cátedra, 1994), 17–45. For a critique of this position, see Vicente Gómez, *El pensamiento estético de Theodor W. Adorno* (Madrid: Cátedra, 1998), 195–218.

up to a catastrophic present whose prospects appear practically closed off; in other words, a way of understanding the possibility of persisting with critique once any hopes of redeeming history have been shattered. Its main purpose is to develop a vision of reality that tears away the veil of "innocuous normality" with which it is presented to healthy common sense, extirpating its banal and falsely familiar semblance so as to allow it to emerge in a new light. It is a matter of introducing a perspective that allows us to look at the world with different eyes and to bring its strangest and most perturbing dimensions into focus. Consequently, the "standpoint of redemption" does not entail a positive affirmation of redemption as some type of "content" that actually appears in historical reality; indeed, so "long as the world is as it is, all images of reconciliation, peace, and quiet resemble the image of death" (ND, 374).[137] Instead, it is a matter of constructing a perspective that, turning its back on transcendence, makes use of its light to illuminate social and historical immanence from a different, displaced viewpoint, under which it becomes decipherable in all its negativity. Hence Adorno's statement: "Perspectives must be fashioned that displace and estrange the world, reveal it to be, with its rifts and crevices, as indigent and distorted as it will appear one day in the messianic light" (MM, 283).[138] It is in this light that the world appears as hell, in all its destitution and damage; since "the light-source which shows the world's crevices to be infernal is the optimal one" (GS 10.1, 284).[139] What this perspective offers is not the *parousia* of the truth, but the demand to put an end to the falsity of a configuration of the present that reveals itself as mutilating all that exists.[140] In this sense, the final fragment of *Minima Moralia* continues: "To gain such perspectives without velleity or violence, entirely from felt contact with its objects—this alone is the task of thought" (MM, 283).[141]

Adorno was aware of what this demand implied. In a certain sense, he was asking something impossible of thought, since thinking itself was affected by the very destitution and distortion from which it sought to emerge. Theoretical

[137]Adorno, *Negative Dialectics*, 381. Translation modified.

[138]Adorno, *Minima Moralia*, 153.

[139]Adorno, "Notes on Kafka," 269.

[140]Gunnar Hindrichs, *Zur kritischen Theorie* (Berlin: Suhrkamp, 2020), 70–2.

[141]Adorno, *Minima Moralia*, 153.

activity could no longer make any claim to purity or transcendence; much less could it consider itself in possession of a redemptive perspective that could only be granted to a praxis that seemed unavailable for the time being. This is the situation of "objective despair" (GS 10.1, 283).[142] How then to adopt "a standpoint removed, even though by a hair's breadth, from a scope of existence" (MM, 283)?[143] For Adorno this perspective can no longer be assumed as positively given; the immanence of an increasingly enclosed and integrated world has become all-encompassing: there is no outside. This is precisely what reinforces the oppressive and suffocating dimension of an order that subjugates those who live under it and whose coercive nature does not always emerge in an explicit way. Yet it is on this basis that philosophy is called upon to look at immanence in a way that can gather something of that messianic light. It is a matter of arriving at a perspective that, without going beyond the sphere of that which exists, opens a viewpoint that transcends it (GS 17, 114).[144] In this sense, it is significant that, when Adorno offers a model of such a perspective, he does not turn to philosophy, but to literature. This is embodied, above all, in the work of Kafka. As early as December 1934 he had written to Benjamin that Kafka "represents a photograph of our earthly life from the perspective of a redeemed life, one which merely reveals the latter as an edge of black cloth, whereas the terrifying distanced optics of the photographic image is non other than that of the obliquely angled camera itself" (ABB, 90).[145] In Kafka the world appears as an inverted image of what a redeemed life would be like; hence a vision of reality as "hell," in all its destitution. This motif returns later in his "Notes on Kafka," in a passage that clarifies and complements the final fragment of *Minima Moralia*. In it, he states that Kafka's work

> feigns a standpoint from which the creation appears as lacerated and mutilated as it itself conceives hell to be. Offenders were hung head down. Kafka, the land-surveyor, captured the surface of the earth just as it must have appeared to these victims during the endless hours of their dying. It

[142]Adorno, "Notes on Kafka," 269.

[143]Adorno, *Minima Moralia*, 245.

[144]Theodor W. Adorno, "Mahagonny," trans. Wieland Hoban, *Night Music: Essays on Music 1928–1962* (London/New York: Seagull Books, 2009), 187.

[145]Adorno and Benjamin, *The Complete Correspondence*, 66.

> is for nothing less than such unmitigated torture that the perspective of redemption presents itself to him. (GS 10.1, 284–5)[146]

Kafka's artistic technique of defamiliarizing earthly reality is, according to Adorno, what allowed him to make "objective alienation" (GS 10.1, 284)[147] visible. Kafka's writing disfigures reality to the point that its very substance becomes intelligible. That this estranged image of reality is achieved through a perspective analogous to that of the Jews, the criminals, and the condemned refers here, once again, to the "polar opposite to the concentration of power" (AHB II, 84). It is the gaze of those who fall under the wheels of history that offers the most accurate understanding of its violent, annihilating dimension, which is alien to meaning; their experience reveals the full force of negativity in an unredeemed world. What Adorno demands from critical theory is an analogous method that allows it to confront a historical situation that he describes as "consummate negativity" (MM, 283).[148] This is what explains his taste for extreme, often paradoxical formulations, sometimes bordering on exaggeration: in this way he seeks to jolt consciousness, to force it to confront what it so often overlooks and to break through the surface of that which seems immutable. This is how his critical theory aspires to preserve a certain transformative energy even in a reality that seems resistant to change, for the "insight that … the horror will come to an end" is "always appropriate" (HGS 5, 306).[149]

Although Benjamin had already said that it is only for the sake of the hopeless that we have been given hope (BGS I, 201),[150] the situation of objective despair now demands a new way of approaching the knowledge of immanence that makes it possible to persevere with critique. This is what leads Adorno to invert Spinoza and affirm that the true cannot be understood as *index sui et falsi*, but that the false must be understood as *index sui et veri*.[151] From this arises the

---

[146] Adorno, "Notes on Kafka," 268.

[147] Ibid.

[148] Adorno, *Minima Moralia*, 153.

[149] Horkheimer, "The Authoritan State," 12.

[150] Walter Benjamin, "Goethe's Elective Affinities," trans. Stanley Corngold, in *Selected Writings, Volume 1, 1913–1926* (Cambridge, MA: The Belknap Press of Harvard University Press, 1996), 356.

[151] Theodor W. Adorno, in Ernst Bloch and Theodor W. Adorno, "Etwas fehlt … Über die Widersprüche der utopischen Sehnsucht," in *Gespräche mit Ernst Bloch* (Frankfurt: Suhrkamp, 1975), 70.

centrality of negativity for his thought; for "the false, once determinately known and precisely expressed, is already an index of what is right and better" (GS 10.2, 793).[152] There is no other means of access to the true than the determinate negation of the false. From the moment Adorno inverts Hegel and considers "the whole"—the constitution of the social fabric—as "the false" (MM, 55),[153] only the negation of what merely is makes it possible to open up a perspective on what must change, and thus on what ought to be. That perspective makes it possible to find, within reality, the trace of something that would point beyond what merely exists. But this requires focusing on what is damaged, unredeemed, and suffering in the world, thus revealing its absurdity (GS 10.1, 284).[154] Hence Adorno's invocation of Nietzsche's line: "Woe says: 'Go.'" (cit. ND, 203).[155] It is the very destitution of the world, the torment of immanence itself, that calls for a redemption at once urgent and unavailable.

Critical philosophy must be expressed in such a way as to ensure this demand is heard. Doing so prevents the decline of awareness regarding the urgent need for radical transformation in a reality where survival comes at the cost of constant increase in fear and in the quantum of avoidable suffering. Of course, this understanding of the task of philosophy marks the specific constitution of Adorno's thought, as well as its unique style—in the first place, because it requires revoking any kind of complicity with the healthy common sense that avoids negativity by minimizing avoidable suffering or by directing attention to other, more palatable aspects of immanence; after all, it is claimed, negativity is only one side of the coin. For Adorno, anyone who thinks in this way has already given up. Such an attitude renounces any standpoint that could do justice both to false objectivity and to the subjects who live in it, and therefore ends up becoming an accomplice to that which exists, in collusion with a logic that couples thought with domination and renunciation. For the rest, the only glimpse Adorno offers of what could constitute an acceptable social configuration is that of a world in which everyone "could be different

152 Adorno, "Critique," *Critical Models*, 288.

153 Adorno, *Minima Moralia*, 50.

154 Adorno, "Notes on Kafka," 251.

155 Adorno, *Negative Dialectics*, 203. Translation modified.

without fear" (MM, 116).[156] Once again, the *telos* of emancipation would be a liberation from fear that allows everyone to live and express themselves without coercion and without the constant suspicion of deviating from the norm relentlessly imposed by anonymous social imperatives. On the other hand, one "cannot be too afraid of the world, such as it is" (GS 10.2, 778).[157] This fear weighs down on individuals each day, in their helplessness and powerlessness in the face of the social apparatus on which their lives depend, and at the same time it is part of the very social logic that constitutes individuals as they are. Fear is a powerful driver of atomization and the destruction of all forms of solidarity, especially in a world permeated by the logic of competition. Thus, if Adorno had stated that "the need to lend a voice to suffering is a condition of all truth," it should not be forgotten that this suffering is defined as "objectivity that weighs upon the subject" (ND, 29).[158]

Adorno's critical theory is grounded in an acute awareness of the crisis confronting the emancipatory hopes initially born of bourgeois modernity. Faith in history as such—or in any subject capable of putting an end to the vast scale of barbarism—was no longer possible, which demanded a fundamentally new outlook on reality. Nor could the emancipatory perspective survive as a purely intellectual concern, limited to proposing new theoretical solutions or paradigms. Adorno understood that remaining in the immanence of the spirit and thought could no longer offer a safe refuge from the historical catastrophe designated by Auschwitz and Hiroshima. How then was it possible to engage with the expectations of emancipation arising from modernity? At the beginning of *Dialectic of Enlightenment*, one can already read: "what is at stake is not the conservation of the past but the fulfillment of past hopes" (DA, 15).[159] To prematurely bid emancipatory hopes goodbye does not solve the problem; rather it eliminates any remaining resistance to the triumph of barbarism. Aspirations of freedom and autonomy, of a life free from suffering and hunger, or of finally being liberated from fear, continued to respond to very real social needs. Hence the importance of continuing to work through the aporias of

[156] Adorno, *Minima Moralia*, 103.
[157] Adorno, "Marginalia to Theory and Praxis," 275.
[158] Adorno, *Negative Dialectics*, 17.
[159] Horkheimer and Adorno, *Dialectic of Enlightenment*, xvii.

emancipatory thought: it is necessary to reread history against the grain to bring to light the factors that had contributed to its historical shipwreck, but one cannot abandon its impulse. "The abundance of real suffering permits no forgetting" (GS 11, 423).[160] In this sense, Adorno's persistence in undertaking emancipatory critique—as well as his recourse to the figures of hell and redemption—is guided by an attitude reminiscent of Beckett's *il faut continuer* with which the novel of *The Unnamable* ends: "Because the end has arrived, 'on ne peut pas continuer,' yet because this end was not liberation but catastrophe, 'il faut continuer.' "[161] Recognizing the enduring potential for catastrophe inscribed in the social logic does not imply a resigned, pessimistic, or ominous theoretical stance; rather, it requires a form of theory that is reflexive about its own historical conditions and its role in the struggle for emancipation. This is not linked to the theorist's professed radicalism, but to the urgency of the historical tasks imposed by the persistence of injustice, heteronomy, and avoidable suffering. Everything else reduces theory to "reconstruction, mere technique" (MM, 283);[162] or else its alleged radicality becomes a sort of mantra that obscures the conditions that would allow it to intervene in historical reality rather than clarifying them.

[160] Adorno, "Commitment," 88.
[161] José Antonio Zamora, *Krise-Kritik-Erinnerung* (Münster: Lit, 1995), 172.
[162] Adorno, *Minima Moralia*, 153.

2

Does It Not Hurt to Be Devoured? The Place of the Critical Intellectual

In the world that society has become, all spirit is a form of neurosis; it is better, then, to turn it to good use than to extirpate it so that the machinery runs more smoothly.

THEODOR W. ADORNO, "Open Letter to Max Horkheimer" (1965)

Adorno's theoretical output is inseparable from the collective project that took shape in the 1930s, organized around Max Horkheimer and the Institute for Social Research. However, what is usually called the "Frankfurt School" is, in no small measure, the result of a misunderstanding. First and foremost, this is because the theory to which this term refers does not constitute a clearly delimited corpus of postulates and methods capable of being transmitted from teacher to disciple. It does not therefore constitute a "school." Moreover, the period during which this theoretical endeavor acquired its most distinctive features did not, strictly speaking, take place in Frankfurt. Its most decisive texts and analyses were conceived during the exile into which these authors were forced by Nazism. In addition, this label includes authors such as Herbert Marcuse and Walter Benjamin, who were only ever briefly in Frankfurt. This is why the term "critical theory," with which Horkheimer tried to capture the specific features of the theoretical output of the Institute for Social Research and the *Zeitschrift für Sozialforschung*, is undoubtedly more appropriate.[1]

[1]Cf. Claussen, *Abschied von Gestern*, 5–12.

It refers to a theoretical project that was formulated in opposition to both academic research (science "free from value judgments") and to a form of Marxism whose aim was not a critique of the existing order, but the legitimization of forms of domination that crystallized in the disastrous drift of the Soviet Union—whose true nature became fully apparent during the great purges in Moscow between 1936 and 1938. Horkheimer's goal was to develop an intellectually and politically autonomous theory, one that did not sacrifice analytic rigor or its emancipatory commitments to the constraints of academic norms or party loyalties. The aim was to develop a line of thought that, starting from the analysis of the concrete social and historical conditions examined by various disciplines—economics, sociology, political science, psychology, history, and cultural theory–would be able to arrive at a theory of society as a whole (HGS 3, 36).[2] However, since the objective was to bring about an emancipatory transformation of social relations, this required attending to the specific features of the different spheres of social life and their potential for friction. While cruder forms of Marxism had tended to consider law, culture, and subjectivity as mere reflections of the economic sphere—a view that, according to Horkheimer, amounted to "an abstractly and therefore badly understood Marx" (HGS 3, 32)[3]—the original goal of the Institute directed by Horkheimer was to integrate contributions from different disciplines into an overarching vision of society and culture so as to grasp their evolutionary dynamics and possibilities for transformation.

Yet this does not imply that the program of critical theory can be equated with the concept of an "interdisciplinary materialism."[4] Attempting to turn the critical theory of society into sociology or social philosophy is—in Horkheimer's own words—"a problematic endeavor" (HGS 4, 213).[5] This is because its objective is not to improve education or to reorganize the way in which scientific research is conducted, but to engage in theoretical work aimed

---

[2]Max Horkheimer, "The Present Situation of Social Philosophy and the Tasks of an Institute for Social Research," trans. John Torpey in *Between Philosophy and Social Science: Selected Early Writings* (Cambridge, MA: MIT Press, 1993), 14.

[3]Ibid., 12.

[4]Cf. Helmut Dubiel, *Wissenschaftsorganisation und politische Erfahrung* (Frankfurt: Suhrkamp, 1978).

[5]Max Horkheimer, "Traditional and Critical Theory," 239. Translation modified.

at transforming the world. Critical theory "never simply aims at an increase of knowledge as such. Its goal is man's emancipation from slavery" (HGS 4, 219).[6] This cannot be understood within the framework of academic work, nor on the basis of the positive role played by knowledge in the current social order; the "profession" of the critical theorist, writes Horkheimer, "is the struggle of which his own thinking is a part, not thought as something independent that might be separated from it" (HGS 4, 190).[7] Critical theory understands itself as forming part of the historical conflict between emancipation and barbarism, and it cannot be separated from this. However, the way in which it serves these struggles is not by adhering to a given political line, but through its commitment to an independent and uncompromising understanding of objective reality. While Horkheimer's theoretical project is to be understood as a framework for collective production involving a certain division of labor (its various members worked in different disciplinary fields in line with their respective training and expertise),[8] what brought these authors together was an interest in emancipatory social transformation and a connection with the legacy of Marx's theory, which was considered essential, but in need of renewal. For critical theory was intended, to a certain extent, as a response to the necessity of renewing Marxism in the face of a new historical situation; if its concepts were not updated to reflect social reality, they ran the risk of becoming "rigid, … abstract and fragile" (HGS 2, 377).[9] The major problem was that, given the increasing integration of workers and the waning desire for social transformation, the link between transformative theory and a subject capable of shaping history had become problematic. This situation, to

---

[6]Ibid., "Postscript," *Critical Theory: Selected Essays*, 246. Translation modified.

[7]Horkheimer, "Traditional and Critical Theory," 216. Translation modified.

[8]While Max Horkheimer and Herbert Marcuse focused on the more strictly philosophical dimension, the intention of which was to integrate the various partial perspectives, Friedrich Pollock and Henryk Grossmann worked on economics, Franz Neumann and Otto Kirchheimer on law and political theory, Erich Fromm on psychological matters, and Leo Löwenthal, Benjamin, and Adorno himself focused on questions of aesthetics and cultural theory. For a comprehensive overview of their collective project, see Martin Jay's classic study, *The Dialectical Imagination: A History of the Frankfurt School and the Institute of Social Research 1923–1950* (Berkeley: University of California Press, 1996), which only covers the period up to the return of Horkheimer, Pollock and Adorno to Germany, or the more complete—but not always reliable—analysis by Rolf Wiggershaus: *The Frankfurt School: Its History, Theories, and Political Significance*, trans. Michael Robertson (Cambridge, MA: MIT Press, 1995).

[9]Max Horkheimer, *Dawn & Decline*, trans. Michael Shaw (New York: Continuum, 1978), 64.

which Lukács attempted to respond through class consciousness and Gramsci through the search for hegemony, led Horkheimer to a growing awareness of the precarious condition of revolutionary theory.[10]

In fact, if anything characterizes critical theory, it is its insistence on the emancipatory impulse, even while recognizing that expectations for social transformation seemed to be receding from the historical horizon. Due to its connection with historical struggles, critical theory could not take the form of a worldview insulated from the course of history, but had to assume that its concepts and analyses were exposed to the shifting conditions of the very reality it sought to transform—including the changing position of those struggles within it. This was to shape the evolution of the theoretical project from the end of the 1930s onward. For sociohistorical upheavals were not just the subject that critical theory had to address, they also permeated its own conditions for the production and transmission of knowledge and threatened the survival of theory itself. Undoubtedly, in a world which is increasingly integrated into ever more vertical power structures, any form of radical critique finds itself in a fragile and vulnerable position. With the rise of fascism and the precarious conditions of exile it imposed, as well as the dominant paradigm for academic research in the United States, the relationship of critical theory with specific disciplines and organized science could no longer be the same as that envisioned at the project's inception. Horkheimer's organizational efforts were therefore aimed at preserving a certain degree of autonomy—also in a financial sense—that would allow the Institute to engage theoretically with the upheavals of the historical moment, without submitting to any academic, political, or economic authority or relinquishing its commitment to social transformation. Because, in a period marked by the decline of emancipatory forces and the concentration of social and political power, independent thought could no longer rely on any form of protection; according to a famous formulation by Horkheimer, such thought had nothing behind it "but its pursuing persecutors" (HGS 4, 224).[11]

---

[10]Cf. Hindrichs, *Zur kritischen Theorie*, 57–9.

[11]Horkheimer, "Postscript," 251.

Even if theory managed to become the placeholder of reason under these conditions, the problem was that this did not necessarily mean that it could influence history. The moment critical theory loses contact with historical praxis, it becomes flawed and lacking: even if it manages to hit upon the truth and express it, that truth remains ineffective and impotent. This means that its analyses—however accurate they might be—can turn out not only to be vain, but also to lack a sense of the actual facts. The point of critical theory was not to harbor true understanding, but to transcend itself through revolutionary praxis. The old understanding of emancipation as the realization of philosophy, which the young Marx linked to the self-abolition of the proletariat, already pointed to this (MEW 1, 391).[12] The damage caused by the rupture of this connection between theory and its historical addressee should not be regarded as merely anecdotal; it was a key factor in the specific configuration that the project of critical theory ultimately assumed, particularly once its fragile link to those striving for a radical transformation of social relations increasingly showed signs of deterioration. It was Horkheimer himself who, as early as 1940, at the height of National Socialism and faced with the crushing defeat of the workers' movement, used the formula of the "message in a bottle" to refer to the meaning of the theoretical project (HGS 16, 726). This image suggests that, given the darkening historical outlook, the critical intellectual could no longer be understood as a vanguard figure or as a kind of guru who must shepherd the masses. Rather, they appear as individuals who, insisting on the autonomy of their thought—linked as it is to a position of relative privilege—formulate an unsparing critique of reality such as it exists. Yet the implication here is that, for all its radicality, this critique can hardly do more than bear witness. Separated from praxis, it continues to serve a truth that aspires to be something more than knowledge. But under the given conditions this yearning cannot be fulfilled. Hence critical theory was formulated with the vague expectation that someone, in an uncertain future, would be in a position to receive it and transform its testimony into a catalyst for praxis. However, as Adorno pointed out (MM, 239),[13] even this expectation of a future recipient could appear naïve

[12]Marx, "A Contribution to the Critique of Hegel's Philosophy of Right. Introduction," 142.
[13]Adorno, *Minima Moralia*, 209.

given the magnitude of the historical catastrophe. Horkheimer himself had already noted that "the most unpleasant discovery materialism leads to is the fact that reason only exists insofar as it has a natural subject behind it … which wants to make use of it" (HGS 16, 235). The lack of a subject capable of halting the transition into the new era of barbarism diagnosed by critical thought is the foundational wound of critical theory.

Perhaps no one gave this question a more central place in his theoretical work than Adorno himself; it is also in this light that his theory can be understood as a "science of mourning." As early as 1939 he had written: "Praxis, which reduces theory to impotence, appears as a destructive element within a theory that does not envisage a possible praxis. Properly, nothing more can be said. Action is the only form left to theory."[14] Indeed, few possessed his foresight in recognizing the deleterious consequences that this blockage of praxis had for theory, and even for what was once called spirit [*Geist*], which now appeared powerless in the face of historical tendencies that imposed themselves with indiscriminate force, as if they were obeying a law of nature. However, it is not so clear what kind of action theory would be capable of. This question is crucial, leading to the core of Adorno's theoretical radicalism. Yet, to understand what is at stake here, it is not sufficient to simply associate Adorno with the collective project of critical theory; it is also necessary to understand his specific position within it.[15] The fact is, both in terms of his intellectual makeup and his theoretical interests, until 1937 Adorno had been a marginal figure in the Institute for Social Research. His contributions to the *Zeitschrift für Sozialforschung* had mainly been reviews and writings on musical topics, although at the same time he had been developing a model of philosophical interpretation aligned with Benjamin's positions as well as epistemological work aimed at clarifying the validity and relevance of dialectics and materialism. To what extent, then, could such an author make a substantive contribution to the development of a critical theory of society? Much has been written about the significance of Adorno's incorporation into the core of the theoretical

[14]Theodor W. Adorno, "Aus einem Schulheft ohne Deckel. Bar Harbor, Sommer 1939," *Frankfurter Adorno Blätter*, 4 (1995), 7.

[15]Cf. IrisDankemeyer, *Die Erotik des Ohrs* (Berlin: Tiamat, 2020), 320, 330–4.

project, the most tangible result of which was the major work coauthored with Horkheimer: *Dialectic of Enlightenment*. It is hard not to notice a shift in tone in this book compared to previous pieces of critical theory, such as the programmatic "Traditional and Critical Theory." But this shift—which can already be discerned in texts from both coauthors from the late 1930s onward—must be understood as a response to diminishing prospects in the face of the triumph of barbarism and as a result of the respective evolution of their theoretical positions in relation to it.[16]

In the first place, the historical catastrophes that struck the world from the late 1930s onward had undermined expectations of emancipation, and the theoretical project that had been built up around Horkheimer had to take stock of this. Although in 1937 he had noted a societal tendency toward barbarism that could still be explained on the basis of the relation between productive forces and relations of production (HGS 4, 201),[17] Auschwitz marked the emergence of a new form of barbarism that could no longer be accounted for by the critique of political economy and the logic of capital accumulation. In this context, the dim hope that a desire for a rational society could be part of the aspirations of every human being (HGS 4, 224)[18] no longer seemed convincing; the horror of extermination was the result of the disinterest and complicit inaction of the people of Europe. On the other hand, since the emergent barbarism was a product of the evolution of modern societies themselves, it also made no sense to see critique as an attempt to recover the unrealized potentials of modernity; all that remained was to highlight its aporias and the destructive character of its contradictions.[19] The critique of society had to dig deeper to understand them. It was therefore connected to a critique of civilization in which the principle of the domination of nature, which was supposed to guarantee self-preservation and set itself up as the motor of progress, revealed itself to be structurally sacrificial insofar as it demanded the strict subjugation of one's inner nature. On this point it was not just Marx who was relevant; Nietzsche and Freud also came into play. To

---

[16]Cf. *infra*, chapter 3.

[17]Horkheimer, "Traditional and Critical Theory," 227.

[18]Horkheimer, "Postscript," 251.

[19]Zamora, *Th. W. Adorno. Pensar contra la barbarie*, 127.

understand the failure of the connection with praxis also required confronting the aporias of the relation between subject and object, which revealed fissures in the constitution of subjectivity. Dialectics turned into something more than a methodology in relation to the historical dimension of the contents of knowledge, instead becoming thought in perpetual movement, resting on no fixed concept, and avoiding any univocal causal links. Adorno's influence in this reformulation was undoubtedly decisive. His model of interpretation, developed in dialogue with Benjamin, with its procedure based on the form of the essay and its dialectical images, would prove particularly fruitful in countering the dogma of progress with an image of history as permanent catastrophe, one more adequate to an understanding of the present as a time of barbarism. His mode of thinking also seemed to promote an emphasis on the tears and fissures in the social fabric as a negative totality, as well as on the possibilities of subverting it.

At the same time, Adorno's own work had been increasingly affirming the need to develop his aesthetic and philosophical analyses in connection with a theory capable of accounting for the composition of capitalist society as a whole: one need only think of texts such as "On Jazz," "The Fetishistic Character of Music and the Regression of Listening" or "Fragments on Wagner." Up until that point it had been sufficient to allude to the analysis of the commodity form in the wake of Lukács' *History and Class Consciousness*, but it now became necessary to incorporate additional elements to unravel how forms of social mediation shaped individual phenomena; this led Adorno to intensify his engagement with the contributions developed within the framework of the Institute. On the other hand, his thought came to place an increased emphasis on the analysis of the constitution of subjectivity and the social modulations of experience. On this basis, Adorno would become a leading exponent of a critical theory of society capable of responding to a particularly bleak historical moment. The "Reflections on Class Theory" or the analyses of the "new type of human being" already point to the emergence of his specific formulation of critical theory, which would be consolidated with *Dialectic of Enlightenment* and *Minima Moralia*. From that moment on, his work assumed an almost frenetic intellectual productivity. This was almost the opposite of what eventually happened to Horkheimer, who, after his *Eclipse of*

Reason, would hardly write anything more than short notes and aphorisms. The consequence of this was that, once he returned from exile, Adorno became the most prominent voice of critical theory in 1960s Europe. He embodied the figure of a committed intellectual capable of raising a dissenting voice in the Germany of the reconstruction period and economic miracle. At the same time, his intellectual profile—marked by his affinity with certain avant-gardes and his insistence on aesthetic questions, his anti-positivist stance, his critique of ontology, as well as his insistence on the importance of style—placed him in a distinctive position. Despite his close collaboration with Horkheimer, the fact is that their approaches were not equivalent. Both authors stated on more than one occasion that what made their work together fruitful was "the tension between the two theoretical temperaments" (DA, 9;[20] cf. GS 20.1, 159). According to Detlev Claussen, the most significant difference between the two consisted in the fact that while Horkheimer emphasized the extra-theoretical dimension of radical thought (i.e., its connection to a practical interest in the transformation of social relations capable of becoming effective in historical praxis), Adorno focused above all on the radicality of theory itself. This is how his thought "took the radical impulses that had mobilized German intellectuals after the collapse of the German empire and reintegrated them into the realm of theory."[21] These impulses were evident, of course, in his understanding of the function of theory and thought, but they also absorbed elements drawn from culture and art.

The Fragile Nonconformity of the Spirit

The distinguishing features of Adorno's intellectual profile stem from a cultural and political sensibility shaped by experiences that differed from those of Horkheimer, Pollock, Löwenthal, and Marcuse. Rather than a childhood in the bosom of a family belonging to the great German-Jewish bourgeoisie, what

---

[20]Horkheimer and Adorno, *Dialectic of Enlightenment*, xi.

[21]Detlev Claussen, *Theodor W. Adorno: One Last Genius*, trans. Rodney Livingstone (Cambridge, MA: Harvard University Press, 2008), 228.

shaped Adorno's primary socialization was the influence of the artistic and musical environment created by his mother and aunt (a singer and a pianist, respectively), which suffused his existence. This also influenced the fact that Adorno's political socialization—shaped by a small age difference that is important to take into account when assessing the impact of events such as the German Revolution of 1918–1919 on their lives—took place in an intellectual milieu more closely aligned with an aesthetic radicalism, one that had been fostered by the disintegration of the European bourgeois tradition and had fueled a revolutionary ferment within the arts. Rather than through exposure to Marxism or the tradition of the workers' movement, Adorno's intellectual experience was influenced by contact with the New Music of the Second Viennese School—above all Arnold Schoenberg and Alban Berg (with whom he would study composition in 1925)—as well as with various avant-garde currents that included both artistic and strictly theoretical works—authors such as Walter Benjamin, Ernst Bloch, Siegfried Kracauer, Karl Kraus, and the early Lukács. All in all, due to his education and personal inclinations, Adorno seemed to move in a sphere where art and theory came together. In fact, the bulk of his writings up to 1933 are musical in subject matter and must be understood above all as militant texts, clearly siding with currents that, according to an expression that appears repeatedly in his letters to Berg, embodied something he considered "important in art-political terms" [*kunstpolitisch wichtig*].[22] Adorno himself would point out that, in retrospect, during these years, the same tension between the possibility of a liberated society and the forces that would later be revealed as fascism was also expressed in conflicts in the field of art (GS 10.2, 501).[23]

Indeed, in the compositions of Schoenberg's school, especially in the free atonal phase, the young Adorno had detected the potential for a liberated music with an implicitly political dimension (GS 18, 96–7).[24] In this sense, his thought succeeded in endowing the analysis of the New Music with an

---

[22]Theodor W. Adorno, letter to Alban Berg on January 30, 1936, in *Theodor W. Adorno - Alban Berg Briefwechsel* (Frankfurt: Suhrkamp, 1997) 69, and *Theodor W. Adorno & Alban Berg: Correspondence 1925–1935*, trans. Wieland Hoban (Cambridge: Polity Press, 2005), 46. Translation modified.
[23]Adorno, "Those Twenties," *Critical Models*, 43.
[24]Theodor W. Adorno, "Against the New Tonality," trans. Wieland Hoban, *Night Music*, 339.

element of social theory that it had previously lacked. It revealed that the composer did not confront musical material from a position of domination or coercion; instead of positioning himself with "sovereign control over the material" (GS 17, 134),[25] he tried to ensure that what Adorno calls "the drive-life [*Triebleben*] of sounds" (GS 17, 201)[26] could claim its due. A music had therefore emerged that was free from the constraints imposed by the tonal system (the resolution of dissonances, the sequencing of consonant intervals in melody, homogeneous sonority, symmetrical relationships, uniform rhythmic development, etc.)—thus opening up sonic possibilities that had previously been unthinkable. In this form of composition Adorno glimpsed a new model for the relationship between subject and object, and the possibility of establishing a "progressive freedom of consciousness in relation to the musical material" (GS 18, 404). However, the actual realization of these potentialities required a different world. In the existing reality, this music had to refuse to make any concession to the audience's taste or to pander to the expectations society imposed on it. This led it to become increasingly isolated, fostering the emergence of neotonal and folkloric tendencies that heralded a restoration of the former sonic order. The consequence of this was a regressive "stabilization of music" (GS 18, 721–8). In his opposition to these tendencies, "the left-wing aesthetic radicalism" embodied by the young Adorno "presupposed a further development of the political, not its abandonment."[27] His position emphasized a notion of enabling a space "for construction out of imagination in freedom" (GS 18, 723), which he understood as a foreshadowing of an emancipated society and which undoubtedly clashed with the rising authoritarian tendencies.

In short, while the experience of the thwarted November Revolution had proved to be crucial for Horkheimer's intellectual formation, for Adorno it was the liquidation of a kind of music that had explored the possibility of a radically new sonority—emancipated from the strictures imposed by the bourgeois society that had engendered it and which was first besieged and then eradicated

---

[25]Adorno, "Reaction and Progress," *Night Music*, 223.

[26]Theodor W. Adorno, "The Dialectical Composer," in *Essays on Music*, trans Susan H. Gillespie (Berkeley: University of California Press, 2002), 205. Translation modified.

[27]Dankemeyer, *Die Erotik des Ohrs*, 42.

from European soil by the rise of the forces that would culminate in fascism—that was decisive.[28] Indeed, Adorno himself was soon forced to realize that no artistic or musical secession could prosper without a radical transformation of the existing social order (GS 18, 730–1).[29] Compositions that had burst through the dams of the prevailing society were forced to return to their former course (GS 18, 725), since they did not have the support of a different social world. From the late 1920s onward, the decline of avant-gardes went hand in hand with the rise of the same elements that—a few years later—Adorno would address in his analysis of the culture industry. For this reason, he would later insist repeatedly that it was not Hitler who put an end to the New Music and the most groundbreaking avant-garde movements, but a broader social development that in Germany ended up leading to National Socialism.[30] The young critical theorist could not but realize that he had to confront the social dynamics that had cut short his intellectual and artistic environment if he wanted to "escape the fate of being reduced to silence in his turn."[31]

Undoubtedly, although Adorno never disavowed his commitment to the New Music, the experiences that marked his intellectual maturation tempered his confidence in the disruptive and emancipatory potential of products of art and culture. Both in the logic of post-liberal capitalism and in the growing influence of the state over more and more spheres of life, society demonstrated a strong tendency toward distinctly vertical forms, characterized by a concentration of power. Thus, while the liberal world had still shown a certain respect for the freedom of what used to be called the realm of the spirit—whose

[28]Cf. Jordi Maiso, "Emancipación o barbarie en la música: Los orígenes de la Teoría Crítica de Th. W. Adorno en sus escritos musicales tempranos," *Daimon* 65 (2015), 21–35.

[29]Adorno, "On the Social Situation of Music," *Essays on Music*, 424.

[30]"Anyone who did not play the game was forced into inner emigration years before the Third Reich broke out: at the latest with the stabilization of the German currency, coinciding with the end of Expressionism, German culture stabilized itself in the spirit of the Berlin illustrated magazines, which yielded little to that of the Nazis, 'Strength through Joy' [*Kraft durch Freude*], Reich autobahns, and jaunty exhibition-hall Classicism" (MM, 64–5 and *Minima Moralia* 57–8). In short, "it was not, as is usually assumed, the pressure exerted by the National Socialist terror that brought, regression, neutralization, and a funereal silence to the arts, for these phenomena had already taken shape in the Weimar Republic, and in liberal continental European society generally." (GS 10.2, 499 and "Those Twenties," 41).

[31]Claussen, *Theodor W. Adorno: One Last Genius*, 111.

flourishing required resistance to all external coercion—by the 1930s, that world already seemed like a thing of the past. Faced with the rise of fascism and a capitalism dominated by monopolies and *trusts*, the fragile realm of the spirit proved utterly powerless before forces that no longer recognized it "as something autonomous, but only as a means to [their] ends, and therefore had no fear of confrontation with it" (GS 11, 686).[32] This was not unique to "totalitarian" political environments; rather, it had to do with a tendency of developed societies to become increasingly "total." In a late text, written in an unusually autobiographical tone, Adorno highlighted how it was the experiences of the most advanced form of capitalism he encountered in the United States that shattered his naive belief in culture, requiring one who had acquired his professional skills through exposure to classical philosophy and avant-garde music to learn "to see culture from the outside" (GS 10.2, 734).[33] It was social reality itself that was turning those who had once been known as men of culture into outsiders, and nothing revealed this more clearly than the emergence of the culture industry.

In the organized capitalism of the post-liberal period, the role of culture had changed. It was no longer driven by the yearning to transcend bourgeois society, which held ideals it could not fulfill,[34] and it became increasingly difficult to maintain the fiction that it could continue to be safe from economic imperatives. Culture and art were assimilated by entertainment, while knowledge itself became an increasingly technical affair: what society demanded was not intellectuals who could think for themselves, but "experts" with specialized knowledge pertaining to the operational network of the social system (GS 10.2, 715).[35] Exiled artists and intellectuals, who had to live off the very society whose demands they turned their backs on in their works, therefore found themselves dependent on an increasingly concentrated economic system. In the emerging total capitalism, they were reduced to

[32]Adorno, "On Benjamin's *Deutsche Menschen*," in *Notes to Literature 2*, 329. Translation modified.

[33]Adorno, "Scientific Experiences of a European Scholar in America," *Critical Models*, 239.

[34]Cf. HerbertMarcuse, "Über den affirmativen Charakter der Kultur," in *Kultur und Gesellschaft I* (Frankfurt: Suhrkamp, 1980), 56–101, and "The Affirmative Character of Culture," in *Art and Liberation* ed. Douglas Kellner (New York: Routledge, 2007), 82–112.

[35]Adorno, "Scientific Experiences of a European Scholar in America," 229.

employees, and this demanded unconditional adaptation to its conditions from them. "Anyone who resists can survive only by being incorporated," as the chapter on the culture industry has it (DA, 153).[36] In this sense, the cases of musicians and authors close to Adorno's circle are instructive. Although Schoenberg, after some effort, was able to take up a position at an American university, Eduard Steuermann (who was Adorno's piano teacher) abandoned his compositional activity while in the United States, and Hanns Eisler (who until 1933 had combined avant-garde composition with political activism) had to survive by composing film music. For his part, Brecht's expectation of making a living writing screenplays for Hollywood did not materialize, and he barely had the chance to run a single theatrical project in the United States. In short, the conditions for working independently were proving increasingly onerous. Expatriates were particularly exposed to the pressures of a society in which "whatever does not present itself here and now as socially useful on the market has no weight, and is forgotten" (GS 10.1, 311).[37]

This situation also had an impact on the possibility of theoretical work itself—all the more so if it had a critical purpose. Indeed, intellectuals forced into exile no longer found the United States to be the country of unlimited possibilities, but "a civilization which absorbs all of life in its system, without allowing the un-regimented mind even those loopholes which European laxness left open even in the epoch of the great business concerns. It is made unmistakably clear to the intellectual from abroad that he will have to eradicate himself as an autonomous being if he hopes to achieve anything or be accepted as an employee of the super-trust into which life has been condensed" (GS 10.1, 98).[38] However, the significance of this experience for the development of Adorno's critical theory should not be misunderstood. The United States does not feature as a counterpart to Europe in his work, but as the vanguard of capitalist development, which is shown here "in its complete purity, without any precapitalist remnants." In that sense, it is not understood as a particular social or cultural model, but as "the most advanced observation post" (GS 10.2,

---

[36]Horkheimer and Adorno, *Dialectic of Enlightenment*, 104.

[37]Theodor W. Adorno, "On Tradition," in *Without Model: Parva Aesthetica*, trans. Wieland Hoban (Chicago: University of Chicago Press, 2023), 22.

[38]Adorno, "Aldous Huxley and Utopia," *Prisms*, 96–7.

736).[39] Anyone who understands Adorno's critique as a commentary on the particularities of American culture or society, marked by European arrogance, should be reminded of the Marxian "*de te fabula narratur*" (cf. MEW 23, 12).[40]

In this regard, Adorno's misadventures in the music division of the Princeton Radio Research Project, which ended in his dismissal, are particularly telling.[41] The project, directed by Paul Lazarsfeld, was a pioneering attempt to marry sociological research and business interests. In retrospect, it seems clear that the position of an intellectual who had taken a strong stand in favor of New Music, characterized by its refusal to make any concessions to the public, was bound to clash with a research project aimed at optimizing the radio system in order to make it, above all, a useful medium for commercial advertising. The study of listeners' reactions to music broadcast on the radio, within which Adorno's contribution was framed, aimed to collect data on listening habits that could provide potential *sponsors* with a better understanding of the public's receptivity to consumer stimuli. Therefore, Adorno's attempt to conduct a more ambitious analysis of the implications of music transmission through radio—taking into account the specific features of the medium and the relationship that listeners established with it, the effect of radio on the transmitted content (i.e., on the musical forms themselves) and the socially mediated character of the resulting listener experience—met with little interest. It was not a question of probing the possibilities of the medium, but of adapting them to fulfill a specific function in the social whole. After several discussions with the project's management, the Rockefeller Foundation refused to continue funding Adorno's position: his work was brought to a halt, preventing him from completing the book he was preparing about music on the radio.[42] The problem was not only that his arguments were not supported by empirical evidence—how could one demonstrate that listening habits were mediated

---

[39] Adorno, "Scientific Experiences of a European Scholar in America," 241.

[40] "The tale is told of you," a citation from Horace's satires. Marx, *Capital Volume 1*, 90.

[41] Cf. in particular David Jenemann, *Adorno in America* (Minneapolis: University of Minnesota Press, 2007), 1–104; also, Robert Hullot-Kentor, *Things Beyond Resemblance* (New York: Columbia University Press, 2008), 94–124.

[42] The materials for this book have been published as part of his posthumous writings in an edition edited by Robert Hullot-Kentor: Theodor W. Adorno, *Current of Music: Elements of a Radio Theory* (Cambridge: Polity Press, 2009).

and conditioned by the social process as a whole?—but also that the model of research in question was invested in obtaining profitable results in the short term and hostile to any reflection that could divert the focus to less tangible issues. The analysis of the new emerging medium and its potential effects was overlooked in favor of its commercial exploitation. It is not surprising that, in later texts, Adorno would document his clash with this way of understanding scientific research:

> The procedure of the official social sciences, which is hardly more than a parody of commercial activity, maintains this model of science, although it only needs it as a form of publicity. The whole apparatus of accounting and administration, of annual reports and balance sheets, of important meetings and business trips is set in motion to endow commercial interests with the veneer of a general need that has been thoroughly studied. (MM, 297–8)

These experiences demanded an evaluation of the extent to which the new conditions of post-liberal capitalism still permitted independent intellectual activity. The work of the spirit, which had never managed to achieve effective autonomy, had now been subsumed under a social logic that kept it "boxed in, isolated in a glass case, for as long as society is itself imprisoned" (MM, 224).[43] Indeed, it was only the privileged conditions of the Institute for Social Research directed by Horkheimer that enabled Adorno to make the way in which the expansion of socializing logic undermined the basis of all critical activity itself an object of reflection. Outside these enclaves of relative autonomy, however, the conditions of employability subjected intellectual labor to ever-increasing pressure to conform. "*Adjustment* was still a magic word, especially to someone fleeing persecution in Europe and from whom it was expected that he would prove himself in the new country and that he would not arrogantly insist on remaining the way he was" (GS 10.2, 702).[44] That situation seems to have plagued Adorno, even in his own dreams. In a transcript of one of them, recorded in 1942, he recounts a succession of encounters with different powerful figures of the era. First, King Ali Fáysal, grants him passage

[43] Adorno, *Minima Moralia*, 197.
[44] Adorno, "Scientific Experiences of a European Scholar in America," 215–16.

through an Arab army parade. Then he arrives by chance in the private office of President Roosevelt. The president kindly welcomes the exiled intellectual, and, with a paternal gesture, allows him to disregard protocol and take a book from the library. When William Knudsen, the then pro-Hitlerian president of General Motors, shows up to discuss national security matters with Roosevelt, Adorno is cordially invited to leave the room, but not before receiving a card with the president's address and telephone number. On leaving, however, Adorno suddenly finds himself in a basement, surrounded by crocodiles that are as menacing as they are seductive, almost like mythical creatures: "their heads were those of extraordinarily beautiful women. One spoke kindly to me, saying that it doesn't hurt to be devoured. To help convince me she promised me the loveliest things beforehand."[45]

The clarity of this image—originally published in the exile magazine *Aufbau*—seems to support Robert Hullot-Kentor's remark that Adorno's dream transcriptions often read like masterpieces of secondary elaboration.[46] In any case, when these unusual crocodiles with the faces of women address their siren songs to him, there is no doubt about the ambivalent attraction that the idea of abandoning all resistance and yielding to whatever the social logic expected of him must have held for the wandering intellectual. However, the very notion of "letting oneself be devoured" suggests that assimilation to social demands entails, above all, a renunciation of one's own individuality, of biographical continuity. It implies abandoning the interests that had given meaning to one's own theoretical work—in Adorno's case, through his close contact with the radicalism of musical and philosophical avant-garde movements—in order to conform to the demands of the academic subsector of the culture industry. The problem is that the imperative to assimilate was not only mediated by consciousness: it was objective and material. It weighed even on theoretical language and the choice of research topics. Thus, even if the intellectual resisted, the inertia of socialization would lead his work to bow to the demands of that which exists. Given this situation, the only option

---

[45]Theodor W. Adorno, *Traumprotokolle* (Frankfurt: Suhrkamp, 2005), 14 and Theodor W. Adorno, *Dream Notes*, trans. Rodney Livingstone (Cambridge: Polity Press, 2007), 8–9.

[46]Robert Hullot-Kentor, "Metric of Rebarbarization," *South Atlantic Quarterly*, 117(4) (2018), 741.

left was critical reflexivity: the intellectual's awareness that he is "as much entangled" in the social logic "as the active participant; the only advantage of the former is insight into his entanglement, and the infinitesimal freedom that lies in knowledge as such" (MM, 27).[47] This is because the social whole "leaves individual consciousness less and less room for evasion, preforms it more and more thoroughly, deprives it *a priori* from the possibility of differencing itself as all difference degenerates to a nuance in the monotony of supply" (GS 10.1, 13).[48]

In this sense, the fact that Adorno spent almost a decade without a regular academic position after losing his job at the Princeton Radio Research Project is also symptomatic. During that time, he collaborated on various research projects funded by American institutions, in studies devoted to anti-Semitism, prejudice, and film music. Most importantly, his comparatively privileged retreat to the California coast allowed him to write *Dialectic of Enlightenment* together with Horkheimer—a text that unquestionably constitutes an attempt to persevere in independent critical intellectual work against all odds. Regardless of the criticism this book may face, nothing in it can be seen as a concession to the standards of accessibility or common sense of the time, nor as an attempt to place his theory in a position that would allow it to gain recognition. For that, one would have to turn, if anything, to works such as *The Authoritarian Personality*. Instead, the joint book by Horkheimer and Adorno is the result of enormous theoretical ambition, seeking as it does to trace the genesis of the most pressing issues of its historical moment: the seemingly inextricable link between thought, fear, and domination, which gave rise to the intertwining of progress and regression; the antinomies of a subjective constitution that facilitated the proliferation of a new barbarism; and, of course, the study of the culture industry and the logic of anti-Semitism, which exposed the limits of the Enlightenment. At the time, however, nothing suggested that the *Dialectic of Enlightenment* would become a classic of twentieth-century thought. In addition to its demanding prose, which assumes extensive prior knowledge on the part of the reader, its first version from 1944 circulated only among the exile

[47]Adorno, *Minimal Moralia*, 26.
[48]Adorno, "Cultural Criticism and Society," 20. Translation modified.

community. In 1947, with its authors still in the United States, the book was published in German by Querido in Amsterdam—but to what public could it have been addressed? Two decades later, when a new generation of students in Frankfurt became interested in the book, its copies were still gathering dust in the cellars of the publishers.

The fate of the collaborative book by Horkheimer and Adorno is certainly unique, but it is not an isolated case in Adorno's oeuvre. Two of his other major publications, *Minima Moralia* and *Philosophy of the New Music*, which contain truly substantial elements of his thought, were written in German during his exile in California, at a time when their publication could not yet be foreseen. The same can be said of *In Search of Wagner*, written in the 1930s between London and New York. This reveals that some of the most decisive writings of Adorno's body of work were conceived without the need for any audience (beyond that of the small community of exiles); the urgency that stirred them was of a different nature. Adorno knew that the materialization of his thought depended on the possibility of preserving the autonomy of intellectual labor, which was socially threatened. This led him to remain stubbornly faithful to the impulses behind his thought and to refuse, as far as possible, to make any concession to the prevailing reality, even at the price of ending up embodying a certain eccentricity (MM, 228f.).[49] But this should not be understood as an attempt to safeguard a presumed "purity" of one's own individuality from the demands of a society whose very character would necessarily defile and contaminate it; after all, it was Adorno himself who wrote that "wrong life cannot be lived rightly" (MM, 43).[50] The critical intellectual is a product of the social circumstances he opposes; this places an inexorable demand upon his thought, lest he constantly run the risk of becoming an accomplice to the very same reality he criticizes (LGF, 84–5).[51] The activity of the intellectual is not free-floating: it is rooted in a social system that separates it from physical labor, and this makes critical theorists "at once beneficiaries of a bad society, and yet those on whose socially useless work it largely depends whether a society

[49]Adorno, *Minima Moralia*, 200–1.

[50]Ibid., 39.

[51]Adorno, *History and Freedom*, 56–8.

emancipated from utility is achieved" (MM, 151).[52] However, the absorption of the spirit into the functional apparatus of society, in line with the logic of the social system, "stands in irreconcilable contradiction to the principle of spirit itself, which is not meant to be absorbed into the reproduction of life" (GS 11, 404–5).[53] Only the exercise of free, unfettered thought makes it possible to become aware of the prevailing (false) social reality, and without this it is not possible to break the crust of an ever more total social logic. In Adorno's work, this becomes nothing less than the impossibility of reconciling oneself with an atrocious world that generates enormous amounts of avoidable suffering. In a lecture delivered in Los Angeles shortly after the end of the Second World War, "Questions on Intellectual Emigration," Adorno addressed the exiled intelligentsia in the following terms: "If our experience places us under any obligation, it is to resist the oppression and injustice that today even a person who is wholly taken up with self-preservation would have to recognize" (GS 20.1, 353).[54] Indeed, if the émigrés had experienced this mutilating dimension of coercion to adapt themselves, this could become a source of knowledge and also of resistance. Adorno recognized that his task as an intellectual also consisted in transforming the wounds that society and history had inflicted on him into a sustaining resource for his critical work.

In this sense, the return to Europe was also motivated by an expectation that the comparatively greater backwardness of German society would offer conditions that were less hostile to this task. However, this did not imply nurturing illusions about the limits that the logic of advanced capitalism imposed on theoretical and critical work: "The more total society becomes, the greater the reification of the mind and the more paradoxical its effort to escape reification on its own" (GS 10.1, 30).[55] The spirit can no longer consider itself sovereign, and its imbrication in social life prevents cultural or theoretical production from being hypostatized beyond its social conditioning factors. That is why, in a crucial passage, Adorno refers to criticism as that activity in

[52] Adorno, *Minima Moralia*, 87.
[53] Adorno, "The Curious Realist: On Siegfried Kracauer," *Notes to Literature 2*, 72.
[54] Theodor W. Adorno, "Questions on Intellectual Emigration," trans. Mark Kalbus, *Social Text* 99, no. 2 (2009), 160.
[55] Adorno, "Cultural Criticism and Society," 33.

which "the mind tears at its bonds" (GS 10.1, 14).[56] The formula is reminiscent of a passage from the *Dialectic of Enlightenment*, which referred to thought as "the servant which the master cannot control at will" (DA, 54).[57] In this sense, the only path open to theoretical and cultural production in the era of its real subsumption into the logic of advanced capitalism consists in the spirit's "critical self-reflection" (GS 10.2, 734).[58] However, as the first sentences of the *Negative Dialectics* reveal, this reflection must also be something more. The imperative for intellectual work is to confront the failure of the spirit to materialize within social and historical reality, that is, to put an end to heteronomy: "Philosophy, which once seemed obsolete, lives on because the moment to realize it was missed. The summary judgement that it had merely interpreted the world is itself crippled by resignation before reality, and becomes a defeatism of reason after the transformation of the world failed" (ND, 15).[59] Although the transition to praxis has failed so far, this does not imply a desperate flight into immediate action, but an even more uncompromising reflection on the very relationship between the activity of thought and the objective shaping of reality, on the constitution of praxis and its mediations; this, for Adorno, is the task of critical theory. To do otherwise would be to succumb to pure defeatism, and to the capitulation of the spirit.

In a passage from *Negative Dialectics*, Adorno himself points out that "grayness could not fill us with despair if our minds did not harbor the concept of different colors, scattered traces of which are not absent from the negative whole" (ND, 370);[60] it is now almost a commonplace to note that, in his thinking, this potential is glimpsed in the promise of art. Indeed, if there is one element that allows us to establish continuity across the different moments of his intellectual biography, it is the living and emphatic experience of art, and, in particular, of music.[61] Even the late monographs on Gustav Mahler and Alban Berg are charged with a remarkable *pathos*. The persistent interest

[56]Ibid., 21.

[57]Horkheimer and Adorno, *Dialectic of Enlightenment*, 29.

[58]Adorno, "Scientific Experiences of a European Scholar in America," 242.

[59]Adorno, *Negative Dialectics*, 3. Translation modified, following Dennis Redmond's version.

[60]Ibid., 377.

[61]Claussen, *Theodor W. Adorno*, 216.

in questions of aesthetics allowed the critical theorist of society to engage with the impulses that had marked his intellectual development since an early age, even shaping his political trajectory. However, the awareness that under advanced capitalism the survival of this understanding of art had been called into question also hindered this relationship. For it raised the question of whether "the concept of culture in which one has grown up has not itself become obsolete; whether what today as a global tendency befalls culture is not what its very own failure brought upon it, the guilt it incurred by isolating itself as a special sphere of spirit without realizing itself in the organization of society" (GS 10.2, 736–7).[62]

The failure of what the young Marx called the realization of philosophy—interpreted by Horkheimer as the revolutionary horizon drawing away—is, for Adorno, compounded by the relapse into barbarism marked by the name Auschwitz and understood as the collapse of culture. Yet, once this failure—which also entails a sense of guilt—is acknowledged, what is the point of defending the potential of art? This question would lead the mature Adorno to critically revisit the positions of his youth: "The concept of radicalness becomes an ideological distraction, a consolation for the real powerlessness of political subjects" (GS 10.2, 506).[63] In a private note, dated 1960, he would go so far as to write: "The bare fact of focusing my interest on aesthetics, which naturally aligns with my personal inclinations, has something evasive, irresponsible, and ideological about it, even before acquiring any specific content."[64] In fact, Adorno himself noted that in the societies of postwar capitalism the meaning of radical art was no longer the same. Even though "during World War I and prior to Stalin, artistic and politically advanced thought went in tandem" (ÄT, 376),[65] the societies of the "economic miracle" seemed to have made peace with supposedly disruptive art. Even German industry was financing abstract painting. This situation had little to do with the formative experiences of Adorno's generation, which were shaped by a very particular historical context in which "art was taken to be what it in no way historically had been: a

[62] Adorno, *Negative Dialectics*, 241.

[63] Adorno, "Those Twenties," 47.

[64] Adorno, "Graeculus II. Notizen zu Philosophie und Gesellschaft," 18.

[65] Adorno, *Aesthetic Theory*, 254.

priori politically on the left" (ÄT, 376–7).[66] These reflections, which the late Adorno formulates in his unfinished *Aesthetic Theory*, require a clarification of the link that his critical theory—marked by a hitherto frustrated interest in emancipation—maintained with the artistic sphere.

Art as a Battlefield

In the decades that followed his death, Adorno was primarily regarded as an aesthete. This ensured him a degree of influence—though not always in a positive sense—in the field of art theory, aesthetics, and cultural studies, but it also contributed to the neglect of his critical theory of society. Indeed, the reception of his aesthetic texts and his musical writings, along with his critique of the culture industry, came to be broadly associated with a defense of "bourgeois high culture" that did not do justice to his position. Adorno's stance was not characterized by an apology for high art as a timeless reservoir of quality and meaning, but by the search for a fragile glimmer of artistic truth amid the omnipresent falsehood of the social. While Adorno's thought was grounded on an awareness of the intertwining of civilization and barbarism, nothing could be further from his approach than the attempt to safeguard an affirmative notion of culture, celebrating its products as valuable in themselves, as if to compensate for how the social logic of advanced capitalism relegates them to an increasingly vestigial role.

Shortly after his return from American exile, Adorno was surprised at the cultural climate that prevailed in Europe: "The word has not yet spread that culture in the traditional sense is dead, that in today's world it has become a collection of catalogued cultural goods, handed over to the consumer and exposed to wear and tear, which are denied the seriousness that today, as yesterday, is paid to them in Germany" (GS 20.2, 455). This failure of culture is a product of society and affects both its "cultivated" side and the so-called "mass culture." But this does not exclude the possibility that accomplished works can emerge under these conditions. In one of the fragments published as a paralipomena to the unfinished *Aesthetic Theory* one can read, "Culture

[66] Ibid., 254. Translation modified.

is refuse, yet art—one of its sectors—is nevertheless serious as the appearance of truth. This is implicit in the double character of fetishism" (ÄT, 459).[67] However, this does not imply that art is able to provide a sphere outside the heteronomy of the social whole in which an undamaged life could manifest itself without contradiction. Nor does it make it possible to affirm that the experience of modern art offers a solution to the aporias of reason and the work of the concept or provides an alternative foundation for criticism.[68] Rather, Adorno's texts argue the opposite. From his earliest writings to his final texts, all his aesthetic theory is formulated against the backdrop of the question of whether an art that would be worthy of the name is still at all possible within the societies of advanced capitalism. As early as 1921, when he was barely 18 years old, a young Wiesengrund-Adorno wrote, "The art of our time is faced with the question of its continued existence. Its necessity threatens to fade into illusion and, when it is screamed out, to become a lie" (GS 11, 611).[69] This troubling issue reappears unaltered in the sentence with which the posthumous *Aesthetic Theory* opens: "It is self-evident that nothing concerning art is self-evident anymore, not its inner life, not its relation to the world, not even its right to exist" (ÄT, 9).[70] The question is: Is art in a position to survive its integration into the socially administered and pacified realm that is culture under capitalism? If so, at what price and how?

Adorno was fully aware that art does not exist or subsist by itself: it has prerequisites that are rooted in social life. In 1932 he had already pointed out that, in the societies of developed capitalism, its function was merely that of a commodity (GS 18, 729).[71] Although in *Aesthetic Theory* he stresses the

---

[67]Ibid., 310.

[68]This has been the claim of some of the self-proclaimed "successors" of the critical theory of the improperly named "second generation." Cf. Jürgen Habermas, "Nachwort von Jürgen Habermas," in Max Horkheimer and Theodor W. Adorno, *Dialektik der Aufklärung* (Frankfurt: Fischer, 1987), 289–92; Albrecht Wellmer, *The Persistence of Modernity: Essays on Aesthetics, Ethics and Postmodernism* (Cambridge, MA: The MIT Press, 1991), vii–ix. For a critique of the mystification of the supposed continuity of critical theory as a procession of generations, cf. Detlev Claussen, "Kann Kritische Theorie vererbt werden?" (T. Frejtag and M. Havel, *Arbeit und Utopie. Oskar Negt zum 70. Geburtstag* (Frankfurt am Main: Humanities online, 2004), 271–85.

[69]Adorno, "Expressionism and Artistic Truthfulness," *Notes to Literature 2*, 259.

[70]Adorno, *Aesthetic Theory*, 1.

[71]Adorno, "On the Social Situation of Music," 391.

dual nature of the work of art, which is both a social fact and an autonomous phenomenon, it is important to emphasize that even its relative autonomy is a result of its condition as a social fact. This already relativizes the very claim to autonomy, which, strictly speaking, would primarily be an appearance, an illusion. Indeed, if works of art managed to conquer a certain independence from their contexts of use in the religious and political spheres, and to emancipate their strictly aesthetic dimension from the demands of their patrons and funders, it was through the division of labor and the anonymous nature of the market. This means that the autonomy of art is not an inherent property of art, a kind of timeless "in-itself" outside social mediation, but is instead made possible by the commodity form and the logic of exchange. From this perspective, Adorno's defense of the autonomy of art appears entirely dialectical. In fact, it is only thanks to reification that works of art can develop their form autonomously, liberating themselves from their social function so as to construct themselves according to their own immanent law. This is a result of late modernity and the development of capitalism. The aporia consists in the fact that in bourgeois society art is integrated to an unprecedented degree, but it is precisely this integration that makes its element of opposition to developed capitalism possible:

> By crystallizing in itself as something unique to itself, rather than complying with existing social norms and qualifying as "socially useful," art criticizes society by merely existing, for which puritans of all stripes condemn it. There is nothing pure, nothing structured strictly according to its own immanent law, that does not implicitly criticize the debasement of a situation evolving in the direction of a total exchange society in which everything is heteronomously defined. Art's asociality is the determinate negation of a determinate society. (ÄT, 335)[72]

In a social logic permeated by absolute functionality, in which the expansion of the commodity form implies that every object must be considered as the embodiment of something abstract in the first instance—value—rather than standing for itself, and therefore that everything is primarily "for another"

---

[72]Adorno, *Aesthetic Theory*, 225–6.

rather than "in itself," art appears as the utopia of a "useless" objectivity, that is, withdrawn from any heteronomous function. Where art is placed at the service of immediate needs, it does not benefit human beings but the social framework of functions that reproduces iniquity: capital as an end in itself. Only by withdrawing itself from the social principle of absolutized utility can art preserve the potential of "correct and fortunate use, a contact with things beyond the antithesis between use and uselessness" (GS 10.1, 392).[73] If art succeeds in doing this autonomously, it is because its products are not mere "things," but move in the sphere of semblance. That semblance is ethereal: it is not in a position to materialize the transcendence it promises, yet it makes possible a certain distance from empirical reality—and thus from the prevailing social logic. Hence Adorno's statement, "Artworks are the plenipotentiaries of things that are no longer distorted by exchange, by profit, and by the false needs of a degraded humanity. In the context of total semblance, art's semblance of being-in-itself is the mask of truth" (ÄT, 337).[74]

However, this intention to withdraw from the realm of utility, which is a condition of its truth, does not come without cost for art either. The price it must pay for this is that, from a practical point of view, its social function becomes increasingly ornamental (GS 10.1, 379).[75] Art is reduced to a mere object of contemplation, often being used for compensatory purposes. Here the dialectical character of autonomy is revealed: this "is not something beyond society, but is produced by it and is imbricated in its web of guilt."[76] The fact that it is detached from utility implies that autonomous art also acquires a fetishistic character that links it to ideology: for, by distancing itself from praxis, it cannot interfere with the very society that horrifies it (ÄT, 335).[77] That is what had always bothered those who were committed to an effectively political form of art. They understand that the self-sufficiency of art, which is what allows it to develop its own immanent logic regardless of the demands of

[73]Theodor W. Adorno, "Functionalism Today," *Without Model*, 111.
[74]Adorno, *Aesthetic Theory*, 227.
[75]Adorno, "Functionalism Today," 96.
[76]José Antonio Zamora, "El arte como lugarteniente de la liberación bloqueada: Th. W. Adorno ante la tesis benjaminiana de la politización del arte. Parte II," *Constelaciones: Revista de Teoría Crítica* 11/12 (2020), 178.
[77]Adorno, *Aesthetic Theory*, 226.

heteronomous society, in turn threatens to condemn it to sterility (ÄT, 459).[78] Adorno was fully aware of this aporia, and yet he continued to defend the specifically aesthetic dimension against the advocates of politically engaged art (GS 11, 409–430).[79] Nevertheless, the debates opposing his positions to the aesthetically reactionary approaches of Georg Lukács or with the more avant-garde ones of Hanns Eisler and Bertolt Brecht arose long before the two camps became mired in the complexities of the Cold War. In particular, the dialogue with Eisler, who aspired to compose music that could be politically effective and yet would not completely relinquish the achievements of Arnold Schoenberg's school (of which Eisler himself had been a prominent disciple), is critical for grasping Adorno's position regarding the relationship between art and politics, which was forged at a time when the conflict between the forces of emancipation and barbarism had not yet been resolved. Indeed, between 1925 and 1933, Eisler and Adorno pursued two different paths in response to the social and political impasse that was stifling the potential of the New Music. Their confrontation is crucial for understanding the impulses behind Adorno's aesthetics, for it is this pre-Nazi scenario, in which aesthetic radicalism and political radicalism could still converge, that shapes the loyalties of his thought and endows it with its distinctive hallmark.

Adorno's and Eisler's differing positions on aesthetic and political matters stemmed from a shared experience: the awareness of "the trap represented by the contradiction of advanced music and the absence of a public."[80] This paradox, which they both witnessed upon arriving at Schoenberg's school when it was past its prime, revealed that the New Music had begun to tread a path that transcended what was feasible within the framework of bourgeois society. What could become of it? While Adorno's radicalism led him to push the logic of the immanent development of musical material to its ultimate consequences—without making any concessions to the public, and thus choosing to persist in this contradiction—Eisler, who would soon distance himself from Schoenberg in favor of his communist militancy, could

[78] Ibid., 310.
[79] Adorno, "Commitment," 76–94.
[80] Claussen, *Theodor W. Adorno*, 154.

not remain indifferent to the almost grotesque isolation in which advanced music unfolded, performing for nearly deserted concert halls: "All this noise takes place in an empty glass bell, no sound reaches the outside. In the absence of any interest and the participation of any kind of audience, this empty activity is host to incestuous orgies."[81] Perhaps the New Music of Schoenberg, Berg, and Webern might have managed to achieve a truth content, but it all remained confined to a small circle of musicians, critics, and concert agents. It was not, of course, that Eisler considered attempts to cling to the already-exhausted forms of bourgeois music to be a more desirable option, for they only produced compositions that he judged to be completely dispensable. Like Adorno, he understood that the decay of bourgeois culture had undermined the foundations of music and its social function. However, he also held that a music that could live up to this situation required a new understanding of its social function and artistic mission, moving beyond the place that had been assigned to it within bourgeois society. Schoenberg's school had undoubtedly taken crucial steps from a technical perspective, but it had not succeeded in responding to the crisis of the social situation of music. That is why, as early as 1925, on the occasion of the master's fiftieth birthday, Eisler had already dubbed him the "reactionary composer."[82] Shortly afterward, already part of the communist movement, he would point out that the way in which the New Music turned its back on the conflicts of its time condemned it to lead "a fictitious existence that can only be maintained artificially."[83] That is what his compositional work sought to respond to: it was about giving new life to the New Music through a political and artistic impulse, one that could overcome its hermetic isolation through forms of composition that would allow for new political uses.

Eisler's stance aroused the interest of the young Adorno, who—despite the break with the master—still pointed to him as "the true representative of the young generation of disciples of Schoenberg and one of the most gifted young composers altogether" (GS 18, 522) in 1927. In fact, it was not difficult

[81]Hanns Eisler, "Zur Situation der modernen Musik," in *Schriften I: Musik und Politik 1924–1948* (Munich: Rogner & Bernhard, 1973), 91.
[82]Eisler, "Arnold Schönberg, der musikalische Reaktionär," *Schriften I*, 13–15.
[83]Eisler, "Über moderne Musik," *Schriften I*, 33.

to recognize an affinity between their political and musical commitments. It is no coincidence that, between 1925 and 1929, Adorno praised compositions by Eisler in no less than three reviews. In the last of these, on the composition "Zeitungsauschnitte, op. 11," Adorno commended him for his interesting attempt at a work for voice and piano that took the growing impossibility of the lyric under capitalist living conditions as its starting point and tried to draw out the consequences of this. Indeed, at a time when social relations held an almost absolute primacy over individual lives, the possibility of subjective expression, which is the precondition for lyricism, seemed to be undermined in advance. Eisler therefore opted for what Adorno calls a "negative lyric" in this piece, which ironically places newspaper clippings and marriage advertisements "in the place that lyric should occupy and no longer does, just as election posters are pasted on the empty plinth of a monument that has been removed" (GS 18, 524–5). His critique did not hesitate to recognize that "the central strength of the songs lies in their tone: at the same time highly differentiated … and concentrated in a will that transcends art: to change the world" (GS 18, 527).

This admiration for Eisler's compositional achievements would persist into the 1960s, after political differences and the Cold War had driven their positions apart; even then, Adorno would highlight the "formidable" character of this composition and other pre-1933 choral works, which he considered "a true musical counterpart to George Grosz."[84] But in his review of the *Zeitungsauschnitte* Adorno had also pointed out a potential threat: namely, that Eisler seemed to have a tendency to sacrifice the differentiation of the composition for the sake of its comprehensibility. The risk here was that the technical and musical means employed would lag behind the level reached by the language of the New Music and could turn "a politically revolutionary attitude into an aesthetically reactionary one" (GS 18, 527). In 1929 Adorno had already noted that the strength of Eisler's compositions came "from politics, not from aesthetic reflection" (GS 18, 524), regarding this as a problem to be solved in his future works. It was, moreover, a question that did not just apply at the level of composition, but also had repercussions in terms of social

[84]Theodor W. Adorno, "Notizen über Eisler," in *Frankfurter Adorno Blätter*, vol. 7 (Munich, 2001), 129.

theory: it implied sacrificing the immanent development of music—which, for Adorno, corresponded to the objective movement of historical reality—in order to foster the conditions for its reception and consumption within the given society.

In fact, at the time Adorno wrote this critique, the differences between the two were already becoming evident. Eisler had joined the workers' music movement, which advocated for a communal music addressed to the proletariat. This move was driven by the conviction that "with the experiences and artistic resources of the bourgeoisie the proletariat must create a proletarian music."[85] This could not help but clash with Adorno's approach. His recognition of the *Zeitungsauschnitte* was in fact an attempt to encourage the tendencies in Eisler himself that were opposed to that position. He had thus lauded his "negative lyric" insofar as it mobilized the "rebellious longing for human immediacy" while assuming the impossibility of postulating "a communal art without community" (GS 18, 525 and 524). For Adorno, the logic of capitalist socialization produces atomization, and within it any immediate form of human community is revealed to be powerless, if not fictitious, ideological, or compensatory (GS 18, 750).[86] "The point of view of the collective cannot be adopted when it is not substantial."[87] Eisler, however, was increasingly turning toward collective and communal music, and he did so in an effort to forge a new relationship with the musical realm that was no longer merely contemplative, but instead emphasized its "use" dimension. Instead of Lieder cycles, he composed choral pieces for the workers' movement and critical ballads, often in collaboration with Brecht. It is at this point that the differences between the two became palpable. With Eisler's commitment to a "politicized music," Adorno saw his fears confirmed: that the technical dimension of the composition would be sacrificed in order to adjust it to the demands and expectations of the public. This also had a political significance: it required the assumption that this proletarian and revolutionary "class consciousness," with which Eisler wanted to connect for the sake of social transformation,

---

[85]Hanns Eisler, "Über moderne Musik," *Schriften I*, 33.

[86]Adorno, "On the Social Situation of Music," 410.

[87]Adorno, "Notizen über Eisler," 127.

was something that was already "given" in the spontaneous socialization of capitalism, and not something yet to be constructed. Hence Eisler overlooked that the requirements to which this type of music was adapted, "singability, simplicity, collective effectiveness," were "necessarily dependent upon a state of consciousness entirely oppressed and subjugated through class domination." Due to this, orienting composition toward this goal "results in fetters placed upon musically productive forces" (GS 18, 751).[88] Adorno thus argued that these concessions to audience preferences rooted in existing social conditions did a disservice to the struggle against domination. While he recognized that Eisler's political compositions could be effective as agitprop—he would later point out that until his agitprop choral pieces, music had not been able to hate—[89] he felt that, as musical compositions, they paid too high a price for this. He certainly valued the attempt to bring the compositional achievements of the Schoenberg school into contact with political and musical impulses outside of it. Nevertheless, he felt that, "if this contact is to be fruitful, it must find dialectic form: this music must intervene actively in consciousness through its own forms and not take instructions from the passive, one-sided position of the consciousness of the audience—including the proletariat" (GS 18, 752).[90]

This brings us to Adorno's specific understanding of what political art is. Adorno argued that, if it was to be emancipatory, the struggle for social transformation cannot be built upon the stigmas with which the prevailing system of domination marks human beings. These are a manifestation of how the social order denigrates human potential and are therefore precisely what should be overcome. Consequently, sacrificing the degree of differentiation achieved in music to turn it into an instrument of revolutionary struggle harms music and does not further the cause of social transformation. It tends to subject the specifically musical dimension to the logic of effect, which entails a capitulation to the social order, and thus undermines the immanent logic of the language of art, its potential for truth, which is no longer deployed

[88]Adorno, "On the Social Situation of Music," 410.
[89]Adorno, "Notizen über Eisler," 123.
[90]Adorno, "On the Social Situation of Music," 411. Translation modified.

on the basis of its own aesthetic criteria but yields to the expectations of the consuming public. In contrast, the radical music of the Schoenberg school yielded nothing to the listener: it demanded "active and concentrated participation, the most acute attention to simultaneous multiplicity, the renunciation of the customary crutches of a listening which always knows what to expect, the intensive perception of the unique and specific, and the ability to grasp precisely the individual characteristics, often changing in the smallest space, and their history, devoid of all repetition" (GS 10.1, 152).[91] Nevertheless, Adorno believed that this music could do more for the cause of emancipation, precisely because it favored a more advanced and awakened consciousness. Hence, he stated that art which is "tightly organized, seamless, and rendered completely sensory precisely through its conscious force—is hardly capable of realization. But it embodies a resistance to the unspeakable pressure exerted on what is human by what merely exists. It acts as the representative of what we might one day be" (GS 11, 125).[92] Rather than promoting explicitly political attitudes, this model of consistent art conveys an attitude of resistance to the expansive character of a social logic that ruthlessly subjugates individual existence. Its sole message is opposition to a conformism that denigrates the human being: "not to become stupid, not to be lulled to sleep, not to go along" (GS 11, 125).[93] Thus, where Eisler opted for the politicization of music, Adorno took a stand for taking artistic autonomy to its ultimate consequences (GS 18, 401–7). Of course, he was aware that neither music nor radical art could, on their own, transcend the sociohistorical reality in which they were rooted, but believed that they had to carry their immanent logic to the very end. To be sure, insisting upon the autonomy of art necessarily led to its own aporias, but renouncing its immanent development did not offer a way out of art's aporetic situation either. Therefore, if radically consistent art was isolated and distant from public interest, this situation should not be remedied aesthetically, since the divorce between artistic development and public consciousness was based on a contradiction that was essentially social (GS 18, 30–1).

---

[91] Adorno, "Arnold Schoenberg 1874–1951," *Prisms*, 149.
[92] Adorno, "The Artist as Deputy," *Notes to Literature 1*, 107.
[93] Ibid.

However, Adorno was also aware of the weaknesses of this position. He himself recognizes that "the separation of art from reality endangers art itself. For even if art persists in itself, it threatens to become ideological—to be self-satisfied in a muffled, petit bourgeois way, to forget its supportive human function, ultimately to become petrified into bad decorum" (GS 18, 830–1).[94] This very problem revealed the moment of truth for positions such as Eisler's. This very choice between autonomy and commitment exposed the social wound that cut through art. While the insistence on autonomy tends to turn art into a mere fetish—"the idle amusement of those who would gladly sleep through the deluge that threatens us" (GS 11, 409)[95]—opting for politically engaged art represents a desperate attempt to escape artistic immanence as such, which undermines its own foundations (ÄT 459).[96] Hence, even in the 1960s, Adorno noted, "Eisler is right from an external perspective, in relation to the religion of art, but this being right turns against his own art, since it is only possible with the same absolute seriousness that he had seen through and ridiculed."[97]

The intransigence of radically autonomous art that prefers to entrench itself in its own hermeticism rather than adapt to the social logic of communicability clearly has an antisocial dimension (GS 10.1, 237).[98] But an art that, under the conditions of advanced capitalism, resigns itself to being degraded into a mere pastime—thus subjecting existence all the more rigidly to the vicarious logic of heteronomous labor (GS 10.1, 153)[99]—found itself in an even less desirable situation. There is no way out of this aporia, which is fundamentally social. Eisler and Adorno recognized the problem, opting for two diametrically opposed responses: if the former sought to resolve this contradiction in reality, through political struggle, the latter called for a renewed insistence on the aesthetic dimension, taking the contradiction to its ultimate consequences. In the long run, neither option would be successful. However, in the adverse

---

[94]Adorno, "Why Is the New Art So Hard to Understand?" *Essays on Music*, 132. Translation modified.
[95]Adorno, "Commitment," 76.
[96]Adorno, *Aesthetic Theory*, 310.
[97]Adorno, "Notizen über Eisler," 128.
[98]Adorno, "The George-Hofmannsthal Correspondence," *Prisms*, 225.
[99]Adorno, "Arnold Schoenberg 1874–1951," 150.

conditions of exile, the two would meet again, and they would end up writing a book together, *Composing for the Films*. Here, a shared interest in the possibilities of employing advanced music in new spaces, beyond the concert halls, outweighed their political differences—at least until the Cold War once again drove a wedge between them. Beyond their disagreements, what united Adorno and Eisler was their shared aesthetic and political socialization in an already distant era that even in the second postwar period evoked "the dream of an unregulated life, the feeling that, for a brief period of time, everything was open, everything was possible" (GS 18, 548).

Throughout his work, Adorno would remain faithful to the impulses of an art that had explored new aesthetic territories as if aspiring to breathe—borrowing a phrase from Stefan George, famously set to music by Schoenberg—"air from another planet." It was this, rather than the defense of high culture, that led him to insist on the transformative potentials of a consistent art—potentials that became all the more urgent in an increasingly integrated world. Undoubtedly, this type of art found it increasingly difficult to go on, and everything in the social logic of advanced capitalism seemed already to undermine the possibility of an art based only on its own premises. In fact, for those who must live in this society, everything that—like art—goes beyond the sphere of reproduction of life and does not serve the most basic needs is, to a large extent, "superfluous." It is not clear on what ground free, autonomous art can still claim the right to exist in a world in which, despite the enormous expansion of productive capacities, hunger, avoidable suffering, and new levels of heteronomy persist. Indeed, in the face of "absurdly incessant scarcity, the expanding and self-reproducing barbarism, the ever-present threat of total catastrophe," there is good reason to distrust phenomena that disregard the crudest and most material interests (ÄT, 362–3).[100] In the world that had made Auschwitz possible, and in which such things were still feasible, one could no longer maintain "an unrefracted relationship to the aesthetic realm" (GS 10.2, 506).[101] Nevertheless, Adorno insisted, "Only for a pacified

[100] Adorno, *Aesthetic Theory*, 243–4.
[101] Adorno, "Those Twenties," 47.

humanity would art come to an end: Its death, which now threatens, would be exclusively the triumph of bare existence over the consciousness that has the audacity to resist it" (GS 12, 24).[102] This must be well understood: such resistance is not capable of diverting the course of the world; at that level, art is powerless. However, the walls of the monadic subject can be broken down by the shudders produced by successful works of art: through a nonconceptual experience, "the irruption of objectivity into subjective consciousness" (ÄT, 363–4)[103] is achieved. This is the potential for resistance that art has preserved within false society and which enables it to set itself up as the language of suffering, "the unconscious writing of history, as anamnesis of the vanquished, of the repressed, and perhaps of what is possible" (ÄT, 384).[104] Adorno would cling to this until the end of his life. The unwavering fidelity to the intuitions he had developed in defense of radical modern art undoubtedly led a part of his aesthetic thought to perish along with it.[105] At the same time, as Robert Hullot-Kentor pointed out, Adorno himself was aware of this situation and may have persisted with it for good reason. "If philosophy only continues because the moment to realize it was missed ..., so aesthetics ... only has any hold on life because art has been entirely misunderstood. The moment of the realization of art has no less been missed. The moment is to be recovered or, failing that, the loss comprehended."[106] This is how Adorno's aesthetics brings us back, once again, to his notion of critical theory as a science of mourning. If art appears in his work as the powerless deputy of a potential society to come—one that is less damaging, less suffocating, and capable of putting an end to heteronomy—this role also serves as a reminder of the failed transition from philosophy to praxis.

---

[102] Adorno, *Philosophy of New Music*, 16.

[103] Adorno, *Aesthetic Theory*, 245.

[104] Ibid., 259.

[105] One might think, for instance, of the notion of a philosophy of art history grounded on the possibility of clearly distinguishing between progress and reaction in artistic proposals.

[106] Robert Hullot-Kentor, "Font Null. The First Sentence of Aesthetic Theory," in *Theodor W. Adorno: Ästhetische Theorie*, ed. Anne Eusterschulte and Sebastian Tränkle (Berlin: De Gruyter, 2021), 27.

Critical Theory and Praxis

"Since utopia was set aside and the unity of theory and practice demanded, we have become all too practical. Fear of the impotence of theory supplies a pretext for bowing to the almighty production process, and so fully admitting the impotence of theory" (MM, 49).[107] Adorno, who wrote these lines in exile in California, could hardly have imagined that less than a quarter of a century later, a young generation of politicized students, raised in the West Germany of the economic miracle and largely influenced by his own reflections, would reproach him for the alleged inconsistency of those who limit themselves to critical thinking without actively engaging in transformative praxis. Did this not contradict the driving impulse of critical theory? As early as 1956, Horkheimer himself had pointed out in a conversation with Adorno that "it is our cursed duty to marry thinking with right praxis" (HGS 19, 59).[108] Even in 1968, when the German protest movement had already reached its height, he recognized that "those who take critical theory seriously have the desire to draw consequences for political action from it" (HGS 3, 14). Certainly, there is no lack of passages in which Adorno himself shows to be fully aware of the inadequacies of a theory that is self-satisfied, admitting that its lack of contact with political praxis represents a genuine mutilation: "Even the most radical reflection of the mind on its own failure is limited by the fact that it remains only reflection, without altering the existence to which its failure bears witness. Hence immanent criticism cannot take comfort in its own idea" (GS 10.1, 27f.).[109] Indeed, his texts often insist that, in the face of a world that constantly demonstrates itself to be the potential or actual harbinger of barbarism, the idea of a neutral and merely contemplative attitude has become a "mockery" (GS 11, 46). What, then, is the reason for his skeptical distance from political praxis, which at the end of his life brought him into conflict with his more politicized students? Despite all the differences, there is no doubt that Adorno was largely sympathetic to the student protests (cf. GS 20.1, 398–401). There

[107] Adorno, *Minima Moralia*, 44.
[108] Theodor W. Adorno and Max Horkheimer, "Towards a New Manifesto," *New Left Review* 65, 51.
[109] Adorno, "Cultural Criticism and Society," 32–3.

is no lack of evidence that he saw the politicized movements of the late 1960s as a sign that the trend toward total integration into the societies of advanced capitalism would not run so smoothly and would meet with resistance along the way (ES, 100–01).[110] Nor did he hesitate to point out that, for German reactionary movements, the students had taken the place once occupied by the Jews.[111] What aroused his reservations was the risk that the impatient radicalism of the students, blind to the actual relation of social and political forces, could not only accelerate authoritarian processes and social regression, but also lead to moments of subjective regression (GS 10.2, 773–779).[112] Accordingly, understanding the reasons for his supposed abstinence from praxis requires taking a closer look at his arguments as to the relationship between theory, politics, and social transformation.

At first glance, Adorno's position may seem irritating, almost stereotypical of someone who stubbornly wants to defend his right to operate from an ivory tower: "Distance from praxis is disreputable to everyone. Whoever doesn't want to really knuckle down and get his hands dirty is suspect, as though the aversion were not legitimate and only distorted by privilege" (GS 10.2, 794).[113] However, the relationship between theory and praxis cannot be approached as an isolated phenomenon; it only acquires its proper meaning once it is framed within the broader framework of social life. This changes the terms of the problem and demonstrates that the primacy of praxis over reflection is not only a claim made by those who demand the urgency of a

[110]Adorno, *Introduction to Sociology*, trans. Edmund Jephcott (Stanford: Stanford University Press, 1999), 58.

[111]Theodor W. Adorno, letter to Günther Grass, November 4, 1968, "Kritik der Pseudo-Aktivität: Adornos Verhältnis zur Studentenbewegung im Spiegel seiner Korrespondenz," in *Frankfurter Adorno Blätter*, vol. 6, ed. Rolf Tiedemann (Munich: Text+Kritik, 2000), 80. The resentment and violence directed at the students eventually materialized in an attack on their most visible representative, Rudi Dutschke, in the middle of Berlin's Kurfürstendamm on April 11, 1968.

[112]Adorno, "Marginalia to Theory and Praxis," 270. See Detlev Claussen, "Konflikte mit Teddie," *Frankfurter Adorno Blätter VI*, ed. Rolf Tiedemann (Münich: text+kritik, 2000) 139–41. The most comprehensive documentation on the relationship of critical theory and the protest movement can be found in Wolfgang Kraushaar (ed.), *Frankfurter Schule und Studentenbewegung* (Hamburg: Hamburger Edition, 1998). For an account of Adorno's relationship to the protesting students in his correspondence, cf. Theodor W. Adorno, "Kritik der Pseudo-Aktivität: Adornos Verhältnis zur Studentenbewegung im Spiegel seiner Korrespondenz," 42–116.

[113]Adorno, "Resignation," 290.

transformative politics, but also one of the features of the blind process that governs life under the current social order. For the reproduction of the social forms of domination and subjugation does not require any consciousness, yet it certainly requires active involvement. Everything in it is dynamism, even frenetic, compulsive action: diligent participation in all the hustle and bustle involved in the exchange of commodities and the logic of competition, as well as in the social forms of work and consumption. Praxis is also the almost automatic reproduction of the respective positions in the different axes of domination. Individuals hardly tolerate being reminded of this situation: they already have enough to do just trying to get by. However, the sole consequence of all this action and all the transformations constantly demanded by the intensive and extensive expansion of economic logic is the constant repetition of the same old thing. Beyond that, subjective activity is socially irrelevant and therefore individual spontaneity is revealed to be trivial (GS 10.2, 764–5).[114] According to Adorno, it is this blind inertia that governs social activity and condemns human beings to effective powerlessness that gives rise to all the suspicions directed at the detachment from bad praxis implied by the reflective attitude: "Whoever only thinks, whoever removes himself, is considered weak, cowardly, virtually a traitor" (GS 10.2, 795–6).[115] In fact, blind participation in the compulsive reproduction of the social logic thrives on the growing disproportion between the social apparatus and the weakened individuals who depend on it. That is precisely the pseudo-natural condition of social life that the reflective, critical attitude aspires to break away from. For "stupidity is not a natural quality, but one [that is] socially produced and reinforced" (MM, 119).[116] In this sense, it would be appropriate here to offer a variation on an old formulation of Walter Benjamin (BGS II, 494):[117] even if consciousness is not necessary to establish certain forms of social domination, it is certainly necessary to overthrow them.

[114]Adorno, "Marginalia to Theory and Praxis," 260.

[115]Adorno, "Resignation," 290.

[116]Adorno, *Minima Moralia*, 105–6.

[117]Walter Benjamin, "Eduard Fuchs, Collector and Historian," in *Selected Writings, Volume 3: 1935–1938*, ed. Howard Eiland and Michael W. Jennings (Cambridge: Harvard University Press, 2002), 276–7.

At this point, it is important to remember that Adorno adheres to an emphatic notion of praxis. This should not be confused with political action in general, but refers specifically to those aimed at radical transformation. In the aforementioned conversation with Horkheimer, he put it quite clearly: "By practice we really mean that we're serious about the idea that the world needs fundamental change. This has to show itself in both thought and action. The practical aspect lies in the notion of difference; the world has to become different" (HGS 19, 61).[118] This notion of praxis refers to conscious action aimed at overthrowing the social relations that subject life to a condition of heteronomy—first and foremost the logic of reproduction of capital. But until that happens, praxis cannot do without theory, since it will remain a product of the realm of necessity, of the struggle for survival, of the absence of freedom (GS 10.2, 762).[119] However, the way in which the link between theory and praxis is formulated should not be misleading. It is not a matter of theory providing the basis for transformative action or offering concrete instructions on how to act. This would imply reproducing the assumption that thought dominates reality and that intellectuals must therefore lead the way and shepherd the masses. On the contrary: "neither theory can be placed at the service of practice nor practice can be understood as the application of theory."[120] In this sense, critical theory remains faithful to an old concept from Marx (MEW 1, 345):[121] thought as such is an integral part of broader historical struggles and, before pointing out or justifying a course of action, it is called upon to clarify the meaning of the struggle itself. This implies respecting the autonomous course of emancipatory praxis, which cannot be imposed on its subjects from outside or determined by thought; the latter can only offer an understanding of reality and its relations of forces and accompany praxis with a reflective attitude. But this also implies that the possibility for theory to have an impact on reality—that what it grasps as wrong in the world might in fact be corrected—does not depend on theory itself. Although Marx had

---

[118]Adorno and Horkheimer, "Towards a New Manifesto," 53.

[119]Adorno, "Marginalia to Theory and Praxis," 262.

[120]Dobbs-Weinstein, *Spinoza's Critique of Religion and its Heirs*, 145.

[121]Karl Marx, Letter to Ruge, September 1843, "Letters From the *Franco-German Yearbooks*," in *Early Writings* trans. Rodney Livingstone and Gregor Benton (London: Penguin Books, 1992), 208.

still been able to believe in the unity of theory and praxis until the failure of the revolutions of 1848, framed by the urgency of a situation that presented itself as a "now or never" (GS 10.2, 781),[122] in the middle of the twentieth century this confidence could no longer be taken for granted. There was no political subject capable of influencing history with which theory could establish a connection, and the societies of advanced capitalism appeared increasingly impenetrable—perfectly integrated despite all their negativity. This required reflecting on the blockage of praxis itself. Adorno is perfectly aware that this situation puts critical thought in a problematic position: if true praxis has become impossible, this undermines the meaning of critical theory itself, rendering it powerless. At the same time, however, whenever reflective activity is suspended, "praxis is damaged and therefore longed for, distorted, and desperately overvalued" (GS 10.2, 760).[123] Any actionism that impatiently rejects all theoretical reflection in order to turn to attempts at immediate action is attempting to flee from the painful awareness of this divorce between theory and praxis. This is what Adorno detects in the attitude of certain sectors of the student movement at the end of the 1960s, and this is what his critique of "pseudo-activity" refers to.

Pseudo-activity is a desperate search for immediate action in an increasingly compacted society in which nothing escapes universal mediation. Adorno interprets it as an attempt to avoid facing up to the frustration produced by a vague presentiment of the difficulty of effectively transforming social relations that are imposed on individuals in a coercive way. Its supporters have realized that theory—even if it is correct—has no direct effect on practice, and for this reason they wield subjective spontaneity against it. However, pseudo-activity is "misguided spontaneity" (GS 10.2, 652),[124] weighed down by powerlessness in the face of the socializing pressure of the administered world. The more-than-legitimate impulse to act against flagrant injustice (e.g., the use of napalm against the civilian population in Vietnam) gives way to a burning need to do anything in order not to stand idly by. Thus, despite its apparent

---

[122] Adorno, "Marginalia to Theory and Praxis," 277.
[123] Ibid., 260.
[124] Adorno, "Free Time," *Critical Models*, 173.

radicalism, the pseudo-revolutionary gesture of direct action seems aimed more at compensating for one's own impotence than at having any real effect. In this way, it fits in perfectly with the disproportion in the balance of power, which highlights the impossibility of a spontaneous revolution: "In relation to real power, which hardly feels a tickle, actionism is irrational" (GS 10.2, 773).[125] The cult of action that refuses to tolerate theoretical reflection runs the risk of losing all contact with its object, that is, with the social reality to be transformed. This gives rise to the suspicion that mobilization, whatever it may achieve, becomes the true end of political activity. Calls for self-sacrifice in the name of lost causes do not bring emancipation any closer. Rather, it suggests that the insistence on praxis functions primarily as a release in the face of a dead-end situation. "People who are locked in desperately want to get out. In such situations one doesn't think anymore or does so only under fictive premises. Within absolutized praxis only reaction is possible, and it is therefore false" (GS 10.2, 796).[126] Ultimately, the cult of immediate action undermines the very foundations of opposition to the current order and ends up promoting resignation: it ceases to safeguard the possibility of a praxis worthy of the name through critical reflection. If there does not seem to be an entity capable of putting an end to a destructive, iniquitous social logic, the possibility of an effective transformation of reality depends on "the full and undiminished awareness of the *blockage* of praxis."[127] Thought "should analyze the reasons and subsequently draw the conclusions. It is up to thought not to accept the situation as final. The situation can be changed, if at all, by undiminished insight. The leap into praxis does not cure thought of resignation as long as it is paid for with the secret knowledge that that really isn't the right way to go" (GS 10.2, 796).[128] It is this situation that led Adorno—even before the student movement—to ironically reformulate a famous observation of the young Marx: "Not only theory, but also its absence becomes a material force when it seizes the masses" (GS 8, 214).[129]

---

[125] Adorno, "Marginalia to Theory and Praxis," 271.

[126] Adorno, "Resignation," 291.

[127] Theodor W. Adorno, *Vorlesung über Negative Dialektik*, 84 and *Lectures on Negative Dialectics*, 54.

[128] Adorno, "Resignation," 291.

[129] Theodor W. Adorno, "Sociology and Empirical Research," in *The Positivist Dispute in German Sociology* trans. Glyn Adey and David Frisby (London: Heinemann, 1976), 84.

"Praxis without theory, lagging behind the most advanced state of cognition, cannot but fail" (GS 10.2, 766).[130] Indeed, how is it possible to arrive at a non-repressive praxis, or at a satisfactory balance between spontaneity and organization without theoretical reflection (GS 10.2, 777–8)?[131] Theoretical-intellectual activity must accompany political movements. If it is to be emancipatory, transformation requires the full labor of consciousness. However, those who judge theory by its immediate practical effect restrict and mutilate the power of thought. After all, Marx's *Capital* does not offer any program of action either. What it presents is an interpretation of the logic that governs the movement of modern capitalist society and a critique of the hegemonic modes of understanding it: it does not offer a solution, but relentlessly analyzes what must be transformed. Adorno's critical theory remains faithful to this model. However, at the same time, it seeks to go beyond Marx. Since it recognizes that the forms of knowledge and those of the society to be transformed are mediated, it becomes aware of the political dimension of thought itself. In fact, theory which has as its main goal the identity of thought itself, thus rigorously deploying deductive reasoning based on ideals of necessity and universality, becomes complicit in domination (MM, 172).[132] This is why Adorno points out that "dialectical thought is an attempt to break through the coercion of logic by its own means" (MM, 171).[133] When the concept levels differences, it proceeds analogously to the abstraction of particulars—of use values—at work in the commodity form. Thus, if the principle of exchange that governs iniquitous social logic is at work even within thought itself, critical theory will have to seek a mode of knowledge capable of surpassing the logic of domination.

---

[130]Adorno, "Marginalia to Theory and Praxis," 265.

[131]Ibid., 274. In this regard, it is no minor detail that the critique advanced by Hans-Jürgen Krahl—the rebellious student who turned against his teacher as the student movement began to wane—was directed precisely at the fact that Adorno's mourning over the demise of the bourgeois individual had led his critical theory to neglect the questions that emerged at a time of political mobilization (Hans-Jürgen Krahl, *Konstitution und Klassenkampf*, [Frankfurt: Neue Kritik, 2008], 300–01). For an analysis of Adorno's and Krahl's positions on the problem of praxis, see Meike Gerber, "Kurz vor der Praxis wiederum in die Theorie," in *Für Hans-Jürgen Krahl: Beiträge zu seinem antiautoritären Marxismus*, ed. Meike Gerber, Emanuel Kapfinger, and Julian Volz (Vienna: Mandelbaum, 2022), 171–97.

[132]Adorno, *Minima Moralia*, 151.

[133]Ibid., 150.

It is here that Adorno's critical theory goes beyond what was proposed by Horkheimer or Marcuse and becomes reflexive about the political implications of the very form of thought. His critique of the principle of identity, for instance, not only points out that it subsumes the particular under the general, but also that it cuts off possibility in reality, it aligns itself with an increasingly hermetically sealed social system, which hardly leaves any room for imagining a better situation (HGS 19, 70).[134] This is where the political impetus in Adorno's critique of ontology and positivism comes from, for they reduce reality to what is the case and, thus, cannot help but naturalize, reify, and fetishize the given.[135] For Adorno, in contrast, "what is is more than it is" (ND, 164);[136] hence "dialectics means intransigence toward all reification" (GS 10.1, 26).[137] It is not a matter of limiting oneself to ordering or classifying the factual, but of arriving at a thought that is not exhausted by the mere reproduction of what there is.[138] "As long as it doesn't break off, thinking has a secure hold on possibility. Its insatiable aspect, its aversion to being quickly and easily satisfied, refuses the foolish wisdom of resignation" (GS 10.2, 798).[139] Adorno's entire body of work, as well as his insistence on the expressive moment of thought as opposed to the purely logical or deductive (ND, 29),[140] is bound up with a form of knowledge that does not reproduce mastery, but which, from coming into close contact with its objects, is capable of reviving spontaneity, consciousness, and the possibility of a less damaged life; in this sense he understands theory as a form of praxis (GS 10.2, 761).[141] If his thought is not satisfied with analyzing the social whole and its developmental tendencies and insists on interpreting singular phenomena—from small daily gestures to linguistic usages or musical scores—this is because he assumes that the possibility of transcending the current order does not depend purely on

---

[134]Adorno and Horkheimer, "Towards a New Manifesto," 61.

[135]Krahl, *Konstitution und Klassenkampf*, 298–300.

[136]Adorno, *Negative Dialectics*, 106. Translation modified.

[137]Adorno, "Cultural Criticism and Society," 31.

[138]On this point, cf. Iain Macdonald, *What Would Be Different: Figures of Possibility in Adorno* (Stanford: Stanford University Press, 2019).

[139]Adorno, "Resignation," 192.

[140]Adorno, *Negative Dialectics*, 18.

[141]Adorno, "Marginalia to Theory and Praxis," 261.

the possibilities it develops, but also on the unassimilated and unassimilable elements within its logic of movement. For "it is in the nature of the defeated to appear, in their impotence, irrelevant, eccentric, derisory" (MM, 172).[142] Hence Adorno's interest in giving voice to the "paralyzed and silenced, whose nuances are both traces of violence and secret messages of potential liberation" (GS 8, 194). In this way he is affirming that "all reification is a forgetting and criticism really means the same as remembrance—that is, to uncover in phenomena how they have become what they are, and thereby recognizing the possibility that they might have become, and could therefore be, something different" (ES, 250).[143]

However, this insistence on the political dimension of theory itself, which attempts to subvert its own entanglement in relations of domination and subjugation and to safeguard the possibility of a different reality, does not imply fetishizing theory as if it were self-sufficient. Adorno is quite clear in this regard: "Praxis is put off and cannot wait; this is what ails even theory" (ND, 242).[144] But the blockage of praxis in turn "grants thought a breathing spell that it would be practically criminal not to utilize" (ND, 243).[145] That is why José Antonio Zamora has pointed out that "only as this breathing spell can theory be the lieutenant of freedom in the midst of unfreedom." Its task is the "critique of false praxis," in the realm of thought, too, "and the unveiling of the form of praxis that is currently blocked. One cannot renounce theory in the name of praxis."[146] Indeed, if the current models of thought and praxis perpetuate the domination of nature and the struggle for self-preservation, true praxis would consist in breaking out of this cycle. In this sense, the insistence on the blockage of praxis should not be understood, along the lines of a certain strain of Marxism, as if the passage to a better society depended solely on the objective conditions being "ripe." Those who remain conscious of the overwhelming reality of suffering understand that praxis cannot be postponed. This is why Adorno insists that, at the level of development of

[142] Adorno, *Minima Moralia*, 151.
[143] Adorno, *Introduction to Sociology*, 150.
[144] Adorno, *Negative Dialectics*, 245.
[145] Ibid.
[146] Zamora, *Krise–Kritik–Erinnerung*, 452.

the productive capacities of advanced capitalism, the conditions for a society liberated from the most basic material deprivations are already available (GS 8, 585).[147] What was lacking was a subject capable of influencing history and breaking down the social relations that impede the realization of what is possible. This is where the limits of theory become visible. For, on the one hand, "true praxis, the totality of acts that would satisfy the idea of freedom, does indeed require full theoretical consciousness … But praxis also needs something else, something physical which consciousness does not exhaust, something conveyed to reason and qualitatively different from it" (ND, 228–9).[148] Criticism arises from a spontaneous impulse that transcends mere thought, closely linked to indignation in the face of a world plagued by violence, injustice, and avoidable suffering. The elements of resistance and nonconformism in an increasingly coercive and hermetically sealed world should not be mistaken for the existence of a subject capable of enacting social transformation. Nonetheless, these elements sow the seeds for the possibility that one day this transformation may become a reality.

Perhaps it was this that aroused Adorno's greatest reservations about the protesting students, in whom opposition to the existing order and the transformative impulse seemed to coalesce with regressive elements that already made it possible to foresee fatal consequences. No one formulated it with as much precision as Samuel Beckett: "*Was ever such rightness joined to such foolishness?*"[149] Adorno was aware of the importance of the subjective moment, of spontaneity, in opening a crack in the hermetically sealed present; but he also knew that this was only one aspect, and that it was far from being a sufficient condition. To confront the oppressive and suffocating character of advanced capitalism's forms of socialization from the standpoint of pure decisionism was "too optimistic even as an expression of despair" (LGF, 226).[150] For this reason, he praised the student protests for their emphasis on the

---

[147]Theodor W. Adorno, "Late Capitalism or Industrial Society?" in *Can One Live After Auschwitz?*, ed. Rolf Tiedemann (Stanford: Stanford University Press, 2003), 122.

[148]Adorno, *Negative Dialectics*, 229.

[149]Letter from Samuel Beckett to Theodor W. Adorno, February 5, 1969, *The Letters of Samuel Beckett, vol. 4* (Cambridge: Cambridge University Press, 2016), 150–1.

[150]Adorno, *History and Freedom*, 161.

pre-theoretical impulse from which true critique originates. However, he was critical of their lack of sufficient reflection, which is crucial for understanding one's own position within social reality and recognizing one's fragility. That is why he insisted, "Praxis is a source of power for theory but cannot be prescribed by it. It appears in theory merely, and indeed necessarily, as a blind spot, as an obsession with what is being criticized" (GS 10.2, 782).[151] Adorno's stubborn insistence on the "happiness that dawns in the eye of the thinking person," which lets a faint ray of light into the gloomy horizon of "the universal tendency of oppression," may be aporetic, and arguably even excessive. Yet perhaps it must be conceded that "anyone who does not let [this happiness] atrophy has not resigned" (GS 10.2, 798–99).[152]

[151] Adorno, "Marginalia to Theory and Praxis," 278.
[152] Adorno, "Resignation," 239.

3

A Farewell to Marx? Unravelling Contemporary Prehistory

While critical theory has a "temporal core," a historical index, this does not entail that it is predetermined by the characteristics of the period from which it emerges—quite the contrary. It is only theoretical activity that can construct an interpretation of a historical moment that allows for the unfolding, clarification, and conceptualization of its constituent features and tendencies. This means that the task of theory cannot be limited to providing a faithful expression of its epoch. In fact, the historical moment to which all critical and emancipatory theory refers "cannot serve as a point of reference to which critical theory is assigned from the outside."[1] Theoretical activity renders its own time intelligible through its very construction, helping to make the signs of a given period and their implications comprehensible. Seeing it this way provides the best means of understanding a book as enigmatic and misinterpreted as the *Dialectic of Enlightenment*. There is no doubt that this work is a response to specific historical circumstances that led to a reformulation of the project of critical theory and that Adorno played a decisive role in this regard. But this reorientation has often been viewed as an abandonment of Marxian influence, where the critique of capitalism

[1]Hindrichs, *Zur kritischen Theorie*, 48.

is replaced by the critique of the domination of nature or the critique of instrumental reason—the latter being more abstract and philosophical, the former more vague and elusive.[2] This reading loses sight of the fact that the *Dialectic of Enlightenment* aspired to develop a theory in keeping with epochal shifts that could no longer be explained solely by applying Marx's interpretative frameworks. It is true that the modifications that the authors introduced in the 1947 edition, with respect to the 1944 original, can be seen as an attempt to do away with the more explicitly Marxist terminology: the proletarian becomes an employee, the capitalist becomes an entrepreneur, exploitation becomes suffering.[3] But this was more likely a response to the fear of being identified with the Soviet side, in what would soon become the Cold War, than a change in their way of thinking with regard to relations of social domination. Either way, up until now, a reading has predominated according to which the *Dialectic of Enlightenment* does not so much articulate a critique of society as a negative philosophy of history that presents a totalizing and pessimistic vision, ranging from Homer to Hitler, from the most remote animism at the dawn of civilization to the cult of facts found in modern positivism, thereby portraying a completely closed-off historical outlook.[4] Since then, numerous studies have shown this interpretation to be a radical simplification, one verging on the grotesque.[5] As a matter of fact, nothing in

[2]Dubiel, *Wissenschaftsorganisation und politische Erfahrung*; Jeffries, *Grand Hotel Abyss*, 235–6.

[3]Cf. Gunzelin Schmid-Noerr, "Nachwort des Herausgebers," in HGS 5, 443–52; and Willem van Reijen and Jan Bransen, "Das Verschwinden der Klassengesellschaft in der *Dialektik der Aufklärung*. Kommentar zu den Textvarianten," in HGS 5, 453–57. For a critique of the simplifications and inadequacies involved in this reading included in the critical apparatus of Horkheimer's complete works, cf. Dobbs-Weinstein, *Spinoza's Critique of Religion and its Heirs*, 118–23.

[4]Among the texts that have helped to consolidate this pattern of reading, the historiography on the so-called paradigm shift in critical theory stands out above all. Cf. Habermas, *The Philosophical Discourse of Modernity*, 135–62; Habermas, "Nachwort von Jürgen Habermas," in Horkheimer and Adorno, *Dialektik der Aufklärung* (Frankfurt: Fischer, 1986), 277–92; Wellmer, *On the Dialectics of Modernity and Postmodernity*.

[5]Carl Cassegård, *Toward a Critical Theory of Nature* (London: Bloomsbury, 2021), 64–73; Gómez, *El pensamiento estético de Theodor W. Adorno*, 25–43; Hullot-Kentor, *Things Beyond Resemblance*, 23–44; Maiso, *Elementos para la reapropiación de la Teoría Crítica de Theodor W. Adorno*, 234–255; Heinz Steinert, *Das Verhängnis der Gesellschaft und das Glück der Erkenntnis* (Münster: Westfälisches Dampfboot), 2007; Rolf Tiedemann, *Mythos und Utopie* (Munich: Text+Kritik, 2009), 102–17; Christoph Türcke and Gerhard Bolte, *Einführung in die kritische Theorie* (Hamburg: Prius, 1994); Zamora, *Th. W. Adorno. Pensar contra la barbarie*, 130–85.

the book suggests that the course of human history is inevitably doomed to plunge into barbarism. Rather, at the time the text was written, barbarism was a consummated reality—one that was manifest and visible to all. In this regard, the major achievement of the book is how, beginning from this awareness of a catastrophic present, it develops the keys for understanding its own historical situation and for comprehending the historical process that has led up to it.

Adorno and Horkheimer were aware that the historical moment they were facing challenged the old certainties of critique. Faced with the spread of fascism and the ease with which the new barbarism had burst through the dams of civilization, the development of the potentials of modernity no longer seemed like a driving force for progress; it had taken on a much more ambivalent quality. On the other hand, the explanatory power of Marx's theory was no longer sufficient to account for some of these phenomena. Hence the need to revise some of Marxism's assumptions, without this necessarily implying an abandonment of Marx. The interpretative framework of the critique of political economy was still vital to account for the structure and dynamics of capitalist sociality, but other elements were necessary to explain its most recent iteration in the post-liberal phase. As Adorno pointed out, it was a question of finding the right way to preserve Marx's intentions under different historical conditions (HGS 12, 524). Indeed, the relations of domination and subjugation that were emerging in fascism and in a capitalism that was increasingly constituted by monopolies and cartels marked the entry into a qualitatively different situation, one which could no longer be explained using the parameters of nineteenth-century capitalism. The powerful forces of social integration that had arisen developed new forms of coercion and belonging—among them the very idea of the national community—that involved new mechanisms of exclusion and domination, but also of persuasion, such as those associated with the culture industry. Meanwhile, the composition of the ruling class and its modes of operation were also changing. As a result, it seemed that the logic of the valorization of value through commodity exchange was no longer sufficient to understand the social process: the relationship between mediation, coercion, complicity, and violence had to be revised. In this scenario, the critique of political economy was still necessary, but it was no longer sufficient to account for the new social and political reality. In response to these circumstances, a reformulation of critical theory took place, the most visible—though not exclusive—result of which was the *Dialectic of Enlightenment*. This work, however, was never intended to be presented as a definitive statement. It was a tentative approach, to be understood within the framework of the debates on the relationship between fascism and the post-liberal configuration of capitalism or on the possibility of rethinking the analysis of social classes on the basis of the theory of rackets.[6] Under the precarious conditions imposed by exile, most of these attempts did not come to fruition, and in 1944 the unfinished nature of Horkheimer and Adorno's work was even reflected in its provisional title: "Philosophical Fragments." In the notes included in the various reprints, both coauthors would insist repeatedly on the tentative and fragmentary nature of their joint book.

But what are the factors driving the reorientation of the theoretical project outlined here? While Marx maintained that the "the anatomy of bourgeois society … has to be sought in political economy" (MEW 13, 8),[7] Adorno and Horkheimer held that the anatomy of fascism offered a key to understanding the societies of the post-liberal era. Fascism is not understood here as a particular phenomenon, confined to countries such as Germany or Italy, but as the form in which the new era becomes legible, with its most salient, menacing features coming into view through it. Indeed, it was fascism that had allowed capitalism to become stable without its antagonisms being eased in the slightest. According to a formulation by Hans-Jürgen Krahl, it embodied "a form of domination that was barbaric but well-suited to the new stage of productive forces."[8] This required a revision of certain assumptions about the historical *telos* of capitalism's development. Marx had already alluded

[6]Horkheimer attempted to provide an analysis of the transformations of class domination during the transition to post-liberal capitalism within the framework of the collective work of the Institute. This project, however, remained fragmentary. Horkheimer's valuable reflections on the tendency of an increasingly verticalized society to converge into rackets or competing gangs emerged out of this idea, as well as Adorno's "Reflections on Class Theory" (GS 8, 373–91; Adorno, "Reflections on Class Theory," 93–110). For a general perspective on the theory of rackets, cf. Fuchshuber, *Rackets: Kritische Theorie der Bandenherrschaft*.

[7]Marx, "Preface (to *A Contribution to the Critique of Political Economy*)," in *Later Political Writings*, ed. Terrell Carver (Cambridge: Cambridge University Press, 1996), 159.

[8]Krahl, *Konstitution und Klassenkampf*, 88.

to the fanaticism "of the valorization of value" which "ruthlessly forces the human race to produce for production's sake," but he justified it insofar as this unbridled productivity appeared as the real basis "of a higher form of society, a society in which the full and free development of every individual forms the ruling principle" (MEW 23, 618).[9] However, at this point, any hope that the unbridled productive capacity of capitalism could lay the foundations for an emancipated society had been shattered. The development of productive forces no longer just implied the promise of a better future, but also new possibilities for coercion and barbarism. Technical progress was no longer opposed to the persistence of prehistory. Moreover, in light of the planned and systematic extermination of millions of human beings, the notion of the unrestricted development of productive capacities could no longer be entertained without a sense of threat (ND, 301).[10] Where did this destructiveness come from that seemed increasingly eager to break out onto the historical stage? Could it be explained by virtue of such absolutized production?[11] This question is not a trivial one, since the caesura marked by Auschwitz implies a breakdown of the certainties on which Marx had still been able to rely. This made it necessary to ask how such a thing could have been incubated in the heart of enlightened bourgeois societies, supposedly based on reason, progress, and technology, and how it had been able to spread so freely across Europe without encountering significant resistance. Indeed, where did this new irruption of brutality come from, demanding a new degree of involvement and submission on the part of the masses, if the forms of sociality based on capitalist circulation were supposed to have banished all direct violence through free agreement and reciprocal recognition between formally free and equal subjects?

These were the new questions that the catastrophes of the mid-twentieth century posed to a critical theory committed to emancipation. They portrayed the devastating violence of fascism not just as a German or even a European

[9] Marx, *Capital Volume 1*, 739.

[10] Adorno, *Negative Dialectics*, 306.

[11] This is what Moishe Postone attempted to argue in his work on the extermination of the European Jews (cf. Moishe Postone, "Anti-Semitism and National Socialism," in *Germans and Jews since the Holocaust*, ed. Anson Rabinach and Jack Zipes [New York: Holmes & Meier, 1986], 302–14). Adorno certainly would not have agreed with this explanation.

problem, but as the "truth of modern society" (HGS 4, 309).[12] Ultimately, the triumph and expansion of fascism demanded a fresh look at how the unresolved contradictions of modern societies, which seemed to culminate in a bloody and brutal regime, had emerged and unfolded. This directed new attention to the dialectic between nature and history, which no longer seemed capable of being addressed in the terms with which Marx had approached it. Marx understood the road to emancipation as a development of productive capacities that amounted to the implementation of a rigid system of social domination over nature. This was the issue with Marx's confidence in history, which unfailingly saw it under the sign of progress and predicted with incorrigible optimism that the end of prehistory was all but imminent. However, his understanding of nature was also considered to be one-sided and insufficient. In most of Marx's writings, nature was seen as sheer passive objectivity, a set of resources that can be appropriated and transformed, valuable as a source of wealth. Yet, nature is also the substratum on which all forms of life are sustained, as well as an inseparable component of spontaneity and subjective need, of one's own will, and therefore something that can also be coerced, repressed, and damaged by the social forms through which survival is mediated. In Adorno's view, Marx's theorizing had overlooked this dimension of nature, and it is precisely this oversight that prevented the recognition that "any attempt to break the compulsion of nature by breaking nature only succumbs more deeply to that compulsion" (DA, 29).[13] Therefore, the prevailing model of domination of nature is structurally sacrificial. No degree of domination over external nature can be achieved without a concomitant domination of nature in the human being. This not only links the subjugation of nature to self-subjugation, but also to social domination—particularly control over the labor of others, who must wrest from nature, through their own exertion, the means to sustain their lives. The triumph of civilization over nature can only be considered as a pyrrhic victory, for its price is mutilation, social antagonism, and renunciation. The logic that allows the subject to dominate nature is a denial of the subject itself

[12]Max Horkheimer, "The Jews and Europe," trans. Mark Ritter in Stephen Eric Bronner and Douglas MacKay Kellner (eds.), *Critical Theory and Society: A Reader* (New York: Routledge, 1989), 78.
[13]Horkheimer and Adorno, *Dialectic of Enlightenment*, 9.

and threatens to destroy nature at every moment. This blind and destructive matrix of the civilizing process proved useful in understanding the genesis of a catastrophic present. If, until then, modernity had been understood as progress, as the overcoming of a past marked by barbarism and heteronomy, leading society toward increasing levels of freedom and justice, it is now clear "that history is at the service of regression, that progress necessarily resurfaces as a vestige of the primitive as long as the principle of history is still the domination of nature."[14] This regression does not, however, imply a return to an earlier period, but a situation in which, with the progressive advance of knowledge, technical means, and the instruments of domination, old conflicts that were never resolved persevere and become increasingly acute.

In this sense, Adorno wrote, "As a rebellion against civilization, fascism is not simply the reoccurrence of the archaic but its reproduction in and by civilization itself" (GS 8, 414).[15] Accordingly, he was interested in developing a theory that could illustrate how the characteristic features of modern society are entangled with archaic elements, apparently "primitive" in character. It has often been pointed out that this strategy, which presents the modern in relation to the archaic past and shows the civilized to be enmeshed with barbarism, may render his theorizing "excessive" and historically unspecific. This objection undoubtedly touches on something important. However, we must not lose sight of the fact that Adorno had a theoretical motive for adopting this perspective. What his approach makes possible is a deepening of the Marxian concept of prehistory, which conceives of all history up to the present day as the realm of unfreedom (GS 8, 234).[16] In *Capital*, there are already concepts that associated the particular characteristics of modern developed societies with archaic elements, revealing a complicity of civilization with barbarism, such as the references to "fetishism" and "wage slavery."[17] These terms, like "prehistory," are intended to express the persistence of heteronomy,

---

[14]Hullot-Kentor, *Things Beyond Resemblance*, 4.

[15]Theodor W. Adorno, "Freudian Theory and the Pattern of Fascist Propaganda," in *The Culture Industry* (London: Routledge, 2005), 137.

[16]Theodor W. Adorno, " 'Static' and 'Dynamic' as Sociological Categories," trans. H. Kaal, *Diogenes* no. 9 (March 1961), 45.

[17]For "wage slavery," see Cristina Catalina, "Trabajo, desposesión y sufrimiento. De la crisis del mundo liberal al neoliberalismo," *Bajo Palabra* 33 (2023), 51–9.

mystification, and unfreedom in supposedly free, rational, and enlightened societies. Under these conditions, no history worthy of the name can be said to have existed so far. It is thus a matter of developing these allusions Marx makes so that this entanglement of modernity with myth and heteronomy can fully unfold its interpretive power in disclosing the true face of the present. With the understanding that capitalist society is simply the most advanced form of prehistory, attention is directed toward developing an interpretation of the present that makes it possible both to illuminate the current image of prehistory and to situate it within a historical trajectory that, up to now, has not succeeded in breaking out of the fatal cycle of domination and subjugation. This is the aim of the genealogical gaze at work in *Dialectic of Enlightenment* and other texts. Its driving force is the attempt to do justice to history as the history of suffering; as a process in which, despite the increasing sophistication of technical progress, the torment borne by subjugated lives has remained unchanged. Adorno articulates this perspective explicitly at the beginning of his "Reflections on Class Theory":

> To recognize the catastrophic violence in the latest form of injustice, that is to say, the latent injustice contained in fair exchange, means simply to identify it with the prehistory that it destroyed. If all the oppression that human beings have ever inflicted on one another culminates in the modern age in the cold inhumanity of free wage labor, then the past is revealed in conditions and things—the romantic contrast to industrial reason—as the trace of past suffering. (GS 8, 373–4)[18]

In this passage, the course of history appears unified from the perspective of domination and suffering, which has never been transcended. According to this, history is the history of subjugation. In light of the new forms of domination that characterize fascism and post-liberal capitalism, a new view of historical reality was needed. The catastrophic dimension of the present meant that any expectations that modern capitalist society could mitigate the coercive element of the relations of direct domination through commodity exchange and contractual agreement were no longer plausible—not only because of the

---

[18]Adorno, "Reflections on Class Theory," 93–4. Translation modified.

mute compulsion underlying these forms of mediation, but also because of the growing dispossession which they had led to, reaching new extremes in the history of subjugation. Understanding the form of the emerging social order also entailed being aware of the dark shadow that loomed over the entire history of the capitalism that had engendered it.

"The Unity of the Epoch"—Capitalism and Fascism

"Whoever is not willing to talk about capitalism should also keep quiet about fascism" (HGS 4, 308–9),[19] Horkheimer wrote in 1939. According to the research carried out by the Institute for Social Research in the 1930s and 1940s, fascism is not an aberration or a deviation from the "normal" course of modern European history, but a result of its internal contradictions that becomes increasingly plausible in the transition from liberal to post-liberal capitalism. Indeed, in 'The Jews and Europe,' one of the first texts in which he directly confronts fascism, Horkheimer's formulation could hardly be more drastic: "Fascism has rescued control over the means of production for that minority which emerged from the competition as the most determined. It is the up-to-date form. Even where fascism is not in power in Europe, strong social tendencies are at work, aimed at adapting the administrative, legal, and political apparatus for the authoritarian model" (HGS 4, 323).[20] These sentences, formulated in the United States, sought to highlight a generalized historical tendency. However, pointing out the growing authoritarian verticalization of post-liberal societies does not imply neutralizing the distinct features of fascism or projecting its characteristics onto democratic regimes. Adorno and Horkheimer never lost sight of the fact that it was only thanks to the elements that distinguished New Deal democracy from the direct and brutal domination of the Nazi regime that they had been able to escape deportation and extermination, and to preserve a minimum of freedom that had allowed them to carry on with their theoretical work. Their interest, however, was

[19] Horkheimer, "The Jews and Europe," 78.
[20] Ibid., 88. Translation modified.

directed at demonstrating the "unity of the epoch" underlying both regimes, and which even tended to blur "the distinctions that constitute the fate, even the moral substance, of individual existence" (MM, 28).[21] Indeed, despite the undeniable differences separating National Socialism, the New Deal, and the Soviet regime, it was possible to recognize a tendency toward the increasing concentration of social, economic, and administrative power, as well as toward a growing capacity of the state (and, through it, of economic imperatives) to impinge on more and more areas of life. "Society is integral even before it undergoes totalitarian rule" (MM, 235),[22] as stated in *Minima Moralia*. This suggests viewing fascism as a possible culmination of certain transformations of post-liberal capitalism that, in other parts of the world, were still at an early stage. Hence the interest in deciphering the new configuration of social life through an analysis of fascism. This new configuration was by no means limited to its authoritarian variant, but it did show signs of a more general tendency to evolve toward increasingly vertical forms of social organization.

"The latest phase of class society is dominated by monopolies; it tends toward fascism, the form of political organization worthy of it" (GS 8, 376),[23] Adorno wrote in his "Reflections on Class Theory." The tendency toward the concentration and centralization of economic power was a result of the dynamics of competition inherent in liberal capitalism, and ultimately of the law of value itself. However, with the formation of large trusts and monopolies, economic activity was entirely transformed, and the growing concentration of social and economic power tends to converge with political power. Some of the conditions for the rise of increasingly authoritarian social forms are rooted in these processes. According to Adorno's formulation, it is the tendency toward absolutized monopolism that "paves the way for the qualitative leap forward involved in fascism. The omnipotence of the monopolies transforms the economy and society, for it implies the elimination of the market which the monopolies had hitherto dominated" (AHB II, 195). This categorical formulation, which emphasizes the weakening of the sphere of circulation

---

[21] Adorno, *Minima Moralia*, 26–7. Translation modified.
[22] Ibid., 206.
[23] Adorno, "Reflections on Class Theory," 96.

in the post-liberal era, seems to echo some of the theses that were being developed by the leading economist of the Institute for Social Research, Friedrich Pollock, in the same period. He considered National Socialism and Roosevelt's United States as the authoritarian and democratic variants, respectively, of a new social, economic, and political order: state capitalism.[24] At this point, it is important to stress that the debates on the relationship between capitalism and fascism within the Institute for Social Research have often been overemphasized. There has been a tendency to focus on polarizing elements above all else, an overemphasis on the points of contention between the authors involved, and this has meant that the broad consensus that prevailed in terms of the basic understanding of the transformations of post-liberal capitalism has been overshadowed. There was, of course, broad agreement on the growing influence of politics in the economic sphere. The members of the Institute also agreed that capitalism in its present situation could no longer be described according to the parameters of *laissez-faire*: the concentration of economic power and the increasing dominance of monopolies had completely transformed the nature of competition. What was at stake was the extent to which these changes heralded a new era of capitalism. It was a matter of clarifying whether the defining features of capitalism—the pursuit of profit that drives the valorization of capital—remained intact or if there was a tendency to replace them with a purely political logic, where the conflicts and contradictions in the process of capital reproduction were supplanted by the growing importance of processes based on the direct exercise of power and domination.

In this sense, Pollock's position in his text "State Capitalism" (1941) was certainly quite drastic. His theses seem to refer to a kind of "economy without economy," in which even the distribution of commodities would be controlled by the state. But his position only makes sense when put into historical perspective. Pollock began to study the Soviet planned economy in the second half of the 1920s, and since the 1930s he had been analyzing the transformations of post-liberal capitalism as an attempt to respond to the great crisis of 1929 by

---

[24]Friedrich Pollock, "State Capitalism: Its Possibilities and Limitations," in *Critical Theory and Society*, 95–118.

intensifying the planning of economic processes, thereby expanding the role of the state in steering the economy. The aim was to overcome the crises without transforming property relations.[25] However, while up to the beginning of the 1940s his texts had analyzed a series of transformative tendencies in capitalism after the 1929 *crash*, in the 1941 text, his approach took a turn toward defining the fundamental features of a new social formation: state capitalism. This is described as the regime toward which the post-liberal phase tends, susceptible of adopting both an authoritarian form as well as a more democratic orientation. Indeed, if the end of liberal capitalism had led to a loss of the centrality of the sphere of circulation and market mediation, now, with the constitution of large trusts and monopolies, the possibility arose of an efficient control of economic processes by means of a planned and vertical management orchestrated by political power. That is what founded the qualitatively new character of state capitalism: "The replacement of the economic means by political means as the last guarantee for the reproduction of economic life changes the character of the whole historical period. It signifies the transition from a predominantly economic to an essentially political era."[26] But Pollock does not merely state this thesis concerning the onset of a new situation where politics takes precedence over economics; he pushes it to its ultimate consequences. What this primacy of politics implies is that the problems and contradictions that the economic sphere produces in social life can now be solved in a purely technical and administrative way: "Economic problems no longer exist in the old sense, since the synchronization of all economic activities no longer takes place through the natural laws of the market, but through conscious planning. Where the economist racked his brains over the exchange process, in state capitalism he finds only administrative problems."[27] As Dirk Braunstein has pointed out, it is hard not to perceive in these words a certain admiration for the state planning apparatus, capable as it seems of containing the risks of crises and ensuring full employment, opening up the possibility that a democratic formulation of state capitalism might be in a position to mitigate social antagonisms. In any case,

[25]See the collection of texts brought together in *Stadien des Kapitalismus*.
[26]Pollock, "State Capitalism: Its Possibilities and Limitations," 101.
[27]Ibid., 91.

"it seems [Pollock's] envisioned state is no longer simply the Engelsian 'ideal personification of the total national capital' but rather the total capitalist in real and unrivalled form."[28]

It is certainly true that Pollock's theses were theoretically bold and controversial. Even when formulating the fundamental features of the new social order as an "ideal type," highlighting the elements underlying quite different political regimes, his statements went to extremes that were difficult to accept, and not only because of the challenge they posed for any possibility of maintaining the validity of Marxist theory. Without a doubt, the most severe response was to be found in the positions adopted by Franz Neumann. But Pollock and Neumann only represent the two extremes of the debate; the other members of the Institute adopted various positions in-between.[29] Hence the widely held interpretation[30] that Adorno and Horkheimer adopted Pollock's theses, which shaped their work in the 1940s—*Dialectic of Enlightenment* in particular—on the basis of an understanding of capitalism as a "totality without antagonisms" is largely unfounded.[31] It is true that Pollock's approaches were largely based on earlier texts by Horkheimer which Adorno had also collaborated on, such as "The Jews and Europe" (1939) and "The Authoritarian State" (written in 1940, published in 1942). But neither Horkheimer nor Adorno, who had different positions on this issue, really endorsed Pollock's theses. Horkheimer always maintained a position of cautious skepticism, due in part to his close relationship with Pollock, but also

[28]Dirk Braunstein, *Adorno's Critique of Political Economy*, 119. Translation modified.

[29]Amaro Fleck and Luiz Philipe de Caux, "Pollock y los frankfurtianos. Notas sobre la recepción del concepto de capitalismo de Estado," *Constelaciones. Revista de Teoría Crítica*, no. 13 (2021), 76.

[30]Among the studies that have defended this thesis are John Abromeit, *Max Horkheimer and the Foundations of the Frankfurt School* (Cambridge: Cambridge University Press, 2011), 405; Dubiel, *Wissenschaftsorganisation und politische Erfahrung*; Jay, *The Dialectical Imagination*; Moishe Postone, *Time, Labour and Social Domination* (Cambridge: Cambridge University Press, 1993), 90–120; Wiggershaus, *The Frankfurt School*; Eva-Maria Ziege, *Antisemitismus und Gesellschaftstheorie* (Frankfurt: Suhrkamp, 2009), 104–08.

[31]Cf. Braunstein, *Adorno's Critique of Political Economy*, 109–37; L. Fischer, "The Frankfurt School and Fascism," in Best, Bonefeld, O"Kane (eds.), *The Sage Handbook of Frankfurt School Critical Theory*, 799–815; Amaro Fleck, *Theodor W. Adorno: um crítico na era dourada do capitalismo*, PhD diss. (Universidad Federal de Santa Catarina, 2015), 75–94; Fuchshuber, *Rackets*, 29–32; Ricardo P. Regatieri, *Capitalismo sem peias* (São Paulo: fflch/Humanitas, 2019), 95–110; Thomas Sablowsky, "Entwicklungstendenzen und Krisen des Kapitalismus," in *Modelle kritischer Theorie*, ed. A. Demirovic (Stuttgart/Weimar: Metzler, 2003), 101–30.

because he perceived the flaws in his approach. It is revealing that, in a letter to Neumann in the midst of the polemic, he only acknowledged the value of Pollock's text as "a basis for the discussion of a current problem, despite all its shortcomings" (HGS 17, 116). In this sense, it is important not to lose sight of the fact that the racket theory that Horkheimer sought to develop during these years, by focusing on competition and the fragmentation of the ruling class, shares more in common with Neumann's thesis on the struggles taking place between elites that underlie the National Socialist State than to the idea of an entirely planned economy. Adorno, for his part, expressed "very serious concern" (AHB I, 139) upon first reading the text, pointing to its weaknesses; behind this was a clear rejection of Pollock's theoretical approach. The text seemed to him to be a flattened and simplified version of some elements of Horkheimer's "Authoritarian State," lacking any dialectic and thus leading to a totally different conclusion (AHB II, 140). Indeed, while Horkheimer had stressed that the transition to an increasingly state-controlled capitalism entailed an increase in exploitation, repression, and social antagonism (HGS 5, 301–2),[32] Pollock depicted it as a stable order capable of resolving all its conflicts through the vertical administration of economic processes. Hence Adorno's comment in a letter to Horkheimer written on June 8, 1941:

> The best way I can summarize my position is that the text represents an inversion of Kafka. Kafka depicted the hierarchy of offices as a hell. Here, hell becomes a hierarchy of offices. Moreover, the whole thing is formulated so much in the form of theses, and in a Husserlian sense "from above," that it completely lacks energy, not to mention the totally un-dialectical assumption that a non-antagonistic economy is possible in an antagonistic society. (AHB II, 139)

This last point was a crucial factor in Adorno's persistent reservations with respect to Pollock's approaches to state capitalism. Indeed, he found the prospect of pacifying capitalism, and liberating it from all its conflicts and crises through comprehensive economic planning, strongly suspect in view of the "antagonistic character of the present" (AHB II, 160). In any case, the motives

---

[32]Horkheimer, "The Authoritarian State," 14.

behind capital accumulation, competition, and profit had not gone away. On the other hand, it should be kept in mind that the thrust of Adorno's critical theory differs completely from Pollock's orientation in this text. For Adorno, "the hell of capitalism must be overcome, not bureaucratically administered."[33]

In short, neither Adorno's nor Horkheimer's theoretical positions can be adequately understood if it is assumed that they endorsed Pollock's theses on the implications of a complete command economy. It is true, however, that their approaches do converge when it comes to the diagnosis of a new form of capitalism in which the mediating role of the market had lost much of its function—their most drastic formulations even speak of a dissolution of the sphere of circulation (HGS 5, 293;[34] GS 8, 385).[35] This leads them to recognize the growing importance of power and domination in the logic of society. Horkheimer goes so far as to point out that "the aspiration for profit today ends in what it always was: striving for social power" (HGS 4, 314),[36] and Adorno refers to economics as "scarcity prepared for the purpose of domination" (GS 8, 381).[37] However, at no point do they go so far as to claim that economic motives have lost their central importance. On the contrary: both Adorno and Horkheimer hold that the new forms of power and social domination—fascism included—respond to the persistence of the economic motives of the extraction of value and the accumulation of capital. In this sense, their texts depict liberal capitalism as a mere "interlude" (HGS 4, 315),[38] an "episode" (GS 8, 380)[39] in which the logics of domination were mitigated by the mechanisms of mediation associated with the market, which still allowed the individual some degree of agency. This interregnum came to an end with the rise of a monopolistic capitalism of a markedly authoritarian nature.[40]

---

[33]Braunstein, *Adorno's Critique of Political Economy*, 128.

[34]Horkheimer, "The Authoritarian State," 1.

[35]Adorno, "Reflections on Class Theory," 104.

[36]Horkheimer, "The Jews and Europe," 82.

[37]Adorno, "Reflections on Class Theory," 100. Translation modified.

[38]Horkheimer, "The Jews and Europe," 82.

[39]Adorno, "Reflections on Class Theory," 100.

[40]"The development of capitalist society, in line with its inherent tendencies, led to the disappearance of the progressive features of competition. It severed the connection between consumer needs and the individual entrepreneur's profit motive; it further diminished the already slim chance for an

In a draft of the prologue to the new edition of the *Dialectic of Enlightenment*, written in 1969, Adorno revisited these transformations. His formulation reveals that the contrast with Marx's theory was intended to signal the specific difference between the features of the new emerging capitalism and those of its liberal phase: "the object of Marx's critique of political economy was liberalism as reality and as ideology. With the transition to an economy which leaves a pseudo-market, but otherwise depends on powers that control production, and which also determine circulation and distribution, the laws of the liberal market lose their meaning; along with them, the economic concept of economics."[41] It follows that, for Adorno, the exclusively exchange-mediated economy of the liberal period analyzed by Marx is only one of the possible forms that the economy can take. The transition to post-liberal capitalism implies the passage to an increasingly compact and vertical social formation, marked by the growing concentration of capital and of political power. In this sense, the concept of the "administered world" does not refer to a predominance of politics over economics, but to a fusion of economic, political, administrative, and cultural motives that respond much more directly to the imperatives of capital. As a result, the influence of the latter penetrates increasingly more domains of social life, giving rise to a society that is much more vertical and subject to the imperatives of the economy. The transition to post-liberal capitalism thus does not so much imply a liquidation of the economy; rather, it leads to "everything, including life itself, becoming the economy."[42] In short, the figure of the new post-liberal order is understood in terms of a capitalism without restraints,[43] marked by "direct control" (GS 10.1, 54).[44] Its most drastic manifestation could be found in the forms of fascist "total mobilization," capable of setting all the energies of the nation in motion

independent person to attain an independent position; it reduced the number of relatively autonomous economic subjects, who, only by virtue of their plurality, were interested in the functioning of a unified legal system and its impartial administration. All of this vanishes in the late stage of capitalism, allowing society to *regress* to forms of direct oppression that had never fully disappeared" (HGS 12, 80–1) [italics mine, JM].

[41]Theodor W. Adorno, "Aus einem Entwurf 'Zur Neuausgabe' der Dialektik der Aufklärung," *Frankfurter Adorno Blätter*, VIII (Munich: Text+Kritik, 2003), 7.

[42]Braunstein, *Adorno's Critique of Political Economy*, 150.

[43]Regatieri, *Capitalismo sem peias*.

[44]Adorno, "Spengler after the Decline," 58. Translation modified.

in a kind of permanent war economy. This demonstrated that forms of social domination that were no longer limited to the anonymous and objectified forms of coercion proper to economic relations had come into effect (GS 8, 584),[45] but they were still driven by the motives of the extraction of wealth and capital accumulation, achieved through an ever more direct exercise of social power. Hence Horkheimer's assertion: "The new order marks a huge leap in the passage from bourgeois domination to immediate domination, and yet bourgeois domination continues" (HGS 5, 332).

This formulation is crucial and establishes both the continuity and the rupture of the new social order in the history of capitalism. In the first place, according to this diagnosis, the increase in the agency of states is not seen as a way of resolving social conflicts by political means, but rather as an unprecedented intensification of the forms of domination. What emerges is a growing confluence of civilized society with barbarism. For critical theory, fascism signified a new strain of capitalism that was no longer limited to the features of its bourgeois form.[46] This is what is implied by the loss of the central position occupied by the sphere of circulation, of money and the market, which also affects the ideals associated with them: freedom and formal equality. Undoubtedly, insofar as liberalism appears primarily as a figure to be contrasted with the emerging order of an increasingly vertical and concentrated capitalism, both Adorno and Horkheimer sometimes tend to idealize certain features of nineteenth-century capitalism. In retrospect, this form of capitalism is associated above all with the progressive features of the sphere of circulation, which allowed the bourgeois subject a certain degree of autonomy and individual agency. However, with the loss of its bourgeois form, capitalism also lost the potential for transcendence that was associated with these characteristics: the atrocious immanence of prehistory thus tends to become total, creating an increasingly suffocating situation for those who must make and reproduce their lives under it. Individuals lose their capacity for agency and tend to become totally dependent on the social and economic

[45]Adorno, "Late Capitalism or Industrial Society?," 116.

[46]Detlev Claussen, "Die amerikanische Erfahrung der kritischen Theoretiker," in Detlev Claussen, Oskar Negt and M. Werz (eds.), *Keine Kritische Theorie ohne Amerika* (Frankfurt: Neue Kritik, 1999), 31. See also Fuchshuber, *Rackets*, 320.

apparatus, "mere administrative objects of the monopolies and their states, on a par with those paupers of the liberal era who have been allowed to die out in our own age of high civilization" (GS 8, 386).[47] This allows economic power to disregard the needs of the subjects it administers: it is in a position to channel them according to its own interests. Hence it is assumed that the greater the efficiency of this social and economic apparatus, "the more useless, vain and destructive" it becomes, "for it serves only the concentration of power" (HGS 12, 414). Here is the key to comprehending fascism: it embodies the passage to a form of total domination that no longer harbors rational features or elements capable of transcending its own crystallization but enforces the imperatives of capital through pure terror. The need to update some of the categories of Marx's critique of political economy stems from this situation, targeting those "such as surplus value, depauperization, even … class."[48] Consequently, in texts from the 1940s, surplus value appears linked to increasingly extractive logics, the growing disproportion between social power and powerlessness is presented as the new form of destitution, and class relations are not only approached from the point of view of the integration of the proletariat, but also through the theory of *rackets*,[49] which denoted a new degree of brutality and violence in the scramble for social wealth.

It is undoubtedly true that some of the reformulations that critical theory undertook in this period led to partial, even exaggerated diagnoses of the new configuration of capitalism. Both monopolies and *rackets* are products of advanced capitalism, but they cannot be regarded as its fundamental explanatory keys. They remain forms of mediation in the reproduction of capital. On the other hand, to speak of a tendency toward the elimination of the market sphere is certainly an exaggeration: it is not the market as such that disappears, but its liberal-bourgeois form. This tendency toward the formation of monopolies and the growing influence of planning and control over demand gives rise to a different type of market, which can no longer be explained or regulated merely by equivalent exchange between formally free and equal

---

[47]Adorno, "Reflections on Class Theory," 105.
[48]Adorno, "Aus einem Entwurf Zur Neuausgabe der *Dialektik der Aufklärung*," 7.
[49]Cf. Fuchshuber, *Rackets*.

individuals. In this sense, Adorno and Horkheimer were wrong when, for a time, they assumed that these more immediate logics of domination could perhaps destabilize the traditional forms of capitalist mediation. Nor were they right in interpreting the signs of the times as indications of a tendency toward the widespread consolidation of authoritarian capitalism. Yet these errors in turn allowed them to "sharpen their gaze on the qualitative transformations of modern domination."[50] Their main task was to clarify the crystallization of new conditions of life marked by a growing polarization between social power and powerlessness. In short: they registered the emergence of a social formation that crossed a new threshold in the degree of subjugation of the individual lives that had to be reproduced through the social and economic apparatus. They were well aware that the elements that had produced these displacements in the social logic might "lie outside the system of political economy," but they were undoubtedly "central to the history of domination" (GS 8, 385).[51]

On the basis of these features of post-liberal capitalism and its most extreme form, fascism, the whole history of capitalism can be seen as a history of coercion and violence. Fascism in particular gave rise to novel forms of subjugation that demanded a rethinking of the relationship between economic and extra-economic coercion. In this sense, for Adorno, the predominance of violent, extractive dynamics transformed the character of the market, as well as that of competition between large concentrations of capital. He thus stated that the notion that these compete on the basis of "equal rights and equal opportunities among the competing parties [is] largely a fiction. Their success depends on the power of their capital outside the competitive process, a power they already possess upon entering the marketplace. It further depends on the political and social power they represent, on old and new conquistador spoils, on their affiliation with feudal property that a competitive economy has never entirely liquidated, and on their relations with the direct governing apparatus of the military" (GS 8, 378).[52] In short, the growing concentration of economic power has made it especially evident that the abstract domination

---

[50]Türcke and Bolte, *Einführung in die kritische Theorie*, 57.
[51]Adorno, "Reflections on Class Theory," 104.
[52]Adorno, "Reflections on Class Theory," 98.

of capital, despite all its mediations, has never ceased to rely on coercion and violence. Of course, the ability to dispose of the time of others was based on the exercise of force from the beginning; Marx himself had already pointed out the processes of dispossession underlying the "free" sale of the commodity labor power. "In the tender annals of political economy, the idyllic reigns from time immemorial," he wrote ironically. By contrast, "in actual history, it is a notorious fact that conquest, enslavement, robbery, murder, in short, force, play the greatest part" (MEW 23, 742–3).[53] In this sense, the reorientation of critical theory in the face of the experiences of fascism and the post-liberal phase does not constitute a departure from Marx, but instead takes up other strands of his thought in which the element of coercion—often direct—appears as the basic principle underlying any anonymous and impersonal mediation through the process of exchange. Hence the continued relevance of the Marxian notion that modern capitalist societies are only the most recent phase in the perpetuation of prehistory. This aims to emphasize the coercive, violent, and even brutal element that continues to pulse within commodity-mediated relations and juridical structures, which, through production and the free purchase and sale of commodities and labor power, reproduces new thresholds of unfreedom.

Protohistory of Contemporary Prehistory

For Adorno, Marx's assertion that all history up to the present has been nothing but prehistory, "gives us a pointer as to how we can recognize what history is" (GS 8, 374).[54] History can no longer be understood as a process of advancement, as "progress" positioning the present and its technical, cultural, and scientific developments as the crowning achievement of a triumphal process. In the light of post-liberal capitalism's new forms of "unmediated control," as well as of the annihilating potential revealed by total war and the extermination camps, historical becoming is prehistorical because it is unified by blind

[53]Marx, *Capital Volume 1*, 874.
[54]Adorno, "Reflections on Class Theory," 94.

violence, the mounting development of a form of social destructiveness that in no way resembles progress in the consciousness of freedom. In this sense, "following Marx, Adorno views previous history from the immediate present, differing from the former by conceptualizing capitalism not as a new form of domination, but as a variant of the oldest form of domination."[55] From this point of view, the "horror consists in its always remaining the same—the persistence of 'pre-history'—but is realized as constantly different, unforeseen, exceeding all expectation, a faithful shadow of developing productive forces" (MM, 267–8).[56] Hence the well-known statement made in a passage from *Negative Dialectics*: "No universal history leads from savagery to humanitarianism, but there is one leading from the slingshot to the megaton bomb" (ND, 314).[57] At base, what the conception of the present as enduring prehistory brings into question is whether the course of history has ever been anything more than a blind perpetuation of forms of domination and subjugation where nothing substantial has actually been altered. "History, as far as it has gone in the present day, remains entangled in myth."[58] Its *telos* remains to devour and be devoured, and the survival of the fittest (GS 8, 237).[59] But the violence that was erupting with fascism and Auschwitz could not be understood solely through the destructive element of capital; rather it seemed to condense "all the mythical violence of prehistory which it had absorbed, and to which it offered a maximum of technical means."[60] This led to an awareness that critical knowledge could not allow itself to be propelled by the driving force of a historical movement that, in essence, is not historical:

> Knowing the new does not mean adapting oneself to it and to the movement of history; it means resisting its inflexibility and recognizing the onward march of the battalions of world history as a movement that remains at a standstill. Theory knows of no "constructive force" but only of one that lights up the contours of a burned-out prehistory with the glow of the latest

[55]Braunstein, *Adorno's Critique of Political Economy*, 164. Translation modified.
[56]Adorno, *Minima Moralia*, 324.
[57]Adorno, *Negative Dialectics*, 320.
[58]Tiedemann, *Mythos und Utopie*, 83.
[59]Adorno, "'Static' and 'Dynamic' as Sociological Categories," 49.
[60]Cf. Türcke and Bolte, *Einführung in die kritische Theorie*, 63–4.

> disaster in order to perceive the parallel that exists between them. (GS 8, 375)[61]

This perspective stands in radical opposition to any understanding of history as theodicy. The notion of a humanity that, to this day, remains captive to a blind historical logic, that pays for each of its advances with enormous sacrifices and presents history as a succession of catastrophes in which "each of its new forms outdoes the old" (MM, 267)[62] challenges the conception that modern societies have of themselves as having overcome a dark past. This perspective can help to clarify some of the stakes of a book like *Dialectic of Enlightenment*. This work sought to render palpable the aporia of a historical moment that, precisely as a result of the advances of the modernizing process, was "radiant with triumphant calamity" (DA, 19).[63] Thus, if the book alludes to elements of a remote past such as magic, myth, or Homeric epics, it is not with the purpose of offering a linear reconstruction of history from its origins to the present; rather, it mobilizes its "constructive force" to trace a protohistory of the present as a perpetuation of prehistory. Such retrospection is driven by the need to grasp a present that can no longer be explained by the patterns that had prevailed up until then. Instead of a teleological understanding of history, viewing the present as the "outcome" of a process, it became necessary to develop a vision of the present and its genesis, demonstrating that its apparently "archaic," even "primitive," elements were a result of the inner, unresolved contradictions of modernity itself. In this sense, even elements that were seemingly far removed from the barbarism that was being unleashed in history—such as the forms of knowledge and the relationship with objectivity—appear as at least potential vehicles of the prevailing iniquity. For "knowledge, which is power, knows no limits, either in the enslavement of its creatures or in its deference to the masters of the world" (DA, 20).[64] So rather than offering a negative philosophy of history, *Dialectic of Enlightenment* lays out a protohistory of the present capable of challenging the narrative that presents the progressive domination

---

[61] Adorno, "Reflections on Class Theory," 95. Translation modified.
[62] Adorno, *Minima Moralia*, 234.
[63] Horkeheimer and Adorno, *Dialectic of Enlightenment*, 1.
[64] Ibid., 2. Translation modified.

of nature—and with it the development of productive capacities—as that which makes it possible to leave myth, violence, and brutality behind in order to establish reason, freedom, justice, and civilization in their place.[65] In short, it was a matter of waking up from the reveries that the Enlightenment had produced about the developmental *telos* of modern societies. But it is not a question of overthrowing the narrative of progress to put a new teleology in its place, this time charting a decadent or negative course, but of critically interrogating the self-exculpatory conception that we tend to have of "normality" in the light of atrocities that no longer permit any trace of naivety. The aim is to expose the fatal logic that has prevailed up to now, in order to finally create the conditions to break its hold.

Ultimately, it is not a matter of reconstructing the historical process, but of casting light on the present in the right way. This requires a theoretical construction capable of giving voice to elements that until now have remained silenced and concealed, eluding a discursive logic based on causal and unequivocal connections. Adorno and Horkheimer thus base some of the key points of their text on protohistorical constellations. The concept of protohistory (*Urgeschichte*) is important for understanding what is at stake in the expository form of the *Dialectic of Enlightenment* and should not be confused with that of prehistory (*Vorgeschichte*). On this point, both authors follow a path opened by Walter Benjamin. When he referred to his unfinished *Arcades Project* (*Das Passagen-Werk*) as a "protohistory of the nineteenth century," he did not intend to produce a prehistory of that century or a history of its origins but an interpretation that, starting from certain of its constituent elements, would be in a position to dissolve certain illusions about capitalist modernity that were no longer sustainable. This involves reviving "a not-yet-conscious

[65]In this sense, the famous thesis that "Myth is already enlightenment, and enlightenment reverts to mythology" (DA, 16; *Dialectic of Enlightenment* 20) refuses to take for granted the view that the advance of reason leads to liberation from the bondage of myth for granted. Rather, myth appears as an initial step in the process of clarifying the world, one that mitigates the uneasiness provoked by the unsettling experience of the unknown by turning the strange into something familiar. Enlightenment, in its blind pursuit of the disenchantment of the world, reduces all objectivity to purely quantitative terms in order to dominate it. In so doing—by sacrificing the natural dimension of the dominating subject itself—it ends up revealing *itself* as mythic. Thus, instead of representing two stages in a linear transition progressing univocally from myth to Enlightenment, the two concepts become poles in a dialectical movement, whose antithesis perpetually reproduces them in a constant conflict and intertwinement.

knowledge of what has been" (BGS V, 572).[66] In short, protohistory looks toward the past from the standpoint of the present, looking for new angles to illuminate history and the results of its becoming by attending to seemingly secondary and forgotten elements. "The point is not to offer an explanation of the genesis of the present based on the temporal past, but to be able to view the present from perspectives that can break away from its own delusions."[67] Protohistory seeks keys to a genealogy of the present that, as Benjamin says, quoting Marx, allow the world to awaken "from its dream of itself" (MEW 1, 346).[68] This requires not falling into a merely chronological or consecutive understanding of history, based on a notion of temporal continuity that leads from the past to the present through linear and irreversible causal chains. In this sense, whatever appears "archaic" or outdated is always the result of the advance of the "historical rhythm," and "everything that has been silenced by history" (ABB, 54)[69] is condensed in it.

Therefore, it is only through certain constellations formed between what is new and what appears as archaic, defying the static conception of epochs, that one can bring to light what has remained buried in the different forms of domination that have succeeded one another across the course of history. This link between the present and traces of the remote past does not involve the search for the origin of a chronological sequence that can be reconstructed in a linear fashion, but an abrupt actualization in which "what has been comes together in a flash with the now to form a constellation" (BGS V, 576).[70] This opens up the possibility of casting new light on the present, making it possible to view it from outside the usual interpretive frameworks. Yet it is the concerns of the present that suddenly render elements of the past legible in a certain context. That would be, for example, the rationale behind the use of the *Odyssey* in *Dialectic of Enlightenment*. It is the awareness of where the internal contradictions of nineteenth-century capitalism had led that makes it possible to articulate this protohistory of the bourgeois subject, master of

[66]Benjamin, *The Arcades Project*, 389.
[67]Zamora, *Th. W. Adorno: Pensar contra la barbarie*, 116.
[68]Marx, "Letters from the *Franco-German Yearbooks*," 209.
[69]Benjamin and Adorno, *The Complete Correspondence 1928–1940*, 38.
[70]Benjamin, *The Arcades Project*, 462.

himself and dominator of nature, paving the way for a critical understanding of the present. Insofar as the story of Odysseus is interpreted as a process of the constitution of the self through his confrontation with mythical forces (i.e., with figures such as Polyphemus, Circe, or the sirens), it is argued that "no work bears more eloquent witness to the intertwinement of enlightenment and myth than that of Homer, the basic text of European civilization" (DA, 63).[71] However, the adventures of Odysseus are not approached with a rigorous, philological analysis of the Homeric epic, but "from the standpoint of the developed exchange society and its individuals" (DA, 74).[72] The purpose is not a hermeneutic reading of the Odyssey that attempts to bring to light the hidden meaning of the text; it is simply an allegorical construction that aspires to make a new understanding of the present possible.[73]

Here, the principle of exchange acquires central importance. Exchange, like the contract, was seen in bourgeois society as the promise of a framework for social relations that was beyond all arbitrariness and violence. In this domain, it was said, what prevailed was voluntary agreement between formally equal subjects. It is true that commodity exchange requires the renunciation of direct appropriation and violent imposition, but at the same time it subjects agents to the logic of the valorization of value, whose inner workings remain opaque to them.[74] Consequently, the bourgeois economy does not neutralize violence, but multiplies it "through the mediation of the market" (DA, 59).[75] Despite the rationalization of legal relations and the exchange of equivalents, the background of coercion and violence not only persists, but expands to ever more dimensions of social life. With coercion separating subjects from their livelihoods, all of existence becomes a struggle for survival. The formal equality of social atoms exacerbates their material inequality. This calls for a critical revision of the very logic of the principle of exchange, and Adorno and Horkheimer seek to focus above all on how this mechanism of

---

[71]Horkheimer and Adorno, *Dialectic of Enlightenment*, 37.

[72]Ibid., 48.

[73]Cf. Gómez, *El pensamiento estético de Theodor W. Adorno*, 32.

[74]Detlev Claussen, *Grenzen der Aufklärung: Zur gesellschaftlichen Genese des modernen Antisemitismus* (Frankfurt: Fischer, 2005), 152.

[75]Horkheimer and Adorno, *Dialectic of Enlightenment*, 33.

mediating social relations intervenes in the constitution of subjectivities. Marx himself, beyond his allusions to individuals as "personifications of economic categories" (MEW 23, 16),[76] had left this question aside. Exchange is, of course, first and foremost an economic category: it points to the structural principle of capitalist social praxis and its impersonal modes of domination. But in Adorno's analysis it implies something else, too. Insofar as it makes it possible to render qualitatively different elements commensurable, equivalent exchange is linked to the very form of bourgeois rationality, which goes hand in hand with the logic of abstraction and the imposition of the principle of identity. In practice, exchange equates what is heterogeneous, distinct, or even irreducible: it reduces it to pure *quantum* so that the principle of equivalence can be established.[77] While it is affirmed that "the 'equivalent form' mars all perceptions," this is because everything that is qualitative in things becomes "the accidental appearance of their value" (MM 259–60).[78] At the same time, from the point of view of the subject's logic of action, exchange appears as the basic principle of someone who only gives because he expects something in return; it is thus inseparable from the model of rationality associated with *homo economicus* (DA, 80).[79]

Although in *Dialectic of Enlightenment* the offerings that the traveler Odysseus gives to his hosts in exchange for hospitality are already interpreted as foreshadowing the logic of transaction, of business (DA, 67),[80] as well as the sacrifices made with the intention of placating mythical powers—one gives something valuable to the gods hoping to secure their protection in return (DA, 68–9)[81]—this should not be taken literally. While both sacrificial exchange and bourgeois exchange involve a moment of deception—since, in truth, there is no exchange between equals (this is why the cunning Odysseus triumphs

---

[76]Marx, *Capital Volume 1*, 92.

[77]"Bourgeois society is ruled by equivalence. It makes dissimilar things comparable by reducing them to abstract quantities. For the Enlightenment, anything which cannot be resolved into numbers, and ultimately into one, is illusion; modern positivism consigns it to poetry. Unity remains the watchword from Parmenides to Russell. All gods and qualities must be destroyed" (DA, 23–4; *Dialectic of Enlightenment*, 4–5).

[78]Adorno, *Minima Moralia*, 227.

[79]Horkheimer and Adorno, *Dialectic of Enlightenment*, 48.

[80]Ibid., 39.

[81]Ibid., 40.

in his encounters with mythical powers, just as the bourgeois sets in motion a process of capital accumulation)—this does not mean that Adorno and Horkheimer aim to derive capitalist rationality from these archaic elements. Rather, given that exchange is interpreted as a "secularization of sacrifice," and sacrifice as a "magic schema of rational exchange" (DA, 67),[82] it is a matter of demonstrating the survival of these vestiges of myth in a practice that is prosaic and secular today.[83] A sacrificial element even persists in the logic of action that seeks only to maximize one's own profit. Therefore, however much Odysseus's cunning allows him to come out on top in his sacrifices to the gods and mythical powers—because "through the calculation of his own surrender he succeeds in defeating the power to which he makes that surrender" (DA, 68[84])—however much his literal compliance with the myth's terms allows him to find the loophole that enables him to escape his fate and preserve his life (DA, 76),[85] Odysseus's adventures show that behind rational action oriented toward individual gain there is still an element of self-denial.

In the end, while Marx had revealed the coercion and injustice that lie beneath the free exchange of equivalents in the economic sphere, the interpretation of the figure of Odysseus offered by Adorno and Horkheimer demonstrates how the way in which he evades the might of mythical powers—to a certain extent through a kind of give-and-take—comes at the price of renunciation and becoming hardened. From the point of view of equivalent exchange, this reveals that the price the subject pays for his self-preservation is always a bad deal. Even if Odysseus's cunning tricks allow him to emerge unscathed from his confrontation with the forces of myth, this is always by sacrificing himself: by denying himself and suppressing his own inclinations for the sake of the domination of external and internal nature and of social domination. This reveals that the renunciations demanded of the subject in order to reproduce his life are not paid back by the fruits that civilization brings; that in this exchange the living subject can never come out ahead, since he sacrifices more than he can get in return: "At the moment when human

[82]Ibid.

[83]Braunstein, *Adorno's Critique of Political Economy*, 164.

[84]Horkheimer and Adorno, *Dialectic of Enlightenment*, 41.

[85]Ibid., 46.

beings cut themselves off from the consciousness of themselves as nature, all the purposes for which they keep themselves alive—social progress, the heightening of material and intellectual forces, indeed, consciousness itself—become void, and the enthronement of the means as the end, which in late capitalism is taking on the character of an overt madness, is already detectable in the protohistory of subjectivity" (DA, 73).[86]

This protohistory of subjectivity, which Adorno and Horkheimer construct through the figure of Odysseus, reveals that in the logic underlying the constitution of the dominating subject, nature already harbors the seed of the reproduction of barbarism through civilization. The way in which the unity of the self is articulated—capable of acting according to certain ends and asserting itself through cunning against more powerful forces—always implies self-sacrifice.[87] The liberation from myth through the rational domination of nature ends up turning rationality itself into myth. This reading is supported by an allegorical construction, which interprets Odysseus's confrontation with the mythical powers through the rationality of exchange, associated with the pursuit of private interest and the cold logic of "egotistical calculation" (MEW 4, 464).[88] The image of Odysseus as the archetype of the bourgeois subject thus makes it possible to link the rationality of the economic agent with the sacrificial logic that enables him to elude the mythical forces, drawing all its expressive power from this capacity for condensation. "The human being's mastery of itself, on which the self is founded, virtually entails the annihilation of the subject in whose service that mastery is carried out, because the substance that is mastered, suppressed, and disintegrated by self-preservation is nothing other than the living entity, of which the achievements of self-preservation can only be defined as functions—in other words, self-preservation destroys the very thing which was to be preserved" (DA, 73).[89] This is also evident in the famous passage interpreting Odysseus's encounter with the sirens, which

[86]Horkheimer and Adorno, *Dialectic of Enlightenment*, 42–3.

[87]Hullot-Kentor, *Things Beyond Resemblance*, 37.

[88]Karl Marx and Friedrich Engels, *The Communist Manifesto* trans. Samuel Moore (London: Penguin, 2002), 222.

[89]Horkheimer and Adorno, *Dialectic of Enlightenment*, 43. Translation modified.

introduces the variable of social domination into the equation between self-preservation and sacrifice: the command over the labor of others (DA, 49).[90]

In this passage, Book XII of the Homeric epic is juxtaposed with the dialectic of master and slave in Hegel's *Phenomenology of Spirit* to depict the prototype of the bourgeois subject as a dominator of himself and of others. This image shows that if Odysseus is in a position to expose himself to the seduction of the sirens' song, which implies a promise of happiness for an already-hardened subject, it is only through a cunning ruse that allows such seduction to be free of consequences. Insofar as Odysseus chains himself to the mast, he can enjoy the sirens' song and at the same time prevent its beguilement from having any effect. But his ruse, which was suggested by Circe, is nothing more than a way to nullify his own desire. On the other hand, his oarsmen, whose ears he has plugged so that they do not succumb to the seductions of the song and whom he has ordered to row without stopping and with their eyes fixed straight ahead, reproduce their lives and that of their master through their efforts. Both the subjugated workers and their master are trapped in their respective social roles (DA, 51–2).[91] The image thus conveys the split between physical labor, subordinate to the demands of self-preservation, and a capacity for pleasure that is only tolerated insofar as it lacks practical consequences. The place allocated to art by bourgeois society neutralizes its promise of happiness in advance, condemning it to remain an object of impotent contemplation. This is an allegorical illustration of the intertwining of self-preservation, mastery over the work of others, and subjugation of one's own inclinations. In the process, both the capacity for experience and thought itself are undermined and reduced to a mere instrument of domination. Insofar as the oarsmen work under duress, with their ears stopped so that no sensuous pleasure might disturb the fulfillment of their task, "the servant is subjugated in body and soul, the master regresses. No system of domination has so far been able to escape this price, and the circularity of history in its progress is explained in part by this debilitation, which is the concomitant of power" (DA, 52)[92]. In this

[90]Ibid., 27.
[91]Ibid., 29.
[92]Ibid., 27.

sense, it can be said that the protohistory of bourgeois subjectivity expounded by *Dialectic of Enlightenment* shows "the dialectic between the constitution of the self and its negation, between the domination of nature and its destruction, between progress and regression."[93]

In this light, rather than a philosophy of history or a "grand narrative," *Dialectic of Enlightenment* offers a set of allegorical images that, arranged in a given constellation, aspire to make legible the aporias that have marked the process leading to a catastrophic present. Adorno was aware of the importance of this methodological resource, whose function is not merely illustrative. If, in the face of the persistence of prehistory, "the age of interpreting the world is over and the point now is to change it, then philosophy bids farewell, and in its farewell, concepts leave off and yet persist and become images" (GS 5, 47).[94] Hence the central role played by these allegorical images, which wield an expressive force that merely conceptual thought often lacks. So when Odysseus is presented as the archetype of the bourgeois subject, the Enlightenment is associated with myth, the hyper-puritanical Kant is interpreted in dialogue with Sade, or culture is analyzed as something produced on an industrial scale, the purpose is precisely to present an image capable of jolting the reader, unsettling their understanding of the world around them. In short: it is a matter of breaking through the automatisms that hinder the critical gaze, since they tend to justify the world as it is and conceal its shamefulness. If conventional thought, adjusted to the reality principle as it is, insists on the exaggerated and eccentric character of some of these constructions, the response must be "only exaggeration is true" (DA, 139),[95] since only exaggeration is commensurate to the horror of the recognition of the present as a perpetuation of prehistory.

"The impartiality of scientific language has deprived what was powerless of the strength to make itself heard and merely provided the existing order with a neutral sign for itself. Such neutrality is more metaphysical than metaphysics" (DA, 39).[96] For this reason, Adorno sought for a different

---

[93]José A. Zamora, "Society and History," in *The Sage Handbook of Frankfurt School Critical Theory*, 636.
[94]Theodor W. Adorno, *Against Epistemology: A Metacritique* trans. Willis Domingo (Cambridge: Polity Press, 2013), 39–40.
[95]Horkheimer and Adorno, *Dialectic of Enlightenment*, 92.
[96]Ibid., 17.

language, and turned to objects and perspectives that escape the logic of the middle ground, since the way in which conventional thought dictates what is normative and what is exceptional should be radically distrusted. Hence the attention paid to the most extreme, to seemingly bizarre elements that tend to escape any kind of thinking that is governed by a tidy sense of factuality. This is what makes it possible to defamiliarize the perspective on the surrounding world and to understand it as the result of a history of domination and subjugation that is seemingly infinite. The purpose is to find a way of presenting problems that stimulates "the spontaneity and energy of thought," provoking "a kind of intellectual short-circuiting that casts a sudden light on the familiar and perhaps sets it on fire" (GS 11, 681).[97] In this sense, the images Adorno seeks are like "allegorical evocations of something that cannot be said in words. They do not want to stop conceptual thought so much as to shock through their enigmatic form and thereby get thought moving, because thought in its traditional conceptual form seems rigid, conventional, and outmoded" (GS 11, 680–1).[98] It is a matter, therefore, of constructing perspectives that can break out of the constraints of conventional discourse so that the result of historical becoming, this damaged and unredeemed reality, loses its presumed self-evidence and thus ceases to appear as unquestionable; in short, it is a matter of opening it up to critique and to a praxis that can put an end to it.

In this sense, one of the fundamental perspectives for the critical interpretation of the present is that of the persistence of myth—of a historical course that seems to impose itself with the inescapability of fate (GS 11, 495–6).[99] This is to be understood as a further clarification of the Marxian reference to the present as the perpetuation of prehistory. Of course, associating an increasingly technological and hyper-rationalized society with blind fatality may seem provocative. Despite all the attempts to resurrect a myth of the twentieth century, there is no doubt that it is not mythical powers or forces of destiny that prevent the realization of the available possibilities for a less dreadful and brutal

[97]Adorno, "Benjamin's *Einbahnstrasse*," *Notes to Literature 2*, 323.
[98]Ibid., 323. Translation modified.
[99]Adorno, "On the Classicism of Goethe's Iphigenie," *Notes to Literature 2*, 154.

life, keeping them "under a spell" (GS 10.1, 27).[100] The mythical or irrational elements that persist in the present are not the product of atavistic forces, but rather something that is mediated by the driving principle of progress itself, underpinned by the forces that propel both the disenchantment of the world and the development of productive forces. In this sense, the diagnosis of Enlightenment's relapse into myth is not solely a philosophical question; it has an eminently social dimension. Adorno emphasized that the contemporary form of myth was the answer to the blockage of the materialization of the possible. That is why he repeatedly alludes to Benjamin's dictum (BGS V, 505)[101] that as long as there remains even one beggar, myth will persist (ND, 203).[102] Even though the level of sophistication that productive forces have attained could put an end to hunger and the most basic deprivations, life remains chained to the struggle for survival. Hence the affirmation that society "grows rigid where it ought to change, because productive relationships resist the change demanded by productive forces; it keeps rolling on like the mythical wheel of fire, because it fails, through rational organization, to put a halt to the logic of fate as one of permanent annihilation" (GS 8, 235).[103] Of course, the allusion to the wheel of fire from Germanic mythology is just a metaphor, but the persistent tendency of society toward annihilation is not. This is what makes history appear under the sign of unalterable fate: it implies the persistence of a form of sociality that perpetuates avoidable misery and injustice, naturalizes domination and suffering, and consequently generates a permanent tendency toward catastrophe. In this sense, Rolf Tiedemann has pointed out that what lies at the heart of this diagnosis is nothing less than the failure of history as such.[104] In large part, the problem stems from the fact that the dynamic that has governed the historical process up to the present day persists in its blind, indifferent course. Its telos has been guided by "ever-increasing control over external and internal nature. This trend takes place in one dimension only, at the expense of possibilities which are not followed up because they do not

[100] Adorno, "Cultural Criticism and Society," 32.
[101] Benjamin, *Arcades Project*, 400.
[102] Adorno, *Negative Dialectics*, 203.
[103] Adorno, "'Static' and 'Dynamic' as Sociological Categories," 46. Translation modified.
[104] Tiedemann, *Mythos und Utopie*, 89.

lead to increased control over nature. Once the dynamic is let loose, it pursues its one goal single-mindedly and like a maniac, devouring everything foreign to it on its way" (GS 8, 235).[105] Once inserted into the social logic, the use of reason is confined to a purely technical register and does not extend to a substantive one. It is directed toward increasing productivity, not to a dignified configuration of labor; it seeks to improve profitability, not the realization and enrichment of genuine human needs or the preservation of nature and its diversity. The difficulty of escaping from a model of domination that destroys what it dominates finds its confirmation in the socio-ecological crisis today: it is a problem whose severity is plain to see, but nothing seems able to stop it. In short, what Adorno makes clear is that, in the current forms of reproduction of life, sociality implies a permanent assault on the individuals who sustain it and of the conditions for reproducing their lives. To accept this sacrificial element—the damage and renunciations it imposes—only to receive in return the persistent coercion of second nature and submission to its imperatives: this is the image of contemporary prehistory, the persistence of myth.

What emerges here is "a pathological constitution of society and individuals of such depth that it demands a radical critique of the rationality that underlies it."[106] Hence the centrality of the allegorical construction around the figure of Odysseus, in which the individual manages to constitute himself as a subject by asserting himself against myth, but, in so doing, ends up inextricably intertwined with it, in what would seem to be a fatal circle. Since his only way of guaranteeing survival is through sacrifice, through self-denial, Odysseus prototypically embodies "the irrationality of totalitarian capitalism, whose technique of satisfying needs, in their objectified form determined by domination, makes the satisfaction of needs impossible and tends toward the extermination of humanity" (DA, 73).[107] His figure anticipates the fundamental traits of the "false society," in which "everyone is too many, and is cheated" (DA, 73).[108] The deception consists in the fact that he sacrifices more for society than he receives from it, and in the face of the growing concentration of the social

[105]Adorno, " 'Static' and 'Dynamic' as Sociological Categories," 46–7.
[106]Zamora, *Th. W. Adorno. Pensar contra la barbarie*, 16.
[107]Horkheimer and Adorno, *Dialectic of Enlightenment*, 43. Translation modified.
[108]Ibid., 43.

and economic apparatus on which his life depends, he reveals himself to be dispensable, replaceable at any moment. The fact is that the living subject can never profit from sacrificing his life for mere survival in a society based solely on self-preservation. This is what leads to a persistent malaise in a civilization that makes individuals susceptible to compensations and, even at the heart of a hyper-rationalized society, leaves them vulnerable to the seductions of myth.[109] Hence the need to complement the critique of society with a critique of civilization that is also capable of probing more deeply: into the relationship between subject and object, history and nature, intellectual and physical labor, hardening and ambivalent sensuality, affirmation of the spirit and negation of the body. From this perspective, the history of civilization is also the history of violence against oneself, against nature, and against others, which is perpetuated under the seemingly more subtle, powerful, and sophisticated forms of modern capitalist sociality.

Absolutized Self-Preservation

"Beneath the known history of Europe there runs a subterranean one. It consists of the fate of the human instincts and passions repressed and distorted by civilization. From the vantage point of the fascist present, in which what was hidden comes to light, even manifest history reveals its connection to that dark underside" (DA, 265).[110] Here, fascism appears as the irruption of a barbarism that allows hitherto buried tensions to rise up to the surface. In this way, the whole of history appears in a new light, revealing its most destructive side. This is what leads to the fact that, in the *Dialectic of Enlightenment*, the critique of society is interwoven with elements of a critique of civilization. The result allows for a deepening of the critique of capitalism. For the motives of the domination of nature and the development of the productive forces were not just the driving force behind the progress of modern societies; they had

[109]Marc Nicolas Sommer, "Exkurs I. Odysseus oder Mythos und Aufklärung," in *Max Horkheimer/ Theodor W. Adorno: Dialektik der Aufklärung*, ed. Gunnar Hindrichs (Berlin: De Gruyter, 2017), 32.
[110]Horkheimer and Adorno, *Dialectic of Enlightenment*, 192. Translation modified.

also exacted a price. In the first place, this entailed a loss of qualities both in the subject dominating nature and in nature itself. For what unifies the different elements designated as "nature" is nothing but their condition as a mere substratum of domination (GS 10.2, 624).[111] Nature is defined by its opposition to its "other," be it society or the spirit, and represents, in the last analysis, that which is to be tamed, subdued, functionalized, and exploited. The problem is that the logic of domination of nature, even as it asserts itself, ultimately fails. For "civilization is the triumph of society over nature—a triumph which transforms everything into mere nature" (DA, 211).[112] Incapable of relating to external and internal nature except through blind domination, the rationality of the domination of nature is clear on the point that it only sees the living as threatening and hostile (LGF, 22).[113] Its driving force is fundamentally fear. But this also reveals the sacrificial character of this logic, which leads to the relentless instrumentalization of one's own body and its impulses to mold them to the discipline of work, to the sacrifice of one's own vitality and mimetic forms of behavior to the demands of the reality principle, to the perfection of social control and discipline, as well as to the patriarchal and violent character that civilization has preserved up to the present.

If the logic of civilization is based on the principle of domination—of nature, of oneself, and of others—its mechanisms tend to conceal the costs that this entails for human beings themselves. For "with the denial of nature in human beings, not only the *telos* of the external mastery of nature but also the *telos* of one's own life becomes confused and opaque" (DA, 73).[114] In a certain sense, the tendency toward increasingly authoritarian and destructive societies must also be read as a reminder of this. In *Minima Moralia* it was already stated that the transition to increasingly total societies is primarily linked to an increase in the pressure of domination (MM, 267).[115] It is important to be aware of what this implies. Despite progress made in the mastery of nature and the growth of technical possibilities associated with it, existence under advanced capitalism

---

[111]Adorno, "Progress," 148–9.
[112]Horkheimer and Adorno, *Dialectic of Enlightenment*, 153.
[113]Adorno, *History and Freedom*, 13.
[114]Horkheimer and Adorno, *Dialectic of Enlightenment*, 42.
[115]Adorno, *Minima Moralia*, 234.

remains trapped in the struggle to meet the most basic needs. Of course, the alleged "abundance" of consumer capitalism offers goods that go far beyond the requirements of physical subsistence, from refrigerators to televisions. However, they entail a narrowing down of what is possible within the current stage of development of productive capacities and, above all, leave individuals increasingly at the mercy of a concentrated and relentless social apparatus. For Adorno, this reveals the wound that continues to afflict civilization: the fact that the perfection of the domination of nature never managed to overcome natural coercion. Even though it aimed at "liberating human beings from fear and installing them as masters" (DA, 19),[116] it generated a new form of coercion, one which was much more implacable: that of society as "second nature." Indeed, "society perpetuates the threat from nature as a permanent, organized compulsion" (DA, 205–6).[117] Under the suffocating weight of this social logic, fear, insecurity, and vulnerability not only persist, but also take on new relevance. At a historical moment in which integration into the fascist collective converged with the transition to an increasingly vertical and authoritarian form of capitalism, it became clear that the promise of a rational and enlightened society, free of violence and fear, had never been fulfilled.

It has already been pointed out that the forms of impersonal coercion characteristic of bourgeois society did not manage to eliminate the background of domination, oppression, and violence that continues to simmer beneath the surface of modern capitalist sociality; that is why history remained prehistory. The belief that free agreement of individual wills within the market could establish some kind of harmony beyond coercion proved to be a mirage with fatal consequences. For "with the spread of the bourgeois commodity economy the dark horizon of myth is illuminated by the sun of calculating reason, beneath whose icy rays the seeds of the new barbarism are germinating" (DA, 49).[118] The calculative reason of the bourgeois world had made it possible to illuminate myth, but it never managed to dissolve it completely. Hence, "blind, quasi-natural conditions live on, even in the enlightened society" (GS 11,

[116]Horkheimer and Adorno, *Dialectic of Enlightenment*, 1.

[117]Ibid., 149.

[118]Ibid., 25.

496).[119] This is the soil from which the seed of this "new barbarism" sprouts, namely fascism and the concentrated capitalism that supports it. But how to explain the process that led to that point? The evolution of capitalism alone did not seem capable of accounting for the features of the new barbarism and, given that its manifestations pointed to logics of mutilation and violence that seemed rooted in deeper strata of subjectivation, Adorno and Horkheimer sought other theoretical keys that could account for it. This is where the centrality of labor appears, which was both the means *par excellence* of the domination of nature and the fundamental pillar of bourgeois capitalist sociality. While vulgar Marxism had considered labor an emancipatory force, "the source of all wealth and all culture" (cf. MEW 19, 15),[120] Adorno and Horkheimer did not see any potential for transcendence in it. Indeed, both in the logic of capitalist subjectivation and in the dynamics of civilization, labor is connected to the principle of self-preservation.

In a way, the logic of the domination of nature could be fully encapsulated in the motto that "work sets you free." Because it is only through work that the subject can free himself from the coercion of overpowering nature, thus realizing the potential for a life that can become something more than mere struggle for subsistence. However, even before fascism made a mockery of the slogan of freedom through work, inscribing *Arbeit macht frei* on the gates of concentration camps that forced their inmates to work themselves to death, there was reason to regard it as highly suspect. For "under the compulsion of domination, human labor has always led away from myth, yet under domination it has always fallen back into its spell" (DA, 49).[121] Indeed, although labor promised freedom from natural coercion, it was a key node at the intersection of social domination and the domination of external and internal nature. At both levels it promotes the enslavement of living beings. At a social level, those who command the labor of others restrict their lives and the development of their needs to the blind struggle for subsistence, regardless of the possibilities for a more comfortable life that

[119]Adorno, "On the Classicism of Goethe's Iphigenie," 154. Translation modified.
[120]Karl Marx, "Critique of the Gotha Program," *Later Political Writings*, 208.
[121]Horkheimer and Adorno, *Dialectic of Enlightenment*, 25. Translation modified.

is not quite so subject to the survival imperative. At this point the image of Odysseus's oarsmen is once again significant. It implies the reduction of the subjected to pure body, to pure capacity for work, which in the history of the modern West is embodied in figures such as galley slaves and subjugated laborers: "The victims of the civilizing process, those whom it oppresses and who pay its bills, are deprived of its fruits, imprisoned in a pre-civilized condition. Civilization, which, historically, leads out of barbarism, has also promoted barbarism, and continues to promote it by virtue of the repressive force exerted by the principle of civilization, the domination of nature" (GS 11, 507).[122] In fact, the effective domination of nature through work requires discipline, hardening the body, subjection of oneself and of others, and adaptation to the requirements of the social apparatus. This reveals, therefore, that the principle of self-preservation, prototypical of the bourgeois subject, was linked to a notion of the self that has eliminated "all natural traces as mythological," which was "no longer supposed to be either a body or blood or a soul or even a natural ego" (DA, 46).[123] Ultimately it refers to a subject that no longer appears as a living entity, but rather "a transcendental or logical subject, [as] the reference point of reason, the legislating authority of action" (DA, 46).[124] That reason, in turn, presents itself as "merely an aid to the all-encompassing economic apparatus" (DA, 47).[125]

This returns us to the strictly social dimension of labor that is associated with self-preservation, which Adorno and Horkheimer explain using the parameters of Marx's critique of political economy: "In the bourgeois economy the social work of each individual is mediated by the principle of the self; for some this labor is supposed to yield increased capital, for others the strength for extra work" (DA, 47).[126] The way they address the consequences of how the reproduction of capital reproduces in turn the different social roles in its service, deepening inequality between social classes, points to the problem of subjectivation, which tends to reduce individuals to mere bearers of

---

[122]Adorno, "On the Classicism of Goethe's Iphigenie," 164.
[123]Horkheimer and Adorno, *Dialectic of Enlightenment*, 22.
[124]Ibid.
[125]Ibid., 23.
[126]Ibid.

social reproduction if they are to have any chance to staying alive: "the more heavily the process of self-preservation is based on the bourgeois division of labor, the more it enforces the self-alienation of individuals, who must mold themselves to the technical apparatus body and soul" (DA, 47).[127] That is to say, the progressive development of society, which allows for ever greater freedom from the realm of natural coercion, places mounting demands upon individuals, who are forced to mold their own nature—their somatic and libidinal substratum—to the social apparatus they serve. If "humanity had to inflict terrible injuries on itself before the self—the identical, purpose-directed, masculine character of human beings—was created, and something of this process is repeated in every childhood" (DA, 50),[128] even greater demands could be expected from an increasingly concentrated and implacable social system. In this regard, it is stated that

> The over-maturity of society lives on the immaturity of the ruled. The more complex and refined the social, economic, and scientific mechanism to the operation of which the system of production has long since attuned the body, the more impoverished the experiences of which the body is capable. The elimination of qualities, their conversion into functions, is transferred by rationalized modes of work to the human capacity for experience, which tends to revert to that of amphibians (DA, 53).[129]

The underlying assumption here is that the development of the social, technical, and economic apparatus that mediates the conditions for survival had become a gigantic machinery that tends to absorb human beings in order to mold them to the demands of its operational framework. This implies an enormous reduction of their life horizons and a mutilation of their capacity for experience. Even though the idea of human beings being reduced to mere Pavlovian reflexes is certainly excessive, it is important not to lose sight of the fact that the meaning of the diagnosis is that the immanence of the social system tends to become total. Here, work no longer sets you free, but, at the

---

[127]Ibid.

[128]Ibid., 26.

[129]Ibid., 28. Translation modified.

same time as it allows one's own life to be preserved by serving the iniquitous logic of capital, it continually reproduces one's subaltern and dependent condition. In this situation, the advance of progress is inseparable from an increased potential for regression:[130] "Through the mediation of the total society, which encompasses all relationships, human beings are being turned back into … mere examples of the species, identical to one another through isolation within the compulsively controlled collectivity" (DA, 54).[131] At this point, Adorno and Horkheimer once again take up the image of Odysseus's oarsmen, which serves as an allegory for the new forms of atomization under the yoke of heteronomous labor. Here, it is associated with a form of subjugation that extends beyond the strictly productive sphere: "The rowers, unable to speak to one another, are all harnessed to the same rhythms, like modern workers in factories, cinemas, and the collective. It is the concrete conditions of work in society that enforce conformism—not the conscious influences which additionally render the oppressed stupid and deflect them from the truth" (DA, 54).[132] In short, the problem of regression and the rise of the new barbarism cannot be explained on the basis of the critique of ideology or culture, but by a form of social constitution that links the mobilization of labor—which obeys the logic of the reproduction of capital, not that of the satisfaction of needs—with the principle of self-preservation. This connection leaves its mark on the physiognomy of subjects and in the models of behavior and rationality that are active in every aspect of their lives. This is all the more harmful insofar as living subjects find themselves in a condition of growing helplessness, since the nexus connecting the reproduction of their individual

[130]However, this should not be confused with a one-sided and non-dialectical view of the socio-technical apparatus, which would imply a total identification of reason and domination. Horkheimer and Adorno rather insist that "The instruments of power—language, weapons, and finally machines—which are intended to hold everyone in their grasp, must in their turn be grasped by everyone. In this way, the moment of rationality in domination also asserts itself as something different from it. The thing-like quality of the means, which makes the means universally available, its "objective validity" for everyone, itself implies a criticism of the domination from which thought has arisen as its means" (DA, 54; *Dialectic of Enlightenment*, 29). For an analysis of these factors, see Marcel Stoetzler, "Wer aber von der Geschichte des Subjekts nicht reden will, sollte auch vom Kapitalismus schweigen," in Gunzelin Schmid-Noerr and Eva-Maria Ziege (eds.), *Zur Kritik der regressiven Vernunft* (Wiesbaden: Springer, 2019), 163–80.

[131]Horkheimer and Adorno, *Dialectic of Enlightenment*, 29.

[132]Ibid.

life to the reproduction of the prevailing social logic is purely contingent. Hence the increasingly coercive effect that the social apparatus has on individuals, which intensifies fear and deepens contemporary prehistory.

Since the reproduction of life depends on a social logic that curtails individual lives, a growing sense of unease spreads, as well as often-unspoken suffering accompanied by feelings of anxiety and powerlessness. Individuals perceive the way social imperatives impose themselves on their lives as something inescapable: the social dimension of their existence appears as blind fate. Therefore, "the denser the weave [of the social fabric], the more one wants to escape it, whereas it is precisely its close weave that prevents any escape" (GS 10.2, 676–7).[133] This generates the potential for regressive dynamics to be unleashed, fostering an "archaic tendency toward violence" (GS 10.2, 680)[134] among the socialized subjects. In this context, it is stated that developed capitalism "cannot exist without disfiguring human beings. Persecution … is inseparable from that order. Its essence, however it may hide itself at times, is the violence which today is openly revealed" (DA, 194).[135] Adorno and Horkheimer insist that the social order was always held up by the threat of coercion and violence; ultimately by oppression. As soon as one is deprived of the shelter of social power, as soon as one loses "money and position," one is left at the mercy of fearsome figures who reinforce the continuity of the history of domination: "the murderer, the killer, the brutalized colossi who are used in secret by the ruling powers" (DA, 268).[136] It is they who sustain "the fear without which there is no domination" (DA, 268).[137] In this light, *Minima Moralia* states that "the barbarians engendered by culture have, however, always been used by it to keep its own barbaric nature alive. Domination delegates the physical violence on which it depends to the dominated. In being allowed the satisfaction of exercising their distorted instincts in collectively approved and proper ways, they learn to do those things which the noble need for the continued indulgence of their nobility" (MM, 207).[138] As a result, the

[133]Adorno, "Education After Auschwitz," 193.

[134]Ibid., 196.

[135]Horkheimer and Adorno, *Dialectic of Enlightenment*, 139. Translation modified.

[136]Ibid., 195.

[137]Ibid.

[138]Adorno, *Minima Moralia*, 182.

brutalization and violence that flourish under the weight of social coercion help to blindly reinforce an order based on violence, which is the root cause of dispossession as such.

The transition to post-liberal capitalism, however, implies a qualitative turning point in this respect. Faced with an implacable and increasingly concentrated social apparatus, the intensity of domination has reached such a pitch that fear hits new heights, and the need to persecute—and not just be persecuted by increasingly anonymous and impersonal mechanisms of coercion—is spreading among those who are dominated. Phenomena such as anti-Semitism can be interpreted as a way of giving free rein to the destructive impulses generated by one's own powerlessness without contravening the social norm. Feeling that one can assert oneself through force, thereby imposing the very principle that governs the social order on those who are more vulnerable, allows one to exorcise the fear caused by seeing oneself as the target of that same senseless violence. Nevertheless, the social mechanisms that make this possible are totally indifferent to individual human beings, who are treated as mere specimens. In this sense, the reduction of individuals to a mere expression of their race or of the stigmas that signify them as suitable targets implies their "regression to nature as mere violence" (DA, 193).[139] Only then can all the brutality be unloaded upon them, all the hostility toward the living that is rooted, in turn, in that hidden downside of progress in the mastery of nature, which accompanies it as its shadow: "The compulsion toward cruelty and destruction stems from the organic repression of proximity to the body" (DA, 266).[140] Living corporeality has been completely subjugated by the social apparatus, which forces the individual to control their own somatic substratum as if it were inert matter. In this sense, subjects that have been hardened and reduced to functions experience a strong revulsion toward anything that arouses the memory of a nature that is living and not completely subdued in them, because it forces them to relive the suffering caused by all that they have had to repress for the sake of self-preservation. Hence the repulsion produced by mimetic behavior, undisciplined gestures, unrestrained

---

[139]Horkheimer and Adorno, *Dialectic of Enlightenment*, 138.
[140]Ibid., 193.

expressiveness, corporeality that evokes something animalistic and primal, that which is not completely filtered by the rules of hygiene: "Whatever is not quite assimilated, or infringes the commands in which the progress of centuries has been sedimented, is felt as intrusive and arouses a compulsive aversion" (DA, 204–5).[141] This is where everything that has become taboo in the natural history of the social order emerges. It unleashes fury because it arouses the memory of one's own repressed impulses, laying bare the logic of toughening and self-discipline that the civilized have had to inflict on themselves. While the social norm tolerates certain avenues for acting out the forbidden desire to yield to impulse and violently suppress those elements and the individuals who embody them, it does so because this further reinforces the logic of submission. It is thus argued that "fascism is also totalitarian in seeking to place oppressed nature's rebellion against domination directly in the service of domination" (DA, 210).[142]

Faced with this situation, in which even seemingly indomitable impulses are redirected toward a further strengthening of domination, the question arises as to whether it is possible to escape the absolutized compulsion of a second nature that reduces social existence to mere "devouring and being devoured" (ND 348–9).[143] The circle of domination seemed to be closing in. This diagnosis clearly acknowledges that the persistence of this logic entails a fatal mutilation of life itself, as well as a curtailment of social and human potential (DA, 297–8),[144] suffocated by fear, domination, and violence. Against this, Adorno and Horkheimer advocated the "remembrance of nature within the subject" (DA, 58).[145] Only that element, "in which the ignored truth of all culture is resolved" (DA, 58),[146] would make it possible to safeguard a notion of progress that would not only entail the indifferent advance of domination, but also "the prospect of its alleviation" (DA, 57).[147] Indeed, without this it would not be possible to put an end to prehistory. Hence the need to develop

[141]Ibid., 147–8.

[142]Ibid., 152.

[143]Adorno, *Negative Dialectics*, 355.

[144]Horkheimer and Adorno, *Dialectic of Enlightenment*, 209–10.

[145]Ibid., 32.

[146]Ibid.

[147]Ibid., 32.

logics of thought and action that do not regard nature and living existence as hostile, that do not impose parameters aimed at their rigid subjugation, but are instead capable of responding to their claims and recognizing themselves in relation to them. In this sense, true progress would not consist in the blind domination over nature nor in the unrestricted development of technical and productive capacities, but in making possible a condition in which human beings could live without harassment or violence, in which the permanent threat of catastrophe that hangs over social life would dissolve, in which lives could be something more than a permanent struggle for self-preservation. In Adorno's own words, "Progress means: to step out of the magic spell, even out of the spell of progress that is itself nature, in that humanity becomes aware of its own inbred nature and brings to a halt the domination it exacts upon nature and through which domination by nature continues. In this way it could be said that progress occurs where it ends" (GS 10.2, 625).[148] However, this requires more than mere self-reflection on the natural and vulnerable dimension of the subject and an appeal to the need for reconciliation. Undoubtedly, restoring the rights of the subjugated is crucial for the critique of the existing, but it cannot be resolved with philosophy alone; rather, it demands transformation at the very roots of the social constitution. In this sense, understanding the motives of Adorno's philosophy requires paying attention to his critical theory of capitalist socialization. Perhaps it is there that his thought, while responding to a historical moment that is no longer our own, proves capable of identifying aporias and sore points that remain unresolved and still lie at the heart of the problems of our time.

[148]Adorno, "Progress," 150.

Part Two

Adorno and the Critical Theory of Capitalism

In the Labyrinth of Social Constitution

In mainstream reception, the image of Adorno as a dark thinker of the "age of catastrophes" of the twentieth century has tended to overshadow his contribution as a critic of capitalist society and the way it configures the lives of human beings. Indeed, Adorno's critique of the forms of total domination that emerged in fascism and Auschwitz cannot be understood in isolation from his analysis of the transformations leading from liberal to advanced capitalism. It was most likely the experience of that catastrophic era that enabled him to sharpen his gaze and perceive what still persisted beneath the apparent prosperity of the so-called golden age of the second postwar period: a ubiquitous tendency toward total integration that marks life in the most developed societies with the sign of heteronomy, of unfreedom. It was the forms of socialization of post-liberal capitalism, with their increasing concentration of social, economic, and political power, that made it possible to affirm that "human beings, in their vital destiny, have become objects" (GS 8, 582). Adorno's contributions to the formulation of a critical theory of capitalism prove fruitful precisely by virtue of this diagnosis. Building on the fundamental insights of Marx's critique of political economy, Adorno attempted to expand and update them in order to account for historical upheavals that were profoundly transforming the makeup of twentieth-century societies. In this sense, his critical theory arose in response to a specific social and historical constellation, coinciding with the genesis of post-liberal capitalism in the 1930s and 1940s. As a result of the experiences of an era marked by the convergence of fascism, the growing concentration of capital in trusts and monopolies, and the increasingly vertical administration of life, Adorno developed a critique of society that pinpointed the transformations and aporias that continue to lie at the heart of contemporary life. These include the trend toward "total socialization" driven by capital, the emergence of the culture industry, the impact of new forms of socialization on the constitution of human beings, and the very transformation of the concept of ideology.

In light of these analyses, capitalism is revealed to be more than an economic system or a mode of appropriating the surplus of production: it refers to the constitution of social life as a whole, in both its objective and subjective dimensions. In this regard, Adorno's critical theory, even when dealing with particular phenomena—including those often dismissed as "subjective" or "cultural"—can only be understood as a critique of the overall social process of the reproduction of life. This entails the formation of social objectivity, of a "system," which imposes itself on individuals by dictating the conditions for their self-preservation. The *telos* of this "system," from which nothing can escape, is the reproduction of capital. To this extent Adorno's social theory should be understood in the Marxian tradition, but he is aware that it is no longer enough to analyze the mode of production. It is also necessary to examine how it affects the constitution of social life. For social logic no longer reigns only in the realm of labor, but also in consumption and in so-called free time. Adorno perceives that the logic of socialization of capital is gaining ground, absorbing ever more dimensions of existence and tolerating ever fewer spaces outside its sphere of influence, but also penetrating the very constitution of subjects, their desires, and their fears. Life becomes a whole integrated into the social logic. However, the focus of his critical theory is not so much the description of the socializing logic of capital, but rather the understanding of the dialectic between the coercive social system and the individuals who have to make and reproduce their existence within it. Ultimately, Adorno exposes how an increasingly powerful social logic—ever more capable of subjugating natural constraints—comes to function as a second nature, disempowering subjects and condemning them to a condition of dependence and powerlessness in relation to the social apparatus.

This is where Adorno's concept of "damaged life" becomes central. It refers to the social mediation of that which is most immediate, including that which is most intimate. It thematizes the experience of how the demands and imperatives of the social system extend throughout one's existence and do so in a coercive way, inflicting suffering. "He who wishes to know the truth about life in its immediacy must scrutinize its estranged form, the objective powers that determine individual existence even in its most hidden recesses" (MM, 17).[1] Nothing could be further from Adorno's critical theory than the notion of a strict opposition between "system" and "life-world" as if they were two distinct and antagonistic logics, as Habermas posited in his *Theory of Communicative Action*. The problem here is not that the "system"—meaning the imperatives of economics and politics—can colonize and impose its logic on the spontaneous spheres of interaction. The analyses of the culture industry, the authoritarian character, or the anthropological transformation of living subjects point in a sharply different theoretical direction. They reveal that, for Adorno, nothing escapes the mediation of the social constitution. Here, life itself is already a product of the overwhelming social process of which it is a part. If he speaks of damaged life, it is because individual existence is relegated to being "dragged along as an appendage of the process of material production, without autonomy or substance of its own" (MM, 17).[2] Living subjects are captured both as producers and as consumers, as employees and as competitors, but

[1]Adorno, *Minima Moralia*, 15.
[2]Ibid.

they also observe how the social fabric ultimately functionalizes needs that go beyond strictly material concerns, such as the search for compensations to offset their renunciations and wounds or the yearning to be recognized as concrete, individual beings. Consequently, what critical theory seeks to transform are the existing conditions of life, while remaining aware that these conditions are not self-contained but are thoroughly embedded in the mode of social constitution as a whole.

In this sense, it is noteworthy that, in recent years, a growing trend has emerged that has refocused attention on the central importance of Adorno's critique of capitalism, which had been overlooked for decades in the reception of his work. At the core of this critique is not just the persistent injustice of class domination—expressed in his formulation of the antagonistic, riven totality—but also the understanding of an autonomized social logic, which turns production into an end in itself and subjects all social activity to the demands of capital accumulation. But, above all, Adorno's critical theory of capitalism attends to what the social system does to the living subjects who keep it running. For the course of society and history ultimately depends on them. Marx had already said that it is not history as such that wages battles; it is not from history that we can expect the advent of emancipation, nor of regression. History has no agents other than living subjects. In this sense, the growing antagonism that Adorno discerned between concentrated social power and increasingly atomized and powerless individuals did not offer particularly hopeful prospects. Transformative praxis seemed blocked. The reinforcement of tendencies that seemed to make individuals prone to tolerate regressive and inhuman behavior seemed instead to be gaining ground, even in the period of the so-called postwar "economic miracles." Adorno read this as a symptom of the objective conditions that weigh on human beings in an increasingly implacable social system, one that integrates its members into a seamless functional network that may open up certain spaces of agency while reproducing their lives under conditions of growing subjugation. This is why his account of the transformations in the conditions of socialization under advanced capitalism is so important—along with his attention to how the internalization of social coercion by individuals takes its toll in terms of resentment, and his analysis of how, following the crisis of classical forms of "ideology," new mechanisms of social cohesion emerge, ranging from the culture industry to authoritarianism, including forms of superstition such as astrology. In this light, it has been pointed out that Adorno's works—whether in philosophy, sociology, aesthetics, or his engagement with psychoanalysis—"should above all be viewed as models of a critique of political economy expanded through social theory."[3]

Undoubtedly, Adorno did not develop a theory of modern society that we can reconstruct as a systematic whole. Rather, his work offers an analysis of a set of particular issues—the mediation of exchange and the commodity form, the increasing concentration of both capital and social power that accompanies the development of productive forces, the social constitution of subjectivity, and the anthropological transformations that these entail—which together suggest a coherent understanding of the forms of sociality in his time. In twentieth-century societies, his thought identifies an expansion of the socializing logic of capital, which exerts enormous influence both on the constitution of social life and on the very formation of living subjects, who are increasingly shaped by it. In this context, it was a question of outlining the key principles of a critical theory of capitalism capable of taking up the Marxian heritage within a different historical stage. In the first place, this involves understanding society as a fundamentally coercive system that imposes itself on the individuals it encompasses. This creates a unique dialectic between the forms of social constitution, shaped by increasingly subtle mechanisms of domination, and the living subjects who sustain them. The tensions between these forces reflect the evolving historical struggle between emancipation and barbarism. In this regard, Adorno's texts evidence a rare ability to perceive the profound social transformations of the last century—from the trend toward total social integration to the growing vulnerability of individuals in the face of the societal structures on which they depend. His analysis did not shy away from the obstacles that these changes posed for emancipatory theory and praxis. It was no longer feasible to postulate an external and "privileged" subject from which to expect a push for social transformation. Rather, the situation seemed to be one where nothing and no one appeared capable of

[3]Braunstein, *Adorno's Critique of Political Economy*, 351.

surpassing the suffocating immanence of the social system. Accordingly, it became necessary to abandon the old illusion that the cause of emancipation swam with the tide of history and to recognize the vulnerability of criticism in confronting the reality it seeks to oppose. Yet this did not prevent Adorno from putting forward an ambitious and demanding critical theory of society. His position is not that of an abstract challenge to the social whole, but one that, without harboring any illusions about its all-encompassing and oppressive power, is also capable of highlighting its contradictions, its fault lines, and its potential points of friction.

4

A New State of Unfreedom: The Logic of Capitalist Socialization

If Adorno can rightly be considered a theorist of advanced capitalism, the basis for this would lie to a large extent in his appropriation of the fundamental categories of Marx's critique of political economy. Certainly, nothing is more alien to Adorno's intellectual profile than Marxism understood as a "worldview" or as a system of "dialectical materialism." His interest in Marx has nothing to do with the Marxist vulgate. However, when he needs to specify what constitutes the negativity of the prevailing social logic, he does so in Marxian terms. This is not to say that Adorno can in any way be considered an epigone of Marx. The distinctive features of his critical theory outline dimensions of social life that go far beyond the scope of Marxian theory. Above all, the difference here has to do with the historical transformations that separate the situation of nineteenth-century liberal capitalism from that of twentieth-century advanced capitalism. During this period of time, the hopes that Marx had still harbored about the development of modern societies, or the existence of a revolutionary subject, had been shattered. Adorno was facing a much more advanced stage in the process of capitalist socialization, with a much higher level of social integration than Marx had known. Nothing in this increasingly hermetic society seemed to nurture the expectations of emancipation that had arisen in the nineteenth century; rather, it presented a seemingly closed historical horizon in which Adorno detected strong regressive tendencies. For this reason, his theory takes the measure of Marxist categories based on a transformed social reality. But it also extends the analysis to new dimensions of the capitalist social condition, ranging from the socialization of "leisure time" to the conflicts that the internalization of an increasingly inescapable social logic entails for living individuals. That is what situates his thought between the critical review of the Marxist legacy, which was already considered insufficient to account for the specific features of twentieth-century capitalist society, and the anticipation of the new readings of Marx that would emerge from the late 1960s onward.

Adorno's understanding of the fundamental features of the social logic based on Marx's critique of political economy bears the imprint of his early reading of *History and Class Consciousness*, the seminal work by Georg Lukács. The approach to Marx proposed in this book had an impact on a whole generation of intellectuals, including authors such as Benjamin and Horkheimer. In it, the commodity form is already seen as "constitutive … of society," capable of penetrating "society in all its aspects," both in its internal and external life, and remolding it "in its own image."[1] This is what opened up the possibility of speaking of society as a totality again, although—in contrast to Hegel—totality was no longer to be understood in a positive sense, but as "negative totality." The influence of Lukács in this regard is evident in the way Adorno deals with the commodity form in his texts of the 1930s, from *Kierkegaard* and "On the Social Situation of Music" to "The Fetishistic Character of Music and the Regression of Listening." From Lukács, Adorno would also take some of the central concepts of his critical theory: reification, fetishism, second nature, and totality. However, Adorno's relationship with Marx cannot be adequately understood if it is viewed solely through the Lukácsian prism, and it undoubtedly extends beyond the critique of reification. The difference lies not only in the fact that Adorno can no longer rely on a salvific role for the proletariat. What he sought in the critique of

[1]Georg Lukács, *History and Class Consciousness*, trans. Rodney Livingstone (Cambridge, MA: MIT Press, 1972), 85.

political economy, as was already evident in *Minima Moralia* and, above all, in his sociological writings from the 1950s and 1960s, up to *Negative Dialectics*,[2] were the keys to developing a theory of the society of his own time, which exhibited distinctive new features.

In this sense, the principle of exchange, which had already been interpreted as a "secularization of sacrifice" (DA, 67)[3] in the *Dialectic of Enlightenment*, takes on central importance for the understanding of the web of socialization in his later writings. But exchange is not primarily understood from the point of view of abstraction here—as analyzed by Alfred Sohn-Rethel[4]—but rather from that of social constitution. When Adorno refers to the "exchange society" he is alluding to the core of the Marxian critique of political economy: the theory of value. In it, Adorno finds the key to an analysis of social objectivity, of capitalist society as a "system." The logic of capital is understood here as an autonomized social relation, one which is reproduced through the actions of individuals, but behind their backs and without their awareness. Undoubtedly, as Helmut Reichelt has pointed out, Adorno's contributions to sociology, his critique of positivism, and even his concept of dialectics can only be understood from this perspective of society as a "whole."[5] For Adorno, capitalism is not simply an economic system, but the global process of the reproduction of life in modern societies. This implies a constitution of social life as a whole, in both its objective and subjective dimensions, which is marked by the subjection of ever more spheres of existence to the logic of capital. In short, what is at stake is the specific understanding of capitalism as a "false totality," as a system that human beings experience, first and foremost, as a form of coercion, and one

[2]For an analysis of the transformation of Adorno's approach to Marx from his youthful writings up to his mature work, cfr. Chris O"Kane, *Fetishism and Social Domination in Marx, Lukács, Adorno and Lefebvre*, PhD dissertation (University of Sussex, 2013), 127–60.

[3]Adorno and Horkheimer, *Dialectic of Enlightenment*, 40.

[4]Cfr. Alfred Sohn-Rethel, *Intellectual and Manual Labour: A Critique of Epistemology*, trans. Martin Sohn-Rethel (London: The Macmillan Press, 1978). In the 1930s, during his exile in Oxford, Adorno had received Sohn-Rethel's early programmatic writings with enthusiasm. However, in his later period hardly any of that initial enthusiasm was to remain, as revealed in the letter in which he responds to Sohn-Rethel's initial reactions to *Negative Dialectics*, clearly setting down the dividing lines at both the theoretical and political levels (cfr. *Theodor W. Adorno and Alfred SohnRethel: Briefwechsel 1933–1969* [Munich: Text+Kritik, 1991], 152–3).

[5]Helmut Reichelt, *Neue MarxLektüre: Zur Kritik sozialwissenschaftlicher Logik* (Freiburg: ça ira, 2011), 22.

which generates anguish and suffering. For Adorno, capitalist societies give rise to a new form of heteronomy.

This is the key to what Adorno's critique of advanced capitalism means. His insistence on the "society of exchange" implies that critical theory cannot fall short of the level of analysis of the Marxian critique of political economy. This is indispensable for understanding contemporary forms of unfreedom. However, Marx's critique alone was not enough to elaborate a critical theory commensurate with the intensification and sophistication of the forms of social domination proper to advanced capitalism; it needed to be updated and expanded to account for an unprecedented degree of concentration of social power. This introduced new coordinates for understanding the growing imbalance of power between the autonomized social logic and the individuals both subjected to it and sustaining it. It also made it necessary to incorporate the study of the subjective factor in order to understand social objectivity, since the conditions of socialization generalized a state of mounting pressure and powerlessness for socialized individuals. Adorno's fundamental diagnosis therefore refers to a logic of "total socialization" that is not only a product of the economic system, but also of the spread of the so-called administered world. But this in no way implies that the critique of political economy ceases to be the fundamental framework for understanding social logic, in favor of explanations based on politics or state power, nor does it suggest that social phenomena can be primarily interpreted through a critique of instrumental reason. Rather, what is at stake is a further expansion of the *ratio* of capital's socialization.

Accordingly, the following pages offer an approach to Adorno's understanding of capitalist society as a regime of unfreedom. Adorno rarely presents this theory in a direct way in his writings, and it often demands "a virtually anamnestic understanding of Marx"[6] from his readers. The purpose is to make explicit the grounding of his social theory in a peculiar appropriation of Marx's critique of political economy to which his texts of the 1950s and 1960s often allude, but which they do not develop. The framework of the Cold War meant that Adorno's relationship with Marx was often somewhat veiled.

[6]Robert Hullot-Kentor, "Moishe Postone and the Essay as Form," *Critical Historical Studies*, 7, no. 1, 15.

Yet without it, it is not possible to understand his critique of capitalism. In this sense, his reading of Marx takes up the central problematics and concepts of Hegel's idealist philosophy, which he retranslates into a foundation for social theory. For Adorno, Hegel had unknowingly articulated the systematic nature of modern society.[7] Hence the importance of revisiting some of his key concepts—mediation and contradiction, as well as the dualities of universal-particular and essence-appearance—along new lines and of demonstrating the peculiar inversion undergone by other concepts—such as totality, spirit, and subject—within the real system that constituted capitalist society. In any case, beyond the references to Hegel and Marx, the core focus of Adorno's social theory is the relationship between the social totality and living individuals. For it is in this tension that the negative and heteronomous character of the social constitution becomes most evident, along with the vital nerve that drives the critique: the experience of damage.

Capitalist Society as a "System": Grappling with Totality

"Society … is as much an epitome of subjects as it is their negation," states Adorno in *Negative Dialectics* (ND, 22).[8] This formulation captures the contradiction inscribed in the social constitution itself. For Adorno—who clearly follows Marx in this respect—society is not merely the sum of the individuals that compose it, but above all the set of relations that they establish among themselves, which has become autonomous from them, confronting and coercing them to the point of ultimately overthrowing them as subjects. The process by which social logic becomes autonomous from the individuals who set it in motion is the central enigma to be explained by social theory (GS 8, 12).[9] When Adorno speaks of society in the strict sense, he is referring to

[7]Cfr. Lars Heitmann, "Society as 'Totality': On the Negative-Dialectical Presentation of Capitalist Socialization," in *The SAGE Handbook of Frankfurt School Critical Theory*, 594.

[8]Adorno, *Negative Dialectics*, 10.

[9]Adorno, "Society," *Critical Theory and Society*, 270.

modern capitalist society—for only this is a truly socialized society, constituted as a web of interdependencies "in which all the members of the society are entwined, and which takes on a certain kind of autonomy in relation to them" (ES, 55).[10] Capitalist society is structured as a system—a totality defined by the way in which relations of reciprocal interdependence among individuals are constituted. "And to this first, still quite abstract approximation, let us add a further qualification, namely, the dependency of all individuals on the totality which they form. In such a totality, everyone is also dependent on everyone else" (GS 8, 10).[11] Adorno therefore conceives of society as an objective structure: a web of interdependencies that could be understood as a "concrete totality" in the Hegelian sense, in which the whole mediates and unifies the singular and heterogeneous elements that compose it and is constituted only through them. Individuals, in turn, are determined by their place within the social whole.

In this sense, Adorno's social theory rests on a retranslation of certain elements of Hegel's idealist conceptualization in light of Marx's critique of political economy. For already in Hegel the figure of totality appears as an all-encompassing system, the dominance of the universal over the particular and the mediation of everything singular. Only these elements do not refer to the unfolding of the spirit, but to the effective constitution of society. Totality is no longer a purely speculative category; neither is it in itself a factual, tangible, or immediately ascertainable entity, but rather "both something abstract and the most real thing of all" (GS 5, 267).[12] The constitution of society as a whole is the result of a specific mode of social mediation: what binds socialized individuals to one another is the universal exchange of commodities. It is the principle of exchange, which is inseparable from the commodity form, that shapes and reproduces the social web of interdependencies. Thus, in his writings of the 1950s and 1960s, Adorno repeatedly refers to the "exchange society" and the "commodity society"; exchange even appears as "the social a priori" (ND, 190).[13] This points to the distinctive feature of a social formation

[10]Adorno, *Introduction to Sociology*, 30.
[11]Adorno, "Society," 268.
[12]Adorno, *Hegel: Three Studies*, 20.
[13]Adorno, *Negative Dialectics*, 190.

in which the whole, which binds together the individuals that make up the social system, is reproduced through their separation, their atomization.[14] But the way in which Adorno understands exchange cannot be confused with that which Hegel, in his *Philosophy of Right*, had called the "system of necessities" of bourgeois society, nor with the so-called simple circulation of commodities (which could be condensed in the Marxian formula of C–M–C). According to his perspective, individuals do not act in exchange as rational beings: their individuality, the rational basis of their action, does not exist in advance of exchange, but is subordinated to it (GS 10.2, 745).[15] When Adorno speaks of exchange, as Marx does in the first chapter of *Capital*, he presupposes a fully developed capitalist society. Thus, he points out that the "universal development" of exchange "happens independently of the qualitative attitudes of producer and consumer, of the mode of production, even of need, which the social mechanism tends to satisfy as a kind of secondary by-product. Profit comes first" (GS 8, 13).[16] Here, exchange occurs under the aegis of the maximization of value, of the reproduction of capital. Therefore, although Adorno insists that society must be understood as a functional network reproduced through the division of labor, the nature of this network ultimately reveals the antagonism of the social system with the individuals who produce and sustain it through their actions: for the interconnectedness of the social system is not oriented toward the fullfillment of its members' needs, but rather toward ensuring the reproduction of capital.

On the basis of this understanding, Adorno is able to affirm that "the law by which the fatality of mankind unfolds itself is the law of exchange" (GS 8, 209).[17] In order to survive, individuals cannot escape it: they depend on the social organization that precedes them, with its division of labor and its

---

[14]"We live within a totality which binds people together only by virtue of their alienation from each other; and which I said that the present society is mediated only through individuation, that also had a critical sense … [it is] through the fact that within the dominant forms of society individual people seek their individual advantage, profit—that the whole is able to survive and reproduce itself at all—even if while moaning and groaning and at the cost of unspeakable sacrifices" (ES, 77–8; *Introduction to Sociology*, 43).

[15]Adorno, "On Subject and Object," *Critical Models*, 248.

[16]Adorno, "Society," 271.

[17]Adorno, "Introduction," *The Positivist Dispute in German Sociology*, 80.

mechanisms for regulating the production and distribution of goods. "Yet, in turn, this does not represent a simple immediacy but is something conceptual. The act of exchange implies the reduction of the products to be exchanged to their equivalents, to something abstract, but by no means—as traditional discussion would maintain—to something material" (GS 8, 209).[18] As is well known, this conceptual, abstract element, by virtue of which what is completely heterogeneous becomes commensurable and therefore interchangeable, is the category of value as developed by Marx in the first chapter of *Capital*. This category, which is crucial for Marx's critique of political economy, also provides the key to Adorno's understanding of the social process. "Above and beyond all specific forms of social differentiation, the abstraction implicit in the market system represents the domination of the general over the particular, of society over its captive membership" (GS 8, 13–4).[19] This offers the key to understanding how the principle of identity gains ground in the logic that governs the social process. For it is the reduction to a mere quantum of value that allows exchange to abstract from the concrete activities of human beings and reduce them to average social labor time, just as it abstracts from the concrete use values embodied in commodities, reducing them to mere magnitudes of value. The activities and needs of living individuals are thus degraded to mere instruments for the valorization of capital. This is also why Adorno refuses to follow Hegel when the latter considers identity as "the ultimate, the absolute"; identity, rather, reveals itself as "the universal apparatus of coercion" (ND 150).[20]

The principle of exchange thus "imposes on the whole world an obligation to become identical, to become total" (ND, 149).[21] In this way society literally becomes a "system," a network of interdependencies. "There is nothing socially factual which would not have its place in that totality" (GS 8, 292),[22] and thus the Hegelian doctrine of the primacy of the whole over the parts is realized. Hence the totality is, "to use Hegel's term, the ether that permeates

---

[18]Ibid., 80.

[19]Adorno, "Society," 271.

[20]Adorno, *Negative Dialectics*, 147. Translation modified.

[21]Ibid., 146.

[22]Adorno, "Introduction," *The Positivist Dispute in German Sociology*, 80.

the whole of society. However, this ether is anything but ethereal; it is, rather, the *ens realissimum*" (GS 8, 364).[23] For Adorno, however, this totality could by no means be understood as pacified and harmonious; quite the contrary. In the first place because "behind the reduction of men to agents and bearers of exchange value lies the domination of men over men" (GS 8, 14).[24] The abstract and impersonal domination of the logic of autonomized value, which has become an "in-itself" (ND, 199),[25] is made possible by class domination, by the appropriation of the labor of others, which is concealed under the guise of equivalent exchange.[26] The system is constituted through the split, the tearing apart of society. Hence the social process, the reproduction of the whole, can only occur through social antagonisms, and not, as the bien-pensants claim, in spite of them: "Society has survived, reproduced, and extended itself, and has developed its forces, only through its division into the opposing interests of those who command and those who produce" (GS 5, 317).[27] Undoubtedly, the system has not ceased to expand, but its machinery can only be maintained by "creaking and groaning on, at unspeakable human cost" (GS 8, 15).[28]

On the other hand, the social totality is not harmonious, since it reveals itself as "that which is unresolved, unreconciled with the subjects" (ND, 22).[29] To

---

[23]Adorno, "Late Capitalism or Industrial Society?," 120.

[24]Adorno, "Society," 271.

[25]Adorno, *Negative Dialectics*, 199. Translation modified.

[26]Marx revealed that, in practice, the social logic of capitalist exchange ultimately fails to fulfill the principle of the fair equivalent exchange. If equal were truly exchanged for equal, surplus value could not be explained—nor, therefore, capital itself. Behind the exchange of equivalents, the appropriation of the labor of others was concealed (MEW 23, 181–91; *Capital Volume 1*, 270). Consequently, Adorno's critique of the exchange process does not seek to return to an earlier state, based on violence or immediate appropriation; rather, he wants exchange to fulfill what it promises: "When we criticize the exchange principle as the identifying principle of thought, we want to realize the idea of free and just exchange. To date, this ideal is only a pretext. Its realization alone would transcend exchange" (ND, 150; *Negative Dialectics*, 147. Translation modified). It is a matter of realizing the principle of exchange—not as a telos that, behind the backs of the actors, turns their actions into a support for the reproduction of capital (see also LGF 237–9; *History and Freedom Lectures 1964–1965*, 170–1). On the importance of this point, see also Hans Georg Backhaus, "Adorno und die metaökonomische Kritik der positivistischen Nationalökonomie," in Andreas Gruschka and Ulrich Oevermann (eds.), *Die Lebendigkeit der kritischen Gesellschaftstheorie* (Wetzlar: Büchse der Pandora, 2004), 27–64.

[27]Adorno, *Hegel: Three Studies*, 79.

[28]Adorno, "Society," 272.

[29]Adorno, *Negative Dialectics*, 10. Translation modified.

speak of society as a "system," as a totality, refers to a form of social constitution that has autonomized itself from the individuals that compose it and keep it in motion. Thus, the concept of totality, which in Hegel was one of the terms for the absolute, referring to the process through which the spirit acts and becomes self-conscious, appears in a very different light in Adorno. Because "a seamless system and an achieved reconciliation are not one and the same; rather, they are contradictory" (GS 5, 273).[30] This social system does not allow any reconciliation between opposites—the individual and the social totality—and continually subsumes the particular under abstract universality—value, capital. The primacy of the whole is therefore produced at the expense of living individuals, at the price of coercion, anguish, and suffering. That which in Hegel appeared as the abstract and impenetrable nature of the world spirit in relation to individuals actually reveals itself as the sign of their heteronomy under the logic of capital.[31] In this sense, Adorno's negative dialectics does not accept the Hegelian notion of identity as the identity of identity and nonidentity, but asserts the rights of the nonidentical, of what is violated as a result of integration into the system. "It is the negative objectivity that is a system, not the positive subject" (ND, 31).[32] It is no coincidence that Hegel's assertion that the "true is the whole"[33] becomes Adorno's apothegm that "the whole is the false" (MM, 55).[34] Ultimately, the formation of society as a whole is flawed, since under the aegis of capital accumulation it cannot but be constituted under the sign of coercion. In the process of the maximization of value, the total social process is everything and individuals are nothing; they are "helplessly dependent on the whole" (ND, 180).[35] Hence in Adorno the category of totality is not affirmative, but fundamentally critical: "Formulated provocatively, totality is society as a thing-in-itself, with all the guilt of reification. But it is precisely because this thing-in-itself is not yet the total societal subject—nor is it yet freedom,

[30] Adorno, *Hegel: Three Studies*, 27.

[31] Zamora, *Krise–Kritik–Erinnerung*, 399.

[32] Adorno, *Negative Dialectics*, 20.

[33] Georg Wilhelm Friedrich Hegel, *Phänomenologie des Geistes. Werke 3* (Frankfurt: Suhrkamp, 1986), 22, and *The Phenomenology of Spirit*, trans. Terry Pinkard (Cambridge: Cambridge University Press, 2018), 13.

[34] Adorno, *Minima Moralia*, 50.

[35] Adorno, *Negative Dialectics*, 178.

but rather extends nature in a heteronomous manner—that an indissoluble moment is objective to it" (GS 8, 292).[36]

To speak of the whole as the "false" implies pointing out that the problem lies in the very constitution of capitalist society. This means that one cannot look for a positive principle in production or in circulation, in labor or in consumption. For this false totality encompasses production and consumption, work and leisure, public and private life, the professional and the political. This totality is not, "as healthy common sense believes, 'the whole world,' but the whole world forced into identity."[37] This is the decisive feature of Adorno's critical theory of capitalism and also that which may be of the most interest today. What is at stake in it is the critique of a form of socialization that tends to align all dimensions of existence with the criteria of the commodity form—which is tangible, for example, in his critique of the culture industry. This compulsion toward identity, which reduces all spheres of life to the homogenizing logic of the social system, in turn undermines the meaning of experience, which has its measure in the qualitatively unique, in the singular (IG, 72). In the consummated world of the commodity, there are no singularities, only embodiments of economic functions: use value as the bearer of exchange value, concrete labor as the manifestation of social labor, and the individual as an embodiment of social functions. However, unlike in idealism, the resulting totality is no longer the absolute and is therefore not seen as an insurmountable horizon, but as something open to transformation. In fact, "dialectical critique seeks to salvage or help establish what does not obey totality, what opposes it, or what first forms itself as the potential of a not yet existing individuation" (GS 8, 292).[38] Totality is no longer the unfolding of spirit, but the coercive integration of more and more dimensions of social life under the formal logic of value valorization; in other words, it is not a positive totality, but a negative one. For this reason, contrary to Hegel, the goal would not be to realize totality, but to abolish it. Only in this way could a liberated society be achieved.

---

[36]Adorno, "Introduction," *The Positivist Dispute in German Sociology*, 12.
[37]Gerhard Scheit, *Quälbarer Leib: Kritik der Gesellschaft nach Adorno* [Freiburg: ça ira, 2016]), 57.
[38]Adorno, "Introduction," *The Positivist Dispute in German Sociology*, 12.

However, at the historical moment when Adorno was writing, some of the certainties that had sustained confidence in the possibility of emancipation in the thought of Marx or, in his wake, in that of Lukács, could no longer be counted on. It could no longer be assumed that this totality, in its unfolding, would necessarily produce its own gravediggers: the proletariat, which in *History and Class Consciousness* still appeared as a unity of subject and object, theory and praxis. In Adorno, this assumption is no longer tenable. First, because it involves siding once again with a constituent part of the "false" whole—namely, the sphere of production and labor. Moreover, this perspective overlooks the coercive nature of labor in capitalism, by which the individual worker can scarcely experience the use value of their labor power as an expression of their own identity. On the other hand, the increasingly oppressive and hermetic nature of the social system no longer allowed for the salvific role that the proletariat had had in Lukács, as its actual position in the societies of the twentieth century did not enable it to transcend the whole or offer a way out. As a result, it was no longer possible to rely on the possibility of challenging negative totality by invoking the "point of view" of a preexisting social group that, by virtue of its position and function within the system, could break the spell.

However, in the absence of a global social subject, the constitution of the social whole remains inverted. The social process does not arise from the organized will of freely associated individuals, but instead follows the blind logic of what Marx called the "automatic subject" (MEW 23, 169).[39] This formulation referred to a desubjectivized subject that was nothing but value itself, which valorizes itself through the social process. Here one could read an inversion of the Hegelian figure of the absolute spirit as subject, which recalls Adorno's understanding of *Capital* as a kind of "phenomenology of the anti-spirit" (*Phänomenologie des Widergeistes*) (ND, 349).[40] However, for anyone with a reasonably attuned philosophical ear, the Marxian reference to the "automatic subject" can only be interpreted as an ironic term; strictly speaking, it is an oxymoron. The philosophical category of the subject, associated with

[39]Marx, *Capital Volume 1*, 255.
[40]Adorno, *Negative Dialectics*, 356.

freedom and autonomy, appears here as the blind compulsion of what is, in principle, a pure abstraction: value. Living individuals, on the other hand, are reduced to the position of "involuntary executors" of the law of value (ND, 259).[41] On this point, Adorno had pointed out "the universal domination of mankind by the exchange value ... which a priori keeps the subjects from being subjects" (ND, 180).[42] Value, of course, does not exist on its own: it requires the action of individuals who, atomized and embedded in a social nexus they do not comprehend, act according to the principle of absolutized self-preservation. For this reason, he also asserts that, regardless of what one thinks or feels, "the living individual person, such as he is constrained to act and for which he was even internally molded, is as *homo oeconomicus* incarnate closer to the transcendental subject than the living individual he must immediately take himself to be" (GS 10.2, 745).[43] This highly provocative statement brings the relationship of identity and nonidentity between empirical individuals and social subjects into sharp relief. As subjects, "individuals perform unconsciously for the whole, under which they suffer as strangers to one another and as in themselves contradictory" (GS 2, 245).[44]

In this same sense, Marx had pointed out that when individuals act within the framework of capitalist socialization—whether as capitalists or as workers, as producers or as consumers—they do not do so as individuals, but as "personifications of economic categories" (MEW 23, 16).[45] In so doing, he addressed the problem of agency. In order to reproduce their life and their position within the social system, individuals have to embody certain roles, which determine the logic of their action in the network of objective mediations. In this sense, they are like mere "component parts of machinery" (MM, 13).[46] However, Adorno, who at this point wants to think the dialectic between the individual and social totality through to its ultimate consequences, does not believe that this implies denying all substance to individual action.

[41] Ibid., 262.
[42] Ibid., 178.
[43] Adorno, "On Subject and Object," 248.
[44] Theodor W. Adorno, "Kierkegaard Once More," trans. Jensen Suther, *Telos* 174 (Spring 2016), 62.
[45] Marx, *Capital: Volume 1*, 179. Translation modified.
[46] Adorno, *Minima Moralia*, 15.

The social field of forces from which the totality emerges does not lie in the fact that the logic of capital restricts individual action, for it depends entirely on such action; rather, it channels it to its own advantage. By virtue of its autonomization from the human beings who sustain it, the social process of capital reproduction has become opaque, but it is realized only through the actions of individuals. The social whole would not exist without the mediation of individual subjects: "the process by which it is maintained is, of course, the process of life, of labor, of production and reproduction, which is kept in motion by the individuals socialized within the society" (ES, 69–70).[47] The problem is that the origin of the autonomized social forms analyzed by Marx in his critique of political economy—value, money, labor, and capital—is no longer recognized as rooted in the very praxis of individuals. As a result, these forms become "second nature." In this sense, Adorno understood materialism as "anamnesis of genesis."[48]

Accordingly, the reference to the "automatic subject" is above all ironic. Because the unconscious process through which it is constituted is forgotten, the social form of value appears as autonomized and endowed with the attributes of a subject. However, this appearance should not be hypostatized. It is not that living individuals are reduced to mere puppets. Rather, the valorization process of capital manages to impose itself insofar as it allows individuals to assert themselves as subjects within the domains of their functional socialization—work, consumption, and competition. Here, capitalism offers channels for personal fulfillment in work or subjectivation through consumption; thus, subjects do not experience their roles solely as something alien, but may come to identify with them entirely. However, these roles circumscribe the scope of their freedom: even where individuals act as free subjects, the meaning of their action is prescribed for them and—in the final analysis—is not in their interest as subjects, but in the interest of the reproduction of capital. For Adorno this reveals a "structural mechanism of society which trains them to pure self-preservation at the same time that it denies them preservation of their Selves"

[47] Adorno, *Introduction to Sociology*, 38.

[48] Cf. "Notizen von einem Gespräch zwischen Th. W. Adorno und A. Sohn-Rethel," in Albert Sohn-Rethel, *Warenform und Denkform* (Frankfurt: Suhrkamp, 1978), 139.

(GS 8, 13).[49] Adorno's entire social theory is grounded in the awareness that the autonomized logic of the "automatic subject," however much it succeeds in mobilizing the action and desires of socialized individuals, ultimately involves a form of domination that inflicts suffering and proves sacrificial for living subjects.

Capitalism as "Natural History"

According to what we have seen so far, Adorno's critique of capitalism is not primarily a critique of exploitation. It is not based solely on the denunciation of material oppression or social injustice, which Adorno in no way denies or downplays. Instead, it shows that the capitalist network of socialization constitutes a very specific mode of heteronomy, of unfreedom. However, freedom is not understood here as an attribute of isolated individuals in the sense in which liberal theory understood it, reducing it to free will or freedom from whom or freedom for what. It has to do with the constitution of social relations, with the shaping of society as a whole. Marx had detected the key to understanding the anatomy of modern society in the field of economics and had stated that the aim of *Capital* was "to reveal the economic law of motion of modern society" (MEW 23, 15–6).[50] Society was thus understood as something inherently dynamic and processual, and its logic appeared to be governed by economic processes that impose their own logic. That is why Adorno stated that individuals primarily experience society "as something nonidentical, as 'coercion'" (GS 8, 12).[51] This coercive character of social mediations is due to the fact that individuals depend on the social whole in order to guarantee their subsistence, and that is why everyday experiences such as difficulties in finding a decent job or being forced to take out a loan are, for Adorno, moments in which society as such becomes palpable (ES, 65–6).[52] It is no coincidence that the distinctive feature of modern forms of socialization consisted "in the

---

[49] Adorno, "Society," 270. Translation modified.

[50] Marx, *Capital: Volume 1*, 92.

[51] Adorno, "Society," 270.

[52] Adorno, *Introduction to Sociology*, 36.

predominance of relations over human beings, the latter coming little by little to be the incapacitated products of the former" (GS 8, 9).[53]

Indeed, for Adorno, if anything explains the logic of modern socialization, it is the autonomization of the social system from the subjects who produce and reproduce it; Marx's concept of the "automatic subject" already alluded to this. In multiple passages of *Capital*, Marx does not hesitate to employ ironic turns of phrase that clearly allude to an inverted social constitution, in which people themselves become things and things become subjects of the social process.[54] That was the *quid pro quo* already implied in the problem of fetishism. All this underscores a specific social condition of heteronomy, one that denies living individuals any form of self-determination. However, the primacy of the maximization of value, of the accumulation of capital, did not stem from an ontological necessity in the organization of human communities, but rather from the specific features of the capitalist social constitution. Ultimately, the socializing logic of capital is based on an inversion between means and ends, between production and the satisfaction of needs. The purpose of production is none other than profitability—in the end the accumulation of capital—while the needs of living subjects "that were potentially functions of the production apparatus have now become such functions in fact, rather than the production apparatus becoming a function of human needs" (GS 8, 361).[55] Production is not arranged in the interests of the socialized individuals, but they must take "what the production line spews out" (LGF, 12).[56] In other words, "The consumers serve the process of production" (GS 11, 144).[57] In the form of sociality constituted by capital, all the ends of human life "become means to a single end: the accumulation of value."[58]

---

[53]Adorno, "Society," 267. Translation modified.

[54]It suffices to mention, by way of example, a passage from *Capital*: "If commodities could speak, they would say this: our use-value may interest men, but it does not belong to us as objects. What does belong to us as objects, however, is our value. Our own intercourse as commodities proves it. We relate to each other merely as exchange values" (MEW 23, 97; *Capital Volume 1*, 176–7). Cf. also MEW 23, 99ff; *Capital Volume 1*, 180.

[55]Adorno, "Late Capitalism or Industrial Society?," 117.

[56]Adorno, *History and Freedom*, 6.

[57]Adorno, "Reading Balzac," *Notes to Literature 2*, 125.

[58]Scheit, *Quälbarer Leib*, 39.

Adorno had already addressed the absurdity of a social system that subsumes life and, along with it, human needs under the demands of capital accumulation at the beginning of *Minima Moralia*. The satisfaction of needs, which is what should justify production, becomes secondary (MM, 13).[59] In this sense Adorno speaks of a "world of unleashed production that forgets its human aims," as "the insatiable and destructive expansive principle of the exchange society" (GS 5, 274). And the fact is that, under the law of the maximization of value, the systemic functionality of exchange does not reside in the use value of the products exchanged, but in their character as embodiments of value. It can thus be affirmed that "exchange value, merely a mental configuration when compared with use value, dominates human needs and replaces them" (GS 8, 209).[60] Undoubtedly, in this social formation, formally free individuals act and exchange based on their interests and in order to satisfy needs; however, through their action and outside their conscious awareness, what prevails is the reproduction of capital. This is why Adorno affirms that they are "the objects and not the subjects of the social process that as subjects they nevertheless sustain" (GS 8, 358).[61] It is their "free" activity that makes them executors of the logic of the "automatic subject." But this freedom is not enough for them to determine their living conditions: only by complying with the logic of value valorization, proving themselves functional to it, will they succeed in satisfying their needs. This is how the logic of the system reduces them to agents of the reproduction of capital and converts the entire life of the majority of the population into a struggle for self-preservation, which barely allows them to articulate horizons that go beyond it. The abstraction of the value form thus becomes a real form of social domination, even more so than any other institution (GS 8, 365).[62] It is no coincidence that Marx had referred to capitalism as "a social formation in which the process of production has mastery over man, instead of the opposite" (MEW 23, 95–6).[63]

---

[59]Adorno, *Minima Moralia*, 15.

[60]Adorno, "Sociology and Empirical Research," *The Positivist Dispute in German Sociology*, 80.

[61]Adorno, "Late Capitalism and Industrial Society," 115.

[62]Ibid., 120.

[63]Marx, *Capital Volume 1*, 175.

In the capitalist constitution of society, the total social process, with its enormous increase in productive capacities, can seem "virtually omnipotent"; but the individual, reduced to a mere agent of the production process, proves himself to be "completely impotent and insignificant" (GS 5, 290).[64] Autonomization designates the fact that structures that have originated in social praxis impose themselves upon—and stand opposed to—the very individuals who set them in motion. This, in fact, was based on Marx's analysis of commodity fetishism, in which the problem of the autonomization, inversion, and naturalization of social relations converge. Marx had revealed that commodities themselves harbor social relations, which are the product of the activity of individuals and thus acquire a "thinglike" character. These relations have no other form of expression outside commodities, and therefore appear to emanate from the commodities themselves. In reality, it is only by virtue of these social relations that objects acquire the form of commodities and become embodiments of value. However, insofar as value, which is nothing but a social relation, appears as an attribute of the things themselves, commodities become "sensuous things which are at the same time suprasensible or social" (MEW 23, 86).[65] What is in fact the result of a given configuration of social relations appears instead as a pseudo-natural quality of objects, independent of any human agency. As Lukács pointed out, the consequence of this process of reification would be that a world of things and reified relations—the world of commodities—confronts the subject "as an invincible power, autonomous in its activity." The product of human labor thus dominates the individual "through laws alien to the human."[66]

The influence of this Lukácsian analysis on Adorno's own approaches is undeniable.[67] Through it, the commodity form can be understood as an increasingly dominant phenomenon in social life, and indeed as a determining factor for the constitution of social objectivity and of living subjects themselves. However, in his *Negative Dialectics*, Adorno explicitly rejected the notion that

---

[64]Adorno, *Hegel: Three Studies*, 46.

[65]Marx, *Capital Volume 1*, 165.

[66]Lukács, *History and Class Consciousness*, 87. Translation modified.

[67]Insightful and succinct commentary on some of Adorno's underlining and reading notes from *History and Class Consciousness* can be found in Braunstein, *Adorno's Critique of Political Economy*, 9–14.

critical theory can be formulated in Lukács's terms. That would imply reducing the problem of social constitution to a phenomenon of consciousness. It is true that Lukács does not consider reification so much the fruit of a "false consciousness," but rather something derived from the very form of social constitution based on exchange.[68] Nevertheless, reification was understood as "the reflexive form of false objectivity" and therefore as "a form of consciousness" (ND, 191).[69] Hence for Lukács the possibility of social transformation depended on awareness: on the proletariat breaking away from the manner it perceives the reality of capital. He assumed that, as soon as the worker recognizes himself as a mere object of the social process, "the fetishistic forms of the commodity structure 'begin' to crumble." However, this means that "Lukács postulates an identity between theory and action founded on knowledge."[70] For Adorno, this identification entails the danger of a relapse into idealism. Although the social constitution has an impact on consciousness, this does not imply that the mere awareness of the social relations of domination can crack the social structure. Reification is not only a problem of consciousness, of the "form of reflection," but fundamentally of "false objectivity," of an inverted social constitution. Consequently, to postulate that the consciousness of the proletariat, as the "identical subject-object of the social and historical processes of evolution,"[71] will succeed in breaking away from the blind and iniquitous character of the social constitution may neutralize the problem at the theoretical level, but it does not solve it in practice. The solution offered is purely speculative. This is why Adorno stresses that "what people suffer under is now more likely to be passed over in the lament about reification than denounced. The evil lies in the conditions that condemn human beings to impotence and apathy and yet could be changed by them; not primarily in people themselves or in the way these conditions appear to them" (ND, 191).[72] This formulation acknowledges that the problem posed by Lukács is central, pointing to fundamental aporias

---

[68] Lukács, *History and Class Consciousness*, 100.

[69] Adorno, *Negative Dialectics*, 190.

[70] José Antonio Zamora, "Materialidad espectral, subjetivación y crítica inmanente del fetichismo," in *Crítica inmanente de la sociedad*, ed. José Manuel Romero (Barcelona: Anthropos, 2020), 181–2.

[71] Lukács, *History and Class Consciousness*, 197.

[72] Adorno, *Negative Dialectics*, 190. Translation modified.

in the social constitution. However, Adorno rejects the fiction that they can be resolved through a merely speculative solution.

In the same vein, Max Horkheimer, in one of the aphorisms from his book *Dämmerung*, had already pointed out that "there are many agents but no conscious and therefore free subjects of social conditions. Human beings must submit to conditions they themselves constantly create as to something alien and overwhelmingly powerful" (HGS 2, 361–2).[73] This idea, which is central for Adorno, connects with Marx's assertion—which was extremely influential also for Lukács's analysis—that capitalist socialization would be a sphere governed by "natural laws" "winning their way through and working themselves out with iron necessity" (MEW 23, 12).[74] The social system of capital appears to be governed by structural laws that have not been deliberately and consciously established, but which govern the logic of the autonomized social process and impose themselves on the individuals acting within it. In fact, the entire preface to the first edition of *Capital* is riddled with flirtations with the language and procedures of natural science, even though what is at stake is a social formation and its historical dimension. How should this be understood? The coercive and pseudo-natural character of the laws that govern the functioning of capitalist society evidences its state of unfreedom. At the same time, Adorno points out again that the blind objectivity that subjugates individuals is imposed through their action: "under the aspect of freedom, necessity stays heteronomous even though predesigned by the autonomous subject" (ND, 338 n.).[75] Yet these laws lend the social realm the appearance of being governed by the same necessity as natural processes, determined by causal mechanisms that no conscious agent is in a position to alter. Of course, Marxian theory sought to show that the supposedly unavoidable necessity of these "natural" laws should not be taken at face value.[76] This "legality is real as a law of motion for the unconscious

[73]Max Horkheimer, *Dawn and Decline*, 51. Translation modified.

[74]Marx, *Capital Volume 1*, 91.

[75]Adorno, *Negative Dialectics*, 345.

[76]"There is a contradiction here: on the one hand, Marx speaks with the scientist's passion of the inexorable laws of nature, in particular of the evolution of the laws of economics. At the same time, however, these laws are shown to be a mystification, an illusion. It is this twin-tracked attitude that provides the key to understanding Marxism as a critical theory, and not the thesis of the natural laws governing society that we need to understand if we are to gain a hold on them" (LGF 170; *History and Freedom*, 117–18).

society" (ND, 349),[77] for the autonomized social system, but its apparent necessity is deceptive. Because "the predominance of economics is not an invariant" (ND, 190).[78] Ultimately, its validity depends on the configuration of social life and, therefore, "the laws of nature [are] capable of being abrogated" (LGF, 167).[79] However, as long as autonomized social objectivity persists and social transformation has not occurred, individuals will not be masters of the conditions necessary to reproduce their lives and their freedom will be reduced to a choice: either submit to market laws or face economic ruin and social marginalization. The heteronomy inscribed in the very constitution of modern societies is manifest in this mute compulsion, which leads "the constitutive forms of socialization" to assert "their absolute supremacy over mankind as if they were divine Providence" (ND 349).[80]

Of major importance for Adorno on this point is the passage in the preface to the first book of *Capital* in which Marx refers to the "development of the economic formation of society" as a "process of natural history" (MEW 23, 16).[81] Here, the analogy with the natural sciences no longer refers solely to the functioning of the mechanisms of the social process, but also to its historical development and evolution. Thus, this notion of capitalism as "natural history" can be understood in the deterministic sense of both the Marxism of the Second International and so-called dialectical materialism, which regard historical movements as governed by laws that ensure capitalist development will inevitably lead to the establishment of socialism. But the passage can also be interpreted in a different, critical sense, and this is how Adorno reads it (ND 347–51).[82] From this perspective, this allusion to "natural history" would, above all, be opposed to human history, that is, conceived as antithetical to the free agency of a conscious and organized will. Its meaning was to be understood in accordance with Marx's observation that capitalism was still a phase—the last one, Marx hoped, with the incorrigible optimism of the

[77]Adorno, *Negative Dialectics*, 355–6.
[78]Ibid., 190. Translation modified.
[79]Adorno, *History and Freedom*, 115.
[80]Adorno, *Negative Dialectics*, 356.
[81]Marx, *Capital Volume 1*, 92.
[82]Adorno, *Negative Dialectics*, 354–8.

nineteenth century—of the "pre-history of human society" (MEW 13, 9).[83] To speak of contemporary society as prehistory was undoubtedly a provocation. It was intended to show that the development of capitalist socialization, like all preceding history, was governed by a necessity that constrains human agency and is antithetical to freedom (GS 8, 234).[84] The historical dynamics of capitalist societies are governed by a model of social synthesis—abstract labor—which "is not yet the total societal subject—not yet freedom, but rather extends nature in a heteronomous manner" (GS 8 292).[85] The social whole is not governed by the conscious will of a collective subject, but blindly and relentlessly follows its own course through crises and the class antagonism. The concept of prehistory therefore refers to the unconscious character of the social process, but also to its implacable and brutal dimension, which, despite the guarantees of law and formal equality, does not prevent its logic from being sustained by violent appropriation, and ultimately by asymmetrical power relations and the use of force. Hence Adorno's assertion: "Human history, the history of progressive mastery over nature, is a continuation of the unconscious history of nature, of devouring and being devoured" (ND 348–9).[86]

When Marx used the concepts of natural history, prehistory, and fetishism—all in a distinctly ironic tone—he was referring to the sore point of a mode of social constitution marked by heteronomy. The subject of this social process would not be a conscious human agency, but rather capital as an "automatic subject." These concepts aimed to subvert the self-portrayal of modern society as the champion of freedom, civilization, and rationality. This ironic subversion also underpins the way in which Adorno's critical theory confronts hyper-rationalized societies, where the very engine of their progress drives them to sink back into mythology. For Adorno —closely aligned not only with Marx on this point but also with Walter Benjamin—capitalism perpetuates an ongoing entrapment in a mythical spell that subjugates human agency and, along with it, history, turning it into inexorable fate. To understand this requires grasping the peculiar dialectic set in motion by capitalist

[83]Marx, "'Preface' to the Critique of Political Economy," *Later Political Writings*, 161.
[84]Adorno, "'Static' and 'Dynamic' as Sociological Categories," 45.
[85]Adorno, "Introduction," *The Positivist Dispute in German Sociology*, 12. Translation modified.
[86]Adorno, *Negative Dialectics*, 355.

development. On the one hand, undoubtedly, its mode of production enables an enormous development of productive forces, allowing human communities to achieve increasing independence from the harshness and constraints of nature. However, since the social organization of production is subordinated to the blind process of capital valorization, capitalism does not break free from natural coercion; instead, it gives rise to a new realm of necessity: a second nature. In it, "authority, bondage, suffering, and ever-present catastrophe" (GS 8, 234)[87] continue to be reproduced as seemingly ineluctable elements of social life.

Although Marx pointed out that every aspect of life in modern society is marked by transformation and perpetual movement—the development of productive forces, the erosion of preexisting social forms, and the growing dynamization of social life—in spite of this, throughout "the transitoriness of its forms and structures" (GS 8, 232–3),[88] the social system does not budge. Modern society persists in prehistory. Coercion, however, no longer stems from the overpowering force of first nature but rather from the autonomized dynamics of a highly integrated social framework. The demands of this framework impose themselves with a mute yet relentless coercion. This creates a blind necessity that dominates society, compelling individuals to live their social existence as an inescapable fate. Its irrational and coercive character is particularly evident during crises. For Adorno, therefore, placing hopes of putting an end to prehistory in the mere increase of productive capacities no longer appeared to be a viable option. In a social formation in which productive activity can only be understood as heteronomous activity, as an end in itself, the understanding of labor as the primary path to emancipation proved untenable; instead, emancipation had to be understood as "liberation from heteronomous labor" (GS 8, 363),[89] seen as a fundamental node of social domination in capitalism.

> The conception of unfettered activity, of uninterrupted doing, of plump insatiability, of freedom as frantic bustle, feeds on the bourgeois concept

---

[87]Adorno, "'Static' and 'Dynamic' as Sociological Categories," 46.

[88]Ibid., 44.

[89]Adorno, "Late Capitalism or Industrial Society?," 119.

> of nature that has always served solely to proclaim social violence as unchangeable, as a piece of healthy eternity. … It is not man's lapse into luxurious indolence that is to be feared, but the savage spread of the social under the mask of universal nature, the collective as a blind fury of production. (MM, 178)[90]

This notion clearly echoes Benjamin's thesis that revolution could no longer be understood as a "locomotive of world history," but rather as an "emergency brake" (BGS I, 1232);[91] indeed, only a break from the blind development of history as mere natural history would rightfully deserve the name of progress (GS 8, 233).[92]

From this perspective on the historical dynamics of capitalist societies, it can no longer be assumed that the realm of freedom will arrive on its own, as something "necessary," as the "natural" development of things allows its objective conditions to mature. On the contrary, emancipation will consist in breaking with society and history as spheres of "necessity," of heteronomy, and in finally overcoming prehistory (LGF 170–1).[93] In Adorno's social theory, this implies much more than transforming the mode of production. Adorno was facing a more advanced stage in the process of capitalist socialization and had to reckon with a level of social integration that was much higher than anything Marx had known. More and more dimensions of existence—from labor to consumption, from production to leisure time, from consciousness to the unconscious—were increasingly subject to the logic of the social constitution. In this ever-expanding social system, whose coercive nature reduces individual agency to a mere function and gives rise to powerlessness and fear, freedom cannot be understood as something "given" or already in place. Because, for Adorno, freedom is not reduced to the free will of each individual, for example, in their choices of consumption or in the way they compete. It cannot be understood as something that springs spontaneously from the individual consciousness. Freedom is not an attribute of the subject,

---

[90]Adorno, *Minima Moralia*, 156.
[91]Benjamin, "Paralipomena to 'On the Concept of History,'" 402.
[92]Adorno, "'Static' and 'Dynamic' as Sociological Categories," 44.
[93]Adorno, *History and Freedom*, 118.

nor a starting point, but something that can only be grasped as a result. In this sense it is "something that must be brought about" (LGF, 167).[94] Individuals are not born free but become free by acting upon what determines them. This involves intervening in the social logic that reduces subjects to mere objects of the social process. Freedom will then be something that is achieved and realized through action. It refers to the outcome of the emancipatory process and is therefore linked to an objective situation, rather than being the inalienable patrimony of living subjects: "Only in a free society would individuals be free" (ND, 261).[95]

The issue is that the social transformation needed to break this heteronomy would require a global social subject, which, for Adorno, cannot be assumed to exist within the "false totality." Social synthesis operates as a blind process; individuals, for their part, act consciously, but in an atomized way, as mere monads. This is why Adorno states that "To this day history lacks any total subject, however construable. Its substrate is the functional connection of real individual subjects" (ND, 299).[96] For Marx, despite his reference to value as the "automatic subject" of the social process, the question of the subject of history still had a clear answer: it was the proletariat. The latter had to bear all the injustices of the social system, and, in principle, this condition of shared oppression made it possible for proletarians to organize and engage in revolutionary struggles. However, Adorno could no longer count on a "given" subject to promote the movement toward social emancipation. The painful experiences of the twentieth century revealed that the proletariat had been integrated. It was no longer in an exterritorial position, and its insertion into the system of employment and consumption had brought it to a position where it had "more to lose than its chains" (GS 8, 384).[97] Indeed, the development of productive forces had improved their living and working conditions, they had coverage protecting them in case of illness or old age, and the advances of industrial society offered them forms of consumption and

---

[94]Ibid., 116. Translation modified.

[95]Adorno, *Negative Dialectics*, 264. Translation modified.

[96]Ibid., 304.

[97]Adorno, "Reflections on Class Theory," 103.

leisure that allowed them to feel like an active part of the new social order. But that was not all: "The deeper reason is that the proletariat is not constituted as a class at the subjective level. One cannot fake a class consciousness that does not exist."[98] Under the forms of socialization of advanced capitalism, the proletariat was defined solely in objective terms, by its position within the capitalist framework of "natural history." It thus remained a figure of the realm of necessity, as traditional Marxism ratified, when it claimed that proletarian consciousness had to rise to the level of its "historical mission." In contrast, for Adorno, the subject of history—meaning the agent capable of transcending prehistory—cannot be based on objective, heteronomous determinations. Instead, it must arise from subjective spontaneity and the impulse to break free from coercion. However, such a collective subject cannot be assumed to exist within capitalist socialization: it must be produced. This marks a major turning point from the certainties upon which Marx still relied: "The emancipation of society from the supremacy of its relations of production has as its aim the real production of the subject that these relations have to date impeded" (AT, 178).[99]

Of course, Adorno's critical theory can do little more than proclaim the necessity of such a subject. This seemed more urgent than ever: not only to make freedom possible but also, in Adorno's historical moment, to avert "the most extreme, total disaster" (GS 10.2, 618).[100] Yet this collective, spontaneous, and conscious subject, which sometimes appears in his writings in the form of a utopian concept that is still a mere abstraction—"humanity" (GS 8, 56)[101]—poses a problem to which theory cannot respond solely in a speculative manner. The development of such a subject is a matter of political praxis, and it has to be forged under the given social conditions—which, in Adorno's historical moment, as in ours, were rather unfavorable. Indeed, for theory to be truly critical, it cannot rely on itself alone; it always depends on its object: society.

---

[98] Adorno, "Notizen über Eisler," 127.

[99] Adorno, *Aesthetic Theory*, 117. Translation modified.

[100] Adorno, "Progress," 144.

[101] Adorno, "Sociology and Psychology. Part I," *New German Critique*, I/46 (November (December 1967), 78.

In the evolution of society, as social power becomes increasingly concentrated and atomized individuals grow ever more powerless, Adorno observed a gradual numbing in moments of spontaneity among living subjects (GS 10.2, 632).[102] This was the critical moment that, in his view, led to the stagnation of praxis.

So far, we have explored the core aspects of Adorno's understanding of capitalism, largely shaped by his distinctive interpretation of Marx's critique of political economy. However, even within this framework, his theory possesses a "temporal core"—an experiential dimension that refers to specific sociohistorical transformations. Capitalism is not a static social formation. Although it is always governed by the blind logic of the valorization of capital, capitalism itself has a historical dynamic. It "must expand in order to survive" (GS 8, 335),[103] and in this way its socializing logic gains ground in both extension and intensity. In so doing, it transforms not only the outward appearance of the world, but also social objectivity and subjectivity as such. For this reason, the main efforts of Adorno's critical theory focused on elucidating the specific phase of "prehistory" that it was his lot to live through. It is in the social transformations that took place in the central decades of the twentieth century that capitalism becomes, for Adorno, a "radically socialized society" and can thus be recognized as a "system" in the strict sense, "satanically" realizing what Hegel had foreseen (GS 5, 273–4).[104] Hence the importance of understanding how Adorno analyzes the implications of these sociohistorical transformations, particularly in his writings of the 1950s and 1960s. In these texts, the contours of a social fabric that no longer admits any "outside" are outlined. This no longer merely meant explaining the laws governing the process of social autonomization, as Marx (and, in his wake, Lukács) had done, but rather illustrating its social reality in a qualitatively transformed sociohistorical situation.[105]

---

[102] Adorno, "Progress," 155.

[103] Adorno, "Introduction," *The Positivist Dispute in German Sociology*, 51.

[104] Adorno, *Hegel: Three Studies*, 27.

[105] Lars Meyer, *Absoluter Wert und allgemeiner Wille* (Bielefeld: Transcript, 2005), 19.

A Social Whole with No Outside: "Total Socialization"

Adorno's critical theory aspires to carry out an immanent critique of society that accounts for the expansion of a network of functional socialization under capitalist criteria. The tendency toward "total socialization" was therefore not the result of the advance of "instrumental reason," as is sometimes assumed, but of the inherently expansive logic of capitalist socialization, which tends to impose the principles of what Adorno called the "exchange society" in a universal and inexorable manner: "To preserve itself, to remain the same, to 'be', [capitalist society] must constantly expand, go beyond itself, advance its frontiers, not respect any limit, not remain the same" (ND, 37).[106] In Adorno's writings, there are many accounts indicating that the defining characteristic of the society of his time was that the framework of functional socialization had become total: nothing escaped its mediation. "The more relentlessly socialization commands all moments of human and interhuman immediacy, the smaller the capacity of men to recall that this web has evolved, and the more irresistible its natural appearance" (ND 351).[107] This entailed new difficulties for any critical theory of society. It was no longer possible to postulate a point of view outside of the social whole. Even the proletariat was no longer in a condition of exterritoriality, since it had become completely integrated into society through work and consumption. "It is no longer possible to adopt a vantage point outside the hurly-burly that would enable us to give the horror a name; we are forced to adopt its inconsistencies as our starting point" (GS 8, 369).[108] Adorno was aware that critical theory lived on the dialectic between identity and nonidentity in the social process. Now, in the face of the advance of a tendentially all-embracing logic of socialization, where could it be located?

In the introduction to *The Positivist Dispute in German Sociology*, near the end of his life, Adorno spoke of capitalist society as a system "which virtually seals itself off" and tolerates nothing qualitatively different (GS 8, 342).[109]

---

[106]Adorno, *Negative Dialectics*, 26. Translation modified.

[107]Ibid., 357–8.

[108]Adorno, "Late Capitalism or Industrial Society?," 124.

[109]Adorno, "Introduction," *The Positivist Dispute in German Sociology*, 57.

Even rudimentary and precapitalist enclaves—such as the family—that persisted within social life, had become necessary components of the stable reproduction of the whole, and therefore could no longer be considered exotic.[110] The fundamental issue here is that there is no longer an outside, and all members of society, including critical theorists, are part of that "false" whole. "The integration of society has increased, in the sense of a growing socialization; the social fabric has become more and more tightly woven, and there are ever fewer areas, ever fewer spheres of so-called subjectivity that are not more or less taken over quite directly by society" (PETG, 106).[111] Even the development of productive forces no longer seemed capable of challenging the relations of production, since production itself had been totally subordinated to them. Yet this totality, subjected to the dictates of capitalist socialization, could not be explained solely in terms of classical liberal market logic. In the decades of the so-called postwar "economic miracles" fostered by the state intervention of Fordism, the functioning of the social machinery was not only based on the expansion of what Adorno calls the "logic of exchange," but also on the rise of the "administered world." This was a process of vertical integration, characterized by logics of concentration, centralization, and standardization in which both the organization of labor and advertising played a role, as well as the mass media and the growing capacity for planning on the part of those who held economic and political power. The social apparatuses of production, distribution, and consciousness formation seemed to merge into a compact and seamless whole (PETG, 208).[112] Thus, a world emerged that was as logically compact as it was bereft of sense (GS 10.1, 268).[113] In short, the web of socialization had become denser because "the growing concentration of the economy, the executive and the bureaucracy has advanced to such an extent that people are reduced more and more to the status of functions" (LGF, 11–2).[114]

---

[110]Institut für Sozialforschung (ed.), *Soziologische Exkurse: Nach Vorträgen und Diskussionen* (Frankfurt: Europäische Verlagsanstalt, 1956), 35.

[111]Adorno, *Philosophical Elements of a Theory of Society*, trans. Wieland Hoban (London: Polity Press, 2019) 64.

[112]Adorno, *Philosophical Elements of a Theory of Society*, 135.

[113]Adorno, "Notes on Kafka," 256.

[114]Adorno, *History and Freedom*, 5.

For Adorno, this situation made it increasingly difficult to develop a coherent and seamless theory of the social logic of advanced capitalism: "Marx had it easier in this respect, since the developed system of liberal economics was available to him. He needed only to inquire whether capitalism fit into this system in order to produce a quasi-systematic theory of his own, in determinate negation of the system he found before him" (GS 8, 359).[115] On the other hand, Marx himself had distinguished between the "mute compulsion of economic relations" (MEW 23, 765)[116]—that is, the "normal" functioning of capital mediated by the commodity form and the logic of exchange—and the forms of coercion and extra-economic violence that could be exercised in certain circumstances, and to which the genesis of the social system was ultimately due (MEW 23, 741–4).[117] As discussed in the previous chapter, Adorno's diagnosis seems to point to the fact that, in advanced capitalism, direct forms of coercion by an increasingly concentrated social power were added to the tacit coercion of the logic of the "automatic subject" mediated by the process of exchange: through the intervention of monopolies, rackets, large business conglomerates, and the state itself. With this, the rules of the economic process seem to change: it can no longer be explained by individual initiative and laissez faire but is increasingly marked by a growing concentration of power and capital that has reached such dimensions that it almost appears "as the expression of society as a whole" (GS 8, 380).[118] In this regard, Adorno goes so far as to affirm: "those were still good times, when a critique of the political economy of this society could be written that judged it in terms of its own *ratio*. For since then the society has thrown its *ratio* on the scrap heap and replaced it with virtually unmediated control" (GS 11, 284).[119]

However, as has already been pointed out, this does not imply that the economy has taken a back seat. If the mechanisms of administration and management are gaining ground, it is as a consequence of the expansion of the socializing logic of capital (GS 8, 125).[120] The criterion of the valorization

[115] Adorno, "Late Capitalism or Industrial Society?," 115.
[116] Marx, *Capital Volume 1*, 899.
[117] Ibid., 873–6.
[118] Adorno, "Reflections on Class Theory," 99.
[119] Adorno, "Trying to Understand *Endgame*," *Notes to Literature 2*, 244. Translation modified.
[120] Adorno, "Culture and Administration," *The Culture Industry*, 110.

of value continues to be the eye of the needle through which everything must pass: society is now more than ever dominated by the laws of the economy.[121] In any case, the intertwining of life's subsumption under the logic of the "automatic subject" with the mechanisms of the "administered world" brings the antagonism between power and social impotence to extreme tension. Human needs were reduced to functions of the productive apparatus, especially in the most profitable sectors, and often at the expense of basic needs such as housing (GS 8, 361).[122] In short, individuals were becoming mere objects of planning and management. Their individuality seemed designed to make them fit into target groups, whether for consumer or political marketing. In this process, the "impenetrability and painfully alien character" (GS 8, 240) of the social for living subjects became increasingly intense; its overtly coercive nature reinforced the experience of unfreedom. In this sense it is stated that it is "the desperate impotence of every single individual" that "now verifies Hegel's extravagant conception of the system" (GS 5, 274).[123] Hence Adorno repeatedly diagnosed that the increasing rationalization of social processes coincided with a manifest objective irrationality of the whole (PETG, 201).[124] Due to these critiques, it has rightly been pointed out that Adorno is a critic in the "golden age of capitalism";[125] that is, that his critical theory of society focuses its attention on the aporias and rifts of a historical moment to which we perhaps tend to look back on a little too fondly after decades of neoliberalism. The genesis of some of the fundamental nodes of domination and servitude in contemporary society can be pinpointed precisely in this historical moment. At the same time, it is important not to overlook that the specific nature of Adorno's contribution is marked by experiences from an earlier historical period: its foundation lies in the upheavals that took place during the 1930s and 1940s.

Indeed, the transition to a form of total socialization had already taken place during the shift to post-liberal capitalist societies after the crash of

---

[121] Adorno, "Die menschliche Gesellschaft heute," 199.
[122] Adorno, "Late Capitalism or Industrial Society," 117.
[123] Adorno, *Hegel: Three Studies*, 27.
[124] Adorno, *Philosophical Elements of a theory of Society*, 130.
[125] Fleck, *Theodor W. Adorno: um crítico na era dourada do capitalismo*.

1929. In this sense, as we have already seen, the work developed within the framework of the Institute in the 1930s and 1940s had revealed that liberalism and totalitarianism were not necessarily antagonistic opposites. Rather, the social models of German National Socialism, the Soviet Union, and the American New Deal revealed—beyond their undeniable differences—certain common features that constituted a disturbing "family resemblance." They were increasingly comprehensive societies, regardless of whether the form of government was democratic or totalitarian. Hence, National Socialism, despite what its proclamations about blood and soil may suggest, can be understood fundamentally as a regime of vertical modernization, responding to processes involving the concentration of social and economic power.[126] Here, the logic of a "total society" is revealed, not so much as a characteristic of certain regimes, but as a sign of an era. The dissolution of the defining elements of classical liberalism—the centrality of the sphere of circulation, as well as the decisive role of the individual—and the growing concentration of capital led to the formation of monopolies and the strengthening of the role of the state, which increasingly took control of many aspects of the economy and social life, becoming an economic actor of the first order.[127] It is striking, in this regard, that Keynes himself—in the 1936 foreword to the German edition of his General Theory—noted that his theory "could be adapted much more easily to the circumstances of a total state" than to a regime of free competition and *laissez faire.*[128] What was at stake was the rise of an economic regime of "total mobilization" vertically organized. Without the power of the

[126]Adorno, *Philosophische Terminologie*, Band I (Frankfurt: Suhrkamp, 1974), 157–8.

[127]Undoubtedly, the most extreme diagnoses in the Institute's orbit—which pointed to the liquidation of the sphere of circulation, the elimination of competition and the establishment of a vertical command economy, allegedly even capable of preventing crises—did not materialize. The most drastic version of this would be F. Pollock's text on state capitalism, which even spoke of a move to the primacy of politics over economics (Pollock, "State Capitalism: Its Possibilities and Limitations"). Adorno, however, was unwilling to recognize Pollock's approach as having any validity—if at all—beyond application to the realm of the Soviet planned economy (cf. Braunstein, *Adorno's Critique of Political Economy*, 127–37). In fact, although certain passages of his work refer to the waning significance of market mediation, his entire social theory is based on an adaptation of the critique of political economy centered on the principle of exchange as a constitutive element of the social, which is simply incompatible with the diagnosis of state capitalism and the primacy of the political.

[128]John Maynard Keynes, *Allgemeine Theorie der Beschäftigung, des Zinses und des Geldes* (Berlin: Duncker & Humblot, 1936), ix.

state, the subjection of social life to the demands of capital would lose its main implementing agent. Hence Adorno's assertion—provocative as it may be—that fascism might be the most suitable form of political organization for that society (GS 8, 376).

It was the anatomy of fascism, understood as a product of the decomposition of bourgeois liberal society, that offered the key to unraveling the implications of post-liberal societies.[129] These could no longer be fundamentally understood in a state or national context, but revealed an increasingly integrated web of interdependencies at the global level.[130] The growing concentration of power in the hands of trusts and big capital meant the tendential decline of what, in the era of bourgeois liberalism, had allowed a margin of self-determination and autonomy for individuals capable of asserting themselves as economic agents in competition. With the transition to post-liberal capitalism, economic reproduction no longer depends on the mediation of individual activity, and individuals are reduced to mere objects, no longer subjects, of social processes. This generalizes the condition of the employee (DA, 176).[131] Social organization no longer demands so much the autonomy of the living subject, but rather its capacity to adapt to the "given" social framework. Whether they want to or not, individuals are forced to "participate as cogs in the machinery" (GS 8, 444). Accordingly, and in the face of the demands of increasingly uncontestable social and economic power, their capacity for action tends to be reduced to "nodal points of conventional reactions and the modes of operation objectively expected of them" (DA, 45).[132] What remains is to look for loopholes, opportunities, or jobs that enable them to get by (GS 8, 16).[133] The increase in social integration was paid for at the price of an intensification of the antagonism between the social system and living individuals. In this regard, Adorno wrote in 1943, "If I had to express in a single sentence the

[129]"That is why totalitarian societies are not the opposites of enlightened liberalism but are contained within it as its consequence. On the other hand, liberalism cannot simply be considered totalitarian, but it is the very thing that fixes down the idea of freedom, the loss of which is the measure of fascism." (Hindrichs, *Zur kritischen Theorie*, 67).

[130]Adorno, "Die menschliche Gesellschaft heute," 195.

[131]Adorno and Horkheimer, *Dialectic of Enlightenment*, 123

[132]Ibid., 21.

[133]Adorno, "Society," 273.

secret of contemporary society, whether monopolistic or totalitarian, I would say that, today, the apparatus for the reproduction of life coincides completely with that of its domination."[134] This notion is central, since it reveals that the whole social process is fueled by the fact that individuals owe their lives to that which the social system inflicts on them; this reveals their enormous vulnerability in the face of concentrated social power. This diagnosis was still valid for Adorno in 1968, when he wrote that the antagonism between the autonomized social totality and the living individuals "has now reached its limits. It has now become fate and finds its expression in what Freud called ubiquitous, free-flowing anguish" (GS 8, 369).[135]

This anguish, for its part, has to do with the impenetrable character of economic structures and their imperatives. It is inseparable from a social constitution that reduces individuals to mere functions and which means that they can only affirm themselves as subjects through them. For once reduced to a mere function of the productive apparatus, any individual becomes a perfectly replaceable entity: "Everyone amounts only to those qualities by which he or she can replace everyone else: all are fungible, mere specimens" (DA, 168).[136] This is already evident in the treatment of individuals as mere numbers—a logic that has not been limited to the tattoos of the concentration camps (GS 8, 243). The majority of the population continues to rely on anonymous and opaque processes.[137] Despite the growing abundance enabled by capitalism, there is an awareness that "society is not in control of itself; there is no overall social subject and its acts of charity are subject to withdrawal" (PETG, 198).[138] This continues to feed sensations of insecurity and anguish that permeate consciousness and the unconscious. Despite the fact that consumer habits tend to homogenize throughout different social classes, the gap between power and social impotence is greater than ever

[134]Adorno, "Graeculus (II). Notizen zu Philosophie und Gesellschaft," 11.

[135]Adorno, "Late Capitalism or Industrial Society?," 124–5. Translation modified.

[136]Adorno and Horkheimer, *Dialectic of Enlightenment*, 116–17.

[137]It is significant that Adorno highlights the inadequacy of Keynesian intervention in this respect: "Keynesianism, that is strengthening the public sector to prevent crises, is rational because it counteracts the explosive tendency of crises. Nonetheless, nothing is changed in the structure of control over the means of production" (PETG, 200; *Philosophical Elements of a Theory of Society*, 129).

[138]Adorno, *Philosophical Elements of a Theory of Society*, 127.

before (GS 8, 16).[139] The identity between objective situation and subjective consciousness, which would be necessary to form a cohesive and seamless totality, cannot be achieved because integration is paid for "with neurosis, suffering and all conceivable phenomena of mutilation" (PETG, 113).[140] Fear, anguish, atomization: the conditions of damaged life had been generalized, and put individuals in an increasingly fragile position. Adorno observed that, as a result of the disproportion between concentrated social power and the powerlessness of socialized individuals, the latter could not help but bend to the demands of social logic, and even fully identified with them. "By virtue of their needs and the omnipresent requirements of the system, men have truly become its products .... The totalizing character of society proves itself in the fact that it does not just take utter possession of its members but creates them in its own image" (GS 8, 390).[141] But these formulations, which are intended to make a certain social tendency visible, are not to be taken literally. They do not intend to claim that the circle of domination has been closed within the all-encompassing framework of socialization, in an increasingly hermetically sealed social system: "The more identical [individuals] are with the system, the less identical they are with it in their turn as helpless executors of its commands. In the individuals themselves it becomes apparent that both they and the totality to which they belong are held together only by antagonisms" (ND, 306).[142] For Adorno, just as living subjects are products of the social totality, they inevitably enter into contradiction with it (GS 8, 49).[143]

On this basis, the question of the dialectic of identity and nonidentity can be revisited as a key to Adorno's critical theory. He understood society as a totality closed in on itself. However, this totality was not monolithic: to continue functioning, the social system and living individuals must mutually reproduce each other. The system needs to reproduce subjective faculties in the individuals it integrates; otherwise, it could not reproduce itself. For this reason, even in a context of growing socialization of internal and external life,

---

[139] Adorno, "Society," 272.

[140] Adorno, *Philosophical Elements of a Theory of Society*, 69.

[141] Adorno, "Reflections on Class Theory," 109.

[142] Adorno, *Negative Dialectics*, 311. Translation modified.

[143] Adorno, "Sociology and Psychology. Part I," 72.

domination cannot be total: it is "impossible for it to extort that complete identity with human beings that is relished in negative utopias" (GS 10.2, 632).[144] The needs of living subjects enter into constant tension with the demands of the social system on which their subsistence depends. It constantly generates friction and creates cracks that allow for opposition and criticism. This does not guarantee anything, but it opens up some spaces for maneuver. For Adorno it implied that, despite its overwhelming power, the substrate on which social logic rests was more fragile than it might seem. Hence his assertion that

> History will not come to rest, as long as there will be antagonism in the social order, and as long as men are not "subjects" of society but remain its agents—whose low status is sometimes disguised by speaking of their "role" instead. Extreme oppression might perhaps force all unreconciled interests into silence; but it could not permanently release the pent-up tension. (GS 8, 237)[145]

These tensions, fissures, and cracks are the traces of an unsatisfied, incandescent vitality. They are marks that a thought that refuses to resign itself must trace beneath the seemingly petrified surface of social life. This holds true even for one of the seemingly least promising areas, at least according to the common interpretation of Adorno's thought: his critique of the culture industry.

[144] Adorno, "Progress," 156.
[145] Adorno, "'Static' and 'Dynamic' as Sociological Categories," 48.

5

The Culture Industry: Integration as Mass Deception

The lie speaks truth.

MAX HORKHEIMER & THEODOR W. ADORNO (1944)

Adorno's critique of the culture industry has undoubtedly been one of the most discussed and commented-upon aspects of his thought, as well as one of the most widely recognized themes in Frankfurt School Critical Theory as such. The very phrase "culture industry," which first appeared in a chapter in the *Dialectic of Enlightenment*, "The Culture Industry: Enlightenment as Mass Deception," appears to have had a remarkable afterlife. Today, cultural managers, art administrators, and secretaries of state speak confidently of the "cultural and creative industries," and it would seem that the ease with which the term is used is indicative of something that is strongly rooted in contemporary society. Yet are these "cultural industries" merely the plural form of the "culture industry" as criticized by Horkheimer and Adorno? Robert Hullot-Kentor has pointed out that these two terms are likely to be a rather peculiar case of accidental homonymy, since they arose independently and refer to different things.[1] The rise of "cultural industries" stems from a type of nominalism that seeks to clothe tertiary-sector activities in the trappings of productive industrial activity, giving rise to terms such as the "tourism

[1]Robert Hullot-Kentor, "The Exact Sense in which the Culture Industry No Longer Exists," *Cultural Critique* 70, 139.

industry," the "environmental industry," or the "education industry." This has also given rise to references to the film, music, and publishing "industries," all of which constitute subsectors of the so-called "cultural industries." This situation illustrates how the recent evolution of capitalist societies has swiftly done away with the irony with which Horkheimer and Adorno once juxtaposed two concepts as antagonistic as "culture" and "industry," which at the time could not be brought together without creating an abrasive contradiction in terms. The deliberate provocation inherent in this term, which once seemed to preclude any affirmative interpretation, hardly registers today.[2] That which has emerged through the expansion of capitalist socialization now appears self-evident, natural, and incontrovertible.

However, what is at stake in the critique of the culture industry is not just culture as such, but also fundamental transformations in capitalist socialization—the expansion of that which has turned society into a "system." This has been overlooked in much of its reception. Instead, what has prevailed is a trivialization of critique, a paradigmatic example of which can be seen in the rigid contrast made between Adorno and Benjamin regarding their supposed positions on so-called mass culture (film, jazz, the media, etc.). In these debates, the positions of both authors have been reduced to exemplary caricatures, adhering to a shallow and easily digestible schema. Benjamin is often depicted as a progressive and visionary intellectual who was able to grasp the emancipatory potential of the new media, while Adorno is seen as embodying the prototype of a cultural mandarin whose criticism should not be taken too seriously, since it was formulated out of elitist disdain toward the same mass culture that heralds the decline of the old bourgeois culture. This dichotomous stylization, as effective as it is misleading,[3] perpetuates a sterile dispute between supporters and detractors, between the apocalyptic and the well-integrated, between cultural "optimism" and "pessimism," and thus overlooks what is fundamentally at stake. The question

[2]"They call themselves industries, and the published figures for their directors" incomes quell any doubts about the social necessity of their finished products" (DA 142; *Dialectic of Enlightenment*, 95).

[3]It ignores the context in which Benjamin affirms the potential of "reception in distraction" (BGS I, 505; Benjamin, "The Work of Art in the Age of Its Technological Reproducibility," *Selected Writings Vol. 4*, 269) and overlooks the fact that Adorno's critique is not shaped by high bourgeois culture, but by the aesthetic radicalism of the first third of the twentieth century and the experience of its social eradication (see Maiso, "Emancipación o barbarie en la música," 29–35).

here is not the subjective position of the critic in the face of the culture industry, nor whether it should be the object of condemnation or celebration: the culture industry is a social reality, regardless of what anyone thinks or feels about it. What critical theory is about is recognizing its implications, the scope of which goes far beyond the realm of art. That is the intention of the chapter on the culture industry, which can only be understood in the fragmented context of the *Dialectic of Enlightenment*. The ironic tone of the chapter is not due to the distance of the snobby intellectual who despises the popular but reveals a certain familiarity with the object being criticized. Adorno was well acquainted with this field through his participation in pioneering research on the radio and his proximity to the Hollywood milieu in the early 1940s—an experience that even led him to cowrite a book with Hanns Eisler on musical composition for films.[4] His criticism does not stem from nostalgia for the glory of bourgeois art—Adorno was, after all, committed to a radically modern art, shaped by avant-garde models—but from an awareness of its implications regarding the emergence of an increasingly "total" society.

The social foundation of the culture industry is advanced capitalism, in which the concentration of social and economic power has reached an unprecedented level. The very phenomena of the culture industry already reveal the implications of the transition to a stage of total socialization and the way in which the "false" whole takes shape. It reveals how the principles governing the socialization of capital are gaining ground in extension and intensity. For the social totality is not only extensive, it not only expands, subjugating more and more sectors of social life, but "as a functional complex, it becomes intensive as well. A dynamic rages in it: society reproduces itself only as a whole, in and through the system, and to do so it needs every last man as a customer" (GS 11, 140–1).[5] It is at this point that the culture industry comes into play. Its specific trait stems from its integrative capacity, which not only incorporates culture into the relentless network of functional socialization and cuts it along the lines

---

[4]Detlev Claussen, *Theodor W. Adorno*, 149–62; Jenemann, *Adorno in America*, 47–147; Viejo, *Música moderna para un nuevo cine* (Madrid: Akal, 2008). The results of these investigations were reflected in Adorno, *Current of Music* and Theodor W. Adorno and Hanns Eisler, *Composing for the Films* (London: Continuum 2007; GS 15, 7–156).

[5]Adorno, "Reading Balzac," 122.

of economic profitability, but also integrates individuals themselves. It does so in a different way than the logic of production: it turns them into clients, into consumers, and that implies a different way of appealing to them as subjects. It implies mobilizing their desires, their ideals, their yearnings, their identity as something to be shaped. Yet that is not all. "The culture industry sprang from the profit-making tendency of capital. It developed under the law of the market, under the compulsion to integrate its consumers, and eventually became the mechanism that shapes and reinforces consciousness in its prevailing forms—the intellectual status quo" (GS 8, 17–18).[6] The culture industry thus significantly shapes existing forms of social consciousness and serves as a crucial key to understanding what comes to count as a social norm. This is closely linked to the constitution of the "lifeworld" in capitalist societies—which can in no way be considered as something alien to the social system—and to the ways in which these norms are internalized by individuals. In this sense, the culture industry emerges as a fundamental instance of socialization. Although the critique of the culture industry has frequently been understood as a mere critique of mass culture, it is clear that what is meant by it is much broader in scope.

From this perspective, it is evident that the culture industry is a fundamental part of the process by which society becomes a totality. Here, it is no longer a question of the old Marxist debates on the relationship between base and superstructure; instead, it concerns understanding a social system that is becoming ever more interconnected (GS 10.1, 29).[7] This means that it leaves nothing and nobody out, and that the culture industry refers to something rooted in the very constitution of capitalist societies. Not even critical intellectuals can consider themselves safe from it since it also affects the very conditions of possibility of intellectual activity. Adorno was well aware of this, and his position on the matter, far from maintaining a purely detached, arrogant stance, is instead reflective:

> He who stands aloof runs the risk of believing himself better than others and misusing his critique of society as an ideology for his private interest.

[6] Adorno, "Society," 274. Translation modified.
[7] Adorno, "Cultural Criticism and Society," 34.

> While he gropingly forms his own life in the frail image of a true existence, he should never forget its frailty, nor how little the image is a substitute for true life. … The detached observer is just as much entangled as the active participant; the only advantage of the former is insight into his entanglement, and the infinitesimal freedom that lies in knowledge as such. (MM, 27–8)[8]

That minimal freedom, rather than arrogance or resentment, is what sustains the reflexive capacity of Adorno's critical theory. Thanks to this, he was able to develop a critique in which the striking aspect is not that, after eight decades, some elements have become outdated—such as his views on popular music and jazz or many of his examples from film and television—but that, despite the evident transformations of capitalist modernization, his analysis still demonstrates remarkable insight and foresight. Undoubtedly, the culture industry itself is dynamic. It evolves along with the transformations of capitalism as such and in response to the shortcomings and expectations for which it must compensate. On the other hand, it is no coincidence that the chapter of the *Dialectic of Enlightenment*, which the authors themselves considered to be especially fragmentary (DA, 17),[9] concluded with a clear exhortation: "To be continued …" That text "was not supposed to be the end of the matter but rather the beginning of an unending analysis of the ways in which the Culture Industry had brought about changes in consciousness."[10] Therefore, an adequate understanding of Adorno's critique of the culture industry cannot be limited to commentary on that chapter, nor can it be restricted to texts written during his exile in the United States. For Adorno, the complex of the culture industry represents a central issue in the socialization patterns of advanced capitalism. This theme forms a backdrop in many of his writings on social theory and cultural criticism from the 1950s and 1960s. Those who only pay attention to the culture industry and its phenomena do not grasp what is truly at stake in it.

---

[8] Adorno, *Minima Moralia*, 26.

[9] Adorno and Horkheimer, *Dialectic of Enlightenment*, 222.

[10] Claussen, *Theodor W. Adorno*, 198.

The Social Position of Culture

In a passage from *Minima Moralia*, Adorno writes that to explain the culture industry system in terms of universal history, "it would have to be defined as the systematic exploitation of the ancient fissure between men and their culture" (MM, 167).[11] Horkheimer and Adorno had coined the concept of the culture industry in order to avoid the possible misunderstandings that the term "mass culture" might cause: after all, what was at stake here were cultural forms that in no way arose spontaneously from the masses (GS 10.1, 337).[12] This is not a kind of contemporary manifestation of popular art, and whatever might remain of the older forms of popular culture takes on a new quality. However, in the first instance, it is important to avoid misunderstandings. The critique of the culture industry is not a critique of specific technical developments (the so-called mass media), nor of certain forms of "popular" culture (such as jazz) or of cultural products designed for "mass consumption" (such as Hollywood films), nor is it merely a critique of "entertainment" as such. There is no doubt that it has something to do with all this, but by restricting it to these phenomena, much of the reception has reduced the culture industry to some of its prototypical manifestations in the in the 1930s and 1940s. The culture industry does not refer to a series of specific forms of culture, but to culture itself, as it unfolds socially in a given phase of capitalist modernity. When Horkheimer and Adorno emphasize that the culture industry forms a cohesive system in which "each branch of culture is unanimous within itself and all are unanimous together" (DA, 141),[13] this is not due to an immanent development of culture itself. Instead, it stems from the expansion of a socializing logic that imposes itself on the cultural sphere, threatening to obliterate what made culture into culture; that is, its capacity to go beyond the sphere of mere functionality that constituted the social fabric and to anticipate an idea of freedom that was not a mere abstraction.

---

[11]Adorno, *Minima Moralia*, 146.
[12]Theodor W. Adorno, "The Culture Industry: A Résumé," *Without Model*, 51.
[13]Adorno and Horkheimer, *Dialectic of Enlightenment*, 94.

The concept of industry is associated with disciplined work, diligence, the organization of production and the generation of value; that of culture, in contrast, refers to leisure, fantasy, personal development that allows for autonomy, and the cultivation of one's individuality.[14] These spheres converge in the concept of the culture industry, but in this combination the former are subjugated to the latter. If "culture today is infecting everything with sameness" (DA, 141),[15] this is because what it conveys is the expansion of the guiding principles of capitalist socialization: culture itself contributes to propagating the regime of identity. This implies an upheaval in the way culture had been understood up until then. If the bourgeois concept of culture had been branded as ideology, this was because it simulated "a society worthy of man which does not exist" (MM, 48).[16] Indeed, this concept affirmed the beautiful and the spiritual as opposed to the useful and the material, and it hypostatized it to a sphere beyond the struggle for subsistence. In this sphere, much as in a nature reserve, social needs that bourgeois society professed as ideals but could not tolerate in practice were preserved: a freedom beyond the merely formal, a humanity and a solidarity beyond the atomized subject of interests within a regime of competition, a truth that was not merely instrumental. Consequently, the sphere of culture was separated from the social process and facticity, imbuing it with a "greater dignity." This sphere was regarded as purer and nobler—perhaps a memento of its separation from physical labor, which rendered culture a privilege for those who could dispose over the labor of others (GS 10.1, 20)[17]—one that resisted the total integration of human life into the logic of the productive mechanism (HGS 12, 194). What is misleading in this conception of culture is that it presented the cultural sphere as if it were autonomous, and the relationship to it appeared as an experience that might be edifying, but was, in any case, separate from "real life." The problem, as Marcuse pointed out, is that the bourgeois notion of culture "exalts the individual without freeing him from his factual debasement."[18] In this sense, the bourgeois notion

---

[14]Hindrichs, *Zur kritischen Theorie*, 121.

[15]Adorno and Horkheimer, *Dialectic of Enlightenment*, 94.

[16]Adorno, *Minima Moralia*, 43.

[17]Adorno, "Cultural Criticism and Society," 26.

[18]Herbert Marcuse, "Über den affirmativen Charakter der Kultur," 71 and Herbert Marcuse, "The Affirmative Character of Culture," in *Art and Liberation*, ed. Douglas Kellner (London: Routledge,

of culture failed to deliver what it promised. However, for Adorno, this does not justify rejecting the element of truth within it—its potential to transcend the logic of bourgeois society by preserving, even if only as semblance, elements that encapsulate the image of possible emancipation.

However, the consolidation of the culture industry seems to signal the historical failure of this role assigned to culture. Indeed, culture was completely subjected to the economic rationality that governs the social process. In this way, culture loses its potential for transcendence and becomes an integrated sphere, administered according to the same *ratio* that governs the rest of the social process, thereby sacrificing its specificity and relative autonomy. What remains of it merely reinforces the social order—either through its nature as a product of entertainment or precisely as something deviant, as a "rarity" that makes it even more appealing in market terms (GS 10.1, 18).[19] In the words of Robert Hullot-Kentor:

> If *culture*, when it is culture, is what potentially goes beyond self-preservation; and if *industry*, meaning considerably more than a device of manufacture, is what reduces this potential to the task of survival, then the *culture* industry—as the production of culture by industry—is the reduction of all that does and could go beyond self-preservation to nothing more than life lived in the violent struggle for survival. *The manufacture of culture as the production of barbarism is the culture industry.*[20]

In other words, with the culture industry, culture tendentially loses the possibility of transcending the realm of necessity and thus sacrifices its specificity and its relative autonomy. The culture industry refers first and foremost to the total subsumption of culture to the commodity form. This is not just a critique of the trade of art or culture. Works of art were already

2007), 92. In this same text, which was published in 1937, a few pages on, one can read: "only in art has bourgeois society tolerated its own ideals and taken them seriously as a general demand. What counts as utopia, phantasy, and rebellion in the world of fact is allowed in art. There, affirmative culture has displayed the forgotten truths over which "realism" triumphs in daily life. The medium of beauty decontaminates truth and sets it apart from the present. What occurs in art occurs with no obligation." ("Über den affirmativen Charakter der Kultur," 82; "The Affirmative Character of Culture" 100).

[19]Adorno, "Cultural Criticism and Society," 22.

[20]Hullot-Kentor, "The Exact Sense in Which the Culture Industry No Longer Exists," 144–5.

commodities: only as commodities could they free themselves from patronage and the direct dependence on sources of finance—be it the church or the courtly sphere—achieving relative autonomy through the anonymity of the market (DA, 180).[21] This relative autonomy allowed art to develop independently of its social function, even if it remained merely tolerated by bourgeois society. What the culture industry entails, however, is a qualitative shift. Cultural and artistic products now tend not to be anything *but* commodities: they cannot transcend the social and economic context in which they emerge so as to cultivate distinctive aesthetic substance.[22] This gives rise to phenomena of an entirely new nature.

The total subsumption of culture to the commodity form is governed by "the principle of commercial exploitation, not by their own specific content and coherent formation. The entire practice of the culture industry transfers the profit motive starkly to products of the spirit" (GS 10.1, 338).[23] When cultural production is subjected to the criteria of the capitalist economy—whose aim is not the satisfaction of needs—it comes to be governed by the same logic that governs the social system of capital. As a result, all consideration for the immanent configuration of individual works is abandoned and the principle of profitability is strictly applied. Culture itself is subjected to the criteria of calculation and planning, and what sets the tone is "the predominance of the effect, the tangible performance" (DA, 146):[24] the whole of cultural production is organized with a view to its consumption. Hence the growing importance

---

[21]Adorno and Horkheimer, *Dialectic of Enlightenment*, 127.

[22]This does not imply that Adorno took it for granted that the products of the culture industry had nothing to offer, or that, as pure commodities, they should be seen as depraved in advance. As early as 1932, speaking of the social situation of music, Adorno was well aware that "the role of music in the social process is exclusively that of a commodity; its value is that determined by the market" (GS 18, 729; "On the Social Situation of Music," 391). However, this did not prevent him from siding with proposals that implied an aesthetic dimension that went far beyond its economic substratum and its social function. This, however, was not the prerogative of the classical forms of "high culture." Whereas in the 1940s he would write a book with Hanns Eisler that aspired to improve the use of music in the medium of film (GS 15, 7–146; Theodor W. Adorno and Hanns Eisler, *Composing for the Films*), in the 1960s Adorno would put forward, for example, some ideas for an aesthetics of film that took the potential of the medium to develop its own aesthetic substance beyond its insertion in the cultural industry seriously (GS 10.1, 353–61; Adorno, "Transparencies on Film," *Without Model*, 68–77).

[23]Adorno, "The Culture Industry: A Résumé," 52. Translation modified.

[24]Adorno and Horkheimer, *Dialectic of Enlightenment*, 99.

of dissemination and reproduction techniques. In accordance with the logic of valorization by which it is governed, the culture industry is not characterized by producing novel cultural content, but by absorbing and processing all the material it finds. It first makes use of the contents of traditional bourgeois culture and elements of popular culture. As it progresses, it also absorbs alternative and "non-commercial" countercultures and subcultures. It always needs some kind of "authentic" cultural material, which it cannot produce on its own. Once it has exhausted its raw materials, it turns to recycling or to half-finished or synthetically produced products; some of them certainly work in terms of the market, but the slightness of their content must be compensated for by the constant supply of novelties. Thus, it has been pointed out that, like capitalism itself, the culture industry consumes its "natural reserves" and thus undermines its own foundations.[25] This affects both "high" and "low" culture, but is particularly evident in products aimed at the general public. There, the demand for profitability gives rise to an increasingly standardized form of production, which classifies its offering according to the customers it addresses and ends up producing its products in accordance with preestablished parameters. The attempt to ensure the public's attention and satisfaction with the minimum effort, and also with the minimum investment, leads to the exhaustive planning of cultural commodities, "from the overall plan down to details" (GS 14, 204).[26] In the case of popular music, for example, that includes everything from the key and the number of bars of the refrain to the type of song, depending on the target audience. The result is a model of cultural production that can almost be seen as an application of the standardized and hyper-rationalized logic of Fordist mass production to the cultural sector: characteristics, patterns, details, and variants are defined in advance and then dosed out and managed by industry "experts" in each case (DA 146).[27] It is based on efficiency, on the calculation and metering out of its effects on the public.

[25]Robert Kurz, "Kulturindustrie im 21. Jahrhundert," *Exit! Krise und Kritik der Warengesellschaft* 9 (2012), 94–100.

[26]*Theodor W. Adorno Introduction to the Sociology of Music*, trans. E. B. Ashton, (New York: The Seabury Press, 1976), 25.

[27]Adorno and Horkheimer, *Dialectic of Enlightenment*, 98–9.

Indeed, the system of the culture industry not only implies coordination between its different sectors, but also the harmonization of production and consumption. Consequently, the counterpart to this model of production is a mode of reception that Adorno interprets as a mere response to stimuli, which leads to a growing difficulty in perceiving the work as a coherent whole and significantly reduces the average audience's ability to differentiate and experience the object as such. In this sense Adorno does not hesitate to speak of a "regression" of the capacity for experience, which maintains the public in an infantile state (GS 14, 34).[28] Cultural products for mass consumption require a particular disposition from the public that, while unrelated to the concentration required by a more traditional relationship with art, resembles something like a state of "alertness." This need to not miss any given stimulus or signal is what enables these products to produce the expected effects. In this mode of attention, which is constantly both tense and dispersed, Adorno detects a tendency toward the "withering of imagination and spontaneity," since the products themselves "are so constructed that their adequate comprehension requires a quick, observant, knowledgeable cast of mind but positively debars the spectator from thinking, if he is not to miss the fleeting facts" (DA, 148).[29] Adorno and Horkheimer had film in mind here first and foremost, but what they detected in it can be applied to the field of audiovisual culture in a broad sense. The overwhelming nature of what happens on the screen, at an increasingly dizzying pace, subjugates the spectator and reinforces the loss of autonomy of the subjects in their own sphere of experience. This is why it is stated that each of the culture industry's products "is a model of the gigantic economic machinery, which, from the first, keeps everyone on their toes, both at work and in the leisure time which resembles it" (DA, 148).[30] In this regard, each product of the culture industry reproduces human beings as what the social system as a whole has turned them into.

[28]Adorno, "On the Fetish Character of Music and the Regression of Listening," 46.
[29]Adorno and Horkheimer, *The Dialectic of Enlightenment*, 100.
[30]Ibid., 100.

However, it would be a mistake to think that Adorno's critique is aimed solely at denouncing the baleful consequences of so-called mass culture. Rather, they point to a notion of culture that "already contains, virtually, the process of identifying, cataloging, and classifying which imports culture into the realm of administration" (DA, 152).[31] At first, even in the 1930s, Adorno still seemed confident that both "high" and "low" culture could resist their integration into the functional logic of the social system and preserve some kind of autonomy. After all, "both bear the stigmata of capitalism, both contain elements of change (but never, of course, simply as a middle term between Schoenberg and the American film). Both are torn halves of an integral freedom, to which, however, they do not add up" (ABB, 171).[32] Over time, however, as the integrative power of the social system fully revealed itself, these hopes proved futile, and the harm caused by the integration of both spheres within the logic of the culture industry became evident: "High art is stripped of its seriousness by aiming for effect, while low art, having been tamed and civilized, loses the wildly resistant quality that inhabited it before society gained total control" (GS 10.1, 337).[33]

Here the price paid for the integration of so-called "popular culture" and "low" art forms was already apparent. For Adorno these constituted "the social bad conscience of serious art" (DA, 157).[34] They were testimony to the failure of culture (ÄT, 32),[35] whose existence was paid for at the price of the exclusion of those subject to heteronomous labor. "Serious art has denied itself to those for whom the hardship and oppression of life make a mockery of seriousness and who must be glad to use the time not spent at the production line in being simply carried along" (DA, 157).[36] For those aware of the implications of the division between physical and intellectual labor, the demand for cultural products that can be consumed without effort, that offer recreation and entertainment, is not reprehensible in itself. Forms of amusement that were

[31]Ibid., 104.
[32]Adorno to Benjamin, London 18/03/1936. Adorno and Benjamin, *The Complete Correspondence*, 130.
[33]Adorno, "The Culture Industry: A Résumé," 51.
[34]Adorno and Horkheimer, *The Dialectic of Enlightenment*, 107.
[35]Adorno, *Aesthetic Theory*, 16.
[36]Adorno and Horkheimer, *The Dialectic of Enlightenment*, 107.

not subject to social normativity—that were truly "untamed"—could in fact become a "corrective to art" (DA, 164),[37] which, with stubborn earnestness and at the price of increasing hermeticism, obstinately sought to safeguard some form of aesthetic truth against the "false" whole. Adorno saw this potential in the absurd, grotesque, and circus-like elements of "low" culture. In its moments of excess, often close to animality, there was an appeal to forms of expression and experience that were increasingly ignored in a society that has subjugated the body to the point of turning it into a mere instrument of labor.[38] However, to the culture industry, these elements are as eccentric and embarrassing as free atonalism or the prose of Karl Kraus. In them, it perceives something that goes against the reality principle that governs an increasingly organized social process, and consequently cannot tolerate them. The problem is not, therefore, that the culture industry offers entertainment, but that—by subjecting it to the demands of the social norm—it sabotages it. "The fusion of culture and entertainment is brought about today not only by the debasement of culture but equally by the compulsory intellectualization of amusement" (DA, 165).[39] Or, in even sharper relief, "The culture industry is corrupt, not as a sink of iniquity but as the cathedral of higher gratification" (DA, 165).[40]

In short, the culture industry attempts a reconciliation of the two split halves of culture, "high" and "low" culture, by integrating them into a diversified offering aimed at different uses and customers: some who aspire to entertain and amuse themselves (albeit without being able to transgress the limits of the reality principle), others who enjoy art as a redoubt of an edifying notion of culture, whose values should be "cultivated." This is how both spheres merge into a single false formula: "the totality of the culture industry" (DA, 158).[41] If the formula is false, it is because, by integrating the two halves that have been divided by social logic, it ruins the best of each: it spoils art and domesticates entertainment. Rather than forcing their

[37]Ibid., 113.

[38]Falko Schmieder, *Ludwig Feuerbach und der Eingang der klassischen Fotografie: Zum Verhältnis von anthropologischen und historischen Materialismus* (Berlin/Vienna: Philo, 2004), 379.

[39]Adorno and Horkheimer, *The Dialectic of Enlightenment*, 114.

[40]Ibid., 114.

[41]Ibid., 108.

reconciliation, we should realize that the two halves are in an "unresolved contradiction" (GS 14, 20).[42] This is caused by the very split constitution of society, in its division between physical and intellectual labor. Only those who enjoy a privileged social position—because their position rests on the labor of others—can develop the capacity for a living relationship with art, which requires time, effort, autonomy, and the capacity for experience; this was the aim of the bourgeois ideal of education [*Bildung*]. In the conditions of total socialization, on the other hand, even if mass media could provide the public with access to works of "high culture," they could not provide the means for actually engaging with them (GS 8, 99–100).[43] Thus, even when motivated by the best of intentions, attempts to democratize access to "culture" could not get to the root of the problem and ended up imposing a normative vision of "cultural goods" that ultimately reaffirmed an increasingly empty ideal of education. Indeed, as Walter Benjamin had already posited, "what is the value of all our culture if it is divorced from experience?" (BGS II, 215).[44] Here "culture" becomes a kind of "value" in itself, hypostatized and detached from the social organization of human affairs; it is thus reduced to a mere status symbol. Adorno's critique of "pseudoculture" [*Halbbildung*] (GS 8, 93–121),[45] which generalizes a relationship to cultural products that is not a first step toward the acquisition of an education, but is instead the product of its decomposition, was directed against this. For Adorno, it made no sense to maintain the fiction "that inducing people to listen to Beethoven symphonies, read Milton and gaze upon Raphael Madonnas is equally 'progressive' and humanistic at all times." (IG, 62)[46] His position is not that of one who defends the need to bring the works of "great art" to the masses at all costs, but rather that of one who recognizes that this notion of "culture" is in a relationship of growing antagonism with the real conditions of life. Adorno is fully aware that, under the conditions of advanced capitalism, the possibility of

---

[42] Adorno, "On the Fetish-Character in Music and the Regression of Listening," 293.
[43] Theodor W. Adorno, "Theory of Pseudo-Culture," *Telos* 95 (March 20, 1993), 21.
[44] Benjamin, "Experience and Poverty," *Selected Writings Volume 2, Part 2*, 732.
[45] Adorno, "Theory of Pseudo-Culture."
[46] Adorno, "The Problem of a New Type of Human Being," *Current of Music: Elements of a Radio Theory*, 462.

"cultivating" human beings through culture is no longer a given; the very ideal of education thus becomes somewhat anachronistic (GS 8, 121).[47]

Ultimately, clinging to the pretensions of culture was of little use. The very experiences of the twentieth century had revealed the bankruptcy of culture, its powerlessness to humanize social life and to put some kind of restraint on the very real irruption of barbarism:

> Auschwitz irrefutably demonstrated the failure of culture. That it could happen in the midst of all the traditions of philosophy, art, and the enlightening sciences says more than merely that these, the Spirit, was not capable of seizing and changing human beings. In those branches themselves, in the emphatic claim of their autarky, dwells untruth. All culture after Auschwitz, including its urgent critique, is garbage. (ND, 359)[48]

This passage undermines any attempt to preserve an affirmative notion of culture that tries to cling to anything substantial in the world of the spirit. The wound that runs through all culture—its complicity with barbarism—is something that cannot be healed by culture itself: it requires a transformation of society as a whole. So long as this does not take place, the social reality of culture in advanced capitalism is nothing but one more field in the production of consumer goods: the culture industry, which has in fact become "second nature" (GS 8, 327).[49] In it, art is integrated, domesticated, and subjected to "functions such as warming people up and drowning out silence …, the commodified negation of the boredom produced by the grey-on-grey commodity world" (AT, 375).[50] Its function is reduced to that of a mere "stimulus," a mood-maker, very often just to the backdrop of everyday life. Today, pop songs set the rhythm for shopping in department stores and shopping malls, and their refrains become intimately associated with the adverts in which they have been used. Under the logic of the culture industry, culture has ended up merging with advertising, design, and marketing.

---

[47] Adorno "Theory of Pseudo-Culture," 20.

[48] Adorno, *Negative Dialectics*, 366–7. Translation modified.

[49] Adorno, "Introduction," *The Positivist Dispute in German Sociology*, 43.

[50] Adorno, *Aesthetic Theory*, 253.

In retrospect, Adorno would say that his experiences in the United States—a country that represented the most advanced vantage point for observing the dynamics of capitalist socialization—enabled him to free himself "from naïve credulity in culture"; by virtue of this, he acquired the ability to "see culture from the outside" (GS 10.2, 733).[51] Without a doubt, among these experiences was that of the culture industry itself, which was undeniably rooted in the expansive dynamics of capitalism. Although Adorno does not renounce the critical potential of an art that does not resign itself to being reduced to guilty complicity with the existing, and which he still regards as an ally of unachieved emancipation, he is also acutely aware of the impotent fragility of an art that can only be developed against the grain of an increasingly overpowering social logic. Art alone cannot undermine the power of the culture industry or counteract what it—as an integral part of the social system—does to human beings. For what is at stake here is not merely the integration of culture, but above all the expansive logic of a form of socialization: the constitution of the "false" whole.

The Culture Industry as an Instance of Socialization

Beyond the possible flaws that may be attributed to Adorno and Horkheimer's critique of the culture industry, it is important to recognize that they were among the first to acknowledge its central importance and its implications for the structural transformation that advanced capitalist societies were undergoing. For their critique of the culture industry is not presented as a critique of culture, but fundamentally as a critique of society.[52] It is a critical reflection on the social conditions of the production and consumption of culture under advanced capitalism: in this case, in its Fordist phase.[53] But what is at stake in it is the expansion of its functional network of socialization, which

---

[51]Adorno, "Scientific Experiences of a European Scholar in America," 239.

[52]Cf. Roger Behrens, *Verstummen: Über Adorno* (Laatzen: Wehrhan, 2004), 56.

[53]Heinz Steinert, *Culture Industry*, trans. Sally-Ann Spencer (Cambridge: Polity, 2003).

no longer only mobilizes socialized individuals as workers and producers, but also as consumers; in this sense, the socializing logic takes over more and more spheres of inner and outer life. The Fordist organization of labor had increased productivity, which strengthened economic growth, and due to this situation, there was a rise in wages and with it a reinforcement of the capacity for consumption. This not only created an outlet for the growing volume of goods that capitalism was able to put on the market, but also completely transformed living conditions. Thus, a mode of social existence marked by the logic of the commodity emerged. The chapter of the *Dialectic of Enlightenment* is an analysis of how, through this process, the functional network of capitalist socialization permeates life in all its dimensions. Notably, the first examples Adorno and Horkheimer use are not works of art, but elements of urbanism; the chapter concludes, for its part, by alluding to the fusion of culture and advertising. The culture industry ultimately refers to life as an integrated whole in capitalist societies, which shows how systemic imperatives are penetrating into more and more dimensions of social existence and shaping the relationship of human beings with the world. As the network of socialization "is drawn ever tighter, modelled after the act of exchange. It leaves the individual consciousness less and less room for evasion" (GS 10.1, 13).[54] In this sense, the first examples on urban planning already reveal how the materialization of social relations in urban space organizes the lives of individuals and defines what corresponds to them in a society marked by the growing concentration of power:

> The monumental, gleaming buildings rising up everywhere represent the logical and unfailing regularity of the large multinational corporations to which the untrammeled entrepreneurial initiative was already tending, the monuments to which are the gloomy residential buildings and businesses in the desolate cities. The older houses around the concrete centers already appear as suburbs, and the new bungalows on the periphery proclaim […] the praise of technical progress, inviting to throw them away after a brief use, like tin cans. But urban projects, which are supposed to perpetuate in small hygienic dwellings the individual as a more or less independent

[54] Adorno, "Cultural Criticism and Society," 21.

> being, subject him all the more radically to his adversary, the total power of capital. As their inhabitants are forced to flock to the centers in order to gain access to work and entertainment, i.e. as producers and consumers, the housing cells crystallize into well-organized complexes. The visible unity of macrocosm and microcosm shows men the false model of their culture: the false identity of the universal and the particular. (DA 3, 141–2)[55]

This identity is false because it erases the difference between the individual and the social whole. Living subjects are not integrated into the social system as autonomous and conscious agents but are subjected to its heteronomous logic. Urban space already gives expression to the growing antithesis between atomized and powerless individuals and a seamless social organization, which turns them into employees and clients—and therefore into subjects dependent on an increasingly concentrated social power. Their needs have been anticipated and captured by the system, integrated into its functional logic, and this is materialized in the very spatial configuration of living environments in the big city. Workplaces, places of consumption, and single-family homes—often mass-produced—whose interiors promise comfort through the proliferation of new gadgets, such as refrigerators, washing machines, and televisions, all of this forms a topology that can be traversed thanks to the star product of the Fordist period: the automobile. The urban landscape, meanwhile, becomes little more than a backdrop for advertisements and billboards, or the emblems of big capital (DA, 186);[56] this was the result of the emerging form of social organization. In fact, the culture industry paradigmatically reflects this process of the subsumption of life, even in its most trivial forms, by the commodity form and the logic of profitability. The culture industry is one of the characteristic features of a form of socialization that integrates all spheres of life into its functional framework, thus dispensing with the need to ask about its justification: the social system becomes total. Even the interior of the home, traditionally a refuge that was relatively sheltered from outside interference, had been abruptly socialized with the rapid diffusion of radio and later television sets, which were to become the center of family and domestic

[55] Adorno and Horkheimer, *Dialectic of Enlightenment*, 95.
[56] Ibid., 132.

life. This is why the critique of the culture industry is not directed at specific forms of life under capitalism, but at the constitution of life itself under the conditions of capital's socialization, in which no sphere escapes the mediation of the social fabric; it does not denounce the "excesses" of the system, but the very logic by which it is governed.

What was at stake here was the understanding of a new phase of capitalism in which its tendency toward expansion had reached a point where economic imperatives practically permeated all of social existence. Central to this development is the consolidation of a new temporal regime that organizes life based on the dichotomy between work and leisure. This imposes a biphasic structuring of social life that separates the dimensions of duty and pleasure with a "puritanical fervor" (GS 10.2, 647).[57] While work required performance, concentration, and effort, free time had to dispense with them at all costs. Although this social structuring of time might recall traditional forms of cyclical time—marked by the succession of day and night, work and weekly rest, the periodic return of festivities and vacation periods—no other social formation had interfered so brutally with the rhythms of tension and relaxation, of concentration and distraction.[58] In a society in which salaried work is the only means by which the majority of the population can access the means of subsistence, working time is perceived as heteronomous time. It is time devoted to activities linked to the obligations of the productive sphere and which is given away in exchange for a wage. In contrast, leisure appears as the "true life," a sphere in which individuals can freely determine the content of their own existence. While the young Marx had already pointed out that men only live when they do not work, and when they work, they do not live (MEW 40, 514),[59] this situation had only been exacerbated by Fordism. This is where the culture industry comes into play, which ties in with the urban wage earners' appetite for fun and excitement, and with their desire to feel as though they are the subjects and protagonists of their own lives. At a time when all social existence bears the imprint of what happens in the office, the factory,

---

[57] Adorno, "Free Time," 169.

[58] Christoph Türcke, *Erregte Gesellschaft* (Munich: Beck, 2012), 246.

[59] Karl Marx, *Economic and Philosophic Manuscripts*, trans. Martin Milligan (New York: Prometheus Books, 1988), 74.

and the business center, for individuals to enjoy the slim margin of "free" time granted to them becomes an end in itself, the purpose of existence as such.

However, Adorno warns that "free time" does not refer to the privileges of a life freed from the constraints of the realm of necessity but is "shackled to its contrary" (GS 10.2, 645).[60] It is a temporal sphere that is equally subject to the functional framework of the social constitution, and therefore reproduces and extends the realm of unfreedom beyond the workplace. "Free time remains the reflex-action to a production rhythm imposed heteronomously on the subject, compulsively maintained in the weary pauses" (MM, 199).[61] What is sought in it bears the imprint of what wage earners want to escape from in their working hours, and thus responds to an increasingly mechanized labor reality. In this regard, Siegfried Kracauer pointed out that "the more monotony holds sway of the working day, the further away you must be transported when work ends. The true counterstroke against the office machine, however, is the world vibrant with color. The world not as it is, but as it appears in popular hits. A world every last corner of which is cleansed, as though with a vacuum cleaner, of the dust of everyday existence."[62] Whereas the world of work generated anxiety at the threat of unemployment or loss of income, entertainment was understood to be a sphere that shied away from both effort and concentration.[63] That is why the products of the culture industry have to be attractive and easy to consume. They are designed to confer a sort of luster on a gray and unrewarding life (GS 10.2, 510),[64] which without them would be difficult to bear. The renunciations demanded by the logic of work must be compensated for in a leisure understood as "escape." Amusement thus becomes "a mere reward for work, and conversely work the mere price of amusement" (GS 8, 159). Thus "free time" is revealed to be a mere reproduction of the capacity to work, and therefore as an extension of the sphere of heteronomy. In this sense, leisure is understood as "the prolongation of work in late capitalism" (DA, 158).[65] The

[60]Adorno, "Free Time," 167.

[61]Adorno, *Minima Moralia*, 175.

[62]Siegfried Kracauer, *Die Angestellten* (Frankfurt: Suhrkamp, 1971), 97 and *The Salaried Masses*, trans. Quintin Hoare (London: Verso, 1998), 99–100.

[63]Adorno, "On Popular Music," *Current of Music*, 309.

[64]Adorno, "Prologue to Television," 52.

[65]Adorno and Horkheimer, *The Dialectic of Enlightenment*, 109.

hopes of transcending the social logic that are mobilized in it are ultimately frustrated, and thus every Sunday is accompanied by the melancholic feeling of "tomorrow already continuing yesterday" (MM, 199).[66]

There is no longer any sphere in which one can escape the imperatives that govern the social process under capitalism. "The whole of life must look like a job, and by this resemblance conceal what is not yet directly devoted to pecuniary gain" (MM, 157).[67] Indeed, the social system confines culture to the realm of leisure. However, by embedding culture within its functional framework, it completely changes its scope and meaning. Because, as fully socialized time, "free time" is structured by the demands of the logic of production: fundamentally, it becomes a time for consuming commodities. Just as Fordist production methods organize labor around efficiency and productivity, leisure must also be made to align with the principles of economic gain. Among the social demands that the new leisure sector is expected to fulfill are evasion and distraction—both of which are transformed into fully organized and professionalized spheres. In this regard, the culture industry is crucial to the integration of leisure into the functional logic of the social whole, since the limited agency it offers to individuals is linked to their role as subjects of consumption. Benjamin traced the genesis of this process back to the great universal exhibitions of the nineteenth century, where masses of wage earners gathered to admire commodities that showcased the productive power of the emerging industrial society—items they themselves could not afford. This contemplation of the marvels of the world of commodities opens "a phantasmagoria which a person enters in order to be distracted." Thus, the nascent entertainment industry fostered "the enthronement of the commodity" and sought to harmonize people's desires with it (BGS V, 50–1).[68] The promise of being included in a world of progress and wealth relegated class antagonisms to the background, even attenuating yearnings for social transformation.[69] However, it was the increase in productivity offered by

66 Adorno, *Minima Moralia*, 175.
67 Adorno, *Minima Moralia*, 138–9.
68 Benjamin, *The Arcades Project*, 18.
69 Susan Buck-Morss, *The Dialectics of Seeing: Walter Benjamin and the Arcades Project* (Cambridge, Massachusetts: MIT Press, 1989), 86.

Fordism that made widespread mass consumption possible, opening up a realm where wage earners could use their income not only for subsistence, but also for movies, dances, vacations, and consumer goods. It is not surprising that this was viewed as an achievement, enabling the vast majority of the population access to goods and pleasures from which they had traditionally been excluded. In this sense, the language and products of the culture industry appealed to the aspirations of a "new middle class that was not a middle class" (GS 11, 399),[70] as access to consumer goods—even for those in predominantly proletarianized conditions—suggested a tendential leveling of lifestyles. The enjoyment of "cultural commodities," reaching beyond mere subsistence, allowed individuals to feel like full members of society. The flip side of this development, however, is that their lives became embedded in the functional fabric of society not only in terms of earning but also in spending. Their entire existence became an integrated whole in the logic of capitalism.[71]

Adorno himself, in one of the rare passages in which he allows himself something resembling a definition, states that "the culture industry is the deliberate integration of its consumers from above" (GS 10.1, 337).[72] Despite all the statements about the culture industry as a service to the customer, in it the customer is not king, "not its subject, but rather its object"; the costumer's position is "secondary, something that has been factored in: an appendage of the machinery" (GS 10.1, 337).[73] However, this situation should not be misinterpreted: the culture industry does not impose itself on individuals against their will. On the contrary, no one consumes the constant influx of new film and music releases or the daily dose of news except by choice. Adorno's point, however, is that the sum of the diverse media that form the

[70]Adorno, "The Curious Realist," 68.

[71]Today, the strict division between work and leisure is being reversed by the very evolution of capitalism. Capitalism no longer aspires to rigidly and meticulously separate work and leisure according to the famous maxim of working while you work and playing while you play, but even aspires to absorb the ludic and imaginative dimension to put it at the service of the logic of production. In some passages Adorno already seems to detect the genesis of this tendency to blur the boundaries between work and leisure. He speaks for instance, of a growing tendency to subject spontaneous moments of interaction and relaxation to the demands of performance and profitability, or at least to the interests of one's own professional career (GS 9.2, 65–6. and *The Stars Down to Earth* (London: Routledge, 2001), 103–104).

[72]Adorno, "The Culture Industry: A Résumé," 51.

[73]Ibid., 52 and 51.

system of the culture industry—from film and television to astrological columns, advertising and pop songs—create a distinct "climate" (GS 10.2, 508).[74] This socially produced climate is what lends the culture industry's offerings their specific appeal. At the same time, this climate enables each individual to perceive their place within the increasingly dense web formed of the culture industry's institutions. In this sense, "to participate in culture means becoming dependent on that network"; "this dependence, however, should not be mistaken for manipulation by powerful industry monopolies, but rather as a form of willingly accepted coercion."[75] Its result is the readiness of most individuals to accept a disposition of the world that turns them into mere spectators and customers. This is how the culture industry is reinforced by the whole system of socialization and how it assigns human beings their functions in the social fabric. In this regard, Adorno and Horkheimer state that "the tendencies of the culture industry are turned into the flesh and blood of the public by the social process as a whole" (DA, 158).[76] For the culture industry does not merely produce cultural artifacts: it produces the audience itself. It shapes the consciousness of individuals so that their dispositions fit the roles of the customer and consumer (GS 8, 474).[77] This is why Horkheimer and Adorno claimed that "the mentality of the public, which allegedly and actually favors the system of the culture industry, is a part of the system, not an excuse for it" (DA, 143).[78]

The culture industry system therefore entails this attempt to synchronize production and consumption. The apparent diversity of supply—both in terms of cultural products, with different types of music and films, and in the nuances that differentiate consumer products in general—is unified in advance and serves the purpose of classifying, organizing, and attracting customers. That makes it possible to assimilate even that which deviates from the norm, tapping into impulses of nonconformity and rebellion. "Something is provided

---

[74]Adorno, "Prologue to Television," 50.

[75]Zamora, *Th. W. Adorno. Pensar contra la barbarie*, 91.

[76]Adorno and Horkheimer, *Dialectic of Enlightenment*, 108.

[77]Adorno, "Contribution to the Theory of Ideology," trans. Jacob Bard-Rosenberg, *Selva: A Journal for the History of Art* (Fall 2022), 31.

[78]Adorno and Horkheimer, *Dialectic of Enlightenment*, 96.

for everyone so that no one can escape; differences are hammered home and propagated" (DA 144).[79] The logic that governs the system is diversification, not diversity. The schematism of the culture industry is organized in such a way that none of its experiential elements can transcend the functional logic of the social system. However, the expansion of the socializing logic is not solely imposed on individuals from outside; they also actively reproduce it in pursuing their own interests. In this regard, the expansion of the sphere of consumption also offers consumers a degree of agency: the capacity to assert themselves as subjects and to make choices, as long as they have purchasing power. In fact, through the system of the culture industry, the music one listens to, the films one watches, the books one reads, or the clothes one wears become more than mere expressions of taste: they become acts of identity construction. That which each person consumes, belonging to one or another market niche, becomes a substitute for his or her individuality. As monetary subjects, socialized individuals find a space of freedom here; it offers them the possibility of self-determination through their habits of consumption. Their integration takes place entirely through this freedom. Of course, this also has its flip side: insofar as their freedom is reduced to that of consumers, their needs are already captured in advance and are therefore restricted to the narrow bounds allowed by the social system. They have some scope for action, but they are not sovereign subjects. In this sense, the only freedom it allows is the "freedom to be the same" (DA, 190).[80] The socializing function of the culture industry helps to internalize this state of affairs, offering gratifications and patterns of identification that allow individuals to align their expectations, desires, and wishes with a social logic that is unilaterally imposed on them. The aim is to soften the friction produced by the antagonism between the social logic and the living individuals who reproduce it by encouraging them to fully identify with the social functions they must embody. It is only because of this that, when individuals pursue their deepest desires and affirm themselves through their actions, they ultimately become agents of the logic of the commodity.

---

[79]Ibid., 97.
[80]Ibid., 136.

This highlights the significance of the rite of social inclusion through consumption. If activities such as going shopping were able to become an intransitive activity, an end in itself beyond whatever goods and products may be acquired, it is because that which is enjoyed in them is consumption itself, the pure exercise of purchasing power. The use value of commodities, that which allows them to satisfy needs, seems to be relegated to the background. This suggests the possibility that the very act of consumption serves to satisfy needs of another kind. Since what is enjoyed in commodities appears to involve what Marx called their "suprasensible" or social dimension (MEW 23, 86),[81] this would indicate a growing identification of individuals with the very logic that governs the process of capital reproduction, on which both their subsistence and their identity ultimately depend. At the root of this identification lies not a perverse attitude on the part of consumers, but rather relations of social power and powerlessness. In this regard, Walter Benjamin spoke of a tendency of individuals to identify themselves with exchange value (BGS V, 65).[82] Adorno detected something analogous in relation to the products of the culture industry (GS 14, 25).[83] Adorno's assertion that the consumption of cultural commodities becomes the consumption of their exchange value is, strictly speaking, unorthodox in Marxian terms and can at best be understood as a metaphorical formulation. However, Adorno aims to reveal something with this claim. If commodities can be understood as "social hieroglyphic[s]" (MEW 23, 88)[84] it is not only because they embody the abstract social labor that enables them to be exchanged, but also because by entering the sphere of consumption we are drawn into a kind of hall of mirrors in which socially disempowered individuals hope to see their image magnified. In this process not only does culture become commodity, but in a way commodity itself takes on a cultural significance. Consequently, the interest in these products lies not so much in what they inherently are but in what they promise to the individual: the opportunity to embody a self-image, to signal belonging, and to avoid exclusion from what is validated by social success and approval. In short,

[81]Marx, *Capital: Volume 1*, 165.

[82]Benjamin, *The Arcades Project*, 18.

[83]Adorno, "On the Fetish-Character in Music and the Regression of Listening," 298.

[84]Marx, *Capital: Volume 1*, 167.

commodities become a source of prestige (DA, 181),[85] a reinforcement of the ego. What is at work here is the logic of substitute satisfaction; underlying it is a need symptomatic of "the wrong kind of social absorption" (MM, 158).[86]

As the social system reduces individuals to functional roles, they constantly fear becoming redundant, acutely aware of their replaceability. This drives them to seek refuge in the emblems of power and social success—whether through the charts of best-selling cultural products, where success itself is the dominant appeal, or identification with brands that serve as modern totems of concentrated capital. They yearn for anything that aligns them with the social logic from which all prestige and recognition emanate, and advertising capitalizes upon this. This situation implies a heightened dependence of individuals on the "false totality," which increasingly anticipates and shapes their needs. In this scenario, any subjective empowerment relies on being sanctioned by the same social logic that relegates subjects to a position of dependence. As Adorno observes, individuals "make common cause with the world against themselves, [...] the omnipresence of commodities, their own conversion into appendages of machinery, is for them a mirage of closeness" (MM, 167–8).[87] Despite the obvious transformations that separate the present moment from Adorno's time, it is hard to believe that this situation has really been reversed.

The "Deception" of the Culture Industry and its Limits

If anything characterizes culture industry's modus operandi for Adorno, it is that it "speculates on the state of (un)consciousness" of its public (GS 10.1, 337).[88] In this regard, the culture industry emerges as a key element for the functional network of socialization, structuring, reorganizing, and channeling

[85] Adorno and Horkheimer, *Dialectic of Enlightenment*, 128.
[86] Adorno, *Minima Moralia*, 139.
[87] Ibid., 146–7.
[88] Adorno, "The Culture Industry: A Résumé," 51. Translation modified.

the conscious and unconscious dispositions of living subjects (GS 10.2, 507).[89] Its purpose is to reinforce a mentality that is prone to capitulate before the overpowering social reality, excluding anything that could foster a shift in that mindset. However, this process involves delicate balances that are not always easy to maintain. Adorno detects an ambivalence that runs throughout the entire culture industry: while it promises an escape from the dull, gray routines of everyday life, it teaches the mores of integration into advanced capitalism. Although its manifest content stirs desires for evasion and escape, what pulsates within it has more to do with fostering a subjective disposition that aligns with the demands of the prevailing social system. In this sense, Walter Benjamin pointed out that the mass reproduction of images was not only related to the mass production of industrial products, but also to the mass reproduction of human attitudes and dispositions (BGS I, 1042). Adorno, therefore, goes so far as to speak of the culture industry as "training for life" (GS 3, 330).[90] Its offerings aim to make the conditions of life more bearable, while at the same time providing models for how to function within the given society. That is why Adorno argued that in the entertainment provided by the culture industry "it is not the bells on the fool's cap that jingle but the bunch of keys of capitalist reason" (DA, 165).[91] Its logic does not accept anything that might undermine the reality principle demanding adaptation to the social norm. This has an impact on the nature of the "dream factory," which cannot transcend the reality from which it wants to flee, not even in the imagination; instead, its dreams aim to engrave the laws of empirical existence onto consciousness (MM, 231–2).[92] If we bear in mind that Adorno posited that the psychosocial substrata on which the culture industry rests are repressed drives of imitation (MM, 229),[93] we can grasp the implications of his claim that "the idea of the successful, conforming, well-adjusted 'average' citizen lurks even behind the fanciest technicolor fairy tale" (GS 9.2, 46).[94] Meanwhile, figures

[89]Adorno, "Prologue to Television," 49.
[90]Adorno, "The Schema of Mass Culture," 91.
[91]Adorno and Horkheimer, *Dialectic of Enlightenment*, 114.
[92]Adorno, *Minima Moralia*, 202.
[93]Ibid., 201.
[94]Theodor W. Adorno, *The Stars Down to Earth*, 81.

less molded by the logic of Fordist capitalism, such as those of the brilliant but seemingly maladjusted individual, or even the subject tormented by his or her own success, have also become models of identification. Individuals cling to them, choosing among the different variants. These patterns allow them to live with the principles around which the social system gravitates and to internalize—even through patterns of "deviation"—what it sets up as the norm and which cannot be called into question. This is how "domination infiltrates human beings" (GS 8, 390);[95] it does not merely influence them but largely constitutes them as that which they are. Its traits are embodied in individuals' dispositions and are evident in many of their gestures and expressions:

> The way in which the young girl accepts and performs the obligatory date, the tone of voice used on the telephone and in the most intimate situations, the choice of words in conversation, indeed, the whole inner life compartmentalized according to the categories of vulgarized depth psychology, bears witness to the attempt to turn oneself into an apparatus meeting the requirements of success, an apparatus which, even in its unconscious impulses, conforms to the model presented by the culture industry. (DA, 191)[96]

Here the central importance of the fusion of culture and advertising is revealed; it manifests itself in the very disposition of subjects. In their way of speaking, presenting themselves, and making themselves visible, even in the private sphere, individuals present themselves as products, as resources conforming to social standards, which makes them fit and employable subjects. Yet dissidence is equally determined in advance. Even models of rebellion and subversion, which also respond to widespread needs of the audience and may appear as antithetic to the culture industry mainstream, are based on stereotypes and seek to encourage mimetic behavior. Through this internalization of the prevailing models of subjectivity and behavior, individuals' attachment to the "ideology that enslaves them" (DA, 155)[97] is established. This attachment, however, is

[95] Adorno, "Reflections on Class Theory," 109. Translation modified.
[96] Adorno and Horkheimer, *Dialectic of Enlightenment*, 136.
[97] Ibid., 106. Translation modified.

fundamentally coercive: it is based on the growing disproportion between power and social impotence. Individuals conform to the prevailing models of the employee and the customer because the social system only recognizes and addresses them insofar as they embody those roles. The pressure to conform to these socially sanctioned criteria is so pervasive that it obscures the suffering and distress caused by this enforced assimilation to the social logic (HGS 12, 573).

This suggests that the traditional understanding of social domination, based on subjection to wage labor and the commodification of labor power, falls short of capturing the demands embedded in the logic of socialization under advanced capitalism. Now the social imperatives reach even deeper and aspire to functionalize individuals at a more fundamental level. In this respect, the culture industry emerges as a key instrument for the socialization of the inner life of subjects. While culture may still retain its role as a means for the "domestication of the animal in the human being" (GS 8, 95),[98] it does so in order to adjust individuals all the more effectively to what the social system demands of them. Its function, therefore, is not limited to entertainment or marketing; instead, it serves as a central mechanism through which the logic of capital ultimately comes to shape the very "lifeworld" of individuals. It marks the patterns of perception and communication, adjusting the perceptual apparatus and the unconscious responses to the tempo required by an increasingly comprehensive social process, ultimately shaping their reactions and forms of self-expression. When Adorno and Horkheimer state that "the whole world is passed through the filter of the culture industry" (DA, 147),[99] they are implying that everyday experience is perceived through its parameters, causing the boundary between the real and the imaginary to blur (GS 10.2, 511).[100] This also has an impact on the configuration of subjects themselves. It contributes to weaving the web of constraints, expectations, and desires that shapes both conscious and unconscious attitudes. It defines the boundaries of what individuals are allowed to dream about. It shapes their

[98]Adorno, "Theory of Pseudo-Culture," 17.

[99]Adorno and Horkheimer, *Dialectic of Enlightenment*, 99.

[100]Adorno, "Prologue to Television," 55.

ways of speaking, thinking, and perceiving, as well as their relationships with others. It also influences their patterns of identification and the ways they compensate for unfulfilled desires. As such, it serves as the fundamental mechanism through which the organizing principles of social order ultimately shape the dispositions of living subjects.

That does not mean that the culture industry imposes itself on people's desires, expectations, and wishes solely from the outside; quite the contrary. The success of its products lies more in their ability to appeal directly or indirectly to diffuse yearnings in the consciousness and unconsciousness of consumers—fundamentally to a repertoire of "repressed, or simply unsatisfied impulses" (GS 10.2, 513).[101] Through the offerings of the culture industry, individuals seek to fulfill "whatever remained unsatisfied in them through the order which takes from them without giving in exchange what it promises" (MM, 168).[102] It is here that the culture industry illustrates its nature as a form of "mass deception," as stated in the chapter's subtitle in the *Dialectic of Enlightenment*. Through its mechanisms of pseudo-gratification, the desire to escape from the world of commodities only draws individuals further into it. Even when Adorno and Horkheimer allow themselves formulations as strong as "to be entertained means to be in agreement" (DA, 167),[103] what lies at the core of that "conformist fun" is not the stupidity of the audience, but rather its effective powerlessness. It is precisely from that sense of nullity and emptiness that they seek relief, turning to promises of escape that resonate with a widespread feeling of dissatisfaction. The problem is that "the culture industry presents that same everyday world as paradise. Escape, like elopement, is destined from the first to lead back to its starting point. Entertainment fosters the resignation which seeks to forget itself in entertainment" (DA, 164).[104] The supposed escape only reinforces the social norm, showing that there is no real antagonism between the work ethic and the supposed hedonism of "mass culture"; both stem from the same rationale.[105] This clarifies that the

[101]Ibid., 54.
[102]Adorno, *Minima Moralia*, 148.
[103]Adorno and Horkheimer, *Dialectic of Enlightenment*, 115.
[104]Ibid., 113.
[105]Hindrichs, *Zur kritischen Theorie*, 130.

issue is not that individuals are deceived, seduced, corrupted, or stripped of agency. Socialized individuals are not passive victims of the social imperatives imposed on them from outside. On the contrary, in order to get hold of them, the culture industry has to mobilize their needs and expectations. The appeal of the culture industry lies precisely in the fact that it "plans for and exploits the need for happiness. The culture industry has a kernel of truth in its fulfillment of a need that originates in the ever-increasing renunciation demanded by society"—that is, from the growing constraints demanded by survival in advanced capitalism, which expose the increasing powerlessness of individuals in the face of the heteronomy that governs their lives; "but the sort of concessions it provides renders it absolutely false" (AT, 461).[106]

The culture industry mobilizes the yearning for a better life—the persistent attachment of individuals to promises of happiness, or at least the need to escape an increasingly intolerable reality—and aligns it with the demands of the reproduction of the existing social order. In this way, it attempts to "channel and integrate the impulses of resistance" that social logic "cannot repress directly and violently."[107] The "deception" lies in how the culture industry responds to the needs it mobilizes in consumers, to whom it appeals precisely as subjects; what it absorbs and co-opts is their own yearning for freedom (GS 10.2, 648).[108] Yet, ultimately, its gratifications can never deliver on what they promise. The culture industry just repeatedly mobilizes the promises to which subjects cling in search of some way out. In this way, "a cycle of manipulation and retroactive need is unifying the system ever more tightly" (DA, 142).[109] Individuals seek to move beyond their dissatisfaction with the given social order, but the way these desires are gratified only reinforces the oppressive immanence of social logic. In this light, Adorno states that the culture industry "speculates on the state of (un)consciousness of the millions it addresses" (GS 10.1, 337).[110] It offers ways to mitigate the antagonism between increasingly weakened individuals and the social apparatus on which their survival depends. Thus, it

---

[106]Adorno, *Aesthetic Theory*, 311.

[107]Dankemeyer, *Die Erotik des Ohrs*, 126.

[108]Adorno, "Free Time," 170

[109]Adorno and Horkheimer, *Dialectic of Enlightenment*, 95.

[110]Adorno, "The Culture Industry: A Résumé," 51. Translation modified.

is not merely a case of "manipulation," and if one can speak of deception, it is a deception that subjects themselves seek out. The gratifications of the culture industry gain strength where the demands of the libidinal economy—which is always inclined to follow the path of least resistance—align with conformism and yield to the pressures of an overwhelming social reality. In this sense, such gratifications should be understood in light of the classic duality of ideology as expressed in the critique of the young Marx: they are not only the "opium of the people," but also the "sigh of the oppressed creature" (MEW 1, 378).[111] They are the expression of "needs, wishes, wants and demands" (GS 9.2, 20)[112] that the socializing logic of advanced capitalism leaves largely unsatisfied. However, the response to these demands is revealed to be "absolutely false," because it weakens individuals and reinforces their dependence on the social apparatus. Hence Adorno does not hesitate to point out that "the vanishing point of the culture industry" is none other than the aim of fostering "dependence and servitude" (GS 10.1, 345).[113] The world, as it is and as it disempowers individuals, appears as the only possible horizon: "ideology today means society as appearance" (GS 10.1, 25).[114]

Since it appeals to the often-unconscious impulses and conflicts of socialized subjects, Adorno argues that the logic of the culture industry operates as a kind of psychoanalysis in reverse (GS 8, 475):[115] "Instead of paying tribute to the unconscious by elevating it to consciousness and thereby simultaneously fulfilling its urge and pacifying its destructive force, the culture industry … reduces people to unconscious modes of behavior even more so than do the conditions of an existence that promises suffering to those who see through it and rewards to those who idolize it" (GS 10.2, 515).[116] Its effect leads socialized individuals, who as living beings inevitably seek satisfaction and relief from suffering, to conform to the existing world, internalizing renunciation and

[111]Marx, *Critique of Hegel's Philosophy of Right*, 131.

[112]Adorno, *The Stars Down to Earth*, 52.

[113]Adorno, "The Culture Industry: A Résumé," 59. Translation modified.

[114]Adorno, "Cultural Criticism and Society," 31. Translation modified.

[115]Adorno takes the term from Löwenthal, see Die techniken des amerikanischen Agitators," in *Das utopische soll Funken schlagen…. Zum hunderten Geburtstag von Leo Löwenthal*, ed. P. E. Jansen (Frankfurt: Klostermann, 1993), 122.

[116]Adorno, "Prologue to Television," 55.

tolerating the logic that condemns them to a life in conditions of increasing heteronomy. In this sense, the culture industry is "advertisement for the world through its duplication" (GS 10.1, 29).[117] At the same time, its influence does not work in only one direction. Capturing subjects—even if only to reduce them to customers—involves appealing to their desires and unmet needs, which are often neglected or even silenced by the performance principle governing the social logic: "When it seeks to grip the masses, even the ideology of the culture industry becomes as internally antagonistic as the society it targets. It contains the antidote to its own lie; this is all that needed to be pointed out to save it" (GS 10.1, 356).[118] Here Adorno reveals himself as the dialectical thinker he always was, a quality often overlooked in discussions of his work. Within the very logic of the culture industry's deception lies the potential for its own subversion. Since individuals, "as subjects [...] still represent the ultimate limit of reification, mass culture must try to take hold of them again and again: the bad infinity involved in this hopeless effort of repetition is the only trace of hope that this repetition might be in vain, that men cannot wholly be grasped after all" (GS 3, 331).[119]

As living subjects with aspirations and interests, individuals are never completely at the mercy of the culture industry's stimuli. This is reflected in Adorno's assertion that the products of the culture industry are undoubtedly "shallower and more standardized than any of its fans can ever be" (AT, 365).[120] In his later writings, Adorno offers more than a glimmer of hope about the limits of the culture industry's ability to apprehend human beings. Although individuals may participate in the gratifications offered by the culture industry, often due to a lack of alternatives, empirical studies by the Institute for Social Research in the 1960s suggested that they did not really believe in its claims and promises. In this regard, Adorno stated that "the real interests of individuals are still strong enough to resist, up to a point, their total appropriation" (GS 10.2, 655).[121] This opens a space for critique

[117]Adorno, "Cultural Criticism and Society," 34.
[118]Theodor W. Adorno, "Transparencies on Film," 72.
[119]Theodor W. Adorno, "The Schema of Mass Culture," 93.
[120]Adorno, *Aesthetic Theory*, 246. Translation modified.
[121]Adorno, "Erziehung nach Auschwitz," 175.

and intervention, even if it does not guarantee success. Although there are limits to the capacity of appropriation of the social system, there is no doubt that it has gained ground. This is evidenced by the authority which the social apparatus wields in managing social needs: "The more strongly the culture industry entrenches itself, the more it can do as it chooses with the needs of consumers—producing, controlling, disciplining them; even withdrawing amusement altogether: here, no limits are set to cultural progress" (DA, 166).[122] Adorno's analysis acknowledges the reality of a historical situation in which "the danger of domination being introduced into human beings through the monopolization of their needs" represents "a real tendency of late capitalism" (GS 8, 393).[123] This underscores the consequences of the tendency toward total socialization for living subjects.

The concept of need relates to nature within human beings, encompassing its most fundamental, instinctual dimension; however, needs are always mediated by social relations. The culture industry caters to the specific needs of the social logic of advanced capitalism: those aimed at reproducing the labor force and aligning individuals' desires with the interests of the social logic upon which their survival ultimately depends. Thus, the satisfaction of these demands becomes a "tie" that binds individuals to the social whole and reinforces their dependence on it: "Nothing may be thought, written, done, or made that transcends a condition which maintains its power largely through the needs of its victims" (GS 10.1, 113).[124] On this basis, Adorno understands that true emancipation would mean transforming the relationship between needs and their satisfaction, as in the current forms of socialization both are locked in a circular situation that ultimately disempowers individuals. While capitalism had developed a high level of sophistication in the means of satisfying needs, it has in fact tethered individuals to the satisfaction of their most basic needs. Ultimately social existence revolves around the mere reproduction of life under the given social conditions, stultifying human beings and hindering

[122] Adorno and Horkheimer, *Dialectic of Enlightenment*, 115.
[123] Theodor W. Adorno, "Theses on Need," 465. Translation modified.
[124] Adorno, "Aldous Huxley and Utopia," 110.

the development of needs that would allow for a richer and more gratifying life.[125] The culture industry plays a substantial role in this regard. The more individuals are required to sacrifice within a system where the production of goods is not aimed at satisfying human needs, but at reproducing capital and sustaining the social processes that support it, the more receptive they will be to offers of escapism, compensation, or strategies that help them cope with living conditions that demand much and offer rather little in return. These needs are indeed real, and no one has the right to deny them. However, theory must still acknowledge that they are a product of the "false" whole. These needs reveal the mutilation of human possibilities in a heteronomous social context. The idea of an emancipated society that "would call for the bad acting of Hedy Lamarr, or the bad soups of Campbell, is absurd. The better the soup, the more pleasurable the rejection of Lamarr" (GS 8, 394).[126]

The critique of the culture industry must therefore be understood within a framework that considers how the logic of socialization in advanced capitalism stifles the development of social needs and possibilities. By focusing on the culture sphere, the analysis sheds light on how the transition to advanced capitalism tendentially eradicated any potential for transcendence. The "cultural" needs addressed here are less about safeguarding an idea of freedom and autonomy, or about the capacity for experience, and more about adjusting individuals to the requirements of the social system. This clarifies why Adorno often refers to the social system of advanced capitalism as a "web of delusion" [*Verblendungszusammenhang*]. This diagnosis implied a severe reduction of the scope of experience in contemporary societies: "The regression of the masses today lies in their inability to hear with their own ears what has not already been heard, to touch with their hands what has not previously been grasped; it is the new form of blindness which supersedes that of vanquished myth" (DA, 53–4).[127]

[125]Few authors have emphasized this point as strongly as Hans-Jürgen Krahl, a disciple of Adorno and a leader of the German student movement. Krahl argued that the struggle for emancipation is rooted in the development of these needs (see Krahl, *Konstitution und Klassenkampf*; and Jordi Maiso, "Hans-Jürgen Krahl: Social Constitution and Class Struggle, B. Best, W. Bonefeld & Ch. O"Kane: *The Sage Handbook of Frankfurt School Critical Theory* (Thousand Oaks: Sage, 2018, 335–350).
[126]Adorno, "Theses on Need," 466.
[127]Adorno and Horkheimer, *Dialectic of Enlightenment*, 28–9.

The culture industry, as an instance aspiring to leave nothing outside its logic of functional mediation, is at the heart of this problem. It contributes toward undermining the subjective capacity to develop desires, intentions, and demands that go beyond the suffocating immanence of a social system that tends to turn socialized individuals into mere objects (GS 20.1, 343). Thus, "the coercive immediacy prevents men from becoming conscious of the very mechanism which mutilates them—it reproduces itself in their pliant minds" (GS 10.1, 227).[128]

However, this tendency toward total integration does not imply that the process itself is without any friction or that everything ultimately fits seamlessly into the system's framework; this can be seen in Adorno's awareness of the limits of the culture industry's "deception." These limits reside in living subjects, who, as inherently antagonistic elements within the social system, cannot be entirely subsumed by it. Critical theory thus aims to connect with the potentials of individuals, to strengthen their faculties as subjects and to counteract the social process that relegates them to a position of weakness and dependence. In this regard, the very logic by which the culture industry seeks to capture individuals offers a foothold for critique. For, in order to get hold of living subjects, it needs to reproduce their needs over and over again, and "even within the needs of those who are registered and managed, something responds in which they are not fully captured—the surplus of the subjective element, which the system never fully mastered" (ND, 99).[129] "Even in the false needs of the living, an element of freedom stirs" (GS 10.1, 390).[130] Adorno never lost sight of the possibility of connecting with that "surplus" element in the participation of subjects as a potential for breaking out of the vicious circle of the always-the-same. Early in *Minima Moralia* he had already written that "the change in the relations of production themselves depends largely on what takes place in the 'sphere of consumption,' which is the mere reflection of production and the caricature of true life: in the consciousness and unconsciousness of individuals" (MM, 13–4).[131] What was at stake in

[128]Adorno, "The George-Hofmannstahl Correspondence 1891–1906," 217. Translation modified.
[129]Adorno, *Negative Dialectics*, 92. Translation modified.
[130]Adorno, "Functionalism Today," 109.
[131]Adorno, *Minima Moralia*, 15.

the very sphere of pseudo-gratifications, the search for satisfaction and the compensations for discomfort was the very possibility of social transformation.

Thus, it becomes crucial to examine the anthropological transformations imposed by advanced capitalism, as well as the vital and psychological mechanisms through which individuals internalized forms of social coercion that confine them to their roles as executors of social functions, rendering them both dispensable and interchangeable. This implies moving from the analysis of social objectivity to the way in which this is sedimented in living individuals. In this way, living subjects themselves emerge as fields of tension between the demands for adaptation and the still-latent potential for emancipation.

6

Toward a "New Type of Human Being": Anthropological Transformation Under Advanced Capitalism

At the heart of Adorno's entire social theory is the relationship between the individual and the social whole. Individuals depend on the social logic to reproduce their lives; in general, they can only "earn a living" and are able to satisfy their needs if they fulfil a useful function in the social system. The totality, for its part, is neither self-sufficient nor does it exist in its own right. It can only perpetuate itself through the action of individuals. This is why it must capture them—shaping their desires and aspirations—so that, through their own agency as subjects, they ultimately reproduce its logic. However, the balance of power between living subjects and the social whole cannot be said to be equal. Since it determines the conditions for existence and subsistence, the social whole always takes precedence. Individuals, on the other hand, depend on it to fulfill their needs. After all, individuation itself is a social process, and not a fact of nature. The very constitution of individual subjects, from their own *ratio* to their ways of apprehending the world and acting within it, responds to the internalization of the social patterns that mediate the conditions for their survival. In this sense "the specific factors which form individuality" can be understood "as internalizations of social compulsions, needs and demands" (ES, 190).[1] This implies that the anthropological constitution and psychological dispositions of individuals are not fixed, but vary depending on their role in and contribution to the reproduction of the social logic. Thus, the bourgeois notion of the individual as a natural, irreducible, and autonomous entity dissolves. It becomes evident that the social logic shapes the very constitution of individuals: the forms of socialization under advanced capitalism extend even into their inner life. However, this does not mean that the illusion of a substantial subject is fully dispelled: "The more individuals are in effect degraded into functions within the social totality through their connection to the system, the more the human being, as a principle, is exalted with the attributes of creative power, absolute rule, and spirit" (GS 10.2, 744).[2]

The critique of the privileging of the individual subject as the substantive and explanatory principle of social logic had already been formulated in Marx's critique of political economy. Marx did not merely contest the "robinsonades" of classical political economy, which treated the individual as a natural entity and not as a product of history (MEW 42, 19–20),[3] but also emphasized that the reduction of living individuals to embodiments of social functions is a defining feature of capitalist socialization. In *Capital*, he observed that when individuals act within the social process, they do not do so in their own right, but rather as "character masks" (MEW 23, 100).[4] More specifically, individuals act as "personifications of economic relations" (MEW 23, 100):[5] as buyers or sellers, capitalists or workers. In this sense, individuals become the bearers of social roles, and it is only by fulfilling these roles—by serving the reproduction of capital, as functionaries of the logic of the "automatic subject"—that they can maintain their social positions and, where possible, reproduce their

[1] Adorno, *Introduction to Sociology*, 112.
[2] Adorno, "Marginalia to Theory and Praxis," 248. Translation modified.
[3] Karl Marx, *Grundrisse*, trans. Martin Nicolaus (London: Penguin Books, 1993), 83.
[4] Marx, *Capital 1*, 179. Translation modified.
[5] Ibid.

lives. By this, Marx did not mean that the mask of the social role conceals or represses the concrete, flesh-and-blood individual. He was referring to the way in which individuation necessarily takes place within the framework of coercive social mediations that structure the functioning of the system as a whole. The individual confronts an intricate web of objective constraints and subjective demands that both enable and limit their capacity to act. This dynamic allows individuals to assert themselves as subjects in different spheres of social life: whether as subjects of work, money, or competition. In this regard, the commodification of labor power is undoubtedly a key catalyst for the social forms of individualization. However, the possibilities offered by consumer capitalism to define one's individuality through market choices—at least as far as purchasing capacity allows—are no less significant. "Expressed using the categories of the critique of political economy, the libidinous and tormentable body is nothing more than the individual who can consume or whose labor power can be consumed."[6] Thus, the social roles, these "masks" of which Marx spoke, are both true and false at once: they are true insofar as flesh-and-blood individuals are inseparable from them, and false insofar as they constitute forms of subjectivation that compel individuals to actively reproduce a social logic of unfreedom.[7]

In this regard, Adorno observed that the ways in which the social logic shapes the agency of the individuals, and even their internal constitution, assimilate them to the *ratio* of *homo economicus*; as such, they "incarnate closer the transcendental subject than the living individual[s] which [they] immediately take themselves to be" (GS 10.2, 745).[8] Precisely where individuals believe themselves to be most fully themselves, they in fact act as bearers of social functions—cogs in the machinery of a seemingly all-encompassing social system. This led Adorno to the provocative claim that "what is supposedly most obvious, the empirical subject, would actually have to be considered as something not yet existing" (GS 10.2, 745).[9] At the same

---

[6]Scheit, *Quälbarer Leib*, 34.

[7]Russell Jacoby, *Social Amnesia. A Critique of Contemporary Psychology from Adler to Laing* (New York: Transaction, 1975), 70–1.

[8]Adorno, "On Subject and Object," 248.

[9]Ibid.

time, Adorno acknowledged that twentieth-century capitalism's scope of socialization extended far beyond what Marx could observe in his own time. Under the conditions of "total socialization," individuals not only embody social functions; they do so amid a growing polarization between increasingly concentrated social power and deepening powerlessness. Living subjects are no longer—and can no longer feel themselves to be—autonomous agents of their own lives. Even if they lack clear awareness of their fragile position in the social whole, they sense that their fate is determined by heteronomous social powers upon which they are utterly dependent. This implies a profound transformation of what individuals are and what they mean. They can no longer be understood as monads, closed unto themselves and clearly differentiated from external reality, but instead increasingly dissolve into the logic of the social system. The line demarcating self from environment becomes blurry (IG, 62).[10] Consequently, individuals find themselves at the mercy of a system whose vast machinery is indifferent to their needs and their existence as concrete beings. That is why Adorno spoke of an antagonism between the social totality and the individuals who compose it, in which anguish and fear become central forces in the new forms of socialization. In response, living subjects, now increasingly weakened and dependent, end up identifying themselves with the social functions they embody and perform. This identification allows them to compensate for the fear and the wounds inflicted in the social process of individuation. Here the social logic can hardly be understood without the help of psychology. This required going beyond Marx, who, despite his allusion to the concept of "character mask," never fully addressed the intertwining of external and inner life within subjects themselves. However, without examining how living subjects internalize the social demands imposed on them, it is not possible to grasp the conditions under which life becomes damaged life. This implies that individuation, rather than being a fully realized process, remains unfulfilled (HGS 12, 592).

Adorno's diagnosis responds to a specific historical juncture: the transition from classical bourgeois capitalism to the post-liberal capitalism that

---

[10] Adorno, "The Problem of a New Type of Human Being," 462.

consolidated in the 1930s and 1940s. During this period, the tendency toward "total socialization" converged with the emergence of increasingly vertical forms of sociopolitical organization, which, regardless of whether the forms of government were authoritarian or democratic, gave rise to increasingly integral societies. In such societies, the classical attributes ascribed to the modern subject—autonomy, freedom, sovereignty, the capacity to be master over oneself—appeared to have lost their basis in social reality and were on the verge of dissolution. However, the implications of this transformation were not only philosophical, nor merely psychological; they pointed to substantive changes in social life and in the very constitution of human beings. Structural transformations of society do not occur only through social dynamics; they also unfold through transformations in the very individuals who sustain and reproduce it (GS 9.2, 362).[11] For this reason, Adorno comes to recognize that the forms of socialization in post-liberal capitalism involve anthropological transformations of far-reaching significance (GS 14, 10). These transformations decisively impacted the way in which human beings relate to their natural, social, and technical environment, as well as to one another and to themselves. The new configurations of social life influenced interpersonal relations, the metabolic exchange between society and nature, and the very constitution of living subjects. However, this is not to suggest that the demands of social logic act upon individuals as an external force, modifying an otherwise intact natural essence. As Adorno remarked, "there is no substratum beneath such 'deformations,' no ontic interior on which social mechanisms merely act externally" (MM, 262).[12] Individuation itself is a social process, and the internal and external dimensions of human life cannot be understood apart from the social mediations in which individuation unfolds. That is why Max Horkheimer, in his inaugural lecture as director of the Institute for Social Research in 1931, had already pointed out the need to carefully examine the interrelation between "the economic life of society, the psychic development of individuals, and the changes in the realm of culture in the narrow sense" (HGS

---

[11]Theodor W. Adorno, *Guilt and Defense*, trans. J. K. Olick and Andrew J. Perrin (Cambridge, MA: Harvard University Press, 2010), 222.
[12]Adorno, *Minima Moralia*, 229.

3, 32).[13] Adorno's critical theory readily took up this challenge. His analyses of the historical fate of the individual in post-liberal capitalism illuminate not only the imbrication of society and nature within socialized subjects, but also the extent to which the emerging social system imposes itself on living subjects in ways that are intrinsically harmful, distorted, and ultimately false.

The Historical Decline of the Individual and the Sacrifice of the Living

"In the age of the individual's liquidation, the question of individuality must be raised anew," Adorno wrote in *Minima Moralia* (MM, 147).[14] The drastic thesis of the annihilation of the individual, which had already been formulated in *Dialectic of Enlightenment* (DA 177),[15] aimed to highlight a far-reaching historical transformation and has been a frequent subject of discussion.[16] At this point, however, it is important to avoid possible misunderstandings. The individual is not understood here as a biological category, in the sense "that human beings do not come into the world like coral colonies but [in general] as single beings" (LGF 104).[17] Rather, individuality as such is conceived as a historical crystallization characterized by features such as singularity, autonomy, self-consciousness, and the capacity for self-determination; in this sense it is "a social category in the fullest sense" (ES, 190),[18] closely tied to the features of bourgeois subjectivity. The individual appears as a monadic entity,

[13]Horkheimer, "The Present Situation of Social Philosophy and the Tasks of an Institute for Social Research," 11.

[14]Adorno, *Minima Moralia*, 129.

[15]Adorno and Horkheimer, *Dialectic of Enlightenment*, 124.

[16]The following stand out amongst the most valuable texts on this issue: Thorsten Bonacker, "Ohne Angst verschieden sein können. Individualität in der integralen Gesellschaft," in Dirk Auer et al. (eds.), *Die Gesellschaftstheorie Adornos* (Darmstadt: Wissenschaftliche Buchgesellschaft, 1998), 117–43; Pablo López Álvarez, "Ocaso del individuo, recuerdo de lo vivo: Sujeto y naturaleza en Adorno," in *Melancolía y verdad*, ed. Muñoz, 33–70; Hermann Schweppenhäuser, *Vergegenwärtigungen zur Unzeit?* (Lüneburg: Zu Klampen, 1986), 42–69; José Antonio Zamora, "Th. W. Adorno y la aniquilación del individuo," *Isegoría* 28 (2003), 231–43.

[17]Adorno, *History and Freedom*, 70.

[18]Adorno, *Introduction to Sociology*, 112.

distinct both from the surrounding reality and from others, and oriented toward the pursuit of relatively autonomous purposes. The capacity of empirical human beings to embody the attributes associated with individuality and to constitute themselves as singular subjects depends on specific social mediations. As Adorno observed, "The individual owes his crystallization to the forms of political economy, particularly to those of the urban market. Even as the opponent of the pressure of socialization he remains the latter's most particular product and its likeness. What enables him to resist, that streak of independence in him, springs from monadological individual interest and its precipitate, character" (MM, 169).[19]

For Adorno, the figure of the individual was rooted in very specific social conditions: it was a relatively late product of European history. Its emergence was linked to the dissolution of the feudal order, which liberated human beings from relations of servitude and direct personal dependence, thereby opening up new spheres of action, primarily through the generalization of mercantile exchange. These transformations made it possible to conceive of human beings not only as members of an estate, social class, or family but, above all, as individuals. In this sense, they were also seen as subjects capable of asserting themselves autonomously within the economic sphere—something that bourgeois society would not only make possible, but actively require of its members. The category of the individual took shape at a time when social relations became structured as monetary relations, and, among socialized subjects, there was "no other nexus between man and man than naked self-interest, than callous 'cash payment'" (MEW 4, 464).[20] The capacity for self-determination associated with this historical figure was thus inextricably linked to the social principle of exchange and property rights, which granted individuals—conceived as relatively autonomous and independent entities, bearers of *private* interests—a certain degree of agency as subjects of commodity exchange. However, this also meant that they were compelled to reproduce their lives within a social logic in which the pursuit of individual interests is mediated through relations of buying and selling.

---

[19] Adorno, *Minima Moralia*, 148.
[20] Mark and Engels, *Communist Manifesto*, 222.

Individuation thus emerges as something intimately tied to the social organization of self-preservation and the struggle for subsistence; this is what keeps it largely associated with biology, despite all the social mediations.[21] The individual is a living creature striving to preserve its life, functioning as a relatively autonomous and self-sufficient entity, capable of forging its destiny through its own action. Yet Adorno insists that, at its core, the form of the individual is nothing but the "reflection of the social process" (MM 261).[22] Although its appearance might suggest "the fictitious claim … that what is biologically one must logically precede the social whole," "what presents itself as an original entity, a monad, is only the result of a social division of the social process. … Not only is the self entwined in society; it owes society its existence in the most literal sense" (MM, 175).[23] In fact, the social fate of each individual depends on its ability, as an autonomous economic subject, to develop its capacities in alignment with the requirements of social logic. If these individuals succeed—and this depends to a great extent on blind mechanisms beyond their control—they will obtain wealth and will see their capacity for action expanded; however, if they do not comply with the demands of the reproduction of capital, they will find themselves isolated, with their individual potentials increasingly restricted. In this regard, the social function, the "character mask," is not external to the individual, but rather enmeshed with their being down to their innermost fibers. Certainly, the logic of universal exchange grants socialized individuals a certain degree of freedom to pursue their own aims and assert themselves as subjects to achieve them. However, this framework of agency does not exist in a vacuum: it is rooted in the functional complex of the social whole. Here, commodity exchange serves not so much the purpose of satisfying individual needs as that of valorizing value. In this sense, Marx pointed out that in capitalist social relations personal independence is based on an objective dependence (MEW 42, 91),[24] which does not allow individuals to free themselves from fear of losing access to the

---

[21]"Self-preservation, the Spinozist *sese conservare*, is truly a law of nature for all living things" (ND, 342; *Negative Dialectics*, 349).

[22]Adorno, *Minima Moralia*, 229.

[23]Adorno, *Minima Moralia*, 153–4.

[24]Marx, *Grundrisse*, 157.

means of survival. Ultimately, their freedom is circumscribed by the blind mechanisms of the reproduction of capital. Thus, the conditions governing the self-preservation of autonomous individuals are largely beyond their control. An economic crisis is enough to leave individuals faced with ruin, cut off from any means of sustenance, regardless of their behavior. Therefore, beneath the autonomy of individual subjects who pursue their interests through the mechanisms of the market and competition, heteronomy still persists; the conditions for the reproduction of life within capitalist socialization remain as unyielding and blind as fate.

Based on this state of affairs, it can be said that capitalist individuality emerges from a logic of "devouring and being devoured" (ND, 349);[25] in it, there is no room for solidarity between social atoms. In this context, Adorno pointed out that individual freedom is also "an image to cover up the total social necessity, which compels the individual to become rugged in order to survive" (ND, 259).[26] Thus, the positive dimension of the individual in bourgeois liberal society—rooted in its capacity for action and scope for self-determination—is inextricably tied to the logic of social atomization and the struggle of all against all. This aspect of competition is closely linked to the monadic nature of the individual, bound to the illusion of being an autonomous and self-sufficient entity, even though everything about them is constituted by the social mediations that allow them to assert themselves as individual subjects.[27] In this sense, "his consciousness of himself as something in-itself" is but the appearance that the social process requires "to raise his level of performance, whereas in fact the individuated function in the modern economy as mere agents of the law of value" (MM, 261).[28] Indeed, the social logic can only operate through the principle of individual self-preservation, "for all its narrowmindedness" (ND, 306).[29] While the individual is associated with self-consciousness and the capacity for self-determination, their degree

[25] Adorno, *Negative Dialectics*, 355.

[26] Ibid., 262. Translation modified.

[27] "Individuals are human beings before they are individuals; they relate to others before they explicitly relate to themselves. They are shaped by the conditions in which they live before they can begin to shape those conditions themselves." (Institut für Sozialforschung [ed.], *Soziologische Exkurse*, 42).

[28] Adorno, *Minima Moralia*, 229.

[29] Adorno, *Negative Dialectics*, 312.

of agency within the social whole reveals them as mere executors of the *ratio* of the "automatic subject" that is imposed through the process of exchange—the valorization of value. From this perspective, their social function is merely derived from the fact that commodities cannot walk themselves to the market and exchange themselves but require the individual's intervention as a "subject of self-interest" whose will resides in commodities (MEW 23, 99).[30]

So, although the individual may have felt free insofar as they stood in opposition to society or other individuals, their role as a subsidiary agent in the reproduction of capital revealed that this freedom was largely an illusion: "The individual was free as the economically active bourgeois subject, free to the extent to which the economic system required him to be autonomous in order to function. Its autonomy is thereby already potentially negated at its source" (ND 259).[31] In reality, this relative and socially conditioned autonomy was the result of individuals having internalized their captivity within the social logic (GS 10.2, 750).[32] For this reason, Adorno argues that in modern capitalist societies individuality has always been, at least in part, a fiction —something illusory. To the extent that individuals only had significance insofar as they could assert themselves by fulfilling their social role within the logic of the whole, they were always fungible and replaceable: they did not matter as unique, concrete beings[33]—that is, as effective individualities. This was already true in the era of bourgeois liberal capitalism, yet it took on new dimensions with the transition toward total socialization in advanced capitalism. Here, social integration had reached such an extreme that it hardly left any room for what might be substantively singular or distinct to unfold. "The social system was becoming increasingly detached from the initiative of individual economic actors," to the point where their conscious interests were no longer the foundation of the market. Instead, "the expectations placed on individual behavior were being dictated by the goals established by economic cartels."[34]

---

[30]Marx, *Capital: Volume 1*, 178.

[31]Adorno, *Negative Dialectics*, 262. Translation modified.

[32]Adorno, "On Subject and Object," 252.

[33]Theodor W. Adorno and ArnoldGehlen, "Ist die Soziologie eine Wissenschaft von Menschen? Ein Streitgespräch," in *Adornos Philosophie in Grundbegriffen*, ed. Friedemann Grenz (Frankfurt: Suhrkamp, 1974), 249.

[34]Zamora, "Th. W. Adorno y la aniquilación del individuo," 233.

The reproduction of the economic system as a whole increasingly depends on impersonal conditions involving the availability of the capital necessary to sustain an increasingly technical and costly system of production. As a result, the possibilities of agency available to individual subjects are substantially reduced. They no longer act as relatively self-sufficient entities forging their own destinies through their actions; instead, their role as economic agents increasingly reveals them to be mere cogs in a vast and overwhelming machine. Competition no longer takes place primarily between social atoms, but between enormous blocs of concentrated capital. In this landscape, individual subjects struggle to secure a niche in which they can reproduce their lives. Their goal is no longer autonomy, but adaptation. As society becomes increasingly organized, administered, and rationalized according to the imperatives of capital reproduction, the economic functions and scope of action available to individuals are established in advance, reinforcing their status as fungible, expendable beings. Their individuality is increasingly confined to the sphere of private life, essentially to consumption, where they can continue to act as subjects as long as they maintain sufficient access to money. "Powerless in the face of a society which is overwhelming, the individual can only experience itself as socially mediated" (GS 4, 288). Hence Adorno concludes that "here, the concept of the individual, having emerged historically, is reaching its historical limit" (GS 8, 450).

In this sense, the historical trajectory of capitalism, which once allowed individuals a certain degree of freedom by introducing a gap between them and the groups to which they belong, allowing them in turn to assert themselves as autonomous subjects, ultimately extinguishes all capacity for self-determination: "The process by which the individual becomes autonomous, which is a function of exchange society, ends in its abolition through integration. That which produced freedom reverts back into unfreedom" (ND, 259).[35] Human beings can no longer autonomously shape their social destiny; they are instead subjected to social forces that lie entirely beyond their control, forces that demand ever more from them. In this sense, integration entails the unconditional subjugation of individual life to the

[35]Adorno, *Negative Dialectics*, 261. Translation modified.

imperatives of an increasingly cohesive social totality; its ultimate consequence is the disintegration of the autonomous subject. As Adorno writes in *Minima Moralia*: "It is the signature of our age that no-one, without exception, can now determine his own life within even a moderately comprehensible framework, as was possible earlier in the assessment of market relationships" (MM, 41).[36] Indeed, everyone—even the most powerful—senses that their lives are in the hands of unbridled and blind economic forces: "Everyone senses that he is somehow at the mercy of society" (GS 9.1, 30).[37]

This, of course, does not suggest that social inequalities have disappeared: rather, it highlights the universalization of unfreedom. Adorno is keenly aware that what is undermined in this process encompasses a range of traits central to the anthropological constitution of the bourgeois subject— traits that had remained a class prerogative:[38] "self-responsibility, foresight, the self-sufficient individual, the fulfillment of duty, and a rigid moral conscience" (GS 8, 450). The character traits that emerge in their place are no longer tied to an idea of autonomy or conscious participation in social life but rather to a disposition to adapt to structures of domination that allow individuals to feel protected by an increasingly concentrated social power. This realistic assessment of power relations drives individuals to capitulate to the social apparatus on which their lives depend (DA, 76);[39] Adorno's diagnosis of the weakness of the ego is rooted here. The growing subjugation of individuals to the demands of social logic, which had become massive and against which they were powerless, was one of the factors that helped explain the emergence of fascism for Adorno, but it was also key to understanding the growing compulsion toward conformity in advanced capitalism. In both

[36]Adorno, *Minima Moralia*, 37.

[37]Theodor W.Adorno, *The Psychological Technique of Martin Luther Thomas' Radio Addresses* (Stanford, CA: Stanford University Press, 2000), 20.

[38]For Adorno, the concept of the individual is inseparable from its class-based imprint, which restricts it to the bourgeoisie. Consequently, the concept of the human being that operates in bourgeois society has a strongly exclusionary character: it leaves out the proletariat, the dependent, women, those unable to fend for themselves, in short, all those who are "denied individuality by the property system" (GS 8, 389; "Reflections on Class Theory," 108). It is precisely this heteronomous and dependent condition that is generalized in the new social framework.

[39]Adorno and Horkheimer, *Dialectic of Enlightenment*, 45.

cases predatory forces are at work, feeding on the lives they subjugate (GS 10.1, 267).

Perhaps the central element of Adorno's analysis of the social process of individuation lies in his awareness that these transformations affect not only the social role of the individual, but also the very constitution of human beings (MM, 261).[40] Now, it is barely possible for anyone to constitute themselves as a self. The new conditions of socialization no longer allow living subjects to maintain any distance from the social apparatus, directly undermining the very conditions of possibility of individuality. It is in this context that one can best understand Adorno's observation that for "many people it is already an impertinence to say 'I' " (MM, 55).[41] While liberal capitalism had fostered and protected individuality, in the "administered world" every manifestation of it becomes suspect (GS 8, 444). Individuality itself becomes a burden for the subject.[42] Their objective weakness leaves them with no alternative but to adapt to the existing social conditions. Yet this adaptation generates a fear of social exclusion, which emerges as a new key to the *principium individuationis* (ND, 355).[43] For this principle has not lost its validity: it simply shifted in meaning. It no longer aligns with the capacity for agency and self-determination but instead reflects a universalization of fear that reinforces atomization. Individuals sense that they have become completely insignificant with regard to the social logic, even as their own weakened state prevents them from fully grasping its implications. If individuation had emerged in connection with the struggle for survival within a social logic shaped by the commodification of labor power and the universal principle of exchange, the conditions of self-preservation in advanced capitalism render obsolete the historical figure of the individual as an autonomous and self-sufficient entity. Consequently, living subjects are forced to annul any distance from social logic and to assimilate themselves to the demands of the apparatus on which the reproduction of their life depends (GS 8, 361).[44] However, while the line separating them from social

---

[40] Adorno, *Minima Moralia*, 228–9.

[41] Ibid., 50. Translation modified.

[42] Th. W. Adorno: "Zum Verhältnis vom Individuum und Gesellschaft heute," *Vorträge 1949–1968*, 146.

[43] Adorno, *Negative Dialectics*, 345.

[44] Adorno, "Late Capitalism or Industrial Society," 117.

imperatives blurs, this does not imply the elimination of the monadic element that pits them against one another: "with the dissolution of liberalism, the truly bourgeois principle, that is competition, far from being overcome, has passed from the objectivity of the social process into the composition of its colliding and jostling atoms, and therewith as if into anthropology" (MM, 28).[45]

The significance of Adorno's observation can hardly be overstated. What is at stake here is a transformation that affects the very constitution of the human. Crucially, this process of the annihilation of the individual does not imply an overcoming of its isolated and atomized character for the sake of solidarity among living subjects (MM, 153)[46]—quite the contrary. As long as the logic of competition persists, other people continue to be perceived either "as enemies or allies, but always as instruments, things" (DA, 81).[47] The decline of the historical figure of the individual is by no means at odds with the resurgence of certain traits that are characteristic of bourgeois anthropology, such as a coldness and indifference toward the fate of others. These traits now give rise to ever cruder and more brutal forms of behavior, which are always linked to the struggle to maintain one's social position and ensure survival. In fact, both the particularism of interests and the right to property remain in place, continuing to exert their influence on character dispositions (MM, 37).[48] This obstructs the possibility of genuine rapprochement between increasingly powerless living subjects, who perceive themselves as merely interchangeable atoms within an increasingly autonomized social apparatus, thereby intensifying isolation and loneliness. The monadic constitution of subjects becomes a prison; more and more, individuals experience their condition as atomized subjects of self-interest as an unbearable burden—one that nevertheless seems impossible to escape.[49]

---

[45]Adorno, *Minima Moralia*, 27.

[46]Ibid., 135.

[47]Adorno and Horkheimer, *Dialectic of Enlightenment*, 49.

[48]Adorno, *Minima Moralia*, 34.

[49]"Every person today, without exception, feels too little loved, because every person cannot love enough" (GS 10.2, 687; "Education After Auschwitz," 201). This lack of affection is rooted in the very structure of social life, which promotes the ruthless pursuit of personal interests in a regime of competition. The problem is that this becomes ingrained in one's character and makes spontaneous relationships difficult, as "the people whom one should love are themselves such that they cannot love, and therefore in turn are not at all that loveable" (GS 10.2, 688; "Education After Auschwitz," 202).

The problem, then, is not that the individual has been annihilated, but that this historical doomed figure persists in a neutralized, impotent, and degraded form (MM, 153).[50] That which was once the embodiment of a certain degree of autonomy becomes the personification of anguish, harm, and impotence. Individuals—who indeed are no longer fully individuals—experience their ongoing individuation with a specific type of fear: the fear of exclusion from the social bond that grants access to the satisfaction of needs and the gratifications of consumption. They sense that they are increasingly replaceable within the logic of the productive apparatus, and this generates a "deep sense of superfluity [that] is really at the heart of the general malaise, the need for security, and uncertainty" (PETG, 99)[51] that dominate social life. They feel worthless in the face of the social whole on which their lives depend (MBP, 170–2).[52] Yet the presentiment of their own fragility leads them to harden themselves and to be willing to do anything in order to avoid losing their position (IG, 76). In their state of growing powerlessness, integration into the existing mode of socialization becomes the only aspiration left to them, leading them to subordinate themselves to the social mechanisms and identify unreservedly with the roles they seek to embody (GS 8, 361).[53] Nevertheless, this pressure continues to weigh heavily upon them, and their atomization inevitably pits them against a social power with which they cannot withstand. In this sense, the historical fate of the individual highlights the transition from a society mediated by universal exchange to a concentration of power tending toward increasingly direct forms of domination (MM, 171).[54] This paves the way for a social formation that, in the 1930s and 1940s, would tend toward authoritarian models. The substratum of an increasingly vertical capitalist economy managed through the levers of state power persisted in the Fordist Keynesianism of the second postwar period, giving rise to an era of stability

---

In the current social order, genuine affection is limited to small enclaves, beyond which any display of love, but also of solidarity, empathy, or recognition, immediately raises suspicion of being purely instrumental.

[50]Adorno, *Minima Moralia*, 135.

[51]Adorno, *Philosophical Elements of a Theory of Society*, 59.

[52]Adorno, *Metaphysics*, 109–10.

[53]Adorno, "Late Capitalism or Industrial Society," 117.

[54]Adorno, *Minima Moralia*, 150.

and prosperity. Adorno, however, never idealized this period, as he saw it as marked by a growing polarization between concentrated social power and individual powerlessness. This sharpened his perception of some of the darker aspects of this phase of capitalism. While it is clear that his analyses cannot simply be applied to present-day society without considering the mediations of a different phase of capitalist socialization, certain passages of Adorno's seem to herald the genesis of some of the most distinctive features of the configuration of contemporary capitalism.

These features primarily reflect the aporias of individuation in advanced capitalism. Under mounting pressure of the social system, socialized individuals increasingly perceive themselves as "means of production and not as living purposes" (MM, 262).[55] To explain what the advance in the socialization of the inner life of human beings entails, Adorno draws an analogy with Marx's concept of the change in the organic composition of capital (MEW 23, 651).[56] By this concept, Marx referred to how, as the process of accumulation unfolds, the mass of the means of production grows in relation to the mass of labor power necessary for their operation. Adorno identified an analogous process in the shaping of socialized individuals. They develop their aptitudes and capacities in line with the productive demands of the social system, allowing the socializing logic of capital to penetrate ever more deeply into them—albeit at the expense of their constitution as living subjects: "If the integration of society … designates subjects more and more exclusively as partial moments in the network of material production, then the 'alteration of the technical composition of capital' is prolonged within those encompassed, and indeed constituted, by the technological demands of the production process. The organic composition of man is growing" (MM, 261–2).[57] This implies that, in the very constitution of the living individual, the imperatives of the social apparatus acquire ever greater force. But what marks them out as living subjects comes across as increasingly residual (GS 8, 60).[58] In this way, the process of absorption into the social logic molds human beings in its image and likeness.

[55]Ibid., 229. Translation modified.
[56]Marx, *Capital: Volume 1*, 773.
[57]Adorno, *Minima Moralia*, 229.
[58]Adorno, "Sociology and Psychology. Part I," 80.

Decades later, Adorno would state that, with this diagnosis of the change in the "organic composition of man," he intended to point out that socialized individuals "are increasingly becoming instruments, means of their own self-preservation ..., at the expense of those parts of their person that the instruments into which they are turning themselves should really be serving" (PETG, 110).[59] Under the conditions of total socialization in advanced capitalism "self-preservation annuls all life in subjectivity. Compared to this, all the achievements of adaptation, all the acts of conformity described by social psychology and cultural anthropology, are mere epiphenomena" (MM, 262).[60] Even those aspects of human beings that elude the functional social framework—their affective and libidinal dimensions—are incorporated into the machinery as a type of lubricant, reducing friction and sustaining its operation. Subjects draw on features of their own "natural" affective resources, instrumentally adapting them to the ends of self-preservation, thereby increasingly distancing themselves from their somatic and libidinal substrates—that is, from their bases as living beings. Hence Adorno's remark that "the living has made itself, as something living, a thing, equipment. The ego consciously takes the whole man into its service as a piece of apparatus" (MM, 263).[61] This implies that the price of total integration is the disintegration of the subject. Insofar as the "ego"—the organon of adaptation—detaches from its own capacities and dispositions, treating them as manipulable objects, it also severs itself from what ought to be preserved. "... because the substance which is mastered suppressed, and disintegrated by self-preservation is nothing other than the living entity, of which the achievements of self-preservation can only be defined as functions" (DA, 73).[62] Split from its own qualities, from what constitutes its individuality, the self "becomes quite abstract, a mere reference-point: self-preservation forfeits its self" (MM, 263).[63]

The irrationality of existence under advanced capitalism lies in the fact that, while individual life becomes a means of self-preservation, the very

---

[59] Adorno, *Philosophical Elements of a Theory of Society*, 66.
[60] Adorno, *Minima Moralia*, 229.
[61] Ibid., 230.
[62] Adorno and Horkheimer, *Dialectic of Enlightenment*, 43.
[63] Adorno, *Minima Moralia*, 230.

social framework on which this self-preservation depends continually affirms the inessential, dispensable, and replaceable character of human beings. Although their weakness prevents them from fully grasping all that this implies, individuals feel that they are replaceable within the reproduction of the social whole, and therefore superfluous as concrete beings. "Individuals are interchangeable both for themselves and for others, like members of serial experiments" (IG, 76). This universal fungibility reveals that living individuals count only as a set of capacities and skills that can be mobilized at will, exposing the effective nullity of any claim to individuality (DA, 168).[64] If integration is achieved despite everything, if individuals are willing to mobilize their capacities, qualities, and dispositions to meet the demands of a social logic that condemns them to the most absolute heteronomy, it is because, as living subjects, they owe their life to that which is inflicted upon them (GS 8, 18).[65] Hence Adorno's insistence that within advanced capitalism self-preservation is achieved at the price of renouncing what ought to be preserved: the subject can only remain alive by sacrificing its self. "In his state of complete powerlessness, the individual perceives the time he has left to live as a brief reprieve" (MM, 188).[66] This affects not only the life of the individuals, but also their experience of death. For the dignity of death is equivalent to that of the individual, and with the degradation of the individual, death itself is also debased (MM, 264–6).[67] Death no longer signifies the end of a singular subject that could be understood as a coherent substratum of the actions and thoughts woven together in a biography; instead, it becomes the "annihilation of a nothing. He who dies realizes that he has been cheated of everything. And that is why death is so unbearable" (MBP, 213).[68] Whereas social transformations have deprived human beings of the only thing that made the experience of death tolerable for them—"the feeling of its epic unity with a full life" (ND, 362),[69] the possibility of a "life lived out to its end" (GS 10.1, 273)[70]—now, "in being seen as no more

[64]Adorno and Horkheimer, *Dialectic of Enlightenment*, 116–117.
[65]Adorno, "Society," 274.
[66]Adorno, *Minima Moralia*, 165.
[67]Ibid., 231–3.
[68]Adorno, *Metaphysics: Concept and Problems*, 136.
[69]Adorno, *Negative Dialectics*, 369.
[70]Adorno, "Notes on Kafka," 260.

than the exit of a living creature from the social combine, death has been finally domesticated: dying merely confirms the absolute irrelevance of the natural organism in the face of the social absolute" (MM, 265).[71]

The point of arrival of this process is the extermination policies of National Socialism, "the parading and patterning of the living like dead matter" (MM, 266).[72] Its machinery of death did not eliminate individuals as concrete singularities, but as "exemplars" of certain categories: the Jew, the political enemy, the life "unworthy of being lived," and so on. This already indicated the growing disregard for the concrete singularity of individual persons, who were eliminated as "deviations from the concept of their total nullity" (ND, 355).[73] But this nullity of individuals is rooted in their thoroughgoing integration into the social logic, and for Adorno this reveals that the forms of socialization of advanced capitalism prepare the ground for the eradication of all singularity: "already in their formal freedom they are as fungible and replaceable as under the boots of their liquidators" (ND, 355).[74] This formulation is characteristic of the way in which Adorno seeks to break through the hardened crust of healthy common sense. It juxtaposes two seemingly heterogeneous elements—the formally free condition of subjects involved in transactions and contracts, and the torment inflicted upon their bodies in the hell of the camps—in order to expose something that a more conventional gaze might overlook. This provocative image seeks to expose how the most annihilatory and brutal forms of violence are rooted in everyday dynamics that appear banal and fully normalized: "Genocide is absolute integration, which is being prepared wherever human beings are made the same—'polished off,'" (ND, 355)[75] to fit seamlessly into the social logic. In fact, the practice of extermination would not have been possible without the total normalization of forms of violence and coercion forged not in some obscure underworld, but within everyday social practice: "What is decisive is the absorption of biological destruction by conscious social will. Only a humanity

[71] Adorno, *Minima Moralia*, 232.

[72] Ibid., 233.

[73] Adorno, *Negative Dialectics*, 362.

[74] Ibid., 362. Translation modified.

[75] Ibid., 362. Translation modified.

to whom death has become as indifferent as its members, that has itself died, can inflict it administratively on innumerable people" (MM, 266).[76]

What, then, is the status of the individual in Adorno's thought? Given its extremely precarious position, the individual is scarcely capable of disrupting the homologizing and coercive logic of the social system; at best, it represents a fragile potential for resistance. If Adorno's critical theory defends the autonomy associated with the figure of the bourgeois individual, it is because this autonomy was more than just an illusion created by the system and could not be fully reduced to its functionality within the framework of social reproduction on which it was based. "Individuality is as much the product of pressure as the energy center which resists it" (ND, 279).[77] Adorno is well aware that, in bourgeois society, the individual never fully came to fruition or attained complete reality; its attributes of autonomy and self-determination were hardly more than a "not yet" [*noch-nicht*][78] However, under the sign of a logic of total socialization that tolerates no outside, what remains of the individual has changed in nature: it no longer reflects socially generated possibilities so far unabsorbed by the system and still awaiting their realization, but rather the sum of the wounds inflicted on living subjects by the social form of the reproduction of life (DA, 277).[79] Consequently, the individual can no longer stand before the social whole "simply as that which is good, or positive. It is merely what is experienced as non-identical in a society where everyone is identical to the extent that they can claim to be potential or actual possessors of their labor power."[80] This nonidentity reveals the inexorably coercive character of the social logic, which appears intent on reducing living individuals to mere functions and, as such, to replaceable specimens. Yet critique draws its vitality from the tension that opens up between the social whole and damaged subjects—albeit under increasingly unfavorable relations of force. In any case, the historical decline of the individual is not only a philosophical problem

[76]Adorno, *Minima Moralia*, 233.

[77]Adorno, *Negative Dialectics*, 283. Translation modified.

[78]Cf. R. Tiedemann, *Niemandsland: Studien mit und über Theodor W. Adorno* (Munich: Text+Kritik, 2007), 23.

[79]Adorno and Horkheimer, *Dialectic of Enlightenment*, 200.

[80]Scheit, *Quälbarer Leib*, 24.

but a situation that "brings the entire construction of bourgeois existence down with it" (ND, 363).[81] Its effects are evident in the shaping of the social conditions of existence and in the very constitution of human beings. Thus, the annihilation of the individual is closely linked to Adorno's diagnosis of the emergence of a new human type, molded by the forms of socialization characteristic of advanced capitalism.

Traits of the "New Type of Human Being"

In his earliest analyses of post-liberal capitalism, Adorno observed that the logic of socialization had reached a new degree of intensity. Now, the social fabric was not limited to functionally harnessing the productive capacity of individuals, but also wove the web of expectations, dreams, and fears that molded their conscious and unconscious dispositions, affecting ever more aspects of their relationship with the world and with themselves. As we have seen, the products of the culture industry do not merely transmit contents of "false consciousness", but rather influence the dispositions of subjects: their capacity of experience, their ways of speaking and relating, and the patterns of identification, catharsis, and compensation for narcissistic wounds. However, these are not phenomena that can be explained in psychological terms, for their causes are fundamentally social. This is captured in the eloquent statement in *Minima Moralia*: "society is seen as an unmediated community of men, from whose attitudes the whole follows, instead of as a system not only encompassing and deforming them, but even reaching down into that humanity which once conditioned them as individuals" (MM, 169).[82] Thus, what defines the specifically human aspect of subjects is not an irreversible achievement, but something entirely vulnerable to the historical transformations of social life. This underscores the importance of examining how integration into the social logic affects living subjects, especially in an era when new forms of socialization seek to functionalize not only their subjective faculties, longings, and fears,

[81] Adorno, *Negative Dialectics*, 370.

[82] Adorno, *Minima Moralia*, 149.

but also the orientation of their attention, the restructuring of their sensibility, and the remodeling of their bodies. These mechanisms of subjection extend far beyond traditional critiques of domination through labor. They signify the penetration of the social system's dynamics into the very anthropological constitution of human beings.

In a passage in *Minima Moralia,* Adorno observes how the historical imposition of wage labor gave rise to the figure of the worker (MM, 261).[83] Similarly, the total subsumption of life in the framework of socialization proper to post-liberal capitalism led to the emergence of a "new human type." In various writings from the 1940s, largely comprising posthumously published notes, Adorno offers an initial outline of this diagnosis.[84] Here, the traits of a new constitution of the human being take shape, replacing the disintegrating figure of the bourgeois individual. Adorno's analyses stem from a comparative observation of the transformations in Europe and the United States. Thus, these writings should not be seen as isolated elements in his work but rather as part of a broader dialectical anthropology outlined in *Dialectic of the Enlightenment* and *Minima Moralia*, as well as to his studies on the subjects' predisposition to authoritarian behavior.

What Adorno is setting out here is the diagnosis of an anthropological transformation in advanced capitalism, one that persists in postwar societies. This notion runs throughout his social theory. In an increasingly integrated society, the fates of individuals increasingly depend on their ability to adjust to the demands of the social system on which their survival depends. Yet this process is not imposed solely from without; rather, subjects internalize social coercion, becoming what they are through this very process. This internalization does not however lessen the pressure exerted upon them. In this regard, Adorno offers crucial insights into how the complete mediation of life by the imperatives of capitalist socialization affects human beings. The first and most fundamental consequence is the growing difficulty individuals

---

[83]Ibid., 228.

[84]These texts include "The Problem of a New Type of Human Being" (*Current of Music*, 461–8), as well as additional drafts published by Rolf Tiedemann in the last volume of the *Frankfurter Adorno Blätter* with the title "Individuum und Gesellschaft. Entwürfe und Skizzen" [Individual and Society. Drafts and Sketches] (IG, 60–94).

face in distancing themselves from the social logic upon which they are increasingly dependent, while experiencing their somatic and libidinal substratum as ever more distant and alien. This results in the weakening of their capacity for experience and spontaneity. As a consequence, their capacity to resist "the impact of the social world as a whole" diminishes (GS 9.1, 20).[85] Here lies one of the key affinities between post-liberal capitalism and the rise of fascism: both are grounded in the same subjective constitution, shaped by new forms of socialization. The elements Adorno identifies in this analysis cannot be directly applied to the present, since the forms of social mediation have evolved. Nevertheless, his diagnosis highlights a series of transformations that cannot be seen as entirely disconnected from the situation today. The following are some of the fundamental features of Adorno's diagnosis of this new human type, captured by four key points.

1. First of all, Adorno insists that "the changes we are examining are those of social reality, of the surroundings we live in" (IG, 63)[86]. Thus, the issue at hand is not primarily one of anthropological transformation, but rather that the very constitution of human beings shifts in accordance with the social circumstances mediating self-preservation. As we have seen, the concentration of social power in post-liberal capitalism establishes an unprecedented supremacy of the social apparatus over increasingly atomized and powerless individuals. This has a decisive impact on their constitution as subjects, affecting even the early stages of child development. Despite technological advancement, socialized individuals remain needy and vulnerable. Their means of orienting and asserting themselves in the world are fragile and delicate, and their development can be irreversibly stunted when they are brutally inhibited. Thus, the development of individuals' capacities and volition requires an enabling environment; without this, fear takes hold (DA 295–6).[87] However, what Adorno detects in post-liberal capitalism is that "reality has taken on such dominance that it suffocates the ego and eats away at its innermost constitution through realistic fear" (IG, 63).[88] Human beings feel themselves

[85] Theodor W. Adorno, *The Psychological Technique of Martin Luther Thomas' Radio Addresses*, 10.
[86] Adorno, "The Problem of a New Type of Human Being," 463.
[87] Adorno and Horkheimer, *Dialectic of Enlightenment*, 213–14.
[88] Adorno, "The Problem of a New Type of Human Being," 463.

to be at the mercy of increasingly opaque social processes, which impose themselves on their lives in an overwhelming way. Their effects can barely be organized into anything resembling a coherent and continuous experience of time (GS 10.1, 50–1).[89] The possibility of conflict between the subject and the social norm is undermined from the outset by the disproportion between the overpowering social logic and the individual's minuscule field of action. This imbalance generates anguish and helplessness, stifling the development of one's potential before it can fully unfold and hindering the formation of a coherent personality; the result is a fractured and damaged subject.[90]

For Adorno, the new human type is characterized by the fact that "he no longer experiences anything himself, but rather lets the all-powerful, opaque social apparatus dictate all experiences to him" (IG, 65–6)[91]; his dependence on this framework, which mediates his relationship with the world, has surpassed a new threshold. Even the capacity for linguistic expression has shrunk, increasingly relying on standardized formulas and stock phrases disseminated through the channels of the culture industry (IG, 64–5).[92] It is also for this reason that the new human type fails to constitute itself as an individual, leading to the dissolution of singularity, continuity, and substantiality of character (IG, 69). His sole aspiration is adaptation: to live up to the demands imposed by social imperatives. At the same time, these demands erupt into his life in ways that can hardly be integrated into the framework of a coherent experience. Adorno speaks of abrupt jolts and shocks that punctuate life trajectories, fragment biographies, and render continuity of experience impossible (GS 8, 24).[93] Here, the shock as a social regime of experience, already identified by Walter Benjamin (BGS I, 613–14),[94] takes on new relevance, describing the traumatic collision between the gigantic forces that shape history and

---

[89]Adorno, "Spengler After the Fall," 55.

[90]Robert Hullot-Kentor, "A New Type of Human Being and Who We Really Are," *Brooklyn Rail*, October 11, 2008, available at [https://brooklynrail.org/2008/11/art/a-newtype-of-human-being-and-who-we-really-are].

[91]Adorno, "The Problem of a New Type of Human Being," 465.

[92]Ibid.

[93]Adorno, "The Revisionst Psychoanalysis," trans. Nan-Nan Lee. *Philosophy and Social Criticism*, 40–3 (2014), 328.

[94]Benjamin, "On Some Motifs in Baudelaire," *Selected Writings* 4, 316–17.

the "tiny, fragile human body" (BGS II, 214).[95] At this point, both Adorno and Benjamin draw a connection between the overwhelming force of social imperatives in everyday life and the destructive capacity unleashed in the two world wars, which exposed a stark disproportion between the socio-technical apparatus and the vulnerable constitution of the human subject. In both cases, experience seemed to have lost its measure, and the individual appeared barely capable of assimilating the unleashed forces looming over their lives. Indeed, confronted with the intransigence with which the imperatives of productive logic impose themselves, individuals are not only reduced to "nodal points of conventional reactions" (DA, 45),[96] but they barely manage to "conceive any aims that go beyond their immediate field of action and their adaptation to present conditions" (IG, 66).[97] Thus, they are confined to a perpetual and precarious present: "Life has changed into a timeless succession of shocks interspaced with empty, paralyzed intervals" (MM, 69).[98]

Under these new conditions of socialization, individuals must stay "unresistingly ready for anything, alert and unconscious at once" (MM, 42)[99]. Such a stance gives rise to a situation characterized by "self-effacement, unconscious dexterity, and adjustment to blind totality" (GS 12, 156).[100] As we have seen, the mobilization of all their vital energy for the sake of self-preservation ultimately results in their own annulment as living subjects. The extreme narrowing of their scope of action leaves them unable to articulate purposes beyond those socially imposed upon them. "Security is glimpsed in adaptation to the utmost insecurity" (MM, 158).[101] The very discontinuity that defines life under the regime of *shock* experience—compelling constant adjustment to ever-changing conditions—becomes a means of shielding oneself from one's own anguish (IG, 71). In this sense, Adorno's diagnosis of ego weakness describes individuals' waning capacity to endure temporal

[95]Benajmin, "Experience and Poverty," *Selected Writings 2.2*, 732.
[96]Adorno and Horkheimer, *Dialectic of Enlightenment*, 21.
[97]Adorno, "The Problem of a New Type of Human Being," 466.
[98]Adorno, *Minima Moralia*, 54.
[99]Ibid., 38.
[100]Adorno, *Philosophy of the New Music*, 126.
[101]Adorno, *Minima Moralia*, 139.

tensions:[102] fear grips them, frustration overwhelms them, and they turn to instant gratification and affirmation. The result is that behavior becomes increasingly unstable, reduced to mere adaptive responses to the demands of a shifting reality. Their limitless malleability in the face of changing circumstances turns individuals into beings without qualities, governed by ever faster, mere reflexive, and reactive impulses. This is not a restoration of lost spontaneity, but rather a transformation of the living into the mechanical: "in the prompt, unresistant reflexes the subject is entirely extinguished" (MM, 264).[103]

It is important to recognize that Adorno's diagnosis is not meant to be taken literally: while the increasing harmonization of living subjects with the social totality is a growing tendency in post-liberal capitalism, it is not yet a *fait accompli*. His critique serves as a warning against this danger, aiming to prevent the realization of a society so integral that it would fully override individuality. The problem lies in the overwhelming demands of external reality, which have become so immense that the sacrifices imposed can no longer be internalized or transformed into elements of personal consciousness.[104] The sheer weight of social pressure bearing down on individuals constantly threatens to overflow their capacity to endure it. This pressure is particularly acute in the sphere of labor, where access to sustenance, as well as the maintenance of status and aspirations, are at stake. The prevailing feeling is that more is demanded of them than they can possibly deliver (LGF, 283).[105] This phenomenon affects all social strata, although the burden is especially severe for those whose basic subsistence is not secured. Strikingly, the development of productive forces has not taken pressure off individuals; on the contrary, the coercion to perform has only intensified. In this light, Adorno's statement that "existence in late capitalism is a permanent rite of initiation" (DA, 176)[106] takes on new relevance.

---

[102]Otto Fenichel, "Ichstärke und Ichschwäche," Aufsätze, vol. 2 (Vienna: Ullstein, 1985), 81.

[103]Adorno, *Minima* Moralia, 231. Cf. Pablo López Álvarez, "La técnica y la escala de lo humano: Sobre un diagnóstico de Th. W. Adorno," in Lorena Acosta Iglesias and Pablo López Álvarez (eds.), *¿Actualidad del humanismo e inactualidad del hombre?* (Madrid: Guillermo Escolar, 2018), 221–43.

[104]Zamora, *Th. W. Adorno: Pensar contra la barbarie*, 110.

[105]Adorno, *History and Freedom*, 205.

[106]Adorno and Horkheimer, *The Dialectic of Enlightenment*, 124.

The principle of formal freedom collides with the material demands of a heteronomous system that obstructs the free development of individual activity and drives individuals to their breaking point: "the libidinal achievements demanded of an individual behaving as healthy in body and mind are such as can be performed only at the cost of the profoundest mutilation" (MM, 65).[107] As a result, psychic pathology loses its exceptional character and becomes just another facet of the "adapted" individual's normality. Beneath the appearance of health and overflowing vitality lies the collapse of individual capacities before they even reach a point of conflict with the social norm (MM, 66).[108] This situation compels individuals to assimilate to the inorganic, to mimic the dead in order to survive. Only by doing so can they withstand the pressures imposed upon them and become, to some extent, insensitive to their own mutilation.[109] This further numbs their subjective capacities; yet, by aligning themselves with the very social logic that degrades them (DA, 176),[110] they manage to preserve a degree of self-esteem and ward off the sense of complete helplessness, abandonment, and powerlessness. Hence Adorno's provocative statement: "underlying the prevalent health is death" (MM, 66).[111] The disproportion between social power and individual powerlessness transforms anguish and fear into full-fledged social forces—forces that, for Adorno, pose constant threats of social regression. Rather than a mere characteristic of the new human type, this should be understood as its fundamental social condition, making the danger of historical involution unmistakably clear. All other attributes of this condition must be understood in relation to this underlying dynamic.

2. The helplessness of the new human type becomes especially apparent when viewed in light of what has been lost. In the new forms of socialization, the mediating instances that once filtered and softened the imposition of social demands have been undermined. Adorno first argues that the new human type inhabits environments devoid of true images. At first glance, this

---

[107] Adorno, *Minima Moralia*, 58.

[108] Ibid., 59.

[109] Schweppenhäuser, *Vergegenwärtigungen zur Unzeit?*, 50.

[110] Adorno and Horkheimer, *Dialectic of Enlightenment*, 124.

[111] Adorno, *Minima Moralia*, 59.

assertion may seem counterintuitive, given that the culture industry—through illustrated magazines, film, and soon also television—had radically reshaped the relationship to the world. However, Adorno understands images here in an emphatic sense, distinct from the mere reproduction of reality's empirical surface. In this stronger sense, images serve as mediators of the meaning of social and communal relations, enabling individuals to assimilate their experiences of the world and to render them commensurable. Images, in this sense, serve as a symbolic filter of social relations—one that is often rooted in tradition. They are forms of mediating the relationship with the world that have now disappeared: "The world no longer offers the child any images, unless one includes the technical *imagines* of the car and the aeroplane. The repertoire of religious imagery has disintegrated. The imagery of bourgeois art never reached most of the population, especially the industrial masses and country people" (IG, 63).[112]

The modern process of secularization brought an end to these traditional ways of conveying meaning. However, the need for such images—essential components of sublimation—has not diminished; on the contrary, it has only increased (MM, 159).[113] In this new stage of capitalism, the status of the image has undergone a radical transformation: "Today, however, images only appear as ready-mades supplied by monopolistic centers, with all the emblems of their own falsity. So far, there has hardly been any serious recognition of what these images mean for people, or of the consequences of their falsity" (IG, 63).[114] Rather than authentic images, Adorno seems to address mass-produced signs that transmit the social norms to which individuals must conform. As products of the culture industry, these images are fundamentally normative: they prescribe individuals their place in social life and the patterns of behavior they are expected to adopt (GS 3, 332–5).[115] Their coercive messages are internalized through identification. "Adjustment means to a large extent imitation" (IG, 71). Yet beneath this model of the socialization of desire lurks a

[112]Adorno, "The Problem of the New Type of Human Being," 463.
[113]Adorno, *Minima Moralia*, 140.
[114]Adorno, "The Problem of the New Type of Human Being," 463.
[115]Adorno, "The Schema of Mass Culture," 93–5.

persistent threat, one that psychoanalysis typified in the castration complex:[116] individuals live in constant fear of deviating from the norm, of harboring desires that exceed what is permitted (GS 3, 335).[117] The result is a shrinking of the Ego's capacities, which is bound up with the erosion of imagination and fantasy. This deprives individuals of any means of distancing themselves from the overbearing social reality and leaves them increasingly helpless before it (IG, 63).[118]

The second element concerns how recent changes in socialization have transformed authority figures, shifting them from the family sphere—traditionally embodied in the figure of the father—to an immediately social form of authority.[119] The disintegration of the traditional family, "the 'germ cell' of bourgeois culture" (HGS 3, 417),[120] eliminates the fundamental mediating instance between individual and society, decisively shaping the development of the self from its earliest stages. Industrialization and the predominance of market relations had already begun eroding the family's social function in the nineteenth century, and the twentieth-century society organized around labor would eventually undermine the very foundations of the family unit and its prototypical roles. No longer the primary agent of socialization—as it once was among the bourgeoisie—the family now plays a diminished role in structuring subjectivity. Consequently, the formation of character and the internalization of social norms no longer occur within a relatively protected sphere capable of filtering out external interferences. Instead, social imperatives are imposed

---

[116]Vladimir Safatle, "Freud em Frankfurt: a funçao da psicanálise no pensamento de Theodor Adorno," in *Por que Freud hoje*, ed. Daniel Kuperman (São Paulo: Zagodini, 2017), 70.

[117]Adorno, "The Schema of Mass Culture," 95.

[118]Adorno, "The Problem of the New Type of Human Being," 463.

[119]At the core of this diagnosis lies the major research of the Institute for Social Research on the transformations in the relationship between authority and the family, the results of which were published in 1936 (Max Horkheimer, Erich Fromm, Herbert Marcuse et al., *Studien zur Autorität und Familie* [Lüneburg, zu Klampen, 2005]). Adorno had not taken part in this project, whose central contributions came from Horkheimer, Fromm and Marcuse, but his thought clearly resonated with its findings, which constituted the first major fruit of the collective research effort organized around the Institute directed by Horkheimer.

[120]Horkheimer, "Authority and the Family," trans. Matthew J. O"Connell, in *Critical Theory: Selected Essays* (New York: Continuum, 2002),128.

on individuals ever more directly and immediately (IG, 64).[121] Human beings have become, in the fullest sense, children of society (GS 10.1, 101).[122]

As a result, the concepts of authority and obedience were radically transformed. In the new modes of socialization shaped by the rise of radio, film, and television, the father figure—whose autonomy had already been weakened by his status as a dependent employee and was further undermined by the growing threat of unemployment—no longer held any authority comparable to that embodied by the automobile, the successful sportsman, or the movie star (IG, 64).[123] These figures represented the social norm in a way that no bourgeois *pater familias* could hope to match. However, this new form of authority also demanded new forms of obedience, eliminating the very possibility of the conflicts through which a relatively autonomous character could develop. The dissolution of family bonds was not, therefore, just a form of liberation; it also signified the disappearance of one of the last enclaves where a certain capacity for resistance might still take root. In the absence of this, "authority is becoming more and more abstract; but also more inhuman and inexorable" (GS 20.1, 306).[124] Confronted with a social reality that asserts itself absolutely, uncontested by any form of mediation, individual development is increasingly marked by fear and anxiety. The result is a weakened and insecure ego, one that is reliant on external validation. Adjusting body and soul to the models of social success becomes the only way to satisfy a need for recognition that can no longer be appeased within the family's sphere of influence. [125] However, by clinging to these images of social power, individuals come to "believe themselves one with the whole whose ubiquity stifles them" (GS 10.1, 99).[126] In such conditions, the forces of socialization appear to have seized the individual's very vital energies.

3. "The new human type cannot be properly understood without awareness of what he is continuously exposed to from the world of things about him,"

[121]Adorno, "The Problem of the New Type of Human Being," 464.
[122]Adorno, "Aldous Huxley and Utopia," 100.
[123]Adorno, "The Problem of the New Type of Human Being," 464.
[124]Adorno, "The Problem of the Family," trans. Jacob Blumenfeld: https://endnotes.org.uk/posts/theodor-adorno-on-the-problem-of-the-family-1955.
[125]Hullot-Kentor, "A New Type of Human Being and Who We Really Are."
[126]Adorno, "Aldous Huxley and Utopia," 99.

wrote Adorno in *Minima Moralia* (MM, 44).[127] Human beings are transformed through their contact with the world of objects that surrounds them. But the massive technification of the object-world gives rise to utensils that are no longer extensions of human intention, but material condensation of concentrated social power. This transformation bears anthropological consequences. At an elementary level it implies that, as the socio-technical environment becomes increasingly complex and refined, human beings must adapt—physically and mentally—to their objects of daily use in an unprecedented way: "The act of driving a car or repairing a radio requires an infinitely greater subordination to the prescribed nature of those objects than the work of a craftsman" (IG, 63).[128] Indeed, interaction with technical artifacts is dictated by their conditions of use and leaves little room for any other form of relation to them. For Adorno this gives rise to "a very peculiar mixture of improvisational ability and obedience" (IG, 67).[129] This tendency is especially pronounced in the workplace, where the logic of the productive apparatus—from the assembly line to the office—expropriates human spontaneity and replaces it with sequences of tightly programmed actions, all of which are subordinated to the imperative of profitability. The new forms of production increasingly dispense with the intervention of a subject acting on the basis of accumulated experience. The result is regression: "The elimination of qualities, their conversion into functions, is transferred by rationalized modes of work to the human capacity for experience, which tends to revert to that of amphibians" (DA, 52–3).[130]

Human beings' capacities to act as subjects develop through their engagement with the objects they use; such interactions cultivate certain aptitudes while others atrophy. In this way, artifacts shape how human beings relate both to the world and to their own subjective dispositions. "Technology is making gestures precise and brutal, and with them men. It expels from movements all hesitation, deliberation, civility. It subjects them to the implacable, as it

[127]Adorno, *Minima Moralia*, 40.
[128]Adorno, "The Problem of the New Type of Human Being," 463.
[129]Ibid., 466.
[130]Adorno and Horkheimer, *Dialectic of Enlightenment*, 28.

were ahistorical demands of objects" (MM, 43–4).[131] A few lines later, after describing how automobiles and refrigerators require their doors to be shut firmly, and after commenting on the cold carelessness encouraged by self-closing doors and the peculiar empowerment a car's powerful engine offers to those tempted to run over anything in their path, Adorno states, "The movements machines demand of their users already have the violent, hard-hitting, unresting jerkiness of Fascist maltreatment" (MM, 44).[132] The technological empowerment of the ego appears tied to the emergence of a subject that seeks to impose itself without regard for its surroundings; one that relishes the ability to assert itself—often violently—without attending to the peculiarities of the objects and persons in its environment. That is why, in this type of subject, there is a withering of "the irreplaceable faculties which cannot flourish in the isolated cell of pure inwardness, but only in live contact with the warmth of things" (MM, 47).[133] What Adorno identifies in these observations is the epochal dimension of a human type whose brutal character—associated with its authoritarian potential—is by no means a specific feature of Germany in the 1930s and 1940s, but a disposition tied to broader trends of socialization, already legible in the most mundane gestures. In the environment of objects and artifacts of the Fordist lifeworld, a new anthropological model takes shape—one in which the capacity to act becomes increasingly detached from attentiveness and sensitivity to the surrounding reality.

As the mechanisms of socialization grow in intensity and scope, society increasingly produces the types of character it requires. In a reality dominated by technology, human beings emerge who are increasingly attuned to it (GS 10.2, 685–7).[134] This means, however, that "the boundary between the human and the world of things is blurred" (GS 10.1, 276).[135] Technical progress undoubtedly holds the potential for a more dignified and humane life. Yet the irrational and pathogenic character of this relationship with technology is evident in the way its products and gadgets come to serve as models for

[131]Adorno, *Minima Moralia*, 40.
[132]Ibid.
[133]Ibid., 43.
[134]Adorno, "Education After Auschwitz," 200.
[135]Adorno, "Notes on Kafka," 262.

the ego. "In the new type's relationship to technique, what is distinct is that for him it is not a question of understanding technical objects, but of identification" (IG, 76). In the period of Fordist "total automobilization," male socialization revolves around knowledge of car brands and the characteristics and performance of various models, and these arouse all the more fascination as the increasing specialization of the division of labor makes the actual mechanics of these cars virtually incomprehensible. The relationship to technical artifacts becomes cultic, echoing the realm of the sacred.[136] Ultimately, these artifacts embody a promise: that disempowered individuals might partake in concentrated social power; as such, they are venerated independently of their utility (GS 10.1, 104).[137] Adorno warns that this leads to a "secret complicity with things, which one would like to resemble oneself" (IG, 66–7).[138] This reframes Günther Anders's idea of "Promethean shame,"[139] suggesting that as social atomization renders deep interpersonal bonds more difficult, and relationships grow increasingly instrumental, libidinal energy is redirected toward tools and machines (GS 10.2, 686)[140] and, ultimately, toward commodities. When voracious consumption coincides with the rapid obsolescence of desired objects, the desire is no longer merely to possess commodities, but to become like them (IG, 71). Weakened individuals search for their reflection in anything that is socially valued, hoping the same logic that negates them as concrete beings might confer some trace of significance. This only deepens their dependence on the social apparatus (LGF, 114–15).[141]

[136]This is how Adorno formulated it in a university course in 1960: "the way that the social order and, above all, the technological apparatus under which we live, together with the technical means and productive forces on which that order depends, have themselves acquired a kind of halo and suggestive power of their own, where the very powerlessness of the individual in relation to these media is in truth reflected. It is very much as Aldous Huxley anticipated in … his prophetic dystopian novel *Brave New World* about thirty years ago. There he imagines a future humanity for which the cross has had its top section removed to leave a simple T as a universal symbol, so that "Model T"—the first Ford model that went into mass production—is a car that now stands in directly for religion" (PhG, 238; *Philosophy and Sociology*, trans. Nicholas Walker [Cambridge: Polity, 2022], 167).

[137]Adorno, "Aldous Huxley and Utopia," 102–3.

[138]Adorno, "The Problem of the New Type of Human Being," 466.

[139]Gunther Anders, *Die Antiquiertheit des Menschen, vol. 1* (Munich: Beck, 2010), 21–95.

[140]Adorno, "Education After Auschwitz," 201.

[141]Adorno, *History and Freedom*, 77.

4. Finally, Adorno emphasizes that a defining feature of the new human type involves a profound transformation of the relationship with the body, which appears especially mutilated (DA, 265).[142] This is significant insofar as the body is the locus where the individual experiences the frictions that arise in the process of having to adjust to a complex of heteronomous social functions. In short, the body is the site where both its nonidentity with the social system and its potential for resistance—however fragile—become tangible. Hence Adorno's insistence on the irreducible somatic aspect of experience: "All pain and all negativity, the moving forces of dialectical thinking, assume the variously conveyed, sometimes unrecognizable form of physical things, just as all happiness aims at sensual fulfillment and obtains its objectivity in that fulfillment" (ND 202).[143] Subjectivity is always rooted in a physical substrate; the subject is, perhaps above all, a subject of needs. Nevertheless, the *Dialectic of Enlightenment* had already identified how the subject's relation to its own body was mediated by the subjugation of inner nature, first and foremost with a view toward the exploitation of labor power. In this way, civilizing logic enables the spirit to distance itself from its own somatic ground, reducing the living body to raw material for domination. As socialization intensifies, so too does the level of discipline required to subjugate and control the *physis*, adjusting it to social imperatives; this is inseparable from the growth in the organic composition of the human being (MM, 261).[144] By this token, the body, as the substrate of life, becomes machinery: an instrument for survival or success. This burdens the relation to one's own physicality with a peculiar ambivalence—one that Adorno sees as emblematic of the new human type.

For Adorno this ambivalence finds a particularly telling expression in the cult of physical corporeality promoted through sport and fitness (IG, 65)[145]. Here, the pleasure of movement, the suspension of utility and the liberation of the living body are preserved, but in a thoroughly distorted form (GS 3, 329).[146] In fact, Adorno argues that sport is not so much a game as a ritual (GS 3, 328).[147] It

[142]Adorno and Horkheimer, *Dialectic of Enlightenment*, 192.
[143]Adorno, *Negative Dialectics*, 202.
[144]Adorno, *Minima Moralia*, 228.
[145]Adorno, "The Problem of a New Type of Human Being," 465.
[146]Adorno, "The Schema of Mass Culture," 90.
[147]Ibid., 89.

initially acquires social significance in the framework of competition, echoing the classical liberal model: it implies the struggle of all against all under the principles of fair play and equal opportunity. Yet in practice, sport channels the energy of living individuals into socially sanctioned forms of activity, tacitly instilling a discipline aimed at taming and functionalizing the body; in this way, the body is trained "all the more inexorably to serve the machine" (GS 10.1, 80).[148] In the new forms of socialization, engaging in sport to stay in shape—purely for the sake of fitness—is not really an end in itself. Ultimately, it is a form of training meant to enable individuals to keep up with the demands of social imperatives, particularly those of the sphere of labor: "*fitness* for labor, however, is one of the clandestine purposes of sport. In sport frequently people first inflict on themselves, and savor as a triumph of their own freedom, exactly what they then must both inflict on and make palatable to themselves under societal pressure" (GS 10.2, 653).[149] The cult of strength and health thus masks a deeper fear and contempt for one's own fragility. What Adorno detects here *in nuce* would become ever more apparent with the further evolution of capitalism, as the function of this civilizing ritual—reframed as an effort at self-improvement—would turn the physical exercise, preferably undertaken at the gym, into a continual test of aptitude and performance for individuals facing increasingly demanding social imperatives. Thus, Adorno considers sport as a ritual of submission. It is a practice of strengthening and hardening of the self, training the individual to endure whatever an increasingly threatening society may demand (GS 10.1, 80).[150]

Yet the living body never fully coincides with the physical body disciplined for work or sport; insofar as it is not inert matter, it resists complete functionalization. This does not mean that the body exists outside of social mediation, or that, as a living body [*Leib*], it can be understood as the antithesis of the reified and functionalized body [*Körper*]. Rather, despite the processes of disciplining and domestication, the somatic cannot be entirely subsumed in the network of social functions. Its persistent ambivalence—as

[148]Adorno, "Veblen's Attack on Culture," *Prisms*, 81.
[149]Adorno, "Free Time," 174.
[150]Adorno, "Veblen's Attach on Culture," 81.

the locus of both pleasure and pain—renders it simultaneously an object of attraction and repulsion (DA, 267).[151] In this somatic stratum, the limits of domestication become apparent, provoking a desire to subject the body to unmitigated control. This is where Adorno identifies a significant shift in the relation to sexuality. In advanced capitalism, control over inner nature no longer aligns with a culture of abstinence and inhibition, but instead coexists with the relaxation of sexual taboos. Sex, which was once restrained and subject to the strictest reproductive functionality, is now tolerated and even encouraged. However, "as the arrangements of life no longer allow time for pleasure conscious of itself, replacing it by the performance of physiological functions, de-inhibited sex is itself desexualized" (MM, 192).[152]

Adorno speaks, in this regard, of a new social situation in which eroticism is promoted as a useful means for physiological release, while its elements of passion and affection—those capable of carrying social monads beyond themselves—are systematically repressed. In this way, the potential of sexual and erotic relations to transcend the functional network of the social logic is neutralized. In the process, what is specifically sexual disappears--while it nevertheless remains a source of aversion and scandal (GS 10.2, 535).[153] Sex is accepted, but only on the condition that it becomes a form of leisure, if not a variant of sport: "Sexuality itself is being desexualized, as it were, by becoming 'fun,' a sort of hygiene. It loses not only its more threatening and ego-alien impact, but also its intensity, its 'flavor'" (GS 9.2, 65).[154] Here, Adorno identifies a paradox: the relaxation of sexual taboos proceeds in tandem with the de-eroticization of sex and even of jouissance itself (IG, 74). Sex is consumed, institutionalized and administered through an entire network of social mechanisms, ranging from the culture industry and fashion to medicine and psychotherapy. Yet this very integration transforms the nature of sex itself. The discourse of *healthy sex life*, along with its corresponding cultural imaginary, tends to eliminate the disruptive force of partial drives (GS

[151]Adorno and Horkheimer, *Dialectic of Enlightenment*, 193.

[152]Adorno, *Minima Moralia*, 169.

[153]Adorno, "Sexual Taboos and Law Today," *Critical Models*, 73.

[154]Adorno, *The Stars Down to Earth*, 102.

10.2, 537–8),[155] with their multiplicitous structures devoid of *teloi*, turning the regulation of sex into a kind of defense mechanism against one's own sexuality.[156] Even in practices where eroticization might seem to persist—as in sunbathing, which many pursue to enhance their attractiveness—Adorno detected processes of desexualization and a new prudishness (IG, 65).[157] Here, the body itself acquires a fetishistic character: libidinal investment is directed toward its exhibition and the self-esteem such displays may generate, rather than toward its condition as the substratum of pleasure and pain. The body appears to be wholly assimilated to the commodity form—and this very assimilation is experienced as a source of pleasure.

According to Adorno, "the path to 'barbarization' is probably connected to this altered attitude to physicality" (IG, 65).[158] The introjection of social discipline not only exacerbates atomization but also leads to estrangement from one's somatic ground—an estrangement that profoundly alters the relationship to pleasure and pain. Among the traits of the new human type, Adorno identifies a diminished capacity for enjoyment that parallels a growing incapacity to suffer. The result is individuals who "are 'hardened', both in the physical and the psychological sense. Their coldness is one of their most conspicuous traits: they are cold in the face of the suffering of others, but also towards themselves" (IG, 66).[159] They are made to withstand blows, hardships, and all kinds of setbacks (IG, 81). Virility is also associated with this capacity for endurance. In this sense, the social process of self-formation reveals itself as a process of toughening up—that is, a growing indifference toward both one's own and others' suffering—grounded in the renunciation of one's own inclinations, leaving a bitter trace of resentment in the social atoms. Often, this frustration seeks an outlet in others, fostering attitudes of cruelty and sadism. For "whoever is hard with himself earns the right to be hard with others as well and avenges himself for the pain whose manifestations he was not allowed to show and had to repress" (GS 10.2, 682).[160] Here, alienation from the somatic

[155]Adorno, "Sexual Taboos and Law Today," 75.
[156]Vladimir Safatle, *Dar corpo ao impossível* (Belo Horizonte: Autêntica, 2019), 182.
[157]Adorno, "The Problem of the New Type of Human Being," 465.
[158]Ibid., 465.
[159]Ibid., 466.
[160]Adorno, "Education After Auschwitz," 198.

basis of life reaches its peak: normality becomes a desensitized mode of living, one increasingly prepared to inflict on others the same violence it has had to internalize. This makes it difficult for the experience of harm to become a motor of social transformation. For, in effect, "it would take living human beings to change the hardened conditions, but the latter have left their mark so deeply on people, have deprived them of so much of their life and individuation, that they scarcely seem capable of that spontaneity on which everything depended" (GS 8, 18).[161] This spontaneity is, at bottom, the impulse toward solidarity with what lives—with vulnerable, tortured, and humiliated bodies that incite resistance and the desire to end unnecessary suffering. Hence the significance of that hypothetical passerby fantasized about by the writer Peter Altenberg, who, upon seeing a coachman mistreat his defenseless horses, loses control of himself and strikes back at him, casting off that "wretched strength" that had previously enabled him "not to have to bother with *other people's* affairs" (GS 10.2, 626).[162] Until such a transformation in subjectivity occurs, the new human type will remain trapped within the dynamics of atomization, competition, and fear—a dynamic that both weakens the individual and subjects them all the more thoroughly to the heteronomous social logic.

The traits that Adorno identifies in the new human type—ranging from the erosion of a unified and coherent self to its altered relationship with the object world and its own body—point to a progressive dissolution of the boundaries between the ego and its social and technical milieu. Here one can discern a mourning for the loss of the autonomous and self-sufficient individual associated with bourgeois subjectivity; this mourning, however, does not turn into a nostalgic lament for an idyllic past. Adorno contends that the bourgeois notion of individuality had already become mere semblance, an ideological construct upheld by specific social configurations that ultimately undermined true individuality. Yet when features of the bourgeois individual are contrasted with those of the emerging anthropological model, the outlines of a new heteronomy become discernible. Hence, these analyses do not refer merely

[161] Adorno, "Society," 275. Translation modified.
[162] Adorno, "Progress," 151.

to the level of cultural critique—or what one might call "superstructure"; the formation of living subjects is itself a socially constitutive moment of life under advanced capitalism. After all, these processes point not to a pathology of individuals, but to a pathology of society itself (MM, 262).[163] At the same time, the diagnosis of these transformations in human constitution points to a real tendency within advanced capitalism, albeit not a fully realized one. The notion of a "pre-established harmony" between the social system and the human beings it encompasses cannot be taken at face value. Adorno employs this concept to illuminate the most threatening aspects of an ongoing social and anthropological transformation—precisely to provoke a response. If the assimilation of living subjects to lifeless functions, their reduction to mere reactive nodes, the absence of friction with social objectivity, or the growing incapacity for genuine experience were simply accepted as accomplished facts, critical theory would be pointless. The cycle of domination and subjugation would be irrevocably sealed. In this context, Adorno's theoretical approach serves as a warning against an observable and escalating trend, not as an expression of pessimistic or nostalgic cultural critique. Rather, it seeks to expose the perils inherent in a new historical situation, aiming to mobilize efforts to counteract them. Moreover, the subjugation of subjects and their internalization of social coercion is not a process devoid of conflict and contradiction, as becomes evident upon examining the inner life of individuals. But this requires reconsidering how Adorno's social theory incorporates psychoanalysis.

Contradiction in the Subject and the Role of Psychoanalysis

"There is nothing in the world that is not social; but nothing is uniquely social, everything has the double character of what it could be and of what the world has turned it into."[164] This reflection, which Adorno jotted down in

[163] Adorno, *Minima Moralia*, 229.
[164] Adorno, "Graeculus (II). Notizen zu Philosophie und Gesellschaft 19431969," 36.

a notebook just weeks before his death, brings us back to the social process of individuation. The logic of socialization plays a central role in the constitution of human beings, providing the very channels through which they can act as subjects. Yet this does not mean that every aspect of individuality can be explained on that basis. The subject is not reducible to what is socially constituted. Socialized individuals are more than mere functions within the social machinery. Although the social logic compels them to act as "character masks" (MEW 23, 100),[165] as embodiments of economic functions, their existence is not therefore exhausted by the patterns contained in the *dramatis personae* orchestrated by the "automatic subject" (MEW 23, 169)[166] of capital. For Adorno, living individuals are fundamentally split beings. On the one hand, they perform functions in the social process; they are "role-bearers." Yet at the same time they remain living subjects, animated by libidinal forces that do not originate in society: in this sense, individuals are also substrata of individual psychology. These two dimensions of the subject point in different directions, often producing a rift within the self. Under the pressure of social coercion, individuals may come to identify with their roles and functions, but this does not mean that they become identical with them. It is from this nonidentity of the subject with himself, as both social being and living creature, that the relationship between social theory and psychology—and particularly the contribution of psychoanalysis—becomes crucial to Adorno. For it is in the clash between the demands of an autonomized social logic and the dynamics of individual libido that the distinctive contribution of Freudian psychoanalysis to the critical theory of society is played out.[167]

---

[165]Marx, *Capital 1*, 179. Translation modified (the translation does not carry over this term).

[166]Ibid., 255.

[167]Among the primary studies on this issue, the following stand out: Wolfgang Bock, *Dialektische Psychologie: Adornos Rezeption der Psychoanalyse* (Wiesbaden: Springer, 2018); Detlev Claussen, *Unterm Konformitätszwang: Zum Verhältnis zur Kritischen Theorie und Psychoanalyse* (Bremen: Wassmann, 1988); Detlev Claussen, "Konformistische Identität. Zur Rolle der Sozialpsychologie in der Kritischen Theorie," in *Soziologie im Spätkapitalismus*, ed. Schweppenhäuser, 27–40; Helmut Dahmer, "Kritische Theorie und Psychoanalyse," in Uwe. H. Bittlingmayer, Alex Demirovic, Tatjana Freytag (eds.), *Handbuch Kritische Theorie* (Wiesbaden: Springer, 2019), 235–275; Jacoby, *Soziale Amnesie*, in particular 42–120; Jordi Maiso, "La subjetividad dañada: Teoría crítica y psicoanálisis," *Constelaciones. Revista de Teoría Crítica* 5 (2013), 132–50; Vladimir Safatle, "Freud em Frankfurt," 63–89; José Antonio Zamora, "El enigma de la docilidad: Teoría de la Sociedad y psicoanálisis en Th. W. Adorno," in *El*

Adorno's relationship with psychoanalysis is marked by persistent ambivalence (cf., for example, MM, 69–74)[168] and is not without a certain theoretical purpose. Horkheimer's dictum that psychology serves as an "auxiliary science" (HGS 3, 57)[169]—though indispensable for grasping social dynamics—remains a guiding assumption in Adorno's work. Nevertheless, he was acutely aware that the insights of sociology and psychology cannot be synthesized into a unified or coherent framework. The split between external and internal life corresponds to a real fracture, a tear that runs through the societies of advanced capitalism which demands theoretical reckoning. "People are incapable of recognizing themselves in society and society in themselves because they are alienated from each other and the totality. Their reified social relations necessarily appear to them as an 'in itself'" (GS 8, 44–5).[170] Undoubtedly, society always refers to relations between human beings—no matter how much they may have acquired autonomy or become reified—and the subject, for its part, is always socially mediated (IG, 87). Still, as Ulrich Sonnemann once observed,[171] sociology remains blind to the inner life of subjects, just as psychology fails to grasp the objective social forces that shape individual behavior. Adorno's enduring engagement with Freud thus always involved an attempt to correct the psychologism inherent in psychoanalysis. It also coexisted with a deep—and arguably excessive—distrust of psychoanalytic therapy, which he regarded as a technique of adaptation: a means of reducing the friction the psyche poses to the smooth functioning of the social order.

Adorno insists that "the divergence between individual and society is essentially social in origin, it is socially perpetuated, and it is in social terms that its manifestations are primarily to be explained" (GS 8, 50).[172] Indeed, psychology cannot account for the autonomized social processes that impose themselves on subjects through the coercive force of the so-called "natural

---

pensamiento de Th. W. Adorno. Balance y perspectivas, ed. Mateu Cabot (Palma de Mallorca: Edicions UIB, 2007), 27–42.

[168]Adorno, *Minima Moralia*, 62–6.

[169]Horkheimer, "History and Psychology," *Between Philosophy and Science*, 119.

[170]Adorno, "Sociology and Psychology, Part I," 69.

[171]Ulrich Sonnemann, *Negative Anthropologie: Schriften 3* (Lüneburg: zu Klampen, 2011), 407.

[172]Adorno, "Sociology and Psychology. Part I," 73.

laws" of society and the economy. Yet the psychic life of individuals cannot be dismissed as incidental or irrelevant. The apparent autonomy of the social logic—its reproduction as if it had a life of its own—rests on the fact that living individuals continue to sustain it through their actions as agents and subjects. This does not imply that psychology can claim any primacy in explaining the processes of social life; on the contrary, Adorno points out, "In view of the present powerlessness of the individual—of all individuals—society and the sciences that deal with it, sociology and economics, take priority when it comes to explaining social processes and tendencies. Even where the individual acts as an individual, and yet socially in Max Weber's sense, the organ of his action, the *ratio*, is a fundamentally social, and not a psychological, instance" (GS 8, 86). The question, then, is not whether psychology can explain social life, but rather to what extent it retains any explanatory power under conditions of total socialization characteristic of advanced capitalism.

For Adorno, the psychological approach is inseparable from the figure of the bourgeois individual of the liberal era, which was conceived as a relatively autonomous agent navigating between the poles of freedom and competition. Even the Freudian topography of the Ego, Id, and Superego, as well as the complex dynamics between consciousness and the unconscious, presuppose that the psychic life of subjects can function as a kind of small autarkic enterprise (DA, 229).[173] This would come into conflict with the new forms of socialization, which no longer tolerated such a model of subjectivity (GS 8, 55).[174] Indeed, the representatives of the new human type could no longer be considered autonomous and self-sufficient entities (IG, 69) but are increasingly shaped by the external social reality upon which their lives were now heavily dependent. In the emerging power relations between the all-encompassing social whole and increasingly powerless individuals, there seemed to be little space left for substantive, autonomous individual action. Adorno had already observed that human beings could scarcely do more than seek out gaps and windows of opportunity in order to reproduce their lives within an increasingly compact and heteronomous social reality.

---

[173] Adorno and Horkheimer, *Dialectic of Enlightenment*, 168.
[174] Adorno, "Sociology and Psychology. Part I," 77.

One might question the value of studying psychic life in such a scenario. If adaptation to social reality undermines the unity of the personality, erodes continuity of experience, and prevents attitudes and dispositions from crystallizing into coherent personality traits, it is difficult to speak of any substantiality of the individual psyche. The psyche, in this context, appears merely as a residue, a leftover that cannot be functionalized. Hence the statement: "The pre-bourgeois world does not yet know psychology, the world of total socialization has already left it behind" (GS 8, 83).[175] However, the drastic tone of this formulation can lead one to mistake a historical tendency for a fait accompli. Adorno often pushes these assertions to the limit, sometimes at the expense of nuance, which can veer dangerously close to crude determinism that no longer seeks to calibrate the balance of forces.[176] It would be a mistake, however, to conclude from this—as some authors have done[177]—that his thought denies any substance to the psychic dimension or that he merely derives it from the social structure. In this respect, Adorno would be inclined to agree with Marcuse's observation that the obsolescence of psychoanalysis does not mean that it is false.[178] The issue at hand is to clarify the precise way in which its contribution remains relevant. On one hand, it is true that individual life can no longer be explained on its own terms. But on the other hand, the increasing dependence of individuals on an overpowering social mechanism means they must tolerate an unprecedented degree of external coercion. It is here that psychoanalysis remains significant: Freudian theory reveals how the destructive logic of society is internalized and proliferates within the individual (GS 8, 83).[179]

For Adorno, Freudian psychoanalysis corresponded to a historical phase that had been surpassed, more attuned to the gradually fading structures of bourgeois subjectivity than to the emergent forms of socialization in advanced capitalism. Yet by concentrating on the psychic life of the atomized

---

[175]Adorno, "Sociology and Psychology. Part II," 95.

[176]Claussen, *Unterm Konformitätszwang*, 24.

[177]Christian Schneider, "Die Wunde Freud," in Richard Klein, Johann Kreuzer and Stefan Müller-Doohm (eds.), *Adorno – Handbuch. Leben – Werk – Wirkung* (Stuttgart/Weimar: Metzler, 2011), 287.

[178]Herbert Marcuse, "Obsolescence of Psychoanalysis," in *Philosophy, Psychoanalysis and Emancipation*, ed. Douglas Kellner and Clayton Pierce (London: Routledge, 2011), 109–21.

[179]Adorno, "Sociology and Psychology. Part II," 95.

individual, Freud succeeded in exposing the violent and mutilating nature of the dynamics of socialization—an insight that became all the more significant in an era when these processes had become pervasive. Indeed, psychoanalysis insists on "the libido as pre-social, phylogenetic as well as ontogenetic, reaches the point where the social principle of domination coincides with the psychological repression of the drive" (GS 8, 27).[180] Hence its capacity to assess the cost that the demands of adaptation to an overbearing social reality impose on living subjects. Only the study of drive dynamics, and not the superficial socialization of psychic phenomena,[181] allows for an in-depth analysis of the "split between the living subject and the objectivity that governs over subjects and which, at the same time, has been produced by them" (GS 8, 44).[182] For Adorno, the central legacy of Freudian theory is metapsychology, insofar as its attention to the dynamics unleashed in the internalization of social coercion makes it possible to bring the centrality of the experience of harm to light. Psychoanalysis offered a key to accessing the "subterranean history" of civilization, consisting of the "instincts and passions repressed and distorted" by it (DA, 265).[183] In this way, it revealed the traces that the internalization of social coercion leaves in the psychic constitution of subjects.

Here, the distance between post-liberal capitalism and the old bourgeois society becomes evident. While Freud had pointed out that, in the process of ego formation, the incompatibility between subjective desires and reality produced "a permanent injury to self-regard in the form of a narcissistic scar,"[184] Adorno contended that, in the new forms of socialization, individual character is constituted as "a system of scars that are only integrated with suffering, and never completely. The infliction of these scars is the way in which society imposes

[180] Adorno, "The Revisionist Psychoanalysis," 330.

[181] Here, Adorno's rejection of Erich Fromm's approach, whose proposal to reconcile social theory and psychoanalysis implied abandoning libido theory in favor, fundamentally, of a typology of social characters that prevents true mediation between social and psychological processes, is fundamental (cf. Claussen, *Unterm Konformitätszwang*; Helmut Dahmer, *Libido und Gesellschaft* (Münster: Westfälsiches Dampfboot, 2013), 312–20; Maiso, "La subjetividad dañada").

[182] Adorno, "Sociology and Psychology. Part I," 69.

[183] Adorno and Horkheimer, *Dialectic of Enlightenment*, 192.

[184] Sigmund Freud, *Jenseits des Lustprinzips: Studienausgabe, vol. 3* (Frankfurt: Fischer, 2009), 230; *Beyond the Pleasure Principle*, trans. James Strachey (New York: Norton & Company Inc., 1961), 14.

itself on the individual" (GS 8, 24).[185] The shift from the "narcissistic scar" to the "system of scars" underscores the damage done to living subjects by a social logic that asserts itself traumatically, through anguish and fear. For Adorno, at the heart of the social logic upon which all survival depends lies coercion, ultimately manifesting as a physical threat to the living body. This does not necessarily entail the direct annihilation of life itself, but it does contribute to the pervasive anxiety of losing access to socially produced wealth. As individuals grow increasingly dependent, they respond with a perpetual desire for security. The resulting disproportion between their powerlessness and the omnipotent power of social objectivity "transcends [...] the intrapsychic libidinal economy" (GS 8, 48).[186]

For individuals are not only the product of the social system, but also its opposite. What society demands of them in order to keep them alive implies renunciations and sacrifices that overflow their psychic economy and find little, if any, compensation (GS 8, 68–9).[187] Although the unquestionable dominance of external reality tends to suffocate conflicts before they can erupt—"the individual has to swallow them" (GS 20.2, 539)—these conflicts persist in the form of anguish and fear, intensifying their antagonism with the social system. Insofar as the ego "has to represent both libidinal needs and the principles of self-preservation, it finds itself constantly overwhelmed. It does not have at its disposal at all the solidity and security that it asserts vis-à-vis the Ego" (GS 8, 71).[188] The mechanisms of ego formation have been weakened, making the tasks of controlling and sublimating drives increasingly precarious. The subject experiences its own weakness both in the face of the overpowering social reality and in the face of drive energy, and this affects its self-esteem: real impotence is experienced as a "narcissistic injury" (GS 8, 72).[189] The libidinal energies directed at the self come into conflict with the objective conditions on which one's existence depends—conditions that impose themselves incontestably and escape all possibility of control; hence the emergence of a sense of helplessness that leads to the proliferation of wounded subjects. For

[185] Adorno, "Revisionist Psychoanalysis," 328.
[186] Adorno, "Sociology and Psychology. Part I," 71–2.
[187] Adorno, "Society and Psychology. Part II," 85.
[188] Ibid., 87.
[189] Ibid., 88.

"what society demands here and now in order to preserve itself as an ordered system demands sacrifices from individuals—sacrifices that they are neither able to rationally process within their own drive economy, nor to recognize as necessary for themselves. They must behave irrationally for as long as such objective irrationality persists" (IG, 89). Indeed, autonomized social logic cannot sustain itself against socialized human beings, but only through the very subjects it produces;[190] this requires some form of internalization of social coercion, no matter how much it comes into conflict with living subjects and their needs. Adorno's conclusion is uncompromising: "Since the reigning objectivity is objectively inadequate to the individuals, it is realized solely through the individuals—that is to say, psychologically" (ND, 345).[191]

Consequently, the consideration of the psychic mediation of social domination becomes one of the constituent elements of the critical theory of society.[192] As Adorno puts it, "the irrationality of the rational system becomes manifest in the psychology of the trapped subject" (GS 8, 48).[193] Only psychologically can one seek the compensations and resources that mitigate the feeling of powerlessness in the face of the conditions on which subsistence depends, the estrangement from one's own life, and the anxiety provoked by social demands that continually produce the sense of not being up to the task. "The weakness of the ego nowadays, which beyond its psychological dimension also registers the effects of each individual's real powerlessness in the fact of the societalized apparatus, would be exposed to an unbearable degree of narcissistic injury if it did not seek a compensatory identification with the power and the glory of the collective" (GS 10.2, 580).[194] The compensation for that narcissistic injury is what leads the subject to capitulate to an overbearing reality and to identify with what society imposes on them, redirecting their libidinal energies toward objects that allow them to feel attuned to social norms and dominant models of success. Their own weakness leads living subjects to internalize the pressure inflicted on them by

[190] Theodor W. Adorno, "Der Begriff der Philosophie," in *Frankfurter Adorno Blätter II* (Munich: Text+Kritik, 1993), 81–2.
[191] Adorno, *Negative Dialectics*, 251.
[192] Zamora, "El enigma de la docilidad," 35.
[193] Adorno, "Sociology and Psychology. Part I," 72.
[194] Adorno, "Opinion Delusion Society," *Critical Models*, 111.

heteronomous society, taking its cause as their own (LGF, 107).[195] Anna Freud had pointed out that through identification with the feared object, "anxiety is converted into pleasurable security";[196] Adorno underscores the importance of this mechanism: instead of opposing the social logic that harms and wounds them, individuals identify with it. Only in this way do they manage to cope with their antagonism toward a social objectivity that traps them in its web of functions and fails to recognize them as concrete beings, declaring them replaceable. Thus, the study of the dynamics of the individual psyche proves indispensable for understanding social phenomena that remain inaccessible to the laws of society and the economy (GS 10.2, 773).[197] These include not only mechanisms of identification, but also the aggressive and destructive impulses that serve as outlets for the frustration and resentment condensed in weakened subjects. In this sense, psychoanalysis demonstrates its significance as the study of "the subjective conditions of objective irrationality" (GS 8, 42).[198] The subjective conditions of social regression are inseparable from the experience of harm.

However, these processes are not predetermined. Psychoanalysis not only reveals that the individual—far from being fully master of itself—is riddled with forms of opacity: repression, censorship, rationalizations, and defense mechanisms; it also shows that, as living and needy beings, subjects cannot help but repeatedly set out in search of happiness and satisfaction. Hence Adorno's assertion: "the concept of the Ego is dialectical, both psychic and extra-psychic, a quantum of libido and the representative of outside reality" (GS 8, 70).[199] The Ego not only embodies the instance of repression and censorship in psychic life, but also—as consciousness—the antithesis of repression. As the meeting point between external and internal reality, the Ego thus reveals itself to be a field of tensions: a privileged stage for the conflicts between domination and servitude, between demands for adaptation and the potential for emancipation. This is why Adorno insists that "psychology is not only relevant as a means of

[195] Adorno, *History and Freedom*, 72.
[196] Anna Freud, *The Ego and the Mechanisms of Defence* (London: Karnac Books, 1993), 111.
[197] Adorno, "Marginalia to Theory and Praxis," 271.
[198] Adorno, "Sociology and Psychology. Part I," 68.
[199] Adorno, "Sociology and Psychology, Part II," 86.

adaptation, but also where socialization finds its limit in the subject" (GS 8, 92). By focusing on the "subterranean history" within the subject, by attempting to illuminate repressed and disfigured instincts and passions, psychoanalysis becomes, for Adorno, a crucial ally in the "remembrance of nature within the subject" (DA, 58)[200] in the age of total socialization. For critical theory thrives on the precarious balance of forces between the diminished subjects and an increasingly overbearing social totality. The potential for resistance depends on the fact that the identity between social objectivity and living individuals has not yet been fully accomplished, that there remains something in them that resists integration.[201] That is where the scars and wounds in the subject become important. They are a memento of nonidentity, of damage, of the "objectivity that weighs upon the subject" (ND, 29).[202] Of course, these wounds do not guarantee anything on their own. However, they must be attended to. Whether the damage becomes entrenched in frustration and resentment or whether it can be mobilized to critical ends depends largely on whether regressive tendencies prevail or whether a potential for resistance takes hold.

[200]Adorno and Horkheimer, *Dialectic of Enlightenment*, 32.
[201]Claussen, *Unterm Konformitätszwang*, 44–5.
[202]Adorno, *Negative Dialectics*, 17.

7

Conscious and Unconscious States: The New Figure of Ideology

The incorporation of the insights of Freudian psychoanalysis opened up new paths for Adorno to develop a critical theory adequate to its time. In his theory of socialization, Marx had assumed that—within socially established frameworks of action—individuals acted on the basis of their particular interests, even when this amount to nothing more than self-preservation. Yet he also understood that in doing so, they perpetuate a mode of sociality hostile to their own interests, "where the possibilities of action are confined to what is socially necessary."[1] Within Marxist theory, the function of ideology is to legitimate the "natural" order that divides society into those who rule and those who labor, presenting it as serving the interests of society as a whole. Adorno recognized that in twentieth-century societies the situation had become more complex. As he puts it, "the cement which once ideologies supplied is now furnished by these phenomena, which hold the massive social institutions on the one hand, the psychological constitution of human beings

[1] Dirk Braunstein, *Wahrheit und Katastrophe. Texte zu Adorno* (Bielefeld: Transcript, 2018), 46.

on the other" (GS 8, 18).[2] Contrary to what some strains of Marxism continued to assume, ideology could no longer be understood merely as manipulation or as a mere matter of "superstructure," but rather as a phenomenon that affects the social process as a whole: it concerns the very constitution of the system, its totality. It has to do with the mechanics of a social process that reproduces itself through the actions of subjects, while simultaneously keeping them in a condition of ignorance and powerlessness. If ideology, nonetheless, can take hold of individuals, it is because of the way it appeals to their needs and psychological constitution. Thus, to understand the dynamics that govern social life in advanced capitalism, it is not enough to analyze society as an objective process; it is also essential to examine how individuals internalize the coercive social logic that they themselves reproduce through their actions. This was the contribution of Freudian theory: insight into how the social forces of individuation shape the needs, desires, and fears of socialized subjects; in short, what moves them to act. The traditional critique of ideology as "false consciousness" was thereby expanded to include considerations of the unconscious.[3]

For this very reason, the way in which Adorno formulates the problem of ideology and its critique is fundamental for clarifying the elements of continuity and rupture between his formulation of critical theory and the tradition of emancipatory thought that emerged in the nineteenth century. Underlying this is the recognition that the societies of post-liberal capitalism—including fascism—emerged from the old bourgeois world but can no longer be explained in its terms. How, then, is one to formulate the critique of ideology, or even critique as such? Adorno was aware that the very concept of ideology is subject to historical transformation, and that both its substance and its function shift in response to changing social relations (GS 8, 458).[4] In his view, Marx had developed the critique of ideology as an immanent critique of capitalist social relations. Through his

---

[2]Adorno, "Society," 152.

[3]Perhaps no one formulated this as clearly as Horkheimer, when he wrote that "the action of numerically significant social strata is determined not by knowledge but by a drive structure that leads to false consciousness" (HGS 3, 59; Horkheimer, "History and Psychology," 120).

[4]Adorno, "Contribution to the Theory of Ideology," 20.

critique of political economy, Marx revealed how the very forms of modern socialization imposed a logic of blind, impersonal domination that subjected the capacity of socialized individuals to act—as well as their needs and the development of productive forces—to the heteronomous demands of the "automatic subject." Nonetheless, this inverted form of sociality could still be confronted with its own normative principles and truth claims. By measuring society against the principles of freedom, justice, and sovereignty that supposedly governed it, there was hope of developing "new principles for the world from the existing principles of the world" (MEW 1, 345).[5] By the mid-twentieth century, however, society had changed dramatically, giving rise to an entirely new historical constellation. With the rise of fascism and the unleashing of a historically unprecedented potential for violence and annihilation—Auschwitz and Hiroshima being the most extreme examples—it was no longer feasible to criticize society by appealing to the unrealized promises of modernization. The task instead became to confront and limit the destructive potential that had emerged in modern societies. Indeed, attempting to confront fascism, racism, or the so-called final solution of the Jewish question using the postulates of immanent critique proved futile. These phenomena no longer sought to explain reality or legitimize prevailing social relations but functioned solely as mechanisms for enacting and justifying violence.[6]

In this context, post-liberal societies also presented other, seemingly more mundane enigmas, such as the widespread resurgence of astrology or the patterns of identification fostered by the culture industry. Did these phenomena not present new challenges for understanding ideology? From this, one might infer that ideology had relinquished its claim to coherent discourse, adopting instead a more flexible form—one capable of aligning with the demands and expectations of individuals within prevailing forms of sociality. Adorno therefore argued that the historical roots of these new forms of ideology "are rather to be found in the general trend toward ever-increasing 'integration' of the individual into the social totality and, economically, the

[5]Marx, "Letters From the Franco-German Yearbook," 208. Translation modified.
[6]Claussen, *Grenzen der Aufklärung*, xxiii.

increasing sacrifices that civilization demands of its supposed beneficiaries."[7] These renunciations cried out for compensation, generating new demands within the libidinal economy. In this sense, the strength of Adorno's thought lies in its capacity to reveal how seemingly secondary aspects of social life illuminate fundamental aspects of the forms of socialization characteristic of advanced capitalism. In his critical theory, the defining features of post-liberal societies cannot be understood without considering phenomena such as the culture industry, superstition, or anti-Semitism. Conversely, none of these phenomena can be fully grasped in isolation from the broader social constitution and its shaping of living subjects. These emergent realities revealed how profoundly the concept, nature, and function of ideology had changed—calling for a corresponding transformation in its critique.

Sociality and Appearance: The Transformation of Ideology

The concept of ideology is one of the most contested legacies of the Marxian tradition.[8] Although concepts such as that of "socially necessary false consciousness" may today sound outdated, the problems they addressed remain unsolved. The importance of the critique of ideology to the project of critical theory developed around Max Horkheimer is well known. From the earliest issues of the *Zeitschrift für Sozialforschung*, there was an effort to reassess and update the problem of ideology, which could no longer be understood merely as the concealment or distortion of social relations. Lukács's analysis of reification was a decisive contribution in this regard, yet it remained largely speculative and insufficiently grounded in a comprehensive analysis of social reality. In this vein, Adorno's contributions to the Zeitschrift, from his initial essay 'On the Social Situation of Music' through later writings

---

[7]Theodor W. Adorno, *Bemerkungen zu "The Authoritarian Personality,"* (Berlin: Suhrkamp, 2019), 27 and "Remarks on "The Authoritarian Personality." *The Authoritarian Personality* (London: Verso, 2019), xliii.

[8]Cf. Sami R. Khatib, "Die Ideologie und ihre Kritik," *Anthropological Materialism*, 2010, available at [https://anthropologicalmaterialism.hypotheses.org/630] (last accessed April 5, 2021).

on Wagner, Mannheim's sociology of knowledge, and 'On the Fetish Character in Music and the Regression of Listening,' largely revolved around this problem. His later analyses of the culture industry, astrology columns, anti-Semitism, prejudice, and the authoritarian personality continued this effort, while fundamentally redefining the terms of ideology critique. In the few texts where Adorno addressed ideology as a theoretical problem, he argued that the social transformations following the collapse of the bourgeois liberal world no longer allowed the concept of ideology to function as Marx had originally intended. This marked a historical rupture that enabled a better understanding of the transformations of capitalism and the role of critique within them. The distance between the historical landscape of twentieth-century societies and the emancipatory horizon Marx was still able to maintain in the nineteenth century becomes particularly evident in the shifting approach to ideology and its critique. Understanding this "tectonic shift" (GS 8, 474)[9] requires situating ideology critique in relation to the critique of political economy, thereby delineating the distinct "temporal core" of Adorno's thought.

First and foremost, Adorno regarded the Marxian concept of ideology as extending beyond the mere concealment of class interests, thus distinguishing his perspective from that of vulgar Marxism. The critique of ideology was not primarily concerned with exposing ideas, beliefs, or positions as mere veils concealing social domination. In Adorno's view, the key lies rather in society's overall constitution and in how it appears to experience. Its foundation lies in the exchange of equivalents as the principle of social mediation, as formulated by classical political economy and economic liberalism. In his critique of political economy, Marx had argued that this logic gave rise to an inverted social reality that turned living subjects into objects of the social process, whose sole *telos* is the reproduction of capital, and which presents the movements of things as if they were endowed with a life of their own. This concept of ideology finds its model in Marx's analysis of commodity fetishism; its key concept lies in the formula of the "socially necessary semblance" (PhS, 144).[10]

[9] Adorno, "Contribution to the Theory of Ideology," 30.
[10] Adorno, *Philosophy and Sociology*, 98.

Above all, it is crucial to note that, for Adorno, Marx does not locate the problem of ideology primarily in consciousness, but in the very constitution of society and the way it unfolds and manifests itself. What defines ideology is not "false" consciousness, but the underlying structure of social interdependencies. This distinction underscores the importance of differentiating between the social logic and its modes of manifestation, between the essence *(Wesen)* and the forms of appearance *(Erscheinung)* of social life. In capitalism, the relationships between socialized individuals are not transparent and open but are mediated through the objects of exchange. Lukács had addressed this in his analysis of reification. In the debates on realism in art, Brecht himself had observed that this reification of social relations could not be grasped merely at the level of empirical appearances.[11] Consequently, the mere representation of reality as it appears in experience no longer corresponds to reality itself. This inverted social constitution creates a deceptive yet socially conditioned semblance that shapes consciousness. As Adorno wrote to Benjamin in 1935, "the fetish character of the commodity is not a fact of consciousness; rather, it is dialectical in the eminent sense that it produces consciousness" (ABB, 139).[12] The notion of "false consciousness" should not be attributed to manipulation or a lack of critical reflection among individuals; rather, it reflects this inverted social constitution. This foundation rests in the mystery of the commodity form, which, as Marx stated,

> reflects, the social characteristics of men's own labor as objective characteristics of the products of labor themselves, as the socio-natural properties of these things. Hence it also reflects the social relation of the producers to the sum total of labor as a social relation between objects, a relation which exists apart from and outside the producers. ... It is nothing but the definite social relation between men themselves which assumes

---

[11] "A photograph of the Krupp works or the AEG reveals almost nothing about these institutions. Reality as such has slipped into the domain of the functional. The reification of human relations, the factory, for example, no longer discloses. .... Whoever reproduces what can be experienced of reality also fails to reproduce it. It has not been possible to experience it as a whole for a long time" (Bertolt Brecht, *Der dreigroschen Prozeß*, in *Schriften I 1914–1923, Werke 21* [Berlin/Frankfurt: Aufbau/Suhrkamp, 1992], 469 and "The Threepenny Lawsuit" in *Bertolt Brecht on Film and Radio*, trans. Marc Silberman [London: Bloomsbury Meuthen Drama, 2001], 164–5).

[12] Adorno and Benjamin, *The Complete Correspondence*, 105.

here [in capitalism, JM], for them, the fantastic form of a relation between things. (MEW 23, 86)[13]

In Marx's understanding of fetishism, appearance is not the antithesis of truth but refers to the conditions under which the "suprasensible" dimension of the commodity—its value—appears as a quality inherent in the things themselves. These conditions are social. This is why such an appearance can be considered "socially necessary": it responds to the objective constitution of social relations.[14] It is both true and false at once. It is true insofar as social relations have really become autonomous from the subjects who set them in motion; and false because these autonomized relations, —constituting a form of abstract, anonymous, and impersonal domination—do not appear as such, but instead present themselves as a "magical" property of things. Marx speaks of a personification of things and an objectification of relations that shapes the spontaneous forms of perception and experience (MEW 25, 838–9).[15] In the same vein, Adorno points out—clearly alluding to classical German philosophy—that the key elements of the social constitution operate as a kind of social *a priori* that determines how subjects apprehend the social web of interdependencies in which their lives are entangled (PhS, 155–6).[16] At its core, however, the problem refers to how praxis is shaped in capitalist society, for "even when we manage to see through appearances, this does not change anything in terms of the fetishism of the commodity."[17] It is the constitution of society itself that leads subjects to take appearances as truth—something

[13]Marx, *Capital Volume 1*, 164–5.

[14]"It is not about the psychological fetishising of individual commodities but about the objective structure of the commodity economy [*Warenwirtschaft*]. In a society in which exchange-value is the dominant principle, this fetishizing is realized necessarily. What is essential is that the commodity disappears as a social relation; all other reactions of reified consciousness [*des verdinglichten Bewusstseins*] are secondary." (Theodor W. Adorno, "Über Marx und die Grundbegriffe der soziologischen Theorie," in H. G. Backhaus, *Dialektik der Wertform* [Freiburg: ça ira, 1997], 508; "Marx and the Basic Concepts of Sociological Theory," trans. Verena Erlenbusch-Anderson and Chris O'Kane, *Historical Materialism* 26, no. 1 (2018), 7.

[15] Karl Marx, *Capital Volume 3*, trans. David Fernbach (London: Penguin, 1991), 968–9.

[16]Adorno, *Philosophy and Sociology*, 107.

[17]Adorno, "Über Marx und die Grundbegriffe der soziologischen Theorie," 509 and "Marx and the Basic Concepts of Sociological Theory," 8. On this point, cf. C. Catalina, "La religiosidad capitalista en Marx y Benjamin: fetichismo y secularización," *Viento Sur*, 158, 2018, 80–1.

that can only be dissolved through an understanding of the social totality that produces to those very appearances. But this requires moving beyond the empirical surface of social life in order to grasp the laws that govern the workings of the system as a whole. Indeed, the concept of ideology as a "socially necessary appearance" implies the possibility of distinguishing appearance from truth and thus entails a notion of objective truth.[18] Marx's critique of political economy rests on the assumption that it is possible to uncover the logic governing the network of interdependencies among individuals, mediated through exchange. This requires a theory capable of accounting for the functioning of society as a whole, which is precisely the aim of *Capital*.

However, once a theory capable of grasping the operation of the social system has been developed, it becomes apparent that this totality fails to fulfill its own concept. What begins as a critique of socially necessary appearance ultimately transforms into an immanent critique of bourgeois society and of the consciousness it generates about itself; that is, of liberal thought. Marx confronts the postulates of the theoretical system of liberalism with the actual logic of bourgeois society, analyzing whether the latter is truly governed by the rules and laws it claims to uphold.[19] For the social logic of capitalism does not generate a harmonious sociality, nor "a justly organized and meaningfully self-reproducing whole." In other words, "the social whole no longer accomplishes precisely what it was supposed to accomplish, for the human beings who are exposed and subjected to this interconnected whole are also mortally and fatefully threatened by the very society to which they owe their life" (PhS, 149–50).[20] Consequently, Marx's critique aims to reveal the *quid pro quo* between production and the satisfaction of needs, along with the inversion of means and ends, and of subject and object. This entails an immanent critique of the social constitution—since the relationships between individuals are neither transparent nor rational, whether in their interactions with one another or in their relation to nature (MEW 23, 94)[21]—rather than simply the unmasking

---

[18]Theodor W. Adorno, "Zur Spezifikation der kritischen Theorie," in *Adorno. Eine Bildmonographie*, ed. Theodor W. Adorno Archiv (Frankfurt, Suhrkamp, 2003), 292.
[19]Adorno, "Über Marx und die Grundbegriffe der soziologischen Theorie," 505–6, and "Marx and the Basic Concepts of Sociological Theory," 6.
[20]Adorno, *Philosophy and Sociology*, 103.
[21]Marx, *Capital Volume 1*, 173.

of false appearances. It is through confronting bourgeois society with its own normative principles—freedom, equality, individuality, and autonomy—that ideology can be understood "as consciousness that is objectively necessary and at the same time false, as the conflation of the true and untrue, differing as much from the whole truth as from barefaced lies" (GS 8, 465).[22]

For Adorno, the clearest example of this is Marx's critique of the doctrine of free and fair exchange underpinings liberalism; once again, this notion is both true and false.[23] At the outset, the critique of political economy highlights the aporetic character of capitalist exchange: if equal value were always exchanged for equal value, there would be no surplus value—and thus no capital. In this sense, the appearance of freedom and justice conceals the systemic dimension of ongoing dispossession, which is the condition for the exploitation of labor. At the same time, however, contrasting commodity-mediated social forms with those based on direct dependence and submission—as under feudalism—makes it clear that, although freedom and equality exist only formally within the exchange process, they are not entirely illusory:

> For although it is true that the process of exchange is neither free nor fair in bourgeois society, and although it is false to say that the employer and the worker encounter each other on nothing but the basis of their own labor in the act of exchange, it is still true that exchange involves some kind of equivalence, and that a more searching investigation—namely the analysis of labor value and the commodity form—is required in order to show that something more is involved in the exchange relation. (PhS, 221)[24]

Thus, if the principle of free and fair exchange becomes ideological—a falsehood—it is because its material realization belies its claim to freedom and justice (GS 8, 473).[25] Yet the semblance of free and fair exchange also contains the potential to transcend its falsity, suggesting that what is merely apparent can become real. In this sense, ideology seems to harbor the antidote to its own lie. Indeed, if the principle of free and fair exchange were really fulfilled—if equal

[22]Adorno, "Contribution to the Theory of Ideology," 24.
[23]On this question, see Braunstein, *Wahrheit und Katastrophe*, 55–68.
[24]Adorno, *Philosophy and Sociology*, 155.
[25]Adorno, "Contribution to the Theory of Ideology," 30.

value were truly exchanged for equal value—the satisfaction of needs would take center stage in the social constitution, rather than the blind reproduction of capital, the logic of the "automatic subject." This would make it possible to overcome the reproduction of class inequality under the guise of fair exchange. Hence Adorno emphasizes that the critique of ideology is not merely negative; it does not simply aim to unmask falsehoods concealing domination. Rather, it seeks to vindicate the moment of truth in the social principle itself, allowing it to claim its rightful place. This was the model of analysis that underpinned Marxian critique: it involved confronting ideology with its own truth (GS 8, 465).[26]

Now, for Adorno, this concept of critique requires a society that can be understood on the basis of its own rational principle, in which "false consciousness appears as a necessary figure of the objective process that binds society together";[27] hence Marx's model of ideology critique is grounded in the formation of bourgeois liberal society (PhS, 222).[28] In this society, the reproduction of social life takes place through commodity exchange—yet it is this very exchange that supports the expanded reproduction of capital. Thus, free and fair exchange among free and equal individuals can be regarded as the driving principle of liberal society, a principle that was at once true and false. For Adorno, this marks the distinctive feature of ideology in its classical sense: "Because *ideology is justification.* It requires two things: firstly, the experience of an already problematic social situation, which therefore must be defended; and second, the idea of justice itself, which has equal exchange as its model, and without which such apologetic necessity would not endure" (GS 8, 465).[29] This is why Marx only needed to develop an immanent critique of the mature system of liberalism in order to prefigure—through the overcoming of its aporias and internal contradictions—the model of a free and just society (GS 8, 359).[30]

[26]Ibid., 25.

[27]Adorno, "Über Marx und die Grundbegriffe der soziologischen Theorie," 508, "Marx and the Basic Concepts of Sociological Theory," 7.

[28]Adorno, *Philosophy and Sociology*, 156.

[29]Adorno, "Contribution to the Theory of Ideology," 24.

[30]Adorno, "Late Capitalism or Industrial Society," 115.

However, this situation no longer held true in twentieth-century societies. In post-liberal capitalism, the concentration of social power led to a society that could no longer be grasped through its own rationality. In the era of monopolies, *rackets,* total states, and large business conglomerates, market rationality proved subordinate to the *ultima ratio* of increasingly concentrated social power. Consequently, freedom and justice—the foundational premises of commodity exchange—ceased to be substantive principles of social life. Though still invoked, they increasingly became hollow shells, detached from actual reality. This applies not only to the fascist period, but also to the Cold War, in which the potential for destruction being wielded at the social and political level—as demonstrated by the escalation of the nuclear arms race—could no longer be explained using rational principles. Adorno's thesis is that this "irrationality of the current social structure resists its rational grasp at the theoretical level" (GS 8, 359),[31] particularly in attempts to account for social dynamics based on consistent, coherent, and internally flawless principles (PETG, 45).[32]

How is ideology to be understood in this new framework? In his "Contribution to the Theory of Ideology," Adorno puts the question rather bluntly: "One can only sensibly speak about ideology as though it were an autonomous, substantial, intellectual entity which has emerged out of the social process and makes its own claims" (GS 8, 474);[33] and, even more drastically: "There really are no ideologies in situations ruled by bare, immediate relations of violence" (GS 8, 465).[34] Of course, even if Adorno speaks of direct power relations or unmediated control, post-liberal capitalism has not ceased to be capitalism. Even the monopoly state or the cartel ultimately represent forms of social mediation. Although these transformations mark major tectonic shifts in the structure of society, neither social mediation nor the commodity form disappears, nor does the valorization of value, which continues to occur through exchange. Yet, social logic can no longer be understood solely via the principle of equivalent exchange, as the concentration of capital and power

[31]Ibid., 237.
[32]Adorno, *Philosophical Elements of a Theory of Society*, 25.
[33]Adorno, "Contribution to the Theory of Ideology," 31.
[34]Ibid., 24.

has given rise to a new social reality. In this context, the profit motive and the drive for valorization are also taken up and enforced by state power and large corporate actors, which assert themselves through prevailing relations of force. Both the profit motive and the valorization of value are increasingly adopted and enforced by political authorities and major corporate powers, which assert themselves through prevailing power relations.[35] This shift alters the concept of ideology, which can no longer be grasped as a substantive theoretical construct with its own inherent logic: "Ideology is … no longer something relatively independent of existence, no longer a theory that idealizes things, yet is also has the aim, however problematic, of explaining reality" (PETG, 209).[36] Ideology had been stripped of any rational foundation. While Marx could still counter bourgeois liberalism's claim to represent society's immanent rationality against itself—by confronting it with its social foundation and exposing its fallacies—in advanced capitalism, such efforts had become pointless. With the transformation of the underlying structures of social life, the significance of theory had been diminished—it became "ephemeral, meager, impotent" (GS 8, 473),[37] ineffective in the face of a reality where the coercive dimension of social relations became increasingly explicit.

For Adorno, fascism offers the clearest evidence for this transformation: it no longer sought legitimation through a rational principle. Indeed, theories of race or the organic *Volkskörper* no longer aimed to explain reality or its governing principles, nor did they rely on a necessary appearance that might still lay any claim to truth. Instead, the outright lie becomes the ruling force, reducing concepts to mere instruments of manipulation.[38] Their effectiveness does not stem from any capacity to persuade, but rather from the threat of force. In this light, Adorno states: "They invoke power with a wink: once you

---

[35]Adorno's texts do not always provide clear-cut explanations in this regard. In his writings up to 1960, there are numerous passages bearing the influence of the experiences of the years following the 1929 crisis, in which he refers to a weakening of market mediation—even within Keynesianism (PhS, 198; *Philosophy and Sociology*, 138). However, particularly in his texts from the 1960s, the principle of exchange increasingly assumes a central role as a constitutive principle of sociality in advanced capitalism.

[36]Adorno, *Philosophical Elements of a Theory of Society*, 135.

[37]Adorno, "Contribution to the Theory of Ideology," 30. Translation modified.

[38]Adorno, "Aspekte des neuen Rechtsradikalismus," *Vorträge*, 448 and *Aspects of the New Right Wing Extremism* (Cambridge: Polity, 2020), 12–13.

try to use reason against it, you will see where you end up. In many cases, the absurdity of its theses is turned against people, so as to test out what they will go along with, so long as they hear the threat that lies behind the phrases, or otherwise accept the promise that they will receive some of the spoils" (GS 8, 466).[39] Put simply, the lies promoted by totalitarian ideologies appear plausible only in light of the growing disproportion between social power and powerlessness. For Adorno, this imbalance—so evident in fascism—also characterizes advanced capitalist societies. Despite the undeniable differences that distinguish democratic regimes from dictatorial ones, both exhibit the oppressive dominance of autonomous social structures, reducing individuals to dependence on the social whole, helplessness, and fear. Such a social framework can no longer credibly lay claim to rationality. This imbalance does not abolish the principle of exchange but strips it of its former centrality. Relations of domination and subjugation become more overt and immediate; accordingly, the notion of ideology—along with its function and meaning—is profoundly transformed. If one can still speak of "false consciousness," it is certainly no longer in reference to a socially necessary appearance or to a hidden underlying logic awaiting discovery through reflection. The absence of freedom and justice, and the coercive dimensions of social mediation, are no longer masked by the principle of exchange but are now glaringly apparent. This was Adorno's point in his 1960 course on *Philosophy and Sociology*:

> I believe that the veil beneath which human beings exist today, beneath which consciousness exists today, is—to put this in an extreme way—the veil of complete unveiledness. It is the veil that consists in the way that human beings certainly experience in themselves the power of the reality that confronts them, without this power being particularly dressed up in any way, although the power in question, through its sheer disproportion to the power and to a considerable extent even the insight of any individual, appears as if it were not itself something that has become what it is, as if it were not itself mediated in and through human beings themselves, as if it were no society itself that ultimately lay behind this power. For this

[39] Adorno, "Contribution to the Theory of Ideology," 25. Translation modified.

> power appears as if it had literally become … a kind of "second nature." (PhS, 234–5)[40]

In a certain sense, it could be argued that there is no longer any veil at all: hence the drastic assertion that "ideology is no longer a veil, but now only the threatening countenance of the world" (GS 8, 477).[41] This is especially true for the societies of advanced capitalism and becomes particularly evident in the duplication of reality effected by the products of the culture industry. The techniques for reproducing the visible appearance of the world, made possible by cinema and television, reveal that "the new ideology has the world as such as its subject." The culture industry "exploits the cult of fact by describing bad existence with utmost exactitude in order to elevate it into the realm of facts. Through such elevation existence itself becomes a surrogate of meaning and justice" (DA, 170–1).[42] This marks a substantive transformation in the relationship between ideology, sociality, and appearance. For here ideology "is no longer a theoretical construct; it is now neither the idealization of something existent nor its complement but, rather, the existent as appearance, the existent in the guise reflected in the total social consciousness, and thus objective spirit" (PETG, 211).[43] This implies that the ideological increasingly coincides with social reality itself in its autonomized form. As a result, consciousness is deprived of its autonomy and is no longer even "false," but merely another node in the circuit of the social totality (GS 10.1, 25).[44] It becomes merely realistic. For, "illusion has become so concentrated that to see through it objectively assumes the character of hallucination" (DA, 231).[45] Although this might suggest that the circle of domination has been fully closed, Adorno contends that the unrelenting dominance of the autonomized social apparatus is actually the first step toward breaking the spell, exposing the fact that this "second nature" confronting individuals is only appearance: "But because ideology and reality converge to such an extent—because reality becomes an

---

[40] Adorno, *Philosophy and Sociology*, 165.

[41] Adorno, "Contribution to the Theory of Ideology," 33.

[42] Adorno and Horkheimer, *Dialectic of Enlightenment*, 119.

[43] Adorno, *Philosophical Elements of a Theory of Society*, 137.

[44] Adorno, "Cultural Criticism and Society," 31.

[45] Adorno and Horkheimer, *Dialectic of Enlightenment*, 170.

ideology of itself in the absence of any other convincing ideology—it would require only a small effort of the mind to throw off the semblance that it is at once both omnipotent and futile" (GS 8, 477).[46]

This is what the new form of the "socially necessary appearance" entails: existing modes of sociality now appear immune to transformation, asserting themselves through naturalized and seemingly indisputable coercion. This coercion contains an element of hypostatized illusion, as the autonomized totality is itself a product of social practice. For Adorno, even individual powerlessness is ultimately a mere semblance, since it is living subjects themselves who sustain the social process (PhS, 236).[47] This is where the characteristic intertwining of truth and falsity in ideology has shifted: reality both is and is not monolithic and unchangeable; individuals are at once utterly powerless and capable of action. Here, too, lies the possibility of transcending the current constitution of social reality. It is striking that this understanding of domination in advanced capitalism still harbors a surprising degree of optimism—perhaps even excessive, inasmuch as what obstructs social transformation is not so much the veiling of its possibility, but rather the very configuration of social life itself, which grips individuals in both consciousness and practice—that is to say, to the precise degree that it constitutes them as subjects. However, because of the subject's nonidentity with the social functions it performs, Adorno does not rule out the possibility that human beings might free themselves from social coercion. He leaves open the prospect that they might take control of their destiny and become the authors of their own biographies. If this fails to occur, it is primarily due to fear, to the social anxiety that weakens individuals whose existence depends on an autonomized social apparatus that confronts them as an overpowering and alien force. This condition compels acceptance of what is socially imposed, leaving little room for dissent between overpowering objectivity—the false whole—and individual consciousness. In their growing powerlessness, individuals resort to defense mechanisms and identification to cope with this reality. Hence Adorno's claim that in advanced capitalism, ideology takes the

---

[46] Adorno, "Contribution to the Theory of Ideology," 33.
[47] Adorno, *Philosophy and Sociology*, 166.

form of a "realism which is supposedly free of ideology" (PhS, 238).[48] Human beings capitulate to a reality that, in principle, remains within their power to change. Hence the conclusion that, insofar as socialized individuals are reduced to mere embodiments of social functions, "we might claim without much exaggeration that present-day human beings serve as such an ideology in their own existence, for they seek of their own free will to perpetuate what is obviously a perversion of real life" (GS 8, 18).[49] Here that the transformation of ideology reaches its most drastic and unequivocal formulation: "Today, ideology is the conscious and unconscious state of the masses as objective spirit" (GS 8, 466).[50] To fully unpack the implications of this thesis requires integrating insights from psychoanalysis and from the diagnosis of the new type of human being, which entails a new mode of character formation. The following pages are devoted to this task.

Critique of Ideology and Analysis of the Self

In some late notes which sought to outline the specific features of critical theory in contrast to traditional theory and even to Marxism itself, Adorno emphasizes that advanced capitalism necessitates "a psychological surplus, beyond the economy, in order to hold society together."[51] Indeed, because social tendencies cannot merely be imposed on socialized subjects but must also be internalized by them and reproduced through their actions, the psychological dimension assumes a new importance in social dynamics: "Ever since the market economy was ruined and is now patched together from one provisional measure to the next, its laws alone no longer provide a sufficient explanation. Without psychology, in which the objective constraints are continually internalized anew, it would be impossible to understand how people passively accept a state of unchanging destructive irrationality and, moreover, how they integrate themselves into movements that stand in rather

[48]Ibid., 172. Translation modified.
[49]Adorno, "Society," 275.
[50]Adorno, "Contribution to the Theory of Ideology," 25–6.
[51]Adorno, "Zur Spezifikation der kritischen Theorie," 292.

obvious contradiction to their own interests" (GS 10.2, 773).[52] For Adorno, psychology attains its full significance as the key to understanding the subjective conditions that render objective irrationality possible (GS 8, 42).[53] Manifestations of this irrationality were indeed pervasive in social life: from the rise of fascism and anti-Semitism in the 1930s and 1940s to the nuclear arms race of the Cold War, extending to the unconditional identification with models promoted by the culture industry, or the coexistence of an increasingly secular, scientific, and rationalized society with institutionalized phenomena like occultism and astrology.

For Adorno, this situation reflects "conscious and unconscious states" that are not merely psychological but point to a broader social condition. Its foundation lies in the "increasing socialization of life, the capture of the individual by the countless appendages of the administered world" (GS 8, 171–2). This gives rise to an antagonism between the autonomized social whole and the individuals who sustain it yet remain entirely dependent on it. The result is an existence reduced to self-preservation, often marked by anxiety, powerlessness, and fear. Living subjects sense the fragility of their condition, but confronting it with full awareness requires fortitude that they often lack. The psychic economy therefore seeks ways to soften this antagonism and render it bearable. Identification with institutions, commodities, and personifications of social power and success enables individuals to feel less dependent on objective processes (LGF, 114–5).[54] This leads to compensatory mechanisms—defenses, rationalizations, and self-deceptions—designed to alleviate frustration without breaking conformity with social norms. These mechanisms reveal how individuals capitulate to an overwhelming reality, while at the same time serving as strategies for navigating and achieving functionality within this reality. Yet these solutions remain illusory. The fundamental antagonism between individuals and an overarching social logic persists, however much it is displaced or rationalized. For Adorno, these psychological mechanisms—intended to soften the structural conflict between the coercive social whole

[52] Adorno, "Marginalia to Theory and Practice," 271.

[53] Adorno, "Sociology and Psychology. Part I," 68.

[54] Adorno, *History and Freedom*, 77.

and the weakened state of individuals—define the new form of ideology in the age of total socialization.

This diagnosis, in turn, reveals the necessity of rethinking the critique of ideology. It is no longer a matter of simply refuting ideological content or exposing the falsity of its claims. Rationally dismantling the national delusions of grandeur, arguing that ethnic traits cannot explain social divisions or imply inherent inferiority, or demonstrating that celestial alignments at birth do determine one's destiny—none of this diminishes the appeal of nationalism, anti-Semitism, or astrology. Those who embrace such attitudes do so not through rational persuasion, but because these "beliefs" answer to latent demands, longings, needs, or impulses—often unconscious. In his empirical studies on authoritarianism and prejudice, Adorno observed that "the acceptance of an ideology is not based upon an understanding of or belief in its content but rather upon what immediate use can be made of it" (GS 9.1, 439).[55] The same applies to affective attachments underlying allegiance to charismatic leaders or the libidinal investment in national symbols, technological gadgets, or sports teams. Thus, Adorno argues that instead of merely refuting the content of these modern forms of ideology—which no longer even pretend to be grounded in truth—that which

> should be analyzed is the dispositions of people upon whom they speculate, and what they strive to call up in people. That is a completely separate matter from the official declamations. Furthermore, the question remains that of why, and in what ways, modern society produces people who respond to such stimuli, indeed who require such stimuli, and whose spokesmen, to a large degree, are Führers and demagogues of all varieties. The development which leads to such transformations in ideologies themselves, and not just their content and structure, is necessary; the anthropological transformations for which the totalitarian ideologies are tailored are consequences of the structural transformations of society. It is only in this way that they are in some way substantial, and not in what they say. (GS 8, 466)[56]

[55]Theodor W. Adorno, Else Frenkel-Brunswik, Daniel Levinson, Nevitt Sanford, *The Authoritarian Personality* (New York: Harper & Brothers, 1950), 733.
[56]Adorno, "Contribution to the Theory of Ideology," 25.

In fact, in his research on the speeches of fascist agitators, Adorno had already observed that "the specific ideas and postulates" being proclaimed "serve merely as bait and hold very little objective weight" (GS 9.1, 38).[57] The manifest content of ideology—particularly in political contexts—serves largely as a pretext. What is truly substantive in its messaging is the attempt to resonate with the discomfort and dissatisfaction arising from individuals' troubled adaptation to the social world that shapes their lives. Ideology appeals to the wounds and scars within the subject—to their anguish, fears, and compensatory needs. This forms its latent content, enabling it to remain functional despite its manifest irrationality and absence of any claim to truth. For, as Adorno puts it, "the conviction that rationality is normality is false. Under the spell of the tenacious irrationality of the whole, the very irrationality of people is normal" (GS 10.2, 587).[58] At root, these new forms of ideology are bound up with the weakening of individuals—a condition of powerlessness and dependency that ideologies not only exploit but also actively reinforce. Their ideologemes draw sustenance from a "state of consciousness and unconsciousness produced in people themselves, both at the objective level, and with their own connivance and the aid of their own drives. This blinds them from seeing their irreconcilability with the state of things and leads them to accept and adopt as their own the very conditions that they feel to be their exact antitheses" (LGF, 115–6).[59] Some features of this dynamic have already been addressed in relation to the culture industry. It mobilizes conflicts, longings, and unsatisfied expectations simmering within subjects, but without allowing them to confront the underlying causes, whose roots lie in the process of socialization. In the end, this mechanism reinforces their condition of heteronomy and dependence.

In short, Adorno's critique aims to expose the social conditions that drive individuals into a state of malaise, weakness, and distress, rendering them vulnerable to ideological stimuli. These derive much of their force from the need to compensate for feelings of powerlessness—or at least to find ways to

---

[57] Adorno, *The Psychological Technique of Martin Luther Thomas' Radio Addresses*, 28.
[58] Adorno, "Opinion Delusion Society," 116.
[59] Adorno, *History and Freedom*, 78. Translation modified.

endure them. Confronted with the diffuse sense of subjection to increasingly omnipotent social and economic powers, individuals seek explanations that allow them to personalize the anonymous and often opaque logic that governs social processes and to identify a culprit to whom to impute the cause of their ills (GS 8, 446–7). They attempt to translate an increasingly abstract yet coercive form of sociality into terms that fit their daily experience. However, integrating the impact of objective social forces on personal existence into a coherent, understandable narrative proves challenging (GS 9.1, 355).[60] In an increasingly organized society, where the web of interdependencies is largely inscrutable, most individuals cannot escape a persistent sense of threat. Their integration as a labor force and as subjects of consumption remains precarious, and they sense that their most vital interests stand in tension with the logic that governs the social whole. Advanced capitalism offers no tangible embodiment of the "automatic subject" that individuals might hold responsible for their malaise. Here social domination is no longer direct; instead, it takes the form of an anonymous compulsion to produce (DA, 197),[61] demanding maximum performance from workers. As a result, conflict often becomes displaced—manifesting in tensions between wage earners who produce against those who monitor production efficiency (GS 8, 187–8). Although both parties are equally dependent, they confront each other through the roles they fulfill. Yet this does not prevent them from uniting in their shared resentment toward the blind coercion they attribute to "those in power," whether politicians, corporate executives, or union leaders. Ideally, they might even succeed in condensing the blame for all their woes into a single, tangible figure. This was the nearly magical role assigned to Jews within the logic of modern anti-Semitism:[62] "This is why people shout: 'Stop thief!'—and point at the Jew. He is indeed the scapegoat, not only for individual maneuvers and machinations but in the wider sense that the economic injustice of the whole class is attributed to him" (DA, 198).[63] With a ready explanation and a designated scapegoat, the anguish of being at the mercy of impersonal, abstract, and inexorable social

[60]Adorno, *Authoritarian Personality*, 671.
[61]Adorno and Horkheimer, *Dialectic of Enlightenment*, 142.
[62]Cf. Claussen, *Grenzen der Aufklarung*.
[63]Adorno and Horkheimer, *Dialectic of Enlightenment*, 142.

forces is alleviated, frustration finds a specific target and the causes of social coercion are further mystified.

Yet anti-Semitism is not the only absurdity that offers a means of coping with a reality that is objectively hostile to socialized individuals. Adorno didn't need to confine himself to explicitly political phenomena to recognize the increasing vulnerability of individuals to the new logic of ideology. It was enough to observe more banal, seemingly innocuous trends—such as the growing popularity of astrology as a mass cultural phenomenon. Here too, a subjective disposition characterized by weakness and dependence emerged—traits that, for Adorno, indicated an affinity with authoritarian tendencies extending beyond the strictly political realm. Just as anti-Semitism had once been labeled the "socialism of fools" at the end of the nineteenth century, Adorno refers to the rising appeal of astrology in the age of total socialization as the "metaphysic of the fools" (MM, 276).[64] It is indeed striking that a disenchanted society—equipped with abundant information channels and shaped by scientific, economic, labor, and administrative rationalization—could still lend any credibility to the pseudo-explanations of astrological columns. Yet when Adorno examined astrology in the postwar period, it was far from marginal or outdated; on the contrary, it had become fully integrated into the fabric of mass communication.[65] In fact, his study, *The Stars Down to Earth* focuses on the astrological columns published between 1952 and 1953 in one of the most "serious" and widely circulated newspapers in the United States, the *Los Angeles Times*.

Adorno examines astrology as an instance of "secondary superstition" (GS 9.2, 16)[66], symptomatic of the immanent contradictions of the process of disenchantment of the world; the latter would seem to find its limit "in the psychological condition of human beings."[67] But psychic dynamics can only be understood on the basis of the dynamics of the social whole: "If, to the

[64]Adorno, *Minima Moralia*, 241. Translation modified.

[65]"More than half the population of the Federal Republic of Germany believes that there is something to the astrology that in the early days of the bourgeois age, when the methods of scientific critique were less developed than they are today, Leibniz already characterized as the only science for which he felt nothing but contempt" (GS 10.2, 586–7 and "Opinion Delusion Society," 116).

[66]Adorno, *The Stars Down to Earth*, 158.

[67]Adorno, "Ist Aberglaube harmlos?," *Vorträge 1949–1968*, 354.

living, objective reality seems deaf as never before, they try to elicit meaning from it by saying abracadabra" (MM, 274).[68] The issue is not that individuals believe in hidden signs embedded in astral configurations offering clues about their daily lives and expectations, but that something within them predisposes them to grant such explanations credibility. If astrology continues to hold sway despite its blatant contradiction with the attained level of scientific knowledge and rational understanding, it is because it provides responses to "very strong instinctual drives" (GS 8, 149–50). The libidinal economy itself appears to draw living subjects into the dialectic of the Enlightenment. In this sense, Adorno's insight is that such forms of "regression to magical thinking in late capitalism" are well attuned to the demands of social logic (MM, 274).[69] Far from contradicting the reality principle, these "explanations" actually facilitate adaptation to a social world that confronts weakened individuals as an inexorable fate, one over which they feel no control (GS 9.2, 110).[70]

Indeed, astrology offers help and guidance, yet its appeal presupposes "ego weakness and real social impotence" (GS 8, 157). Beyond the specific advice it provides, the underlying message of astrology columns provides individuals with the illusion of escaping the arduous task of orienting themselves autonomously within a society dominated by abstract and coercive mediations that loom over them like a constant threat. This illusion is sustained by the tacit assumption that some kind of authority "ought to know more about themselves and what they should do than they can decide for themselves" (GS 9.2, 19).[71] If the stars' guidance is nevertheless *down to earth*, it is because, instead of calling irrational social conditions into question, astrology trains individuals to "make the most of them" (GS 8, 153). Destiny, in this view, is already inscribed in the stars; as long as one adheres to astrological predictions and prescriptions, there is nothing to fear.[72] Thus, astrology functions as a kind of secular, low-cost substitute for divine providence, offering a means to alleviate uncertainty and lend a semblance of meaning to the blind forces governing social life in

---

[68]Adorno, *Minima Moralia*, 240.

[69]Ibid., 239. Translation modified.

[70]Adorno, *The Stars Down to Earth*, 156.

[71]Ibid., 52.

[72]Adorno, "Ist Aberglaube harmlos?," 357.

advanced capitalism. The notion that one's life is written in the stars reflects the opaque and arbitrary logic of society as experienced by the individual—a perpetual source of anguish and distress. Astrology's task, in this sense, is "to channel the growing horror into pseudo-rational forms, to stabilize the rising tide of anxiety by consolidating it into fixed patterns, institutionalize it, as it were" (GS 8, 173). Adorno's critique of astrology mirrors the duality of the young Marx's critique of religion: it exposes astrology as both the "sigh of the oppressed creature" and the "opium of society" (MEW 1, 378;[73] cf. GS 8, 157).[74] This duality reveals the entanglement of compensation and legitimation, a hallmark of modern ideology. From this perspective, reading astrological columns as a normalized superstition within the totally administered society is not merely a symptom of dependency, but a practice that obscures, justifies, and perpetuates it. Astrology's distinct ideological function lies in its ability to enshroud existing reality in an aura of fatality (GS 9.2, 109),[75] thereby facilitating the reproduction, and reinforcement of the dominant "conscious and unconscious states."

Adorno's analysis also examines how phenomena such as astrology or anti-Semitism, take root within the psyche of the individual. Their overt irrationality compels individuals to rationalize them as mere "opinions." This notion of "opinion," however, is tied to a late-liberal relativism that has abandoned any commitment to binding truth: "Insofar as everyone is allowed to think what he will, regardless of whether it is really true, because each will choose to think whatever is most favorable for his or her benefit or self-advantage" (GS 8, 470).[76] In a context where the inner workings of social objectivity have become increasingly opaque, such "opinions" function as tools

[73]Marx, *Critique of Hegel's "Philosophy of Right,"* 131.

[74]One of the primary figures to develop this line of thought in the critique of ideology has been Detlev Claussen. Drawing on a formula from Marx, Claussen has proposed understanding the new forms of ideology as forms of "everyday religion." In doing this, he has not only preserved the link between Adorno, Marx, and Freud, but has also established a contemporary mode of critique based on a diagnosis of failed secularization (see Detlev Claussen, *Kritik der Alltagsreligion. Ideologiekritik unter veränderten gesellschaftlichen Verhältnissen* [Frankfurt, Neue Kritik, 2000]).

[75]Adorno, *The Stars Down to Earth*, 155.

[76]Adorno, "Contribution to the Theory of Ideology," 28. For a perspective on the current relevance of a critical theory of opinion grounded in Adorno, see Eric-John Russell, "Certainty in an Uncertain World: Toward a Critical Theory of Opinion," *Critical Sociology* 50, nos. 4–5 (2023), 691–706.

for navigating a world perceived as alien and threatening—a way of mitigating helplessness. When someone claims, for instance, that Jews must have done something to warrant such hatred, or that a person's behavior can be attributed to their being a Gemini or Taurus, the "opinion" ceases to function as a step toward autonomous knowledge. Instead, it assumes a primarily psychological function. "Here the 'in my opinion' does not qualify the hypothetical judgment, but underscores it" (GS 10.2, 574).[77] In this context, "opinion" operates as a form of self-affirmation, charged with a significant affective investment. When subjects perceive their "opinions" as integral to their selves, they will resist any attempt to question or refute them—whether through facts or reflection—since doing so would inflict a narcissistic wound that may be intolerable. That is why astrology, racism, conspiracy thinking, and anti-Semitism cannot be countered by reasoning or explanation alone; their root causes must be addressed. These lie in a social model of subjectivation that undermines the ego, numbs the capacity for experience, and fosters the psychological needs that sustain such beliefs. For "what the subject, in the name of opinion, takes for his personal prerogative is in every respect merely the reproduction of the objective relations in which he is entangled" (GS 10.2, 591).[78] This psychological search for compensation or relief from the symptoms of narcissistic injury also has broader implications. First, it challenges the liberal assumption that "normal" and reasonable opinions will inevitably prevail over "pathological" or "delusional" ones (GS 10.2, 573). In hyper-rationalized societies under advanced capitalism, individuals learn to coexist not only with a "normal" degree of astrological superstition, but also with other socially sanctioned forms of irrational opinion. Hence the attachment to national symbols, the scapegoating of Jews for all misfortunes, or in the assertion of the supposed natural inferiority of racial or cultural groups. Adorno's diagnosis is clear: the need for such "opinions" is embedded in the very structure of "normality" in advanced capitalist societies. As he asserts, "If there really is no correct life in the false life, then actually there can be no correct consciousness in it either" (GS 10.2, 591).[79]

---

[77] Adorno, "Opinion Delusion Society," 107.
[78] Ibid., 120.
[79] Ibid.

Astrology and anti-Semitism are, for Adorno, paradigmatic instances of the new form of ideology, as they reveal how ideology appeals to latent needs and longings within individuals—needs that signal deep malaise—while fabricating an illusory harmony between the wounds of the individuals and the social objectivity that produces them. Adorno frequently emphasizes the structural affinity between these forms of superstition and anti-Semitism (GS 20.1, 366–7; MM, 275[80]), observing that their logic mirrors the "deception" perpetrated by the culture industry. In these cases, however, the connection to a numbed capacity for experience—and to a repetitive, stereotyped, and often magical thinking—is even more evident. For Adorno, modern forms of superstition and scapegoating are symptoms of diffuse psychic conflicts that reveal the precarious condition of an individual who "shows that psychologically he is no longer a match for the world and is thrown back upon an illusory inner realm" (GS 10.2, 566).[81] What is particularly striking is that this kind of "belief" or "opinion" does not lead to social pathologization but instead exerts a normalizing effect (GS 9.1, 282).[82] These "ideologies" function as psychically adaptive mechanisms, enabling certain individuals to navigate social reality and integrate into it. The gratifications and outlets they provide do not disrupt social adaptation or violate societal taboos, since their aggression is consistently directed at the most vulnerable groups. Accordingly, such ideological stimuli exploit wounds within the subject, offering what Freud called "crooked cures" [*Schiefheilungen*].[83] These mechanisms compensate for feelings of inferiority, fabricating an illusion of reconciliation between the reality principle and the pleasure principle. Whether this takes the form of belief in astrology, conspiratorial thinking, or fascist aggression depends on shifting configurations of social life and individual psychic needs. What matters is that these ideological stimuli offer modes of integration that are not enforced through coercion but derive their power from their ability to resonate

---

[80] Adorno, *Fighing Antisemitism Today*, trans. Wieland Hoban (Cambridge: Polity, 2025), 11–2; Adorno, *Minima Moralia*, 241.

[81] Adorno, "The Meaning of Working Through the Past," 98.

[82] Adorno, *The Authoritarian Personality*, 618.

[83] Sigmund Freud, *Massenpsychologie und Ich-Analyse. Studienausgabe, vol. 9* (Frankfurt, Fischer, 2009), 132 and *Group Psychology and the Analysis of the* Ego, trans. James Stratchey (London: The Hogarth Press, 1949), 124.

with "long-established patterns of hopes and aspirations, fears and anxieties that dispose them to certain beliefs and make them resistant to others" (GS 9.1, 161–2).[84] In so doing, they alleviate discomfort and anxiety, reducing psychic friction and aligning the individual with the demands of the social order. As Wolfram Stender aptly puts it, "in the pseudo-logic of the ideological, objective obfuscation and individual scars come to form a stable short-circuit."[85] In this process, social and psychological conflicts are concealed; although they persist, they are displaced and hidden. As a result, individuals can coexist with these conflicts without being incapacitated or forced to confront their underlying causes. In this way, such ideological stimuli function as "cures," enabling individuals to attain an illusory harmony with the social norm.

This capacity to provide psychic compensations—whether through identification, collective narcissism, or scapegoating—helps explain how seemingly disparate phenomena such as anti-Semitism, nationalism, fascist agitation, as well as sports fandom, as well as identification with culture industry celebrities, can all function as libidinal bonds to unite large numbers of atomized, powerless, and needy individuals. In this sense, Adorno refers to these phenomena as "mass media" (GS 20.1, 366)[86]: their modes of gratification act as cohesive forces that link together individuals who often feel misunderstood and alone, offering them the longed-for sense of belonging to a "community." For this reason, Adorno interprets these new forms of ideology as a kind of "psychoanalysis in reverse." They appeal to emotional needs, to conflicts, and to often primary and irrational dispositions. However, rather than confronting them, they "constantly reinforce a defensive stance instead of working on a resolution; [they] play around with the unconscious and preconscious instead of raising [the issue] into the consciousness in any way" (GS 8, 155). As a result, libidinal energies slip from the ego's control. Since the unconscious tends to follow the path of least resistance, reinforced fears and inclinations capitulate to the overwhelming demands of social objectivity. As Adorno writes, that which "actually wanted to get beyond the unconscious then re-enters the service of

[84]Adorno, *The Authoritarian Personality*, 10.

[85]Wolfram Stender, *Kritik und Vernunft, Studien zu Horkheimer, Habermas und Freud* (Lüneburg: Zu Klampen, 1996), 79.

[86]Adorno, *Fighting Antisemitism Today*, 10.

the unconscious and may thus even strengthen its force" (GS 8, 71–2).[87] In this way, the psychic functioning of ideological mechanisms reveals a central feature of the "permanent rite of initiation" that defines life under advanced capitalism. By exploiting longings and fears—while offering gratifications that require minimal effort—these mechanisms entrench individuals in a state of growing dependence, reinforcing a vicious cycle of conformism, docility, and powerlessness. For Adorno, resisting authoritarian tendencies embedded in the normality of advanced capitalism depends on counteracting the socializing forces that perpetuate dependency and powerlessness. Only by achieving this can the persistent danger of social regression be averted.

"Normal Monsters": The Persistent Potential for Authoritarianism

Adorno's theorization of the transformations of ideology is inseparable from the experiences of fascism and anti-Semitism. These were not mere aberrations in the trajectory of modern society; rather, they had been incubated within it. This required a careful analysis of "conscious and unconscious states" without trivializing any of their symptoms, and an examination of the role played by the psychic-libidinal economy in the process through which certain individuals came to embrace specific "ideologies." For if fascist and anti-Semitic self-affirmation succeeded in taking root in the mentality and praxis of certain individuals, it was due to its ability to address widespread subjective needs. Authoritarian tendencies, therefore, were neither confined to Germany nor unique to Europe. In fact, the studies on prejudice, anti-Semitism, authoritarianism, and fascist propaganda conducted by Adorno, Horkheimer, and Löwenthal in the 1940s were focused on American society, undertaken while the country was actively engaged in fighting fascism and in the years following its victory.[88] During this period, the main representatives

---

[87] Adorno, "Sociology and Psychology. Part II," 87.

[88] Theodor W. Adorno, *The Psychological Technique of Martin Luther Thomas" Radio Addresses* GS 9.1, 7–142; Theodor W. Adorno, Else Frenkel-Brunswik, Daniel J. Levinson, and R. Nevitt Sanford, *The Authoritarian Personality* (the parts written by Adorno are collected in GS 9.1, 143–509); Leo Löwenthal,

of critical theory tended to interpret the anthropological transformations linked to the growing integration of the individual into post-liberal capitalism as an evolution that gave rise to subjects particularly susceptible to fascist and authoritarian behavior. The new form of ideology seemed to have "as it were, eaten its way deeper into human substance. Today, probably more than ever, it lies in people's very make-up, in their abilities and shortcomings, their preferences and interests" (HGS 17, 496). Indeed, Horkheimer would later state unequivocally that what these investigations revealed was

> the emergence of a new "anthropological" species: the authoritarian human type. Unlike the old-fashioned fanatic, he seems to amalgamate the ideas and aptitudes of a highly industrialized society with irrational or anti-rational convictions. He is at the same time enlightened and superstitious, proud of his individuality and constantly worried about not being like others, suspicious of his independence and prone to blind submission to power and authority. (HGS 5, 415)[89]

Here, authoritarianism is not understood primarily as a political program, but as the emergence of an increasingly total society that tends to cultivate subjective dispositions aligned with its demands.[90] This diagnosis led to the insight that authoritarian or overtly fascist tendencies were not necessarily phenomena confined to a few European countries. Rather, they were also latent in the democratic societies of the post-liberal period. The concentration of social and economic power affected individuals at the most intimate level of their lives. Socially, they were not regarded as singular beings in their

---

Vorurteilsbilder. Antisemitismus unter amerikanischen Arbeiter, in *Schriften 3* (Frankfurt: Suhrkamp, 1990), 175–237; Leo Löwenthal and Norbert Guterman, *Prophets of Deceit* (New York: Harper & Brothers, 1949). The *Studies in Prejudice* series, edited by Max Horkheimer, also included two volumes based on research carried out in the United States: Nathan W. Ackerman and Marie Jahoda, *Anti-Semitism and Emotional Disorder* (New York: Harper & Brothers, 1950); and Bruno Bettelheim and Morris Jannowitz, *Dynamics of Prejudice* (New York, Harper & Brothers, 1950). An important, though unpublished, study, *Anti-Semitism Among American Labor*, was conducted through interviews in various industrial cities in the United States between June and November 1944. This research revealed that 30.8 percent of respondents expressed "active hostility to Jews," while 38.5 percent displayed a rejecting attitude without engaging in active discrimination (see Rolf Wiggershaus, *The Frankfurt School*, 460–78).

89 Horkheimer, "Preface," Adorno et al., *The Authoritarian Personality*, ix.

90 Hullot-Kentor, "Metric of Rebarbarization," 741–2.

individuality, but primarily as producers and consumers of commodities. This contributed to the proliferation of weakened, increasingly dependent subjects who sensed their potential expendability. As a result, "a general state of ignorance and confusion" emerged, generating psychic dispositions and needs that could be redirected to serve authoritarian discourses (GS 9.1, 338).[91] These offered strong identity patterns and forms of affirmation that compensated for the sense of powerlessness, while deflecting blame onto groups perceived as responsible for social ills. In this way, authoritarianism facilitated navigation through a world increasingly perceived as hostile (GS 9.1, 269),[92] and thus became psychically "functional" for a growing number of individuals. This revealed a structural relationship between the forms of socialization under advanced capitalism, the shaping of subjective needs, and the effectiveness of authoritarian, fascist, and anti-Semitic ideologies. The underlying issue was not the character of specific individuals or social groups, but a deeper problem rooted in the very constitution of post-liberal society. As Adorno observed, the true danger lay in the fact that "fascist propaganda has only to *reproduce* the existent mentality for its own purposes" (GS 8, 429).

An initial approach to understanding what makes individuals receptive to such stimuli and susceptible to falling under the sway of fascism can be found in the famous study, *The Authoritarian Personality*. In this work, in which Adorno played a leading role, the tendency to adopt authoritarian, fascist, or anti-Semitic positions was linked to a particular configuration of character. The central hypothesis is that "the political, economic, and social convictions of an individual often form a broad and coherent pattern, as if bound together by a 'mentality' or 'spirit,' and that this pattern is an expression of deep-lying trends in his personality" (GS 9.1, 149).[93] The study aimed to uncover latent psychic dispositions that could be activated under certain conditions, revealing the proclivity of certain individuals to join fascist movements or engage in ethno-racial persecution—even in a country like the United States (GS 9.1, 153).[94] The determining factor, in this regard, was thought to lie not so much

[91] Adorno, *The Authoritarian Personality*, 662.
[92] Ibid., 608.
[93] Ibid., 1.
[94] Ibid., 4.

in a person's explicit political stances as in their character dispositions (GS 9.2, 365). The idea was that the subject's precarious psychic equilibrium shapes their conscious mentality and positions, rather than the reverse.

The explanatory key to the authoritarian personality is, therefore, purely psychoanalytic. Its predominant feature is an extreme weakness of the ego, understood in the Freudian sense as the psychic instance "that governs the relations between self and outer world, and between self and deeper layers of the personality" (GS 9.1, 201).[95] In these subjects the ego is so diminished that it can no longer achieve a synthesis capable of integrating the various elements of the personality into a coherent whole. The internalization of the moral conscience, what psychoanalysis refers to as the superego, fails and proves incapable of regulating the demands of the drives. As a result, this moral instance operates as a foreign body within the personality. Instead of internalizing the social precept "the individual identifies him or herself promptly and directly with the stereotyped scales of values" (DA, 224).[96] The result is a rigid, numb, and unstable character, which affects both their attitude toward the social norm and their capacity to relate to external and internal reality (GS 9.1, 188–210).[97] On the one hand, the authoritarian individual exhibits a conventional and uncritical behavior that venerates everything that embodies power, submits to the social norm, and is ready to persecute anyone who violates it. This is a subject who praises harshness and strength, organizing their entire perception of reality "in hierarchical terms: above and below, strong and weak."[98] This type of character is also marked by an increasing incapacity for experience. Its primary trait is resistance to all forms of introspection. This reveals a detachment from one's own emotional and psychic life, which fosters coldness and emotional constriction, while simultaneously diminishing imagination and sensitivity. Moreover, the resulting relationship to the world is governed by rigid, stereotyped, and often pathos-laden patterns of perception, reinforced by a tendency to project onto others all the inner impulses they themselves have had to repress in order to adapt.

---

[95] Ibid., 234.

[96] Adorno and Horkheimer, *The Dialectic of Enlightenment*, 164. Translation modified.

[97] Adorno, *The Authoritarian Personality*, 224–41.

[98] Adorno, "Die autoritäre Persönlichkeit," *Vorträge 1949–1968*, 258.

The outcome is a personality structure whose experience of reality is increasingly detached from "a spontaneous and vital relationship to people and things" (GS 9.2, 369). This is compounded by an unstable character, marked by a fragile balance and underlying aggressive tendencies, which are intensified through a hyper-identification with social power. As a result, the capacity for autonomous and differentiated judgment is undermined, and susceptibility to "prejudice" is heightened. Indeed, the authoritarian personality is receptive to rigid patterns for interpreting and navigating reality, patterns that allow the ego to operate sovereignly in the world without the need for reflection or sifting through experience, even at the cost of blurring the boundaries between reality and fantasy. These patterns become even more effective when they provide an outlet for the frustration and discomfort generated by increasingly coercive, impenetrable, and opaque forms of socialization. Naturally, the weakened subject will not dare to rebel against omnipotent social power, but their anger can be redirected toward a substitute target, thereby discharging compressed aggression without challenging dominant social forces or jeopardizing their own adaptation. Consequently, the authoritarian personality is defined by an ambivalence that reconciles "blind belief in authority and readiness to attack those who are deemed weak and who are socially acceptable as 'victims'" (GS 9.1, 475).[99] At its core lies the unconditional acceptance of prevailing power relations, ultimately culminating in an embrace of social Darwinism. Hence, Adorno's statement: "The potentially fascist character ... consists not only of crude outside factors, such as economic and social conditions, but of opinions, ideas, attitudes, and behavior which appear to be the individual's but which have originated neither in his autonomous thinking nor in his self-sufficient psychological development but are due to his belonging to our culture" (GS 9.1, 465–6).[100] The conclusion, then, is that it was the very normality of post-liberal capitalism—not a deviation from it—that provided the fertile ground for the proliferation of a model of personality that was at once submissive, conformist, and aggressive, in which authoritarian discourse could firmly take root.

---

[99]Adorno, *The Authoritarian Personality*, 759.
[100]Ibid., 752.

Beyond its clear merits, the study on *The Authoritarian Personality* also presents several weaknesses. The most obvious of these, of which Adorno was fully aware, was the tendency to derive political positions from character structure, a move that risked falling into psychologism. In addition, the methodology of scales, typologies, and syndromes—designed to classify different personality structures and their potential for fascist, ethnocentric, or anti-Semitic tendencies—did not yield coherent results. For instance, individuals who scored high on scales measuring ethnocentric character displayed liberal dispositions, while others who exhibited a low tendency toward prejudice instead exhibited psychic dispositions highly susceptible to conformity.[101] This seemed to suggest the need to introduce additional variables to enhance the explanatory potential of the findings. Perhaps the most significant difficulty, however, was the attempt to mediate between objective forms of socialization and psychic processes through the structure of character. Erich Fromm had introduced this strategy into the work of the Institute for Social Research,[102] developing a typological analysis of character aimed at explaining the forms of action, reaction, and the drive economy in different personality models. While this approach helped to account for certain reactive formations, it overlooked the conflicts and drive dynamics through which social processes impose themselves on psychic life. Ultimately, it subsumed concrete individuals into a typological classification of social characters: a schematism that was often excessive.[103] Adorno, despite being sharply critical of Fromm, nonetheless adopted this methodological framework in *The Authoritarian Personality*. As a result, the personality model that emerges functions like a Weberian ideal type. While it possesses undeniable heuristic value for analyzing certain traits in the evolution of character structures in post-liberal capitalism, it proves more limited when it

---

[101]Hullot-Kentor, "Metric of Rebarbarbarization," 735–41.

[102]In fact, in *Studies on Authority and the Family*, Fromm had already spoken of an "authoritarian-masochistic character" (Horkheimer, Fromm, Marcuse *et al.*, *Studien zur Autorität und Familie*, 110–35).

[103]Cf. Erich Fromm, "Die psychoanalytische Charakteriologie und ihre Bedeutung für die Sozialpsychologie," in *Analytische Sozialpsychologie und Gesellschaftstheorie* (Frankfurt: Suhrkamp, 1970), 65–9.

comes to identifying how specific biographical experiences might promote or inhibit the consolidation of violent and authoritarian dispositions.[104]

All in all, Adorno introduced a crucial approach that helped illuminate the psychodynamic logic underlying receptivity to fascist and anti-Semitic "ideologies." This insight would define the direction of his contributions, enabling a connection between the analysis of objective social dynamics and a focus on the subjective dimension of these regressive social phenomena. His key contribution lies in recognizing that Freud's diagnosis of civilization's discontents had a distinctly social dimension and that its symptoms had intensified under advanced capitalism. Individuals now found themselves caught in an increasingly dense social fabric where pressure mounted in tandem with the growing intensity of socializing imperatives (GS 10.2, 676). For Adorno, this tendency endured even in times of prosperity.[105] As socioeconomic power becomes increasingly omnipotent and the space for individual agency contracts, "the necessity of … adaptation, of identification with the given, the status quo, with power as such, creates the potential for totalitarianism" (GS 10.2, 567).[106] Unwavering adherence to authority and the social order is only one side of the coin. Its reverse is a condition of dependence that demands from individuals increasingly intolerable levels of renunciation, along with a relentless harshness toward their own needs and the ambivalences of psychic life—ultimately fueling the frustration and anxiety simmering within them. Thus, the desire to escape the suffocating web of coercion grows stronger: "this intensifies the fury against civilization. The revolt against it is violent and irrational" (GS 10.2, 677).[107] Hence the growing prominence of destructive, violent, and even sadistic impulses, which gain momentum as the pressure of civilization intensifies. At this point, the "archaic tendency toward violence" (GS 10.2, 680)[108] increases in individuals. These subjective dispositions toward aggression and destructiveness are significantly linked

---

[104]For a critique of the implications of this, see Claussen, *Unterm Konformitätszwang*, 22–5; Paul Parin, *Der Widerspruch im Subjekt* (Frankfurt: Syndikat, 1978), 72–7.

[105]Adorno, "Die autoritäre Persönlichkeit," 264.

[106]Adorno, "The Meaning of Working Through the Past," 99.

[107]Adorno, "Education After Auschwitz," 193.

[108]Ibid., 196.

to authoritarian discourse. For, "as a rebellion against civilization, fascism is not simply the reoccurrence of the archaic but its reproduction in and by civilization itself" (GS 8, 414).

In July 1943, while collaborating with Adorno on a joint theory of anti-Semitism, Horkheimer observed that "the tendencies which make human beings susceptible to the propaganda of terror are themselves the result of terror, physical and spiritual, of actual as well as potential oppression" (HGS 17, 464). For Adorno, a key psychic mechanism in this process was identification with the aggressor, which enables individuals to shift from feeling threatened to feeling empowered by threatening others—from a passive to an active stance.[109] Few passions favor this identification with social power as effectively as those arising from the very wound inflicted by capitulating to that power: resentment. Those who have internalized harsh demands on themselves often demand the same iron discipline for others. They cannot tolerate the thought that someone might evade the pressures they were forced to endure. As a result, such individuals identify with the oppressive forces that shaped them and, in the name of those forces, seek to punish anyone who seems to evade their grip. Nietzsche famously described this dynamic as the tendency to "sanctify *revenge* with the term *justice*."[110] The envy aroused, for example, by the representation of a life freed from heteronomous labor leads to anger directed precisely against "the most unfortunate group, the unemployed, because they are conceived of as being exempted from the hardship of labor" (GS 9.1, 128).[111] Adorno was quick to detect the peculiar allure of calls to act ruthlessly against those allegedly unwilling to work: they offer a form of compensation to those who have had no choice but to comply with coercive demands: "They find relaxation unbearable because they do not know fulfillment" (DA, 195).[112] This reveals that persecution targets not only the vulnerable, but particularly also those who appear less constrained

---

[109]Freud, *The Ego and the Defense Mechanisms*, 125.

[110]Friedrich Nietzsche, *Zur Genealogie der Moral*, in *Kritische Studienausgabe, vol. 5* (Munich: dtv/de Gruyter, 1988), 309–10. and *On the Genealogy of Morality*, trans. Carol Diethe (Cambridge: Cambridge University Press, 2006), 48.

[111]Adorno, *The Psychological Technique of Martin Luther Thomas' Radio Addresses*, 119.

[112]Adorno and Horkheimer, *Dialectic of Enlightenment*, 1410.

by the social norms from which one could not escape (GS 10.2, 677).[113] The intensity of the fury directed at them reveals their status as figures of forbidden desire, whose uncanny appeal, in the strict Freudian sense,[114] can only be exorcised through violence. In this way, they reconcile the need to vent inner rage with obedience to social prescriptions.[115] Their supposed rebellion is, at root, conformist; their apparent insubordination is merely a release valve. In modern societies, the Jews became the most common targets of such resentment, perceived as incarnating a form of happiness deprived of power (DA, 196).[116] Having been relegated to the sphere of circulation, commerce, and the liberal professions, the rise of capitalism was perceived as a social ascent of the Jews. In fact, the processes of assimilation left them in a position of singular ambivalence: they appeared as a group that was at once well-adapted and vulnerable. This led to their being targeted both as beneficiaries of a coercive, abstract, and impenetrable social order and as the hidden power behind Bolshevism. Thus, the Jews came to be "the group which, in practice and in theory, draws to itself the destructive urge which the wrong social order spontaneously produces" (DA, 192).[117]

It has occasionally been argued that Adorno's analysis of anti-Semitism does not sufficiently account for the specific nature of violence against Jews compared to other forms of "prejudice."[118] While this critique contains a kernel of truth, it overlooks an essential dimension of his contribution. Adorno's framework not only identifies parallels between anti-Semitism and other types of discriminatory violence but also embeds these phenomena within a broader social theory that considers the socio-psychic constitution of individuals. For Adorno, "anti-Semitism is not a matter of individual psychology"; rather, it is an attitude, a feeling that accompanies "the actualized consciousness of

[113]Adorno, "Education After Auschwitz," 193.

[114]Sigmund Freud, "Das Unheimliche," in *Studienausgabe*, vol. IV, Frankfurt, Fischer, 1994, 242–74 and "The Uncanny," *The Standard Edition of the Complete Psychological Works of Sigmund Freud Volume XVII*, trans. James Strachey (London: The Hogarth Press, 1955).

[115]Fenichel, "Elemente einer psychoanalytischen Theorie des Antisemitismus," *Aufsätze 2*, 375.

[116]Adorno and Horkheimer, *Dialectic of Enlightenment*, 141.

[117]Ibid., 137.

[118]Ziege, *Antisemitismus und Gesellschaftstheorie*. For a closer analysis of the question of anti-Semitism in Adorno, cf. Jordi Maiso, "The Critical Theory of Antisemitism and the Limits of Enlightenment," in *Critical Theory and the Critique of Antisemitism*, ed. M. Stoetzler (London: Bloomsbury, 2023), 29–49.

power. Anti-Semitic situations arise whenever power must be asserted over someone weaker, and such situations arise only under the pressure of power. German anti-Semitism since Hitler bears in all its traits the mark of an induced phenomenon, where the threat from above suggests that failing to conform to anti-Semitic views can result in power being turned against the individual" (IG, 84). From this perspective, anti-Semitism serves as the prototype for conformist rebellion. Its violent eruptions are essentially a "tolerated excess," in which the possibility of giving in to the drives and indulging in aggression is implicitly regulated. In truth, pogroms and lynchings are not spontaneous or impulsive, but respond to the strategies of those who sustain fascist discourse.[119] As Adorno puts it, anti-Semitism is "an induced scheme, even a ritual of civilization, and pogroms are real ritual murders." For "anti-Semitic behavior is unleashed in situations in which blinded people, deprived of subjectivity, are let loose as subjects" (DA, 195).[120] In this regard it is telling that empirical studies revealed those most inclined toward anti-Semitic actions were often individuals who perceive themselves as victims of social injustice (GS 9.1, 302).[121] Their sense of having been wronged—cheated, even—leads them to demand that others endure the same suffering. Indeed, in outlining the characteristics of the anti-Semitic personality, Adorno describes them as "people who suffer injustice as a result of social competition but who also, in their own way, identify with that competition. They are Darwinists. They believe in the survival of the fittest and always feel that they are 'fitter' than the Jews, and that the Jews are naturally doomed to collapse. When nature does not work as expected, they lend it a hand" (IG, 85–6).

These reflections are not exclusive to anti-Semitism; they could also apply to violence directed against other social or ethnic groups. This is because the psychic dynamics underlying authoritarian aggression do not hinge on the specific characteristics of the object of hatred but rather on its functionality in providing an outlet for destructive impulses of certain individuals, thereby compensating for the frustration that fuels them. In this context, the unique

[119]Adorno, *Bemerkungen zu "The Authoritarian Personality,"* 38–41. and "Remarks on 'The Authoritarian Personality,'" xlviii–l.

[120]Adorno and Horkheimer, *Dialectic of Enlightenment*, 140.

[121]Adorno, *The Authoritarian Personality*, 632.

position of Jews lies in their ambivalent characterization, which enables them to be paradoxically perceived both as a figure of power and of pure powerlessness. This duality facilitates the projection of arguments that serve to justify violence inflicted upon them.[122] The alleged content of anti-Semitic or racist "ideologies"—whether the affirmation of the natural inferiority of Jews or their supposed role as shadow architects of a global conspiracy—are rationalizations that no longer even strive for any appearance of truth but instead fulfill a purely psychic function: the legitimization of violence. Fundamentally, what is at work here is a projective mechanism, for "those impelled by blind murderous lust have always seen in the victim the pursuer who has driven them to desperate self-defense, and the mightiest of the rich have experienced their weakest neighbor as an intolerable threat before falling upon him" (DA, 212).[123] This allows individuals to suspend self-restraint and give free rein to their destructive impulses under the guise of self-defense.

Yet this same projective mechanism drives aggressors, almost inexorably, to inflict upon their victims precisely what they unconsciously fear most for themselves: "those who express what everyone craves—peace, homeland, freedom—will be denied it, just as nomads and traveling players have always been refused rights of domicile. Whatever someone fears, that is done to him. . . . Those evicted compulsively arouse the lust to evict them even here. The marks left on them by violence endlessly inflame violence" (DA, 208).[124] Once the social mechanism has branded them with the stigma of exclusion, the victims are often presumed to bear some form of guilt—this remains, to this day, the rationalization used to legitimize the calls for authoritarian

[122]"Some of these features, such as 'clannishness' aid rationalization; others, such as the expression of weakness or masochism, provide psychologically adequate stimuli for destructiveness. There can be hardly any doubt that all these requirements are fulfilled by the phenomenon of the Jew. This is not to say that Jews must draw hatred upon themselves, or that there is an absolute historical necessity which makes them, rather than others, the ideal target of social aggressiveness. Suffice it to say that they can perform this function in the psychological households of many people. The problem of the 'uniqueness' of the Jewish phenomenon and hence of anti-Semitism could be approached only by recourse to a theory which is beyond the scope of this study. Such a theory would neither enumerate a diversity of 'factors' nor single out a specific one as 'the' cause but rather develop a unified framework within which all the 'elements' are linked together consistently. This would amount to nothing less than a theory of modern society as a whole" (GS 9.1, 269–70; *The Authoritarian Personality*, 608).

[123]Adorno and Horkheimer, *Dialectic of Enlightenment*, 154.

[124]Ibid., 150.

aggression. Their mere presence becomes justification enough to deem them unwelcome, not "one of us," and therefore subject to expulsion—as if their very existence undermined the possibility of feeling "at home" (GS 9.1, 139).[125] Beneath this dynamic lies a deep drive for self-affirmation and the exercise of power. For racism, xenophobia, and anti-Semitism are not aberrant deviations from the prevailing social order, but rather manifestations of how that order molds individuals and perpetuates harassment and violence (DA, 194).[126] In a society governed by blind and relentless coercion, individuals come to perceive violence as the foundation of the social order itself. Accordingly, authoritarian rhetoric functions as a call to aggression, offering dispossessed and resentful individuals the chance to participate actively in the very system of violence that they are ordinarily forced to endure.[127] This dynamic allows those only marginally better off to assert a sense of privilege over the even more disadvantaged. As Adorno notes, "rage is unleashed on those who are both conspicuous and unprotected. And just as, depending on the constellation, the victims are interchangeable: vagrants, Jews, Protestants, Catholics, so each of them can replace the murderer, in the same blind lust for killing, as soon as he feels the power of representing the norm" (DA, 195).[128] Though such violent outbursts leave the root of discontent untouched, they offer an outlet for pent-up aggression. The manipulative genius of fascist propaganda lies in its ability to "place oppressed nature's rebellion against domination directly in the service of domination" (DA, 210).[129]

Adorno observes that what individuals seek in authoritarian "ideologies" is a palliative to mitigate the "suffering generated by rational civilization."[130] While the "manifest content" of such ideologies is undeniably irrational, their appeal lies not in any factual accuracy, but in their capacity to facilitate the internalization of social coercion for a significant number of individuals. This, in turn, implies that "what is 'pathological' today may with changing social

[125]Adorno, *The Psychological Technique of Martin Luther Thomas' Radio Addresses*, 120.

[126]Adorno and Horkheimer, *Dialectic of Enlightenment*, 139.

[127]Cf. Löwenthal, "Falsche Propheten," in *Schriften* 3, 122.

[128]Adorno and Horkheimer, *Dialectic of Enlightenment*, 140.

[129]Ibid., 152.

[130]Adorno, *Bemerkungen zu "The Authoritarian Personality,"* 29 and "Remarks on 'The Authoritarian Personality,'" xliv.

conditions become the dominant trend of tomorrow" (GS 9.1, 157).[131] A mere shift in the sociopolitical climate can render permissible what was previously taboo. In the opening sentences of the final fragment of "Elements of Anti-Semitism" in *Dialectic of Enlightenment,* written after the fall of Nazism, Adorno and Horkheimer describe precisely this process—only in reverse. After Hitler's death, open expressions of hatred toward Jews were no longer socially acceptable. The military defeat of fascism and the exposure of the extermination of European Jews reimposed a taboo on such displays. Hence the bitter irony with which they begin the passage: "But there are no longer any anti-Semites. They were just liberals who wanted to express their antiliberal opinions" (DA, 226).[132] Under the new conditions that regulate what may and may not be said, anti-Semitism becomes crypto-anti-Semitism, a "rumor about the Jews" (MM, 125),[133] a form of "non-public opinion" that can no longer be explicitly articulated.

In this sense, Adorno notes that "gossip, rumor …, opinions that are not made entirely explicit in public, have always been the medium in which different forms of social discontent that did not dare step into the light in a social order were active. Anyone who adopts such opinions or rumors immediately seems like a member of a secret, truthful community that is merely suppressed by the surface forms of society" (GS 20.1, 363).[134] Those who violate the social taboo may feel rebellious, presenting themselves as bold individuals who dare to voice the "truth" that others fear to express. Yet this supposed bravery rests on the tacit assurance that their "opinion" will find resonance with a broad, complicit social majority. In this context, the taboo exists precisely to protect the vulnerable and to counter the inertia of a population that once acquiesced to extermination. Rumors and insinuations that challenge this prohibition effectively vindicate the harm already inflicted and affirm the supposed right to continue persecuting, albeit without openly stating it. This is why Adorno asserts that veiled insinuations and hints, "can sometimes be more dangerous

[131]Adorno, *The Authoritarian Personality*, 7.
[132]Adorno and Horkheimer, *Dialectic of Enlightenment*, 165.
[133]Adorno, *Minima Moralia*, 110.
[134]Adorno, *Fighting Antisemitism Today*, 5–6.

than an open expression" (GS 20.1, 378)[135]. Such indirect statements are instantly understood by those in the know, fostering an undercurrent of hostility beneath the façade of "democratic normality." This strategy bides its time, waiting for a shift in the balance of power that will once again render overt aggression socially acceptable.

Even in the 1950s and 1960s, precisely during the period of the "economic miracles" and welfare expansion, Adorno remained acutely aware of the enormous fragility of democratic regimes. Under the forms of socialization characteristic of advanced capitalism, democracy had managed to assert itself only on a formal level, failing to embed itself meaningfully in the material conditions of everyday life. For democracy to truly flourish, it required individuals who were genuinely autonomous and independent, capable of acting as subjects of their own lives. Yet the social logic of individuation under capitalism seemed to preclude this possibility, reducing individuals to positions of increasing dependence. In this context Adorno referred to fascism as the "the wounds, the scars of democracy."[136] Its persistent threat signaled an unresolved problem in the relationship between democracy and capitalist socialization. Moreover, fascism's defeat in 1945 had been achieved solely on military terms. In the late 1950s, Adorno wrote: "National socialism lives on, and even today we still do not know whether it is merely the ghost of what was so monstrous that it lingers on after its own death, or whether it has not yet died at all, whether the willingness to commit the unspeakable survives in people as well as in the conditions that enclose them" (GS 10.2, 555).[137] Adorno had no doubt that the conditions enabling fascism's rise remained intact—not necessarily at the overt political level but certainly within the social sphere. The ongoing trend toward capital concentration continued to intensify polarization between social power and individual powerlessness. This dynamic also posed a constant threat of downward mobility, prompting well-situated groups to cling anxiously to their status and privileges. Despite the era's apparent prosperity and near full employment, the rise in productive

[135]Ibid., 32.

[136]Adorno, "Aspekte des neuen Rechtsradikalismus," 445 and *Aspects of the New Right Wing Extremism*, 9.

[137]Adorno, "The Meaning of Working Through the Past," 89–90.

capacities left many individuals feeling as though they were potentially unemployed—essentially surplus to the needs of the social system. Against this backdrop, Adorno issued the following warning:

> The more our society tends to become "integral," i.e. a thoroughly organized totality, the more increases the pressure it exercises upon comparatively impotent individual. And it is exactly this process which enhances psychological defence mechanisms which are bound up with prejudice. It may be quite possible that even the most horrifying manifestation of discrimination, the Nazi policy of "genocide," is deeply connected with the economic fact that today's form of economic organization proves incapable of reproducing the population living under such conditions.[138]

As long as this pressure and this latent anxiety remain in force, social life harbors a destructive potential that can explode at any moment. This is why Adorno warned of a danger of regression lurking beneath the prosperous surface of the societies of the economic miracle. As late as 1966, he stressed that, "as far as peoples' conscious and unconscious is concerned," the possibility that something like Auschwitz could be repeated could not be ruled out:

> Barbarism continues as long as the fundamental conditions that favored that relapse continue largely unchanged. That is the whole horror. The societal pressure still bears down, although the danger remains invisible nowadays. It drives people toward the unspeakable, which culminated on a world historical scale in Auschwitz. (GS 10.2, 674)[139]

Adorno does not regard Auschwitz as an isolated aberration but as the culmination of a historical process. Systematic extermination represents the endpoint of a trajectory rooted in specific social and historical conditions—conditions that gave rise to various forms of violence, exclusion, and barbarism, ultimately reaching their most brutal expression in Auschwitz.[140]

---

[138]Adorno, *Bemerkungen zu "The Authoritarian Personality,"* 47 and "Remarks on 'The Authoritarian Personality,'" lii.

[139]Adorno, "Education After Auschwitz," 191.

[140]As Detlev Claussen has pointed out, in reality, the machinery of death that made Auschwitz possible is not explained by the logic of anti-Semitism, but by the logic of violence. Anti-Semitism cannot do

These conditions not only shape socialized individuals but also teach them to adapt to and coexist with such realities. This insight underscores the need to understand, without illusions, how contemporary conditions of socialization produce what Adorno terms "normal monsters" (ND, 282).[141] These are not merely frustrated individuals seeking an outlet for their aggression, but fully integrated members of society: emotionally hardened, cold, and prone to dividing the world into rigid categories of friends and enemies—willing to employ any means necessary to achieve their ends. Adorno suspected that this type of character was even more prevalent under fully developed advanced capitalism than during the period of Nazism itself (GS 10.2, 683).[142]

According to a formulation by Adorno, fear had been "the ultimate lesson of the fascist era" (GS 3, 335).[143] However, this fear did not dissipate along with the military defeat of the Nazi regime. It persisted, not only because of the ongoing antagonism between the social system and the weakened individuals, but also due to the broader evolutionary tendencies of the social system itself, which continued to breed fear of catastrophic outcomes. Consequently, social unrest and anxiety continued to intensify. In a text published posthumously, Adorno voices the suspicion that the treatment of Jews in the extermination camps, where they were reduced to "mere objects of manipulation, living corpses, virtual 'cakes of soap,' may easily have been the projection of the prejudiced person's dim awareness of his own social situation, an awareness which he could suppress successfully only if he could prove to himself and others that it is the other fellow who could be dispensed with."[144]This, for Adorno, represents the destructiveness of conscious and unconscious states. It is not merely a matter of "false consciousness," but of the blind perpetuation of the social logic of violence. In a crucial passage from *Negative Dialectics*, Adorno writes that the state of freedom would be one in which instincts

without the Jews. Total annihilation follows a different logic, which makes use of the ways of intimidating and fighting the enemy to the point of taking a qualitative and brutal turn in the extermination of millions of unarmed and defenseless human beings (Claussen, *Grenzen der Aufklärung*, 49–50).

[141]Adorno, *Negative Dialectics*, 287.

[142]Adorno, "Education After Auschwitz," 198.

[143]Adorno, "The Schema of Mass Culture," 96.

[144]Adorno, *Bemerkungen zu "The Authoritarian Personality,"* 48 and "Remarks on 'The Authoritarian Personality,'" liiv.

and inclinations would no longer have to express themselves destructively (ND, 281).[145] Achieving this would require a form of social existence that no longer generates fear—one that no longer deems human lives as worthless nor reinforces the idea that human history follows the brutal logic of natural history: to devour or be devoured. Only in such a world could a spontaneous vital impulse emerge, capable of fostering a genuine solidarity with "torturable bodies." Until then, all that remains is the old maxim: "not allowing oneself to be stupefied by the power of others or by one's own impotence"; without forgetting that Adorno himself warned that this is an "almost insoluble task" (MM, 63).[146]

[145] Adorno, *Negative Dialectics*, 285.
[146] Adorno, *Minima Moralia*, 57.

Coda: The "Limit of Reification": Adorno and Late Capitalism Today

> "What would be different has not yet begun."
>
> THEODOR W. ADORNO (1966)

Adorno's critical theory sets out to chart the struggle between emancipation and barbarism under the conditions of advanced capitalism, which signaled the end of the bourgeois world. Undoubtedly, the experiences of the so-called age of catastrophes deeply informed his thought, even shaping his stance toward the apparent prosperity of the postwar era. However, rather than consigning Adorno to the ranks of incorrigible prophets of doom, this perspective may in fact bolster his relevance in an era in which the catastrophic dimensions of capitalism are becoming increasingly apparent. Adorno's work opens up a model of critique that is no longer oriented toward a time "before the revolution," but rooted in a "time of resistance." Those who resist find themselves at odds with the prevailing historical trend. In this case, resistance largely involves opposition to the normalization of barbarism. The awareness of the immense costs of total socialization in the 1930s and 1940s—which eradicated everything that deviated from the absolutized functionality of the social system, from the annihilation of the individual to the suppression of New Music—kept Adorno from succumbing to the siren songs of economic growth as a supposed path to social prosperity. One of the defining traits of Adorno's stance in the postwar period was his unwavering skepticism toward the so-called golden age of capitalism. Beneath the surface of material prosperity during the "economic miracles," his critical theory perceived the persistence of heteronomy, the intensification of fear, and the reduction of human beings to mere instruments of a social logic they were compelled to uphold as its subjects. To him, it was evident that the threat of regression persisted. While Adorno's thought may at times appear excessive or bleak, his analyses have proven more enduring than those of critics who dismissed him in favor of self-proclaimed "paradigm shifts" within critical theory.[1] Adorno's concern was not to establish a normative foundation for critique, but to guard emancipatory thought against complicity in the deceptive inertia of "healthy common sense." He was therefore convinced that the "evil eye is fertile. It strikes phenomena which are overlooked or deemed harmless when one does not linger over them but merely dispenses with them from above as nothing more than the façade of society" (GS 10.1, 78–9).[2] This critical gaze, which strove to resist the complacency of generally accepted opinion, enabled him to detect decisive transformations in seemingly innocuous phenomena—from the culture industry to the emergence of new human types, as well as shifts in forms of consciousness and subjectivity, manifested in authoritarian tendencies or astrology. Confronted with the extreme events of the twentieth century, Adorno concluded that "there is nothing innocuous left" (MM, 26).[3] Today, his keen ability to discern how the seeds of barbarism take root in the most ordinary aspects of life is not something that can be dismissed lightly.

Nevertheless, Adorno's stance cannot be adequately understood as a seamless, monolithic expression of negativity. Even in his most somber and despairing analyses, he identifies evolving tendencies within social transformations, rather than fully accomplished processes. Adorno himself acknowledged that his emphasis on the bleak was intentional, "following the maxim that only exaggeration per se can be the medium of truth today" (GS 10.2, 567).[4] For him, exaggeration was a deliberate method designed to unsettle consciences and strip away illusions about the harmlessness of normality, revealing "a tendency concealed behind the smooth façade of everyday life"

[1]Cf. Maiso, *Elementos para la reapropiación de la Teoría Crítica de Theodor W. Adorno*, chapter 3; Safatle, *Dar corpo ao impossível*.

[2]Adorno, "Veblen's Attack on Culture," 80.

[3]Adorno, *Minima Moralia*, 25.

[4]Adorno, "The Meaning of Working Through the Past," 99. Translation modified.

(GS 10.2, 567).[5] In light of the extreme horrors that culminated in Auschwitz—with the active or passive complicity of broader society—no provocation could be deemed excessive. Yet this approach also demands caution. Its aim is not to reinforce the increasingly one-dimensional nature of social reality with a theory that fosters one-dimensional thinking. Adorno's insistence on dialectics and his commitment to a theory that refuses to settle on any fixed position—not even on absolute negativity—must equally be applied here. While his work does not offer a systematic theorization of social reality, it nevertheless does not shy away from formulations that make it clear that advanced capitalism is far from a homogeneous and uniform entity. As Adorno put it in the context of the so-called positivism dispute: "Society is full of contradictions and yet determinable; rational and irrational in one, a system and yet fragmented; blind nature and yet mediated by consciousness" (GS 8, 548).[6] Formulations such as these challenge any attempt to portray social objectivity as an unyielding, unbroken whole, whose ultimate triumph is predetermined. Adorno's ability to render social logic intelligible stems not only from his recognition of its overwhelming and coercive nature, but also from his refusal to hypostatize it as a reality "in itself." By underscoring its dependence on living subjects for its ongoing reproduction, he reveals that it stands, in a certain sense, on feet of clay. In short, Adorno's emphasis on the menacing dimension of certain sociohistorical tendencies does not stem from a belief that the path toward barbarism is inevitable or irreversible. Rather, by laying bare the gravity of the threat without softening it, he aims to provoke a response capable of preventing its full realization.

Adorno's critical theory, in its analysis of advanced capitalism, brings a troubling tendency into focus: the forces capable of restraining the most destructive potentials embedded in the social constitution are steadily losing ground. The very basis of critique has grown increasingly fragile, as intellectual production becomes ever more entangled in the system's expanding integrative dynamics. In light of the most horrific experiences of the first half of the twentieth century, the prospect of emancipatory social transformation seemed to vanish from the realm of possibility, as history appeared irrevocably

---

[5]Ibid., 99.

[6]Adorno, "On the Logic of the Social Sciences," *The Positivist Dispute in German Sociology*, 106.

bound to a catastrophic course. In this sense—and in line with Benjamin's insight—Adorno understood catastrophe not as a looming future event, an ominous disruption of the "normal" order, but as the very mode by which life is reproduced under advanced capitalism: a kind of "permanent catastrophe."[7] Despite his acute awareness of the destructive nature of normality, Adorno does not regard the catastrophic present as immutable. However blind the course of social life may be in perpetuating the brutality of "prehistory," however much "the whole" is "the false" (MM, 55)[8] and "wrong life cannot be lived rightly" (MM, 43),[9] the reproduction of social logic remains mediated by individual action—and thus by consciousness. This perspective precludes any notion that the existing order is inexorable or entirely impervious to human agency. The problem, rather, lies in the growing powerlessness of living subjects in the face of the social machinery upon which their lives depend, leading to a widespread capitulation to its overwhelming reality. The ego, which Freud described as the faculty responsible for reality testing, increasingly withdraws and aligns itself with the dynamics of unconscious drives, thereby fulfilling the function of adaptation at the price of self-consciousness (GS 8, 71).[10] This dynamic facilitates the proliferation of mechanisms that operate as a kind of "psychoanalysis in reverse," disempowering individuals, reinforcing their dependence on the social totality, and fostering what Adorno called a "web of delusion" (*Verblendungszusammenhang*). For Adorno, this web constitutes a tangible sociological reality—manifested, for instance, in the phenomena underpinning the new forms of ideology. Even as it obstructs all avenues of transformative praxis, it does not necessarily signal the closure of history. Indeed, Adorno's work contains numerous passages suggesting the opposite: "Every individual trait in the web of delusion is nonetheless relevant to its possible end. Good is what wrenches itself free, finds a language, opens its eyes" (GS 10.2 622).[11] Accordingly, the task is not merely to engage in a "ruthless criticism of the existing order" (MEW 1, 344),[12] but also to identify

[7]Adorno, "Contra Paulum," 477.
[8]Adorno, *Minima Moralia*, 50.
[9]Ibid., 39.
[10]Adorno, "Sociology and Psychology. Part II," 87.
[11]Adorno, "Progress," 148. Translation modified.
[12]Marx, "Letters from the Franco-German Yearbooks," 207.

moments within the asphyxiating immanence of the social system where the potential for transformation can emerge. Without this, criticism risks devolving into mere impotent lamentation. This is why Adorno insists: "The means employed in negative dialectics for the penetration of its hardened objects is possibility—the possibility of which their reality has cheated the objects, and which is nonetheless visible in each one" (ND, 62).[13]

Where, then, might one discern the possibility capable of mobilizing transformative energies? For Adorno—especially in his later work—this potential lies primarily within living subjects, who are never entirely identical to the social objectivity that shapes them. Any critique that refuses to sever its connection with history must remain attentive to this. The social system of capitalism cannot function without reproducing individuals as subjects of needs and interests; without this, its logic would grind to a halt. This suggests that capitalist domination is not purely coercive but also operates through strategies of incorporation—appropriating and functionalizing the nonidentical within the subject. As a result, the logic of social domination not only intensifies alienation but also exploits the very desire to overcome it. Hence it needs to absorb and redirect needs, shaping how they are expressed and satisfied within the confines of its own immanence. For Adorno, this is the greatest danger of a "total society" (GS 8, 393):[14] its capacity to infiltrate the constitution of human beings, channeling their vital impulses—their pursuit of gratification and avoidance of suffering—into paths that serve the reproduction of the social whole. His diagnosis reveals how the socializing logic of capitalism entraps living subjects in an endless cycle of renunciations, frustrations, compensations, and substitute gratifications. This cycle deepens their dependency on the oppressive immanence of the system, which they long to escape in search of relief. In so doing, it perpetuates anxiety, suffering, and fear, leaving individuals at the mercy of a social order driven by the mute compulsion of capital valorization. This logic fails to recognize individuals as concrete beings, reducing them to fungible, interchangeable entities for the sake of its own perpetuation. Arguably, this tendency has not been reversed

[13] Adorno, *Negative Dialectics*, 52.

[14] Adorno, "Theses on Need," 465.

but has only expanded in scope and intensity in the subsequent development of capitalism up to the present.

In some writings from his later work, Adorno emphasizes the importance of a "turn to the subject" (GS 10.2, 676).[15] This does not stem from any naïve faith transformative potential of currently existing individuals, but from a recognition that the constitution of subjectivity is a crucial battleground. It is here that the fate of critique is decided: whether it gains ground and fosters resistance or surrenders to conformism. This struggle is central to determining whether history will open toward emancipatory possibilities or continue its complicity with barbarism. Living subjects—upon whom social objectivity weighs heavily, leaving behind scars, anxiety, and suffering—remain the locus where demands and needs continue to assert themselves. Critique can transform these into the seeds of a struggle to transform the social conditions of life. This is how Adorno put it in one of his last lectures, given in the spring of 1968:

> It might be said that under present conditions the subject is both: on one hand, ideology, because in reality the subject does not matter, and because there is something illusory about even believing oneself a subject in this society; on the other, however, the subject is also the potential, the only potential, by which this society can change, and in which is stored up not only all the negativity of the system but also that which points beyond the system as it now is. (ES, 254–5)[16]

Of course, this fragile potential for transcendence must not obscure the fact that the subject in question is shaped in the image and likeness of the social system and its coercions. This is a weakened, dependent subject whose capacity for experience has been diminished—a subject hardened and rendered increasingly cold by a reality governed by the principle of ruthless competition. Nevertheless, Adorno insists on the possibility of overcoming this model of subjectivation because it can never fully capture the living individual. As such, it does not constitute a final or irrevocable reality. Within the very

---

[15]Adorno, "Education After Auschwitz," 193.

[16]Adorno, *Introduction to Sociology*, 152.

constitution of the subjects, there remain elements—however faint, even if only manifesting as wounds or discomforts—that resist complete assimilation to the system, thus pointing "beyond the system as it now is." For Adorno, the potentials that the system has frustrated within individuals cannnot be considered entirely extinguished, at least so long as human beings retain some degree of spontaneity. The system does not merely harm subjects; it must also continually mobilize their desires and their search of gratification to sustain itself. This mobilization undoubtedly involves the artificial production of desires and the social manipulation of needs. Yet, as Adorno notes, "even in the false needs of a human being an element of freedom stirs" (GS 10.1, 390).[17]

This dimension of striving—the surplus of subjectivity that can never be fully functionalized—constitutes a source of what Adorno calls "the potential of a not-yet-existent individuation" (GS 8, 292).[18] This is why individuals, as subjects of needs, interests, and expectations, represent for him "the ultimate limit of reification" (GS 3, 331),[19] the point where "socialization finds its limit within the subject" (GS 8, 92). As long as the social logic requires the mobilization and capture of individuals to sustain itself, the circle of domination cannot be entirely closed. Hence, Adorno's wager is to address subjects and help develop their potential. This entails fostering their awareness of their position and needs within the social whole, strengthening their capacity for experience, and sharpening their critical faculties.[20] Only by recognizing that their potential cannot be reduced to what the system has made of them, and that the oppressive reality that diminishes and intimidates them is not an inescapable necessity, can they begin to challenge and reverse the processes that confine them to mere embodiments of functions within the logic of the "automatic subject." For Adorno, the potential for resistance lies in the individual subject—in the wounds and scars left by socialization. As he puts it, "only from within does one issue forth"

---

[17]Adorno, "Functionalism Today," 14.

[18]Adorno, "Introduction," *The Positivism Dispute in German Sociology*, 12.

[19]Adorno, "The Schema of Mass Culture," 93.

[20]As Detlev Claussen has noted (*Mit steinernem Herzen*, [Bremen: Wassmann, 1989], 110), this defined the praxis of the critical theorists following their return to the German Federal Republic. Their efforts focused on educating a younger generation in a spirit resolutely opposed to all forms of conformism.

(AT, 411).[21] Even in this damaged and diminished subject, Adorno detects a force capable of cracking the seemingly monolithic surface of the system. It is within their unfulfilled vitality that the hope for a break from conformity can take root. Perhaps this helps explain his insistence on the figure of the individual and his suspicion toward forms of community; for Adorno, "the zoon politikon is something yet to be realized" (GS 11, 266).[22]

Anyone aware of this state of affairs will find resources for revitalizing critique in Adorno's work. However, it is important to remember that his theory is rooted in the "age of catastrophes" and offers one of the most incisive critiques of the so-called golden age of capitalism—a period that has long since passed. The historical tensions from which Adorno's critique takes shape are those that oppose the emergent form of post-liberal capitalism—marked by tendencies toward total socialization and the functionalization of more and more spheres of life—to the elements of immanent critique within the bourgeois world, particularly the notion of the autonomous individual capable of asserting their singularity in opposition to the social totality. Today, however, these tensions seem to have irreversibly collapsed: the subsequent development of capitalism has swept away the historical vestiges that once enabled its rise. The present now increasingly appears disconnected from any historical dimension, and individual agency in the new forms of deregulated labor is continually subsumed under the demands of the "automatic subject." Yet that is not all. The fact that we no longer live under a capitalism of splendor and prosperity, but rather one of diminishing expectations and looming catastrophe, carries significant implications for how we receive Adorno's legacy. For Adorno was able to anticipate many of today's present

---

[21] Adorno, *Aesthetic Theory*, 276.

[22] Adorno, "Extorted Reconciliation," *Notes to Literature 1*, 226. Translation modified. At this point, Hans-Jürgen Krahl's critique becomes particularly relevant. Krahl argued that one of the greatest weaknesses of Adorno's critical theory was its preoccupation with mourning the decomposition of the bourgeois individual, which led to the question of organization being neglected (Krahl, *Konstitution und Klassenkampf*, cit., 292). As Benjamin observed, organization is both the medium in which the reification of social relations is most clearly revealed and the only medium through which such reification could be overcome (BGS III, 221; "An Outsider Makes His Mark," *Selected Writings 2.1*, 306). Krahl"s efforts within the German anti-authoritarian movement of the late 1960s can thus be seen as an attempt to address this critical gap in the history of critical theory—an attempt shaped by a very specific and historically determined set of circumstances.

concerns, from the growing insignificance of the individual lives to their crude superfluity. He perceived the rising tide of anxiety and fear, even when it was not yet fully apparent. However, his critical theory was grounded in the assurances of full employment and mass consumption, which underpinned the tendency toward "total integration." His late work repeatedly reflects on the end of utopia, noting that the development of productive capacities could, in theory, meet basic needs—such as food, housing, clean water, and medicine—and eliminate extreme deprivation. His conception of dialectics as "ontology of the wrong state of things" (ND, 22)[23] was based on that concrete possibility. Yet today that scenario seems increasingly out of reach. However, even as deprivation and hardship re-emerge in a society whose productive capacities seem to defy all limits, Adorno's warning endures: "The satisfaction of material needs is the necessary, but not sufficient, condition of a liberated society."[24] Such a society would demand that needs evolve beyond dependence on blind material interests and surpass the sacrificial logic that reduces life to a mere struggle for survival. If the present seems to drift ever further from this horizon, diminishing any hope of escape from the suffocating immanence of the system, what then becomes of the prospects for critique?

Adorno himself recognized that the few remaining elements of social life still capable of harboring some form of transcendence were confined to the sphere of consumption. This led him to assert in *Minima Moralia* that "only by virtue of opposition to production, as still not wholly encompassed by this order, can men bring about another more worthy of human beings. Should the appearance of life, which the sphere of consumption itself defends for such bad reasons, be once entirely effaced, then the monstrosity of absolute production will triumph" (MM, 13–4).[25] The current state of affairs seems to confirm the most unsettling aspects of this diagnosis. The semblance of life and subjectivity that consumption once preserved is now fracturing, as growing numbers of people struggle to meet even their most basic needs. Capitalism's capacity for integration is waning, and despite massive growth in productive capacities, even

---

[23]Adorno, *Negative Dialectics*, 11.
[24]Adorno, "Zur Spezifikation der kritischen Theorie," 292.
[25]Adorno, *Minima Moralia*, 15.

employment no longer guarantees access to the basics. Adorno did not foresee such a scenario, and this underscores the need to acknowledge the specific difference between his historical experience and our own. His insistence on the aporias of a civilization rooted in the domination of external and internal nature has become all the more urgent in light of the increasingly inescapable problem of the socio-environmental unsustainability of the prevailing model of life's reproduction. Although Adorno's time was marked by anxiety over integration into an implacable social machinery, today's pervasive fear stems from the opposite: the fear of exclusion—of being unable to secure even a minimal share of social wealth. This dynamic fuels the fierce competitiveness of our time, which has grown increasingly ruthless.[26] As inequality spreads, the immediate exercise of force ever more frequently eclipses the mediation of law, with a growing tendency to eliminate surplus populations rather than exploit their labor power. Although Adorno diagnosed the growing nullity, interchangeability, and superfluity of individuals in his own time, these trends have now reached unprecedented extremes.

Similarly, the degree of economic and extra-economic coercion imposed on individuals shows no sign of abating, nor has the indifference of those who still feel protected by the prevailing "normality." The survival of critique undeniably relies on the existence of individuals who refuse to bow to the stark realism of prevailing relations of force—those who will not resign themselves to social relations that repress, exploit, abuse, or abandon human beings to death. It depends on subjects who—despite pervasive social atomization—remain open to solidarity with "tormentable bodies." Of course, this offers no guarantee—only a fragile point of departure. The central question is whether the hopes Adorno places in the unresolved dialectic between individual and social totality—whose nonidentity is the very condition of his critical theory—can withstand the transition to a social system that increasingly requires fewer human beings for its reproduction. Can there still be any hope for the potential transcendence of individual needs, as more and more human lives are rendered

[26]On this point, cf. C. Catalina, "La herida de la integración fordista. Notas para una genealogía del darwinismo social neoliberal," in *Republicanismo, Nacionalismo y Populismo como formas de la política contemporánea*, ed. J. L. Villacañas and A. Garrido (Madrid: Dado, 2021), 207–53.

superfluous by the all-encompassing demands of capital's self-perpetuation? What can be expected of those not yet crushed under its wheels, if the system's imperatives seem to ensnare them ever more thoroughly? Paradoxically, it would seem that what remains most relevant in Adorno's diagnoses is precisely their bleakest dimension: the tendencies toward total integration and the relentless reproduction of socially avoidable suffering have not abated. On the contrary, all signs appear to confirm Benjamin's old insight that the very fact that "things keep going on like this *is* the catastrophe" (BGS I, 683).[27]

Ultimately, the extent to which possibilities for resistance still subsist cannot be determined on the speculative plane of theory alone; it can only be clarified within sociohistorical reality. As Horkheimer and Adorno observed, "not the good but the bad is the subject matter of theory. Theory presupposes the reproduction of life in its existing forms. Its element is freedom, its theme oppression" (DA, 247).[28] Consequently, the aim of emancipatory thought is not to realize the latent potentials of the social totality, but to abolish its violent and coercive dimensions. Adorno emphasizes that while nothing in social life escapes the mediation of the system, the potential for transcendence lies in the singular—in that which the system can only integrate through force and coercion. Thought, which moves within the realm of the identical, of the concept, lacks the power to determine in advance where the unfolding of such singularity might lead if freed from systemic determination. To do so would betray the dialectic, which "is based on the experience of the impotence of a criticism that keeps to the general and polishes off the object being criticized by subsuming it from above under a concept as its representative" (GS 5, 318).[29] This principle holds true for the analysis of any social phenomenon, which cannot be fully grasped if considered solely through the lens of the system's crushing objectivity. Critique must also attend to what within the system appears destined to be cut short: the potentials and latencies that at first seem to hold no promise of success. As early as 1935, Adorno articulated the "salvation of the hopeless" as the guiding program of his entire philosophy

---

[27]Benjamin, "Central Park," in *Selected Writings 4*, 184. Translation modified.
[28]Adorno and Horkheimer, *Dialectic of Enlightenment*, 181.
[29]Adorno, *Hegel: Three Studies*, 80.

(AHB I, 35)—a commitment he upheld until the end of his life.[30] For the desire to transcend the false totality clings to the insight that its seemingly absolute closure is itself an illusion: "What is, is more than it is. This 'more' is not imposed upon it but remains immanent to it, as that which has been pushed out of it. In that sense, the nonidentical would be the thing's own identity against its identifications" (ND, 164).[31] From this understanding emerges a fundamental insight of Adorno's dialectic: "Only the critical idea that unleashes the force stored up in its own object is fruitful" (GS 5, 318).[32]

[30]This is what connects Adorno's critical theory—otherwise aligned with that of Benjamin—with a certain profanation of theological motifs (cf. Zamora, *Th. W. Adorno. Pensar contra la barbarie*, 279–97).

[31]Adorno, *Negative Dialectics*, 161.

[32]Adorno, *Hegel: Three Studies*, 80.

Bibliography

Works by Theodor W. Adorno

Collected Works

Adorno, T. W. *Gesammelte Schriften*, 20 vols. Edited by Rolf Tiedemann in collaboration with Gretel Adorno, Susan Buck-Morss, and Klaus Schultz, Frankfurt: Suhrkamp, 1970–86. All volumes were reprinted in 2003; the year given in parentheses indicates the original publication date of the respective volume of the *Gesammelte Schriften*.

Vol. 1: *Philosophische Frühschriften* (1973).

Vol. 2: *Kierkegaard: Konstruktion des Ästhetischen* (1979).

Vol. 3: *Dialektik der Aufklärung: Philosophische Fragmente* (with Max Horkheimer, 1981).

Vol. 4: *Minima Moralia: Reflexionen aus dem beschädigten Leben* (1980).

Vol. 5: *Zur Metakritik der Erkenntnistheorie. Drei Studien zu Hegel.* Edited by Gretel Adorno and Rolf Tiedemann (1970).

Vol. 6: *Negative Dialektik. Jargon der Eigentlichkeit: Zur deutschen Ideologie* (1973).

Vol. 7: *Ästhetische Theorie.* Edited by Gretel Adorno and Rolf Tiedemann (1970).

Vol. 8: *Soziologische Schriften I* (1972).

Vol. 9.1: *Soziologische Schriften II* (Part 1). Edited by Susan Buck-Morss and Rolf Tiedemann (1975).

Vol. 9.2: *Soziologische Schriften II* (Part 2). Edited by Susan Buck-Morss and Rolf Tiedemann (1975).

Vol. 10.1: *Kulturkritik und Gesellschaft I* (1977).

Vol. 10.2: *Kulturkritik und Gesellschaft II* (1977).

Vol. 11: *Noten zur Literatur* (1974).

Vol. 12: *Philosophie der neuen Musik* (1975).

Vol. 13: *Die musikalischen Monographien (Versuch über Wagner; Mahler: Eine musikalische Physiognomik; Berg: Der Meister des kleinsten Übergangs).* Edited by Gretel Adorno and Rolf Tiedemann (1971).

Vol. 14: *Dissonanzen. Einleitung in die Musiksoziologie* (1973).

Vol. 15: *Komposition für den Film* (with Hanns Eisler). *Der getreue Korrepetitor* (1976).

Vol. 16: *Musikalische Schriften I - III* (1978).

Vol. 17: *Musikalische Schriften IV* (1982).

Vol. 18: *Musikalische Schriften V.* Edited by Rolf Tiedemann and Klaus Schultz (1984).

Vol. 19: *Musikalische Schriften VI.* Edited by Rolf Tiedemann and Klaus Schultz (1984).

Vol. 20.1: *Vermischte Schriften I* (1986).

Vol. 20.2: *Vermischte Schriften II* (1986).

Posthumous Writings

Adorno, T. W. *Nachgelassene Schriften*, edited by the Theodor W. Adorno Archive, Frankfurt and Berlin: Suhrkamp, 1992–(publication still ongoing).

I. Fragmentary Writings

Vol. 1: *Beethoven. Philosophie der Musik. Fragmente und Texte*, edited by Rolf Tiedemann, 1993.
Vol. 2: *Zu einer Theorie der musikalischen Reproduktion*, edited by Henri Lonitz, 2001.
Vol. 3: *Current of music. Elements of a radio theory*, edited by Robert Hullot-Kentor, 2006.

II. Lecture Courses

Vol. 1: *Erkenntnistheorie* (1957–8), edited by Karel Markus, 2018.
Vol. 2: *Einführung in die Dialektik* (1958), edited by Christoph Ziermann, 2010.
Vol. 3: *Ästhetik* (1958/9), edited by Eberhard Ortland, 2009.
Vol. 4: *Kants «Kritik der Reinen Vernunft»* (1959), edited by Rolf Tiedemann, 1995.
Vol. 6: *Philosophie und Soziologie* (1960), edited by Dirk Braunstein, 2011.
Vol. 7: *Ontologie und Dialektik*, edited by Rolf Tiedemann, 2002.
Vol. 8: *Ästhetik (1961–62)*, edited by Anne Eusterschulte, 2025.
Vol. 9: *Philosophische Terminologie*, edited by Henri Lonitz, 2016.
Vol. 10: *Probleme der Moralphilosophie* (1963), edited by Thomas Schröder, 1996.
Vol. 11: *Fragen der Dialektik (1963–64)*, edited by Christoph Ziermann, 2021.
Vol. 12: *Philosophische Elemente einer Theorie der Gesellschaft* (1964), edited by Tobias ten Brink and Marc Phillip Nogueira, 2008.
Vol. 13: *Zur Lehre von der Geschichte und von der Freiheit* (1964–5), edited by Rolf Tiedemann, 2001.
Vol. 14: *Metaphysik. Begriff und Probleme* (1965), edited by Rolf Tiedemann, 1998.
Vol. 15: *Einleitung in die Soziologie* (1968), edited by Christoph Gödde, 1993.
Vol. 16: *Vorlesung über negative Dialektik*, edited by Rolf Tiedemann, 2003.
Vol. 17: *Kranichsteiner Vorlesungen*, edited by Klaus Reichert and Michael Schwarz, 2014.

III. Talks and Conversations

Vol. 1: *Vorträge 1949–1968*, edited by Michael Schwarz, 2019.

Correspondence

Adorno, T. W. *Briefe und Briefwechsel*, edited by the Theodor W. Adorno Archive, Frankfurt and Berlin: Suhrkamp, 1994–(publication still ongoing).
Vol. 1: *Theodor W. Adorno–Walter Benjamin. Briefwechsel 1928–1940*, edited by Henri Lonitz, 2020.
Vol. 2: *Theodor W. Adorno–Alban Berg. Briefwechsel 1925–1935*, edited by Henri Lonitz, 1997.
Vol. 3: *Theodor W. Adorno–Thomas Mann, Briefwechsel 1943–1955*, edited by Christoph Gödde and Thomas Sprecher, 2002.
Vol. 4: *Theodor W. Adorno–Max Horkheimer. Briefwechsel* (4 vols.), edited by Christoph Gödde and Henri Lonitz, 2003–6.
Vol. 5: *Briefe an die Eltern*, edited by Christoph Gödde and Henri Lonitz, 2003.

Vol. 6: *Theodor W. Adorno–Ernst Krenek Briefwechsel 1929–1964*, edited by Claudia Maurer Zenck, 2020.
Vol. 7: *Theodor W. Adorno–Sigfried Kracauer, Briefwechsel 1923–1966*, edited by Wolfgang Schopf, 2008.
Vol. 8: *Theodor W. Adorno–Gershom Scholem Briefwechsel 1939–1969*, edited by Asaf Angermann, 2015.
Vol. 9: *Theodor W. Adorno–Rudolf Kolisch Briefwechsel 1926–1969*, edited by Claudia Maurer Zenck, 2023.

Other Cited Editions of Adorno's Works

Adorno, Theodor W. "'Static' and 'Dynamic' as Sociological Categories." Trans. H. Kaal. *Diogenes* 9 (March 1961): 28–49.
Adorno, Theodor W. "Sociology and Psychology. Part I." *New German Critique* I/46 (November/December 1967): 67–80.
Adorno, Theodor W. "Sociology and Psychology. Part II." *New German Critique* I/47 (January/February 1968): 79–97.
Adorno, Theodor W. *Philosophische Terminologie* (2 vols.). Frankfurt: Suhrkamp, 1974.
Adorno, Theodor W. *Introduction to the Sociology of Music*. Trans. E. B. Ashton. New York: The Seabury Press, 1976.
Adorno, Theodor W. "Introduction." In *The Positivist Dispute in German Sociology*. Trans. Glyn Adey and David Frisby, 1–67. London: Heinemann, 1976.
Adorno, Theodor W. "Sociology and Empirical Research." In *The Positivist Dispute in German Sociology*. Trans. Glyn Adey and David Frisby, 68–86. London: Heinemann, 1976.
Adorno, Theodor W. "On the Logic of the Social Sciences." In *The Positivist Dispute in German Sociology*. Trans. Glyn Adey and David Frisby, 105–22. London: Heinemann, 1976.
Adorno, Theodor W. *Prisms*. Trans. Samuel and Shierry Weber. Cambridge, MA: MIT Press, 1981.
Adorno, Theodor W. "Society." In *Critical Theory and Society: A Reader*, edited by Stephen Eric Bronner and Douglas Kellner, 267–75. London: Routledge, 1989.
Adorno, Theodor W. *The Culture Industry*. Trans. Nicholas Walker. London: Routledge, 1991.
Adorno, Theodor W. *Notes to Literature* (2 vols.) Trans. Shierry Weber Nicholsen. New York: Columbia University Press, 1992.
Adorno, Theodor W. *Hegel: Three Studies*. Trans. Shierry Weber Nicholsen. Cambridge, MA: MIT Press, 1993.
Adorno, Theodor W. "Theory of Pseudo-Culture." *Telos* 95 (1993): 15–38.
Adorno, Theodor W. "Der Begriff der Philosophie." In *Frankfurter Adorno Blätter* II, edited by Rolf Tiedemann, 9–91. Munich: Text+Kritik, 1993.
Adorno, Theodor W. *Aesthetic Theory*. Trans. Robert Hullot-Kentor. New York: Continuum, 1997.
Adorno, Theodor W. "Über Marx und die Grundbegriffe der soziologischen Theorie. Aus einem Seminarmitschrift im Sommersemester 1962." In H. G. Backhaus, *Dialektik der Wertform*, 501–13. Freiburg: ça ira, 1997 [Adorno, Theodor W. "Marx and the Basic Concepts of Sociology." From a Seminar Transcript in the Summer Semester of 1962. Trans. Verena Erlenbusch-Anderson and Chris O'Kane. *Historical Materialism* 26, no. 1 (2018): 1–11.]

Adorno, Theodor W. *Critical Models*. Trans. Henry W. Pickford. New York: Columbia University Press, 1999.
Adorno, Theodor W. *Introduction to Sociology*. Trans. Edmund Jephcott. Stanford, CA: Stanford University Press, 1999.
Adorno, Theodor W. *The Psychological Technique of Martin Luther Thomas' Radio Addresses*. Stanford, CA: Stanford University Press, 2000.
Adorno, Theodor W. "Kritik der Pseudo-Aktivität. Adornos Verhältnis zur Studentenbewegung im Spiegel seiner Korrespondenz. Eine Dokumentation." In *Frankfurter Adorno Blätter* VI, edited by Rolf Tiedemann, 42–116. Munich: Text+Kritik, 2000.
Adorno, Theodor W. *Metaphysics: Concepts and Problems*. Trans. Edmund Jephcott. Stanford, CA: Stanford University Press, 2001.
Adorno, Theodor W. *The Stars Down to Earth*. London: Routledge, 2001.
Adorno, Theodor W. "Notizen über Eisler." In *Frankfurter Adorno Blätter* VII, edited by Rolf Tiedemann, 121–34. Munich: Text+Kritik, 2001.
Adorno, Theodor W. *Essays on Music*. Trans. Susan H. Gillespie. Berkeley and Los Angeles: University of California Press, 2002.
Adorno, Theodor W. *Can One Live After Auschwitz? A Philosophical Reader*. Trans. Rodney Livingstone and others. Stanford, CA: Stanford University Press, 2003.
Adorno, Theodor W. "Aus einem Entwurf 'Zur Neuausgabe' der Dialektik der Aufklärung." In *Frankfurter Adorno Blätter* VIII, edited by Rolf Tiedemann, 7–8. Munich: Text+Kritik, 2003.
Adorno, Theodor W. "Graeculus (II). Notizen zu Philosophie und Gesellschaft." In *Frankfurter Adorno Blätter* VIII, edited by Rolf Tiedemann, 9–41. Munich: Text+Kritik, 2003.
Adorno, Theodor W. "Individuum und Gesellschaft. Entwürfe und Skizzen." In *Frankfurter Adorno Blätter* VIII, edited by Rolf Tiedemann, 60–94. Munich: Text+Kritik, 2003.
Adorno, Theodor W. "Zur Spezifikation der kritischen Theorie." In *Adorno. Eine Bildmonographie*, edited by the Theodor W. Adorno Archiv, 292. Frankfurt: Suhrkamp, 2003.
Adorno, Theodor W. *Negative Dialectics*. Trans. E. B. Ashton. London: Routledge, 2004.
Adorno, Theodor W. *Minima Moralia*. Trans. E. F. N. Jephcott. London: Verso, 2005.
Adorno, Theodor W. *Traumprotokolle*. Edited by Christoph Gödde and Henri Lonitz. Frankfurt: Suhrkamp, 2005. [*Dream Notes*. Trans. Rodney Livingstone, Cambridge: Polity Press, 2007.]
Adorno, Theodor W. *Philosophy of New Music*. Trans. Robert Hullot-Kentor. Minneapolis: University of Minnesota Press, 2006.
Adorno, Theodor W. *History and Freedom*. Trans. Rodney Livingstone. Cambridge: Polity, 2006.
Adorno, Theodor W. *Lectures on Negative Dialectics*. Trans. Rodney Livingstone. Cambridge: Polity, 2008.
Adorno, Theodor W. *Current of Music: Elements of a Radio Theory*. Edited by Robert Hullot-Kentor. Cambridge: Polity Press, 2009.
Adorno, Theodor W. *Night Music: Essays on Music 1928–1962*. London: Seagull Books, 2009.
Adorno, Theodor W. "Questions on Intellectual Emigration." Trans. Mark Kalbus. *Social Text* 99, no. 2 (2009): 159–64.
Adorno, Theodor W. *Guilt and Defense*. Trans. J. K. Olick and Andrew J. Perrin. Cambridge, MA: Harvard University Press, 2010.

Adorno, Theodor W. *Against Epistemology: A Metacritique*. Trans. Willis Domingo. Cambridge: Polity Press, 2013.

Adorno, Theodor W. "The Revisionist Psychoanalysis." Trans. Nan-Nan Lee. *Philosophy and Social Criticism* 40, no. 3 (2014): 326–38.

Adorno, Theodor W. "Theses on Need." Trans. Devi Dumbadze. *Constelaciones: Revista de Teoría Crítica* 6 (2014): 464–7.

Adorno, Theodor W. "Kierkegaard Once More." Trans. Jensen Suther. *Telos* 174 (Spring 2016): 57–74.

Adorno, Theodor W. *Philosophical Elements of a Theory of Society*. Trans. Wieland Hoban. London: Polity Press, 2019.

Adorno, Theodor W. "Bemerkungen zu *The Authoritarian Personality*." *Bemerkungen zu "The Authoritarian Personality" und weitere Texte*, edited by Eva-Maria Ziege, 21–70. Berlin: Suhrkamp, 2019. ["Remarks on *The Authoritarian Personality*." In *The Authoritarian Personality*, xli–lxvi. London: Verso, 2019.]

Adorno, Theodor W. *Aspects of the New Right Wing Extremism*. Trans. Wieland Hoban. Cambridge: Polity Press, 2020.

Adorno, Theodor W. *Philosophy and Sociology*. Trans. Nicholas Walker. Cambridge: Polity Press, 2022.

Adorno, Theodor W. "Contribution to the Theory of Ideology." Trans. Jacob Bard-Rosenberg. *Selva: A Journal for the History of Art* (Fall 2022): 19–33.

Adorno, Theodor W. *Without Model: Parva Aesthetica*. Trans. Wieland Hoban. Chicago: University of Chicago Press, 2023.

Adorno, Theodor W. *Fighting Antisemitism Today*. Trans. Wieland Hoban. Cambridge: Polity Press, 2025.

Adorno, Theodor W. "On the Problem of the Family." Trans. Jacob Blumenfeld: https://endnotes.org.uk/posts/theodor-adorno-on-the-problem-of-the-family-1955.

Adorno, Theodor W., et al. "Diskussionen aus einem Seminar über die Theorie der Bedürfnisse." HGS 12: 559–86, 1985.

Adorno, Theodor W., and Walter Benjamin. *The Complete Correspondence 1928–1940*. Trans. Nicholas Walker. Cambridge, MA: Harvard University Press, 1999.

Adorno, Theodor W. and Alban Berg. *Correspondence 1925–1935*. Trans. Wieland Hoban. Cambridge: Polity Press, 2005.

Adorno, Theodor W. and Ernst Bloch. "Etwas fehlt … Über die Widersprüche der utopischen Sehnsucht." In *Gespräche mit Ernst Bloch*, edited by Rainer Traub and Harald Wiese, 58–77. Frankfurt: Suhrkamp, 1980.

Adorno, Theodor W., and Hanns Eisler. *Composing for the Films*. London: Continuum, 2007.

Adorno, Theodor W., and Arnold Gehlen. "Ist die Soziologie eine Wissenschaft vom Menschen?" In *Adornos Philosophie in Grundbegriffen. Auflösung einiger Deutungsprobleme*, edited by Friedemann Grenz, 224–54. Frankfurt: Suhrkamp, 1974.

Adorno, Theodor W., Else Frenkel-Brunswik, Daniel J. Levinson, and R. Nevitt Sanford. *The Authoritarian Personality*. New York: Harper & Brothers, 1950.

Adorno, Theodor W. and Alfred Sohn-Rethel. *Briefwechsel 1936–1969*. Edited by Christoph Gödde. Munich: Text+Kritik, 1999.

Horkheimer, Max, and Theodor W. Adorno. *Dialectic of Enlightenment: Philosophical Fragments*. Trans. Edmund Jephcott. Stanford, CA: Stanford University Press, 2002.

Horkheimer, Max, and Theodor W. Adorno. "Diskussionen über Sprache und Erkenntnis, Naturbeherrschung am Menschen, politische Aspekte des Marxismus." HGS 12, 493–525, 1985.

Horkheimer, Max, and Theodor W. Adorno. "Diskussionen zu den 'Elementen des Antisemitismus' der Dialektik der Aufklärung." HGS 12, 587–92, 1985.

Horkheimer, Max, and Theodor W. Adorno. "Diskussion über Theorie und Praxis." HGS 19, 32–72, 1986. ["Towards a New Manifesto." Trans. Rodney Livingstone. *New Left Review* 65 (September/October 2010): 33–61.]

Further Sources

Abromeit, John. *Max Horkheimer and the Foundations of the Frankfurt School.* Cambridge: Cambridge University Press, 2011.

Ackerman, Nathan W., and Marie Jahoda. *Anti-Semitism and Emotional Disorder.* New York: Harper & Brothers, 1950.

Anders, Günther. *Die Antiquiertheit des Menschen.* 2 vols. Munich: Beck, 2010.

Backhaus, Hans-Georg. "Adorno und die metaökonomische Kritik der positivistischen Nationalökonomie." In *Die Lebendigkeit der kritischen Gesellschaftstheorie*, edited by A. Gruschka and U. Oevermann, 27–64. Wetzlar: Büchse der Pandora, 2004.

Becker, Jens, and Heinz Brakemeier, eds. *Vereinigung freier Individuen. Kritik der Tauschgesellschaft und gesellschaftliches Gesamtsubjekt bei Theodor W. Adorno.* Hamburg: VSA, 2004.

Beckett, Samuel. *The Letters of Samuel Beckett.* Vol. 4, 1966–89. Edited by George Craig, Martha Dow Fehsenfeld, Dan Gunn, and Lois More Overbeck. Cambridge: Cambridge University Press, 2016.

Behrens, Roger. *Verstummen. Über Adorno.* Laatzen: Wehrhahn, 2004.

Benjamin, Walter. *Gesammelte Schriften.* 8 vols. Edited by Rolf Tiedemann and Hermann Schweppenhäuser, in collaboration with Theodor W. Adorno and Gershom Scholem. Frankfurt: Suhrkamp, 1972–99. (All volumes reprinted in 2006.)

Benjamin, Walter. *Goethes Wahlverwandschaften.* BGS I, 123–201, 1991. [*Goethe's Elective Affinities.* Translated by Stanley Corngold. *Selected Writings.* Vol. 1, 1913–26, 297–359. Cambridge, MA: Harvard University Press, 1996.]

Benjamin, Walter. "Das Kunstwerk im Zeitalter seiner technischen Reproduzierbarkeit. Dritte Fassung." BGS I, 471–508, 1991. ["The Work of Art in the Age of Its Technological Reproducibility. Third Version." *Selected Writings.* Vol. 4, 1938–1940, 251–283. Cambridge, MA: Harvard University Press, 2006.]

Benjamin, Walter. "Über einige Motive bei Bauldelaire." BGS I, 605–54, 1991. ["On Some Motifs in Baudelaire." *Selected Writings.* Vol. 4, 1938–40, 313–55. Cambridge, MA: Harvard University Press, 2006.]

Benjamin, Walter. "Zentralpark." BGS I, 655–690, 1991. ["Central Park." *Selected Writings.* Vol. 4, 1938–1940, 161–199. Cambridge, MA: Harvard University Press, 2006.]

Benjamin, Walter. "Über den Begriff der Geschichte." BGS I, 691–704, 1991. ["On the Concept of History." Translated by Howard Eiland and Michael W. Jennings. *Selected Writings.* Vol. 4, 1938–1940, 389–400. Cambridge, MA: Harvard University Press, 2006.]

Benjamin, Walter. "Notizen und Vorarbeiten zu den Thesen Über den Begriff der Geschichte." BGS I, 1228–1252, 1991. ["Paralipomena to 'On the Concept of History.'" *Selected Writings.* Vol. 4, 1938–1940, 401–411. Cambridge, MA: Harvard University Press, 2006.]

Benjamin, Walter. "Erfahrung und Armut." BGS II, 213–219, 1977. ["Experience and Poverty." *Selected Writings*. Vol. 2, 731–736. Cambridge, MA: Harvard University Press, 2005.]

Benjamin, Walter. "Eduard Fuchs, der Sammler und der Historiker." BGS II, 465–505, 1977. ["Eduard Fuchs, Collector and Historian." *Selected Writings*. Vol. 3, 1935–1938, 260–302. Cambridge, MA: Harvard University Press, 2002.]

Benjamin, Walter. "Ein Aussenseiter macht sich bemerkbar. Zu S. Kracauer. 'Die Angestellten.'" BGS III, 219–225, 1996. ["An Outsider Makes His Mark." *Selected Writings*. Vol. 2, 305–311. Cambridge, MA: Harvard University Press, 2005.]

Benjamin, Walter. *Das Passagen-Werk*. BGS V. 2 vols. Frankfurt: Suhrkamp, 1996, [*The Arcades Project*. Translated by Howard Eiland and Kevin McLaughlin. Cambridge, MA: Harvard University Press, 2002.]

Bettelheim, Bruno, and Morris Jannowitz. *Dynamics of Prejudice*. New York: Harper & Brothers, 1950.

Bock, Wolfgang. *Dialektische Psychologie. Adornos Rezeption der Psychoanalyse*. Wiesbaden: Springer, 2018.

Bonefeld, Werner, and Chris O'Kane, eds. *Adorno and Marx. Negative Dialectics and the Critique of Political Economy*. London: Bloomsbury, 2022.

Braunstein, Dirk. *Adorno's Critique of Political Economy*. Translated by Adam Baltner. Leiden: Brill, 2022.

Braunstein, Dirk. *Wahrheit und Katastrophe. Texte zu Adorno*. Bielefeld: Transcript, 2018.

Brecht, Bertolt. *Der dreigroschen Prozeß. Werke* 21. Edited by Werner Hecht, Jan Knopf, Werner Mittenzwei, and Klaus-Detlef Müller. Frankfurt: Suhrkamp, 1992. ["The Threepenny Lawsuit." In *Bertolt Brecht on Film and Radio*. Translated by Marc Silberman, 147–99. London: Bloomsbury Methuen Drama, 2001.]

Buck-Morss, Susan. *The Dialectics of Seeing: Walter Benjamin and the Arcades Project*. Cambridge, MA: MIT Press, 1989.

Cassegård, Carl. *Toward a Critical Theory of Nature. Capital, Ecology, Dialectics*. London: Bloomsbury, 2021.

Catalina, Cristina. "La religiosidad capitalista en Marx y Benjamin: fetichismo y secularización." *Viento Sur* 158 (2018): 78–86.

Catalina, Cristina. "La herida de la integración fordista. Notas para una genealogía del darwinismo social neoliberal." In *Republicanismo, nacionalismo y populismo como formas de la política contemporánea*, edited by J. L. Villacañas and A. Garrido, 207–53. Madrid: Dado Ediciones, 2021.

Catalina, Cristina. "Trabajo, desposesión y sufrimiento en el capitalismo. De la crisis del mundo liberal al neoliberalismo." *Bajo Palabra* 33 (2023): 49–80.

Claussen, Detlev. *Abschied von Gestern. Kritische Theorie heute*. Bremen: Wassman, 1986.

Claussen, Detlev. "Nach Auschwitz. Ein Essay über die Aktualität Adornos." In *Zivilisationsbruch. Denken nach Auschwitz*, edited by Dan Diner, 54–68. Frankfurt: Fischer, 1986.

Claussen, Detlev. *Unterm Konformitätszwang. Zum Verhältnis von Kritischer Theorie und Psychoanalyse*. Bremen: Wassmann, 1988.

Claussen, Detlev. *Mit steinernem Herzen. Politische Essays*. Bremen: Wassmann, 1989.

Claussen, Detlev. "Konflikte mit Teddie." In *Frankfurter Adorno Blätter* VI, edited by Rolf Tiedemann, 139–41. Munich: Text+Kritik, 2000.

Claussen,Detlev. "Konformistische Identität. Zur Rolle der Sozialpsychologie in der Kritischen Theorie." In *Soziologie im Spätkapitalismus*, 27–40. Darmstadt: Wissenschaftliche Buchgesellschaft, 1995.

Claussen, Detlev. "Die amerikanische Erfahrung der kritischen Theoretiker." In *Keine Kritische Theorie ohne Amerika*, edited by D. Claussen, O. Negt, and M. Werz, 27–45. Frankfurt: Neue Kritik, 1999.

Claussen, Detlev. *Aspekte der Alltagsreligion. Ideologiekritik unter veränderten gesellschaftlichen Verhältnissen*. Frankfurt: Neue Kritik, 2000.

Claussen, Detlev. *Theodor Adorno: One Last Genius*. Translated by Rodney Livingstone. Cambridge, MA: Harvard University Press, 2008.

Claussen, Detlev. *Grenzen der Aufklärung. Zur gesellschaftlichen Geschichte des modernen Antisemitismus*. Frankfurt: Fischer, 2005.

Dahmer, Helmut. *Libido und Gesellschaft*. Münster: Westfälisches Dampfboot, 2013.

Dahmer, Helmut. "Kritische Theorie und Psychoanalyse." In *Handbuch Kritische Theorie*, edited by U. H. Bittlingmayer, A. Demirovic, and T. Freytag, 235–75. Wiesbaden: Springer, 2019.

Dankemeyer, Iris. *Die Erotik des Ohrs. Musikalische Erfahrung und Emanzipation nach Adorno*. Berlin: Tiamat, 2020.

Dobbs-Weinstein, Idit. *Spinoza's Critique of Religion and its Heirs: Marx, Benjamin, Adorno*. Cambridge: Cambridge University Press, 2015.

Dubiel, Helmut. *Wissenschaftsorganisation und politische Erfahrung. Studien zur frühen Kritischen Theorie*. Frankfurt: Suhrkamp, 1978.

Eagleton, Terry. *The Ideology of the Aesthetic*. Cambridge, MA: Basil Blackwell, 1990.

Eisler, Hanns. *Schriften I. Musik und Politik 1924–1948*. Munich: Rogner & Bernhard, 1973.

Elbe, Ingo. *Paradigmen anonymer Herrschaft*. Würzburg: Königshausen & Neumann, 2015.

Fenichel, Otto. *Aufsätze*. Vol. 2. Vienna: Ullstein, 1985.

Fischer, Lars. "The Frankfurt School and Fascism." In *The Sage Handbook of Frankfurt School Critical Theory*, vol. 2, edited by B. Best, W. Bonefeld, and C. O'Kane, 799–815. London: Sage, 2018.

Fleck, Amaro. *Theodor W. Adorno. Um crítico na era dourada do capitalismo*. PhD diss., Centro de Filosofia e Ciências Humanas, Universidade Federal de Santa Catarina, Florianópolis, 2015.

Fleck, Amaro, and Luiz Philipe de Caux. "Pollock y los frankfurtianos. Notas sobre la recepción del concepto de capitalismo de Estado." *Constelaciones. Revista de Teoría Crítica* 13 (2021): 71–92.

Freud, Sigmund. "Das Unheimliche." In *Studienausgabe*, vol. IV, edited by Alexander Mitscherlich, Angela Richards, and James Strachey, 242–74. Frankfurt: Fischer, 1994. ["The Uncanny." *The Standard Edition of the Complete Psychological Works of Sigmund Freud*, vol. XVII, 219–252. London: The Hogarth Press, 1955.]

Freud, Sigmund. *Jenseits des Lustprinzips*. In *Studienausgabe*, vol. III, edited by Alexander Mitscherlich, Angela Richards, and James Strachey, 213–72. Frankfurt: Fischer, 1994. [*Beyond the Pleasure Principle*. Translated by James Strachey. New York: Norton & Company, 1961.]

Freud, Sigmund. *Massenpsychologie und Ich-Analyse*. In *Studienausgabe*, vol. IX, edited by Alexander Mitscherlich, Angela Richards, and James Strachey, 61–134. Frankfurt: Fischer, 2009. [*Group Psychology and the Analysis of the Ego*. Translated by James Strachey. London: The Hogarth Press, 1949.]

Freud, Anna. *The Ego and the Mechanisms of Defence*. London: Karnac Books, 1993.

Fromm, Erich. *The Working Class in Weimar Germany: A Psychological and Sociological Study*. Translated by Barbara Weinberger. Cambridge, MA: Harvard University Press, 1984.

Fromm, Erich. *Analytische Sozialpsychologie und Gesellschaftstheorie.* Frankfurt: Suhrkamp, 1970.

Fuchshuber, Thorsten. *Rackets. Kritische Theorie der Bandenherrschaft.* Freiburg: ça ira, 2019.

Fuchshuber, Thorsten. "Más allá del autoritarismo. La teoría de los rackets de Max Horkheimer." *Constelaciones. Revista de Teoría Crítica* 13 (2021): 36–70.

Gerber, Meike. "Kurz vor der Praxis wiederum in die Theorie." In *Für Hans-Jürgen Krahl: Beiträge zu seinem antiautoritären Marxismus*, edited by Meike Gerber, Emanuel Kapfinger, and Julian Volz, 171–97. Vienna: Mandelbaum, 2022.

Gómez, Vicente. *El pensamiento estético de Theodor W. Adorno.* Madrid: Cátedra, 1998.

Habermas, Jürgen. "Nachwort von Jürgen Habermas." In M. Horkheimer and Th. W. Adorno, *Dialektik der Aufklärung*, 272–92. Frankfurt: Fischer, 1986.

Habermas, Jürgen. *The Philosophical Discourse of Modernity.* Translated by Frederick G. Lawrence. Cambridge: Polity Press, 1987.

Han, Sangwon. *Konstitutive Negativität. Zur Rekonstruktion des Politischen in der negativen Dialektik Adornos.* Bielefeld: Transcript, 2016.

Hegel, Georg Wilhelm Friedrich. *Phänomenologie des Geistes*, Werke 3. Frankfurt: Suhrkamp, 1986. [*The Phenomenology of Spirit.* Translated by Terry Pinkard. Cambridge: Cambridge University Press, 2018.]

Hegel, Georg Wilhelm Friedrich. *Grundlinien der Philosophie des Rechts*, Werke 7. Frankfurt: Suhrkamp, 1986. [*Elements of the Philosophy of Right.* Translated by H. B. Nisbet. Cambridge: Cambridge University Press, 2003.]

Heitmann, Lars. "Society as 'Totality': On the Negative-Dialectical Presentation of Capitalist Socialization." In *The Sage Handbook of Frankfurt School Critical Theory*, vol. 2, edited by B. Best, W. Bonefeld, and Ch. O'Kane, 589–606. London: Sage, 2018.

Hindrichs, Gunnar. *Zur kritischen Theorie.* Berlin: Suhrkamp, 2020.

Hindrichs, Gunnar, ed. *Max Horkheimer / Theodor W. Adorno. Dialektik der Aufklärung.* Berlin: De Gruyter, 2017.

Honneth, Axel. *The Fragmented World of the Social.* Translated by Charles W. Wright. New York: SUNY Press, 1995.

Horkheimer, Max. *Gesammelte Schriften* (19 vols.), edited by Alfred Schmidt and Gunzelin Schmid-Noerr. Frankfurt: Fischer, 1985–96.

Horkheimer, Max. *Dämmerung. Notizen in Deutschland.* HGS 2, 309–453, 1987. [*Dawn & Decline.* Translated by Michael Shaw. New York: Continuum, 1978.]

Horkheimer, Max. "Vorwort zur Neupublikation." HGS 3, 14–19, 1988.

Horkheimer, Max. "Die gegenwärtige Lage der Sozialphilosophie und die Aufgaben eines Instituts für Sozialforschung." HGS 3, 20–35, 1988. ["The Present Situation of Social Philosophy and the Tasks of an Institute for Social Research." Translated by John Torpey. *Between Philosophy and Social Science: Selected Early Writings*, 1–14. Cambridge, MA: The MIT Press, 1993.]

Horkheimer, Max. "Vorwort [zu Heft 1–2 des 1. Jahrgangs der Zeitschrift für Sozialforschung]." HGS 3, 36–39, 1988.

Horkheimer, Max. "Geschichte und Psychologie." HGS 3, 48–69, 1988. ["History and Psychology." Translated by Frederick Hunter. *Between Philosophy and Social Science: Selected Early Writings*, 111–28. Cambridge, MA: The MIT Press, 1993.]

Horkheimer, Max. "Materialismus und Metaphysik." HGS 3, 70–105, 1988.

Horkheimer, Max. "Autorität und Familie." HGS 3, 336–418. ["Authority and the Family." *Critical Theory: Selected Essays*, translated by Matthew J. O'Connell, 47–128. New York: Continuum, 2002.]

Horkheimer, Max. "Traditionelle und kritische Theorie." HGS 4, 162–216, 1988. ["Traditional and Critical Theory." Translated by Matthew J. O'Connell. *Critical Theory: Selected Essays*, 188–243. New York: Continuum, 2002.]

Horkheimer, Max. "Nachtrag." HGS 4, 217–25, 1988. ["Postscript." Translated by Matthew J. O'Connell. *Critical Theory: Selected Essays*, 244–52. New York: Continuum, 2002.]

Horkheimer, Max. "Die Juden und Europa." HGS 4, 308–31, 1988. ["The Jews and Europe." Translated by Mark Ritter. *Critical Theory and Society: A Reader*, edited by Stephen Eric Bronner and Douglas Kellner, 77–94. London: Routledge, 1989.]

Horkheimer, Max. "Autoritärer Staat." HGS 5, 213–319, 1987. ["The Authoritarian State." *Telos* 15 (1973): 3–20.]

Horkheimer, Max. "Vernunft und Selbsterhaltung." HGS 5, 320–50, 1987.

Horkheimer, Max. "Vorwort zu den *Studies in Prejudice*." HGS 5, 406–11, 1987. ["Foreword to *Studies in Prejudice*." In T. W. Adorno, Else Frenkel-Brunswick, Daniel J. Levinson, and R. Nevitt Sanford, *The Authoritarian Personality*, lxvii–lxx. London: Verso, 2019.]

Horkheimer, Max. "Zur Soziologie der Klassenverhältnisse." HGS 12, 75–104, 1985.

Horkheimer, Max. "Deutschlands Erneuerung nach dem Krieg und die Funktion der Kultur." HGS 12, 184–94, 1985.

Horkheimer, Max. *Späne. Notizen über Gespräche mit Max Horkheimer in unverbindlicher Formulierung aufgeschrieben von Friedrich Pollock*. HGS 14, 172–549, 1988.

Horkheimer, Max. *Briefwechsel 1937–1940*. HGS 16, 1995.

Horkheimer, Max. *Briefwechsel 1941–1948*. HGS 17, 1996.

Horkheimer, Max, Erich Fromm, J. Gumperz, Herbert Marcuse, Franz Neumann, and Friedrich Pollock. 'Die Marxsche Methode und ihre Anwendbarkeit auf die Analye der gegenwärtigen Krise.' HGS 12, 398–416, 1985.

Horkheimer, Max, Erich Fromm, Herbert Marcuse, et al. *Studien über Autorität und Familie*. Lüneburg: zu Klampen, 2005.

Hullot-Kentor, Robert. *Things Beyond Resemblance. Critical Essays on Theodor W. Adorno*. New York: Columbia University Press, 2006.

Hullot-Kentor, Robert. "A New Type of Human Being and Who We Really Are." *Brooklyn Rail*, 10/11 (2008): https://brooklynrail.org/2008/11/art/a-new-type-of-human-being-and-who-we-really-are.

Hullot-Kentor, Robert. "The Exact Sense in which the Culture Industry No Longer Exists." *Cultural Critique* 70 (2008): 137–57.

Hullot-Kentor, Robert. "Metric of Rebarbarization." *South Atlantic Quarterly* 117(4)10 (2018): 721–56.

Hullot-Kentor, Robert. "Moishe Postone and the Essay as Form." *Critical Historical Studies* 7, no. 1 (2020): 9–18.

Hullot-Kentor, Robert. "Font Null. The First Sentence of *Aesthetic Theory*." In *Theodor W. Adorno: Ästhetische Theorie*, edited by Anne Eusterschulte and Sebastian Tränkle, 21–8. Berlin: De Gruyter, 2021.

Institut für Sozialforschung (ed.). *Soziologische Exkurse. Nach Vorträgen und Diskussionen*. Frankfurt: Europäische Verlagsanstalt, 1956.

Jacoby, Russell. *Social Amnesia. A Critique of Contemporary Psychology from Adler to Laing*. New York: Transaction, 1975.

Jameson, Fredric. *Late Marxism. Adorno, Or, The Persistence of the Dialectic*. London: Verso, 1990.

Jay, Martin. *The Dialectical Imagination: A History of the Frankfurt School and the Institute of Social Research 1923–1950*. Berkeley: University of California Press, 1996.

Jeffries, Stuart. *Grand Hotel Abyss*. London: Verso, 2016.
Jenemann, David. *Adorno in America*. Minneapolis: University of Minnesota Press, 2007.
Keynes, John Maynard. *Allgemeine Theorie der Beschäftigung, des Zinses und des Geldes*. Berlin: Duncker & Humblot, 1936.
Khatib, Sami. "Die Ideologie und ihre Kritik." *Anthropological Materialism* (2010): https://anthropologicalmaterialism.hypotheses.org/630.
Kołakowski, Leszek. *Main Currents of Marxism*, vol. III. Oxford: Oxford University Press, 1978.
Krahl, Hans-Jürgen. *Konstitution und Klassenkampf*. Frankfurt: Neue Kritik, 2008.
Kraushaar, Wolfgang (ed.). *Frankfurter Schule und Studentenbewegung. Von der Flaschenpost zum Molotowcocktail* (3 vols.). Hamburg: Hamburger Edition, 1998.
Kurz, Robert. "Kulturindustrie im 21. Jahrhundert." *Exit. Krise und Kritik der Warengesellschaft* 9 (2012): 60–100.
Kracauer, Siegfried. *Die Angestellten*. Frankfurt: Suhrkamp, 1971. [*The Salaried Masses*. Translated by Quintin Hoare. London: Verso, 1998.]
López Álvarez, Pablo. "Ocaso del individuo, recuerdo de lo vivo. Sujeto y naturaleza en Adorno." In *Melancolía y verdad*, edited by Jacobo Muñoz, 33–70. Madrid: Biblioteca Nueva, 2011.
López Álvarez, Pablo. "El tiempo y las cosas. Observaciones sobre el sujeto." *Constelaciones. Revista de Teoría Crítica* 5 (2013): 362–7.
López Álvarez, Pablo. "La técnica y la escala de lo humano. Sobre un diagnóstico de Th. W. Adorno." In *¿Actualidad del humanismo e inactualidad del hombre?* Edited by Lorena Acosta and Pablo López, 221–43. Madrid: Guillermo Escolar, 2018.
Löwenthal, Leo. *Mitmachen wollte ich nie. Ein autobiographisches Gespräch mit Helmut Dubiel*. Frankfurt: Suhrkamp, 1980.
Löwenthal, Leo. "Vorurteilsbilder. Antisemitismus unter amerikanischen Arbeitern." In *Falsche Propheten. Studien zum Autoritarismus. Schriften* 3, 175–237. Frankfurt: Suhrkamp, 1990.
Löwenthal, Leo. *Judaica, Vorträge, Briefe. Schriften* 4. Frankfurt: Suhrkamp, 1990.
Löwenthal, Leo. "Die Techniken des amerikanischen Agitators." In *Das Utopische soll Funken schlagen… Zum hundertsten Geburtstag von Leo Löwenthal*. Edited by Peter-Erwin Jansen, 116–24. Frankfurt: Klostermann, 1993.
Löwenthal, Leo, and Norbert Guterman. *Prophets of Deceit*. New York: Harper & Brothers, 1949.
Lukács, Georg. *The Theory of the Novel*. Translated by Anna Bostock. Cambridge, MA: MIT Press, 1971.
Lukács, Georg. *History and Class Consciousness*. Translated by Rodney Livingstone. Cambridge, MA: MIT Press, 1972.
Macdonald, Iain. *What Would Be Different. Figures of Possibility in Adorno*. Stanford: Stanford University Press, 2019.
Maiso, Jordi. *Elementos para la reapropiación de la Teoría Crítica de Theodor W. Adorno*. Salamanca: Ediciones Universidad de Salamanca, 2010.
Maiso, Jordi. "La subjetividad dañada. Teoría crítica y psicoanálisis." *Constelaciones. Revista de Teoría Crítica* 5 (2013): 132–50.
Maiso, Jordi. "Emancipación o barbarie en la música. Los orígenes de la Teoría Crítica de Th. W. Adorno en sus escritos musicales tempranos." *Daimon* 65 (2015): 21–35.
Maiso, Jordi. "Zur gesellschaftlichen Produktion von Kälte." In *Grenzsteine. Beiträge zur Kritik der Gewalt*, edited by Theodora Becker, Andreas Franze, Jakob Hayner, and Arne Kellermann, 71–85. Munich: Text+Kritik, 2016.

Maiso, Jordi. "Hans-Jürgen Krahl: Social Constitution and Class Struggle." In Beverley Best, Werner Bonefeld, and Chris O'Kane (eds.), *The Sage Handbook of Frankfurt School Critical Theory*, vol. 1, 335–50. London: Sage.

Maiso, Jordi. "Sismografías de la edad de oro: Adorno y Beckett." *Laocoonte. Revista de estética y teoría de las artes* 7 (2020): 189–202.

Maiso, Jordi. "The Critical Theory of Antisemitism and the Limits of Enlightenment." In Marcel Stoetzler (ed.), *Critical Theory and the Critique of Antisemitism*, 23–49. London: Bloomsbury, 2023.

Maiso, Jordi and Breixo Viejo. "Imágenes en negativo. Notas introductorias a 'Transparencias cinematográficas.'" *Archivos de la Filmoteca* 52 (2006): 122–9.

Marcuse, Herbert. "Über den affirmativen Charakter der Kultur." *Kultur und Gesellschaft*, vol. 1, 56–61. Frankfurt: Suhrkamp, 1980. ["The Affirmative Character of Culture." In *Art and Liberation*, edited by Douglas Kellner, 82–112. London: Routledge, 2007.]

Marcuse, Herbert. "Das Veralten der Psychoanalyse." *Kultur und Gesellschaft*, vol. 2, 85–106. Frankfurt: Suhrkamp, 1980. ["Obsolescence of Psychoanalysis." In *Philosophy, Psychoanalysis and Emancipation*, edited by Douglas Kellner and Clayton Pierce, 109–21. London: Routledge, 2011.]

Marx, Karl. "Briefe aus den 'Deutsch-Französischen Jahrbüchern.'" *MEW* 1, 337–346. [Berlin: Dietz, 1981. "Letters from the Franco-German Yearbooks." In *Early Writings*, translated by Rodney Livingstone and Gregor Benton, 199–210. London: Penguin Books, 1992.]

Marx, Karl. "Zur Kritik der Hegelschen Rechtsphilosophie. Einleitung." *MEW* 1, 378–91. Berlin: Dietz, 1981. ["A Contribution to the Critique of Hegel's Philosophy of Right. Introduction." In *Critique of Hegel's "Philosophy of Right,"* translated by Anette Jolin and Joseph O'Malley, 129–42. Cambridge: Cambridge University Press, 1977.]

Marx, Karl. *Zur Kritik der politischen Ökonomie, MEW* 13. Berlin: Dietz, 2015.

Marx, Karl. "Preface (to A Contribution to the Critique of Political Economy)." In *Later Political Writings*, edited by Terrell Carver, 158–62. Cambridge, MA: Cambridge University Press, 1996.

Marx, Karl. "Kritik des Gothaer Programms." *MEW* 19, 11–32. Berlin: Dietz, 1987. ["Critique of the Gotha Program." In *Later Political Writings*, edited by Terrell Carver, 208–26. Cambridge: Cambridge University Press, 1996.]

Marx, Karl. *Das Kapital. Kritik der politischen Ökonomie*, vol. 1, *MEW* 23. Berlin: Dietz, 2005. [*Capital: A Critique of Political Economy*, vol. 1. Translated by Ben Fowkes. London: Penguin, 1990.]

Marx, Karl. *Das Kapital. Kritik der politischen Ökonomie*, vol. 3, *MEW* 25. Berlin: Dietz, 2005. [*Capital*, vol. 3. Translated by David Fernbach. London: Penguin, 1991.]

Marx, Karl. *Ökonomisch-philosophische Manuskripte aus dem Jahre 1844, MEW* 24, 465–588. Berlin: Dietz, 1968. [*Economic and Philosophic Manuscripts.* Translated by Martin Milligan. New York: Prometheus Books, 1988.]

Marx, Karl. *Grundrisse der Kritik der politischen Ökonomie, MEW* 42. Berlin: Dietz, 1983. [*Grundrisse: Foundations of the Critique of Political Economy.* Translated by Martin Nicolaus. London: Penguin Books, 1993.]

Marx, Karl, and Friedrich Engels. *Manifest der Kommunistischen Partei, Marx Engels Werke*, vol. 4. Berlin: Dietz, 1977, 459–93. [*The Communist Manifesto.* Translated by Samuel Moore. London: Penguin, 2002.]

Meyer, Lars. *Absoluter Wert und allgemeiner Wille: Zur Selbstbegründung dialektischer Gesellschaftstheorie*. Bielefeld: Transcript, 2005.

Morgan, Alastair. *Adorno's Concept of Life*. London: Continuum, 2007.

Nietzsche, Friedrich. *Zur Genealogie der Moral*. In *Kritische Studienausgabe*, vol. 5. Munich: dtv, 1988. [*On the Genealogy of Morality*, trans. Carol Diethe. Cambridge: Cambridge University Press, 2006.]

O'Kane, Chris. *Fetishism and Social Domination in Marx, Lukács, Adorno and Lefebvre*. PhD diss., Centre for Social and Political Thought, University of Sussex, 2013.

Parin, Paul. *Der Widerspruch im Subjekt*. Frankfurt: Syndikat, 1978.

Pollock, Friedrich. *Stadien des Kapitalismus*. Munich: Beck, 1975.

Pollock, Friedrich. "State Capitalism: Its Possibilities and Limitations." In *Critical Theory and Society: A Reader*, edited by Stephen Eric Bronner and Douglas Kellner, 95–118. London: Routledge, 1989.

Postone, Moishe. "Anti-Semitism and National Socialism." In *Germans and Jews since the Holocaust*, edited by Anson Rabinach and Jack Zipes, 302–14. New York: Holmes & Meier, 1986.

Postone, Moishe. *Time, Labour and Social Domination*. Cambridge: Cambridge University Press, 1993.

Regatieri, Ricardo Pagliuso. *Capitalismo sem peias*. São Paulo: fflch/Humanitas, 2019.

Reichelt, Helmut. *Neue Marx-Lektüre: Zur Kritik sozialwissenschaftlicher Logik*. Freiburg: ça ira, 2013.

Reijen, Wilhelm van and Jan Bransen. "Das Verschwinden der Klassengesellschaft in der Dialektik der Aufklärung." HGS 5 453–57, 1987.

Rose, Gillian. *The Melancholy Science: An Introduction to the Thought of Theodor W. Adorno*. London: Verso, 2014.

Russell, Eric-John. "Certainty in an Uncertain World: Toward a Critical Theory of Opinion." *Critical Sociology* 50, nos. 4–5 (2023): 691–706.

Sablowsky, Thomas. "Entwicklungstendenzen und Krisen des Kapitalismus." In *Modelle kritischer Theorie*, edited by Alex Demirovic, 101–30. Stuttgart/Weimar: Metzler, 2003.

Sacristán, Manuel. *Seis conferencias*. Madrid: El Viejo Topo, 2005.

Safatle, Vladimir. "Freud em Frankfurt: a função da psicanálise no pensamento de Theodor Adorno." In *Por que Freud hoje*, edited by Daniel Kuperman, 63–89. São Paulo: Zagodini, 2017.

Safatle, Vladimir. *Dar corpo ao impossível: O sentido da dialética a partir de Theodor Adorno*. Belo Horizonte: Autêntica, 2019.

Schmid-Noerr, Gunzelin. "Nachwort des Herausgebers." HGS 5, 423–52, 1987.

Scheit, Gerhard. *Quälbarer Leib: Kritik der Gesellschaft nach Adorno*. Freiburg: ça ira, 2016.

Schmieder, Falko. *Ludwig Feuerbach und der Eingang der klassischen Fotografie: Zum Verhältnis von anthropologischen und historischen Materialismus*. Berlin: Philo, 2004.

Schneider, Christian. "Die Wunde Freud." In *Adorno–Handbuch: Leben - Werk - Wirkung*, edited by Richard Klein, Johannes Kreuzer, and Stefan Müller-Doohm, 283–94. Stuttgart: Metzler, 2011.

Schwarz, Roberto. "On Adorno (An Interview)." Trans. Simone Fernandes and Mariana Fidelis. *Dissonância: Revista de Teoria Crítica: Dossiê Teoria Decolonial e Teoria Crítica* 4 (2020): 436–47.

Schweppenhäuser, Hermann. *Vergegenwärtigungen zur Unzeit? Versammelte Aufsätze und Reden*. Lüneburg: zu Klampen, 1986.

Sohn-Rethel, Alfred. *Warenform und Denkform*. Frankfurt: Suhrkamp, 1978.

Sohn-Rethel, Alfred. *Intellectual and Manual Labour: A Critique of Epistemology*. Trans. Martin Sohn-Rethel. London: The Macmillan Press, 1978.

Sonnemann, Ulrich. *Negative Anthropologie*. Schriften 3. Lüneburg: zu Klampen, 2011.

Steinert, Heinz. *Culture Industry*. Trans. Sally-Ann Spencer. Cambridge: Polity, 2003.

Steinert, Heinz. *Das Verhängnis der Gesellschaft und das Glück der Erkenntnis: Dialektik der Aufklärung als Forschungsprogramm*. Münster: Westfällisches Dampfboot, 2007.

Stender, Wolfram. *Kritik und Vernunft: Studien zu Horkheimer, Habermas und Freud*. Lüneburg: zu Klampen, 1996.

Stoetzler, Marcel. "Wer aber von der Geschichte des Subjekts nicht reden will, sollte auch vom Kapitalismus schweigen: Zur Radikalität der Dialektik der Aufklärung." In *Zur Kritik der regressiven Vernunft: Beiträge zur 'Dialektik der Aufklärung'*, edited by Gunzelin Schmid-Noerr and Eva-Maria Ziege, 163–80. Wiesbaden: Springer, 2019.

Tiedemann, Rolf. *Niemandsland: Studien mit und über Theodor W. Adorno*. Munich: Text+Kritik, 2007.

Tiedemann, Rolf. *Mythos und Utopie: Aspekte der Adornoschen Philosophie*. Munich: Text+Kritik, 2009.

Traverso, Enzo. *Left-Wing Melancholia: Marxism, History, and Memory*. New York: Columbia University Press, 2016.

Türcke, Christoph. *Erregte Gesellschaft: Philosophie der Sensation*. Munich: Beck, 2012.

Türcke, Christoph, and Gerhard Bolte. *Einführung in die kritische Theorie*. Darmstadt: Primus, 1994.

Vidal, Vanessa. *Esto no tiene sentido: La interpretación materialista del arte*. Valencia: Publicacions Universitat de València, 2021.

Viejo, Breixo. *Música moderna para un nuevo cine: Eisler, Adorno y el Film Music Project*. Madrid: Akal, 2008.

Wellmer, Albrecht. *The Persistence of Modernity: Essays on Aesthetics, Ethics and Postmodernism*. Cambridge, MA: The MIT Press, 1991.

Wellmer, Albrecht and Vicente Gómez. *Teoría crítica y estética: Dos interpretaciones de Th. W. Adorno*. Valencia: Publicacions Universitat de València, 1994.

Wiggershaus, Rolf. *The Frankfurt School: Its History, Theories, and Political Significance*. Trans. Michael Robertson. Cambridge, MA: The MIT Press, 1995.

Zamora, José A. *Krise – Kritik – Erinnerung: Ein politisch-theologischer Versuch über Adorno im Horizont der Krise der Moderne*. Münster: Lit, 1995.

Zamora, José A. "Theodor W. Adorno y la aniquilación del individuo." *Isegoría* 28 (2003): 131–43.

Zamora, José A. *Theodor W. Adorno: Pensar contra la barbarie*. Madrid: Trotta, 2004.

Zamora, José A. "El enigma de la docilidad: Teoría de la Sociedad y psicoanálisis en Th. W. Adorno." In *El pensamiento de Th. W. Adorno: Balance y perspectivas*, edited by Mateu Cabot, 27–42. Palma de Mallorca: Edicions UIB, 2007.

Zamora, José A. "Theodor W. Adorno: Crítica inmanente del capitalismo." In *Melancolía y verdad*, edited by Jacobo Muñoz, 71–94. Madrid: Biblioteca Nueva.

Zamora, José A. "Society and History." In *The Sage Handbook of Frankfurt School Critical Theory*, vol. 2, edited by Beverley Best, Werner Bonefeld, and Chris O'Kane, 625–41. London: Sage, 2018.

Zamora, José A. "Materialidad espectral, subjetivación y crítica inmanente del fetichismo." In *Crítica inmanente de la Sociedad*, edited by José M. Romero and José A. Zamora, 171–204. Barcelona: Anthropos, 2020.

Zamora, José A. "Th. W. Adorno: Filosofía frente a la catástrofe." *Sociología histórica* 10 (2020): 464–80.

Zamora, José A. "Teoría Crítica: Reflexiones en torno a su (in)actualidad." *Diálogo filosófico* 108 (2020): 361–86.

Ziege, Eva Maria. *Antisemitismus und Gesellschaftstheorie: Die Frankfurter Schule im amerikanischen Exil*. Frankfurt: Suhrkamp, 2009.

Index